Corruption

Corruption

Causes, Consequences and Control

Edited by

Michael Clarke

St. Martin's Press, New York

All rights reserved. For information, write:
St. Martin's Press, Inc., 175 Fifth Avenue, New York, NY 10010
Printed in Great Britain
First published in the United States of America in 1983

Library of Congress Cataloging in Publication Data
Main entry under title

Corruption—causes, consequences, and control.

    Based on a conference held June 1982, at the Gracie
Conference Centre of the University of Aston, Birmingham.
    1. Corruption (in politics)—Congresses.   I. Clarke,
Michael, 1945–
JF1081.C67   1983   350.9'94   83–9712
ISBN 0–312–17007–6

Contents

Preface

The chapters in this book are the outcome of a conference held in Birmingham in June 1982 at the Gracie Conference Centre of the University of Aston, which provided a most congenial setting; it was funded most substantially by the Barrow and Geraldine S. Cadbury Trust, and additionally by the British Academy and the National Association for Soviet and East-European Studies, to whom the organisers and participants are most grateful.

The impetus to arrange the conference came from parallel interests in corruption, my own with respect to Britain and Nick Lampert's in the USSR, and our suspicion that there were a number of other people working in this field whose work we did not know. Our objective was to assemble a wide range of people working on corruption in the industrialised West, the Third World and the Soviet bloc, in order to take a comparative view of the phenomenon and to bring together people with common interests who had so far not been in touch. To this end we co-opted our former colleague Robin Cohen, and in due course secured the commitment of some thirty participants—from both sides of the Atlantic, from Europe East and West—many of whom, after the usual delays and discussions, produced papers. I was sufficiently impressed with the quality of many of the papers and pleased with the liveliness and strong interest in many of the conference debates at which they were presented to offer to seek collective publication. Whether our collective enthusiasm was intellectually justified we must leave the reader to judge, but I must express my gratitude to participants for their work in presenting and revising papers, and for making the conference a success.

Michael Clarke
Birmingham, November 1982

1 Introduction

MICHAEL CLARKE

In a recent cartoon in the London *Times* Mark Boxer (Marc) depicted one member of the British establishment saying to another, against a background of press posters announcing increases in rail fares and postal charges, 'I won't be able to afford to go to the office to post my personal letters'. A few months earlier Marc drew a similar couple against a background of press notices showing Mrs Thatcher's announcement that the Falklands War had cost £700,000,000, with one saying to the other, 'Luckily she doesn't have to put it down to election expenses'. Coming during the period of a seemingly unending series of frauds and rip-offs by members of insurance syndicates of Lloyds of London, a pervasive cynicism was to be expected, a sense that everyone is corrupt; and that the higher up the political and economic order one is, opportunities are greater and the chances of detection or public objection fewer. In the case of Lloyds such cynicism is perhaps justified. Only a year or so previously it had vigorously defended itself as the doyen of city rectitude, where a gentleman's word is his bond; conflicts of interests, even where they apparently exist, could not remotely be claimed to act against clients' interests. For this reason the divestment of broking and underwriting interests demanded by parliament was plainly unnecessary and any policing of members could be undertaken by the rather informal procedures of the Council of Members. The outcome of the series of revelations of serious abuses by members has led not only to the acceptance of divestment, but to the appointment of a chief executive with substantial disciplinary and investigative powers, committed to introducing firm regulations enforcing much wider disclosure of members' interests and commitments.

Do these examples point unequivocally to a corruption no less rampant in the British establishment than in the American, or indeed Soviet, or Indian one, whose presence has been the more artfully concealed, and where investigation, accusation, and definition have been delayed and diverted by an astute ruling class? Such a view is not, on a more detailed examination of the evidence, wholly implausible, but in practice a number of pertinent questions are begged. Britain generally sees itself as less subject to corruption than other comparable countries, yet as some of the chapters in this book demonstrate, corruption is endemic in certain areas (cf. Fennell), epidemic in others (cf. Miers). Such a demonstration is likely to incite the alarmed British commentator, anxious not to be caught out again, into the opposite error of supposing corruption to be pandemic. But, it must be asked, if everyone is at it, are they all at it to the same extent, all the time? Are all societies the same in this respect? At all levels? At all times? Can no finer discriminations be made about what kinds of corruption different social, economic and political systems produce, about the extent of corruption and its variations in different sectors of society; about whether opportunity always results in exploitation and about problems of spread and control?

The chapters that follow indicate the complexity and diversity of corruption and its meanings and implications in a wide range of countries, and hence the difficulty of generalisation. But it is clear that different political economies permit and even require differing kinds and extents of corruption and that these opportunities and practices change over time. All societies will present some opportunities, but these will often vary from sector to sector. And control, while often possible, may at times require political and social changes that are quite substantial, particularly given that corruption is much harder to eliminate once established than to prevent in its formative stages.

But there are still difficulties. What conduct do we call corrupt? Of course Marc's implication that Mrs Thatcher's Falklands War was an electoral gambit was only a joke—or was it? After all, political unpopularity because of a disintegrating economy was a frequently cited reason in the British press for Galtieri's invasion. This, however, is to risk reducing the term corruption to the level of pure political accusation, a 'boo-word'. The question is not whether such accusations are a means of moral and political castigation and leverage, but whether that is all they are. More precisely, we have to distinguish between the sense in which corruption can be defined and understood as a social scientific term applicable to all societies, and that in which it is one which is closely tied to the sense of superiority of Western industrialised societies, which created modern bureaucracies and with them abuse of office as a permanently sensitive issue.

Much concern about corruption is a direct reflection of the increasing dominance of bureaucratic administration in industrialised and semi-industrialised societies. One tempting definition of corruption, therefore, is the abuse of bureaucratic office for personal or factional gain. It is important to recognise that this definition, in the sense in which such abuse is understood today as illegitimate, reflects not so much the existence of actual bureaucracies as the acceptance in modern societies of the bureaucratic principle central to what Max Weber called formal legal rationality, that decisions should be reached by functionaries, both public and private, according to the merits of each case as determined by the application of publicly identified universalistic criteria. This is not the place to rehearse Weber's arguments[1] regarding the derivation of the formal and impersonal machinery of bureaucracy from the rational universalistic calculations of bourgeois capitalism, and thence from the inner-worldly asceticism of Protestantism. The significant matter is that, as Weber was keen to establish, this disinterested formal approach to decision making was developed on a hitherto unheard of scale as one of the foundations of modern bourgeois capitalism and is not necessarily more 'natural' or 'just' than the traditional and particularistic mode of decision making.

Thus, whilst we now take it for granted that the bureaucrat who refuses to process our case or to provide us with appropriate service would be the subject of complaint to his superiors simply on the grounds that he has failed to treat us in the same way as everyone else according to established rules, such a reaction would have been inappropriate to the patrimonial bureaucrat given personal authority (as well as the authority of office) in a feudal system of administration. To cite a more precise example, we take it for granted that we may challenge the bureaucracy to justify its actions in the assessment of income tax, and likewise assume that all of the tax gathered will be transmitted to the Exchequer. This is quite at variance with the traditions of tax farming prevalent until modern times, in which the right to collect taxes was sold or allocated as a patronage post, and seen as an opportunity to extract from the population as much tax as possible above that required by the sovereign, with officials at all levels taking a cut.

The principal advantage of the modern bureaucracy, Weber pointed out, was that its impersonal universalistic procedure was efficient. This has often seemed a rather poor joke to those who have struggled in the Kafkaesque entrails of contemporary bureaucracies, but in macro-social and economic terms, it is true. It is true, however, only if the conditions Weber specified as characteristic of the modern bureaucracy obtain, most notably that officials are properly paid, so that they do not need to supplement their income by bribery; where formal and effective supervision of subordinates exists; and where adequate training is given to ensure technical competence. He might have also added two other vitally important conditions: that the workload of the official is such that he can discharge it effectively and according to due process in the time available to him; and that there is an effective procedure for clients to complain about gross inefficiency, incompetence and corrupt behaviour. Where pay and competence are inadequate, workloads too high, supervision lax and complaints ineffective, modern bureaucracies cannot function, and are necessarily adapted along the lines of particularistic and political pressures. Palmier discusses these problems most directly in Chapter 12.

A further background condition necessary for a modern bureaucracy to work properly is that the economy should function at a level adequate to supply the goods and services which the bureaucracy administers. Where shortages and bottlenecks occur, as they do in almost all developing economies, and, as the chapters on the Soviet Union indicate, as may happen in a planned economy, bureaucratic administration is impaired and pressures to particularistic solutions are generated.

Now all the preceding remarks are couched very much in an idealised Weberian understanding of bureaucracies. The past two generations of research on public and private bureaucracies have explored in great detail the way in which they really work, and pointed to the importance of informal relations and unofficial routines in overcoming 'red tape', or the obstructive consequences of formal rules, which are required to deal with a very diverse and constantly evolving reality.[2] What is striking about this research in relation to corruption is its stress on the functionality of such particularistic and informal habits: they are used to manage workloads, reduce delays and establish friendly relations with colleagues and so humanise Weber's impersonal bureaucracy, but their collective aim is not the exploitation of the advantages of office, but rather the effective delivery of an adequate service—getting the job of the bureaucracy done. More recent research has identified some of the more deviant habits of officials in some bureaucracies in making illegitimate use of official time and resources—a matter which is one of South's concerns in Chapter 4—but whilst this might be a deviation from perfection, it need not seriously compromise the efficiency of the bureaucracy as a whole.[3] It consists in making life more comfortable for officials rather than abandoning the commitment of the officials as a body to providing an adequate service.

To those familiar with the heyday of Empire this argument must by now seem a trifle laboured. Much attention was devoted in the Imperial civil service to the ethic of service, and many discriminations made as to the capacity of native populations to understand and absorb it. Much was said of the virtues and satisfaction of a job well done. Whilst no doubt overblown in its moral, religious and patriotic connotations, the service ethic still remains significant in any understanding of corruption. For all that it is now very much more implicit than explicit in bureaucratic culture, and overt emphasis on a service ethic unfashionable, it is still the case that social security clerks in Birmingham seem more likely to suffer individual collapse and to take strike action over increased workloads rather than to seek bribes as a way of handling the problem;[4] and although private medicine still exists as a safety valve (a role which has been neglected in recent debates on it), queues for National Health Service beds continue to lengthen without stories of corrupt queue-jumping arising; even in the field of council housing waiting lists (many notoriously long), bribery and special influence stories are few, and there is no evidence that cases are more than isolated. We should compare this with the situation Smart describes in Sicily where, because everyone regards the world as divided into the cunning and the mugs and is convinced that, in order to get things done, cunning and particularistic alliances and influences are essential, the resources of public (and, though he says less of it, private) bureaucracies are inevitably diverted to deal with 'special' cases whilst the rest languish: cultural traditions and expectations are critical in subverting bureaucratic due process (see Chapter 8).

Whilst we should be aware, then, that there is one definition of bureaucracy that is ethnocentric in deriving from a rather idealised form of modern bureaucracy, this feature should not distract us from the fact that given a number of, in practice, quite stringent conditions, such bureaucracies can function in a reasonably efficient and disinterested way, and that having done so, an expectation about bureaucracy and official positions is established which constitutes quite a substantial bulwark against the encroaching pressures of corruption as circumstances change. Conversely, where corruption has long been widespread it will be hard to eradicate not only because bad practice drives out good, but because, just as it is hard for the average British bureaucrat to see his office as an opportunity for individual gain, so it is hard for the Sicilian one to see it otherwise, since to do so would come dangerously close to abandoning the cynicism necessary for cunning and to become a dupe of rectitude, a mug.

This however, is only half the story—the strong half, as it were. The other half concerns the political character of corruption and of allegations of corruption. I can best indicate its breadth by a somewhat indirect approach. All bureaucracies, as has been noted, tend to develop informal relations which not only ease the life of officials, but often enhance efficiency. Where bureaucracies and their officials have public clients, especially clients who come into regular contact with the same officials, this tendency to informality is likely.

A bond of friendship and goodwill may develop on this basis, and it is likely that the official will see that his client's affairs are given adequate attention. From the point at which that attention is greater than that given, on the merits of their cases, to other clients, corruption formally arises. The point at which the law intervenes is another matter. Official sanctions may follow if clients become friends, and for this reason police are segregated from the public in special housing and discouraged from having civilian friends, and British civil servants are discouraged (though on a remarkably 'understanding' basis) from taking jobs with former clients until two years after retirement. In France the practice is so well established as to have a special name—'*pantouflage*'.[5] Under British law (cf. Fennell) an official who accepts a material favour (cash or kind) from a client is liable to be accused of the crime of corruption, though 'understanding' has to be exercised here in respect of limited Christmas gifts of alcohol (though cf. Murphy), and other matters that might be termed 'trivial' or 'normal practice' or 'goodwill'. At this stage the official becomes a 'grass eater' in American police parlance, that is he accepts the favours, whether offered as outright bribes for a specific purpose or not, which are offered him. In the most developed form of corruption he becomes a 'meat eater', going out aggressively and, in the words of one notorious operator, 'organising things like they have never been organised before',[6] laying down the terms for clients on which normal services will be rendered and on which special favours will be granted.

Few would dispute the criminally corrupt character of 'meat eating', which is why such cases involve lavish publicity, solid sentences and ringing court-room denunciations. Where the line is to be drawn as regards the myriad of other cases down towards the weak end of the continuum is a political matter. It is political in that regulatory, including criminal, legal definition is laid down by the legislature, and such rules and definitions vary both with time and place and are frequently the outcome of scandals, vigorous accusatory campaigns aimed at outlawing a hitherto legal practice. Thus there is some evidence to suggest that, although the laws on corruption have not been altered, a widespread tightening of business and financial practice has taken place in Britain over the past twenty years, as a result of government intervention and self-regulation[7] (often through government pressure and scandal, as in the recent case of Lloyd's insurance syndicates). The culmination of a series of scandals displaying what a Conservative prime minister called 'the unacceptable face of capitalism' was the Poulson affair, with its wide ramifications among civil servants, local government officers and MPs, and the consequent Royal Commission on standards of conduct in public life.[8]

Thus corruption is political not only in the broad sense that formal definitions of it change according to a developing political consensus, but in individual cases. The cry 'You are corrupt!' is moral and political more than a legal accusation, and the connotations of decay, depravity, secretiveness and self-interest are well understood as grossly incompatible with official position in public office: public trust is betrayed. It is not merely that such accusations lead to general changes in the definition of corruption, but that, even within a stable definition, who is accused and who succumbs to the accusation, and whether by legal indictment or public antagonism, is a matter of political struggle, a struggle ultimately concerned with moral character rather than technical deviation. The fate of the late Reginald Maudling is particularly pertinent in this connection.[9]

When we recognise this, we may also recognise that, politics being what it is, the motives for accusations may by no means be the moral altruism and defence of public interests that are so overtly trumpeted. There may be political advantage and self-interest in smearing an opponent. As Szeftel's and Riley's chapters on African countries show, where corruption is present successful accusations may be made from a mixture of motives: it may be that the extent and notoriety of corruption have mobilised public opinion, but often the advantage of successful accusation to the accusers, who aspire to benefit by others' loss of office, is plain. On the other side, effective measures may be taken to contain an anticorruption campaign to limited numbers of fall guys; and the more widespread and entrenched corruption is, the more likely this is to be successful.

A further consequence of the political character of corruption claims is that they lead, with the support of the legal system, towards a concern with individuals engaged in corrupt practices and their removal from office, instead of the conditions which give rise to their behaviour. Fennell's account of the extraordinary sequence of events in South Wales, where long established Labour councillors were ousted after a corruption scandal, only to be replaced by their political opponents, who were in turn convicted of the same abuses, is a striking example of this. The bewildering and ineffective reformative consequences of an anticorruption campaign upon police is graphically described in Punch's account of events in Amsterdam (Chapter 7); media publicity and individualisation led to loss of morale and cynicism among officers when self-righteous accusers failed to recognise the pressures towards corrupt practice and the occupational necessity for close contacts with criminals, the hazards in fact of those required publicly to be 'good men' but occupationally involved in 'dirty work'.[10] Anticorruption campaigners may effectively 'rout out' individuals and even repress the practice temporarily, but unless they concern themselves with causes they are unlikely to prevent a recurrence.

In the case of the 'meat-eater', an individualistic emphasis is justified, and accounts for these cases being given such prominence. For here it is not so much a matter of yielding to temptation, which leads to questions being asked about the nature of the tempting circumstances, as extortion. Eliminate the corrupt entrepreneur and you eliminate the corruption, since it is from him that the impetus comes. And the best, or the worst, of it is that such determined entrepreneurship carries with it a very strong tendency for everyone below the rank of the entrepreneur to be corrupt too. Where the entrepreneur, the chief meat-eater, is the head of state, as in the cases Whitehead discusses, the consequences in terms of the distortion of the entire economy are dramatic. When considering the causes of corruption one should not neglect the very powerful impact of individuals, though such individuals can only have a great impact where circumstances favour even if they are not directly conducive to corruption. Just as politics and private enterprise produce their great figures, so in a different way may corruption—and at times they may be also politicians and/or business men.

Corruption in another sense is political: its success, even locally, is a manifestation of power. This power is manifested negatively, in the effective insulation of the corrupt appropriators of income and advantage from denunciation and removal, but it is power nevertheless. If the activity is small scale, secrecy is necessary to protect the operation, but secrecy is backed by the black-mailing power provided by the complicity of others in corruption, as well as by the carrot of illicit privilege or income. Where corruption is well established, it may be more or less public, and the impotence of those who protest at its depredations is publicly plain. We thus return to the point made above about the political character of corruption accusations, but this time from the other side: those who participate in and, still more, organise corruption are power holders.

In this light the moral character of corruption and some important means of controlling it become evident. The fact that large-scale corruption has been the basis of successful campaigns (often military coups) to overthrow regimes is an indication of the costs it imposes upon the population at large. Corruption involves the diversion of public funds into private hands, and inefficiency in the use of manpower and resources. Not only does it lead to the enrichment, often to grotesque levels, of those who find or get themselves into positions where they can exercise corrupt influence, but it involves the exclusion of those unable to participate in paying for corruptly given favours. Its essential objective is to eliminate competition, to create a charmed circle, an inside track. As such it is profoundly anti-democratic. Those who doubt its negative character should refer to the trenchant analysis of the positive theories by Smart and Whitehead.

If the effect of corruption is to create a large outgroup who are excluded from access to services and opportunities to which they have a formal right, it is likely that at least some of this excluded group will want to protest. Control of corruption hence requires a population sufficiently alert, self-confident and politically aware to, in Lampert's terminology, 'blow the whistle', and determined enough to require effective redress. At the same time the state must be sufficiently open to allow such protests and to act effectively upon them, since in many cases state agents will be the objects of the protest and serious accusations of corruption are always politically embarrassing. Because the state has an obligation to prevent corruption, it is not likely that in practice it will look kindly upon such complaints; the press becomes the principal effective medium of complaint. Even in Britain, where the press is not subject to direct political control, enormous obstacles stand in the way of complaints being publicised and followed up by journalistic investigation, as Murphy and Doig document. The power of the corrupt to control information, to influence potential informants and to deny journalists access to sources is supported by the powerful laws on contempt, official secrets and especially libel.

I have so far suggested:

(1) that bureaucracies must be given adequate resources and training and a reasonable workload and that the economy must operate in a reasonably balanced and effective way to avoid creating pressures towards corruption;
(2) that where cultural traditions accepting of corruption exist they are hard to eliminate and conduce to corruption, but where bureaucracies are well founded and established, a service ethos can develop that forms a cultural barrier against corruption;
(3) that the efforts of skilled and determined entrepreneurs of corruption are often an important factor where circumstances are at all permissive of corruption; and all societies will contain some quarters which invite corruption;
(4) that the political capacity of the excluded population to protest vigorously against corruption is a vital preventive force;
(5) that state may be more or less willing to process such complaints effectively, but is unlikely to act with enthusiasm; hence
(6) the media, and the press in particular, are vitally important as channels of protest.

The following chapters suggest a number of additional points about the causes and extent of corruption, though perhaps less decisive than those above. First, in relation to point three, the role of individual initiative versus conducive circumstances, it should be said that conditions in particular societies at given times and in limited sectors vary in the extent to which they conduce to corruption. At one extreme we find the society whose entire political economy requires corruption in order to function at all adequately, as outlined by Katsenelinboigen for the USSR, and commented on in specific aspects by Lampert, Shenfield and Mars. It is worth noting in this connection however, the point made by Katsenelinboigen that a practical if not a legal distinction is made in the USSR between necessary and normal deviation from the rules, and exploitative corruption, where such deviations are clearly more for the purposes of private gain than public good. One should not neglect in this connection the clearly political character not only of individual corruption cases, their progress as far as the courts, and the protection afforded by local influential officials (cf. Lampert), but also the political character of anti-corruption campaigns, which may be concerned with general efficiency and morale, or may be also concerned with the purging of 'undesirables'. Much the same could be said of such campaigns in many Third World countries.

The requirement of corruption in the USSR for political–economic reasons —the inadequacies of the planning machine—is one end of a continuum of opportunity, exercising decided pressures towards corruption on a very wide, almost comprehensive scale, since the entire economy is planned. In addition, these pressures remain relatively constant since the regime is stable and not evolving rapidly. By contrast, in Szeftel's account of Zambia there are similar political-economic sources of pressures to corruption, but they are the product of transition, as political independence from Britain has been succeeded by the new African ruling class's attempts to follow political victory with the appropriation of economic opportunities.

If we turn to industrialised Western societies there are several examples of both relatively stable and historically developing sectoral opportunities for and pressures towards corruption. In British local government, the practice of contracting public works privately has provided a long-term basis for corrupt relations, as Fennell indicates. This is apparently much less the case for central government, first because no one party has monopolised power for long periods, and secondly because senior councillors, as chairmen of resource allocating committees, can dominate decision making and local civil servants in a way that is not possible in central government and administration—ministers' tenure of office is very often less than even the short span of a government's term. In Amsterdam by contrast, the circumstances giving rise to police corruption were the historical changes in the inner city consequent upon the arrival of a substantial and in part wealthy Chinese population and other ethnic migrants, and the rise of the Netherlands as an important centre in the international narcotics trade.

Perhaps the most interesting example of these considerations is Miers's account of casino corruption in Britain. The nature of gambling is such that it provides a long-term sectoral opportunity for corruption on a very lucrative scale. On the available evidence, however, this appears to have been reasonably well contained in Britain by the recognition of the dangers and the imposition of stringent controls and surveillance. This points up the importance in low- and medium-level or sectoral corruption of effective surveillance to penetrate the secrecy with which such operations are necessarily conducted. Where it is more widespread, secrecy is less important (cf. Whitehead), since there is higher-level and more comprehensive political protection. The spread of casino corruption beyond a quite limited sector and the possibility of involving members of the judiciary, senior police, politicians and the regulatory agencies is inhibited in Britain's case by the structurally and economically disinterested position of those surveillance and regulatory agents. Unlike Nevada and Atlantic City in the USA,[11] revenue from gambling is not a key element in local or national revenue, does not involve a significant number of local jobs and secondary employment, and hence there are no financial and political–economic pressures to condone dubious practices in order to keep vital tax income flowing. The history of casino corruption in Britain also illustrates the way in which historical change may act to increase or reduce pressures to corruption. As Arab oil money flowed into London casinos on a vast scale in the early 1970s their number expanded accordingly; when this flow declined towards the end of the decade, it sharply increased competitive pressure between casinos, which led directly to corrupt practices to retain the allegiance particularly of the high rollers. In the last few years the regulatory agencies have taken the opportunity provided by cases of corruption which have emerged to close down casinos to a level more nearly in line with market demand.

It is tempting to try to go beyond these remarks to a more comprehensive analysis of political economies and their relative tendencies to require, permit and control corruption. The very diversity of the examples in this book counsels caution in this connection; but in addition the remarks above perhaps indicate other reasons why such an attempt is fraught with danger. The first is the vague and morally accusatory character of corruption—not only does it include a multitude of sins, but it is inventive in defining sins and rectitude for both altruistic and politically self-interested reasons. Secondly, corruption appears to have an alarming tendency to appear in all societies at all times, even if not to the same extent, and especially where administration by formal modern bureaucracies is a significant feature of them. Since this is true to an ever-increasing extent of all societies today, both those already industrialised and those aspiring to be so, it seems that it behoves any society, even those, such as Britain, with an apparently low incidence of corruption, not to be complacent: not only can it happen here, almost certainly it already is. Finally, historical developments, both dramatic and public, and less obvious and unremarked, provide constantly changing opportunities for and pressures towards corruption even within the same political economies. None of this should, I think, make us unduly pessimistic about understanding corruption, and thereby understanding its consequences and the means necessary to control it. That the measures necessary to control it may in some cases be beyond the capacities of the society concerned or the government that rules it should not lead us to abandon interest, but should at least lead us further than the dramatic pointed finger, the corruption exposé.

Notes

1. Mainly in G. Roth and C. Wittich (eds), *Economy and Society*, Berkeley, University of California Press, 1979. See also *The Protestant Ethic and the Spirit of Capitalism*, London, G. Unwin, 1930.
2. It is impossible to cite all the research here: two reasonably representative selections can be found in A. Etzioni (ed.), *Complex Organizations*, New York, Holt Reinhart, 1966; O. Grusky and G. A. Miller (eds), *The Sociology of Organisations*, New York, Free Press, 1970.
3. See e.g. S. Henry, *The Hidden Economy*, London, Martin Robertson, 1978; and J. Ditton, *Part-time Crime*, London, Macmillan, 1977.
4. See S. Keeble, 'Social security on strike', *New Society*, 28 October 1982.
5. G. Jordan and J. Richardson, Pantouflage: a civil service perk', *New Society* (22 February 1979).
6. B. Cox, J. Shirley and M. Short, *The Fall of Scotland Yard*, Harmondsworth, Middx., Penguin, 1977.
7. M. J. Clarke, *Fallen Idols: Elites and the Search for an Acceptable Face of Capitalism*, London, Junction Books, 1981.
8. Royal Commission on Standards of Conduct in Public Life, 1974–6 *Report* (Chairman Lord Salmon), Cmnd 6524, HMSO, 1976; See M. Tomkinson and M. Gillard, *Nothing to Declare*, London, John Calder, 1980, for an account of the Poulson affair and Maudling's involvement in it.
9. Tomkinson and Gillard, op. cit. On the general question of political accusations of corruption see S. Chibnall and P. Saunders, 'Worlds Apart: Notes on the Social Reality of Corruption', *British Journal of Sociology*, **28** (1977), 138–77.
10. E. Hughes, *Men and Their Work*, New York, Free Press, 1958.
11. J. Skolnick, *House of Cards*, Boston, Little, Brown, 1978.

2 Local government corruption in England and Wales

PHIL FENNELL

Throughout British history local government has carried a traditional association in the minds of the public with opportunities for corrupt practices. All the diverse organs of local government of the eighteenth century—the select vestries, municipal corporations, manorial courts, and justices of the peace, as well as the local statutory authorities established for special purposes such as the Court of Sewers—were objects of criticism on account of the jobbery that pervaded every aspect of the amorphous structure. The Webbs, in their detailed historical account of local government (1963, p. 380), refer to the corruption of parish government in the following terms:

> In the majority of urban parishes where select vestries were started, this close body fell from the outset into the hands of small shopkeepers, master craftsmen and builders, to whom the opportunities for eating, drinking, and making excursions at the public expense, and the larger gains of extending their little businesses by parish work offered an irresistible temptation.

Indeed Joseph Merceron, the notorious 'boss' of the parish of Bethnal Green, has been likened by one writer to the legendary Chicago gangsters, on the basis of his domination of the parish for a period of almost fifty years from 1787 (Smellie, p. 13). Justices of the peace were also prone to abuse of their office, as is evidenced by the stigmatisation of the Westminster justices by Edmund Burke as 'the scum of the earth'.

This chapter begins with a brief outline of the structural development of local government and the private sector of the economy. Included in this section is a brief summary of the development of the criminal statutes relating to corruption. This is followed by a section dealing with the areas of local government operation where opportunities occur for corrupt practices. The third part deals with the reports of the two bodies that investigated the question of corruption as a result of scandals that came to light in the early 1970s, namely the Redcliffe-Maud Committee and the Salmon Commission. This is followed by three case studies of local government in South Wales, each of which illustrates different aspects of corruption. The chapter concludes with some general remarks on corruption as an object of social scientific inquiry.

Historical introduction

It was not until 1835, with the passage of the Municipal Corporations Act, that a rudimentary basis of a system of local government, founded on a rather limited form of democratic franchise and under a form of central government direction and inspection, was established. Before that date, where government at a local level was not conducted through royal nominees in the shape of lords lieutenant and justices of the peace, it was in the hands of manorial or municipal corporations comprising agricultural or craft and trade representatives. At the most local level select vestries consisting of churchwardens and vestry-men ran the government. A common feature of these bodies was their oligarchic character, with ownership of property the major qualification for membership. Referring to the operation of the corporations, the Webbs (1963, p. 368) have this to say:

> What emerges from our analysis of these manorial and municipal exceptions from the common rule of the government of the country by the King's Lieutenants and the King's Justices is the fact that practically all the regula-tive activities of these organs of independent authority seem to be con-nected, at least by traditional origin, not with the common interests of all men as citizens and consumers, but with the particular interests of the members as locally privileged groups of agriculturalists, traders and manu-facturers . . .

Beyond the dictates of self-interest the functions of local government were limited by modern British standards, usually confined to the provision of a volunteer constable, licensing, and the administration of indoor and outdoor pauper relief. Some model authorities such as Manchester provided an organised police force before this was required of them by law, and quite a few ran their own fire service.

The Industrial Revolution threw into sharp focus the need for a more effic-ient and democratic means of local government than that which for the most part the corporations were either capable of providing or inclined to provide. The great massing of population in the towns and cities and the concomitant problems of overcrowding, poor housing and sanitation leading to outbreaks of typhus and cholera; the lack of an adequate police force to cope with rising crime, as well as the dramatic rise in pauperism; all contributed to the radical urge to reform the structure of local government along Benthamite lines. Well before the Act of 1835, the increase in the magnitude of the traditional tasks of local government had all but rendered obsolete the traditional method of performance through a few officials who owned the freehold of their offices and remunerated themselves through the customary fees and duties attached to the discharge of their functions, supplemented by a larger number of con-scripted 'volunteers' to perform the undesirable duties such as that of constable.

The Benthamite formula for efficient government (directed to the greatest good of the greatest number through the application of modern scientific methods at the least cost), was based upon the principle of 'putting out to contract' the various functions of local government at the lowest price yielded by competitive tender, resulting in a projected increase in efficiency of government through the virile influence of market competition. To ensure that the self-interest of the contractors remained enlightened, Bentham adapted his Panopticon principle to the purpose of exercising supervision and surveillance over local government through a central chamber that would have the function of inspecting the affairs of local bodies. Well before any of this achieved legislative fruition in the nineteenth century, the practice of 'putting out to contract' was widely established, but with such an absence of effective supervision that the phrase 'putting out' seems infelicitous, since there took place what the Webbs refer to (1963, p. 426) as an unashamed 'orgy of corruption'. The distribution of contracts among the members became so widespread that in 1782 it was made an offence for churchwardens and overseers of poor law institutions to contract for or supply goods to be paid for out of public funds. It was not until 1835, however, that this was made a ground for disqualification from office. Although there had been in force in many areas standing orders for the prevention of this kind of favouritism, these were frequently suspended by bodies whose tender-hearted concern for the mutual prosperity of their membership exceeded their desire to adhere·to regulations.

The importance of this period is that it was at this time that the principle of 'putting out to contract' created a significant interface between local government and the private sector, which increased the opportunities for unjust enrichment. As the range and importance of local government functions increased so central boards of control were established, together with auditors, as a means of keeping a check on the financial dealings of the authorities. Although it was established that members of local government bodies could not themselves enter into contracts with those bodies, there appeared to be no penal provision directed against the giving or the receipt of a bribe to influence the conduct of members of public bodies in the exercise of their duties. This gap was exploited to the full in London in the period leading up to the 1880s.

At that time the body which exercised the vast bulk of the functions of government for London was the somewhat cumbrous Metropolitan Board of Works, which, as Herbert Morrison (1949, p. 88) put it with some understatement, 'acquired a possibly exaggerated reputation for jobbery'. The Board was a body elected from the parishes and districts of London that had been established in 1855 as a structure through which not only could the local government of London be conducted, but also the widespread re-construction and renovation of the city could be co-ordinated. It had power to build, widen or repair roads, to demolish buildings, to control building, to buy and sell land and to make improvements to buildings. Financial controls were exercised by the

Commissioners of Works where sums of more than £50,000 were involved, and by Parliament where sums in excess of £100,000 were involved. In 1887 the Metropolitan Board, under duress, appointed a Select Committee to inquire into allegations of corruption concerning the sale of land. The Committee was something of a non-event, since no witnesses would turn up, preferring instead to make the case for the appointment of a Royal Commission with the power to subpoena witnesses, and equally important, to grant them immunity from prosecution. Eventually, in March 1888 a Royal Commission was established and reported in November of the same year. The Commission found that the Board had frequently failed to invite public competition for the sale and lease of premises and that premises so disposed of were often vested in pauper nominees of Board members. It also reported that payments had been received from tenants found for public houses, and that bribes had been taken by members of the Board in return for relaxing their standards as music hall censors. In conclusion, the Commission recommended (1888, par. 94):

> that it would be well if it were made a criminal offence to offer any member or official of a public body any kind of payment or reward in relation to the affairs of the body of which he is a member and also if the person accepting it were made amenable to the criminal law . . .

It was the report of the Royal Commission which provided the basis for the Public Bodies (Corrupt Practices) Act 1889. As a piece of criminal legislation it was unambitious, as the following remarks from its sponsor, Lord Randolph Churchill, show (his Lordship was responding to the criticism that the Bill was not widely enough drafted in that it only extended to public bodies and not private corporations):

> I fear that if the scope of the Bill were extended, no progress would be made on any legislation on the subject. There is an essential difference between a private body and a public one. A private body had a direct interest in looking after its servants, but in the case of a public body, what is everybody's business is nobody's business. . . . At some time, perhaps, Parliament may take into consideration the mischievous practice of giving commissions and tips; but it is too much to attempt now. This Bill is the direct offspring of the Commission to inquire into the Metropolitan Board. The Commission found that persons had been guilty of corrupt practices for which they could not be got hold of in any way . . . [1]

The provisions of the Act were limited to 'local public bodies', with reference to which two classes of corrupt transactions were declared to be misdemeanours. The first is the giving of a bribe, and the second the receiving of a bribe by 'any person . . . to induce a member, officer or servant to do anything in relation to his public duties'. No prosecution is permitted under the Act without the consent of the Attorney-General. At the time the Act was introduced it was a fairly recent innovation, which had become increasingly common since the mid-nineteenth century, for Parliament to restrict the right of a private citizen to bring a private prosecution by requiring the consent of one of the Law Officers of the Crown (of whom the Attorney-General is the most senior) before criminal proceedings may be set in train. This means that the Attorney-General (who is also a Member of Parliament and of the Cabinet) acts as a sort of filter through which cases must pass before they reach the courts. Since the Attorney-General is an executive officer, this has implications for classical rule of law theory because decisions involving the interpretation and application of the law are taken out of the hands of the judges. This, although it is said to bring with it a measure of uniformity in the enforcement of the law, is in principle open to objection, even from incumbent Attorney-Generals like Sir Reginald Manningham-Buller, who objected to the practice in the following passage from his evidence to the Select Committee on Obscene Publications (1958, pp. 53–4): 'Uniformity in the administration of the law is a matter for the courts themselves and should not, in my view, be achieved by interposing the decisions of officers of the executive between them and the law they administer'. The original stated reason for the introduction of the requirement of the Attorney-General's consent was to avoid bribery, collusion, blackmail and other improper practices which frequently surrounded the private prosecution. By the 1970s, as Dickens notes (1974, pp. 50–1), the Home Office was able to offer five justifications for the extension of the practice:

(1) to secure consistency in practice in bringing prosecutions, for instance where it is not possible to define the offence very precisely, so that the law is potentially very broadly applicable, or is open to a variety of interpretations;
(2) to prevent abuse of process or the bringing of the law into disrepute through the bringing of trivial cases;
(3) to enable account to be taken of mitigating factors;
(4) to provide some central control of the use of the criminal law when it has to intrude into sensitive or controversial areas;
(5) to ensure that decisions on prosecution take account of important considerations of public policy.

In sum, the Attorney-General's consent was required to enable the prosecution process, as well as the interpretation of the law, to be kept under tight control by central state authority. In the particular case of corruption law such consent proved a bone of contention during the early years of the twentieth century between the government and the interest groups involved in further legislative ventures.

The Prevention of Corruption Act 1906 was intended to deal with corruption in connection with all agents, whether agents of public bodies or private principals. It was aimed at the then prevalent practice of offering and receiving secret commissions. The term secret commission refers to the situation where an agent acts as a buyer for his principal, and without the principal's knowledge, receives a percentage of the purchase price from the seller. The Act was preceded by ten years of lobbying for legislation by the Secret Commissions Committee of the London Chamber of Commerce, which had published a report on the subject in 1898. The Act was extremely carefully worded, and its major effect, apart from making the giving or receipt of a secret commission a criminal offence, was to include crown agents and people serving under local authorities as agents, thus extending the ambit of the 1889 Act. The latter reform had been necessitated by difficulties with the 1889 Act, particularly those resulting from counsels' opinions given to the Attorney-General in two cases where the advice was that the bodies to which the corrupt person belonged did not fall within the rather limited definition of 'public local body'. The Attorney-General had saved these provisions for the appropriate legislative opportunity; the Prevention of Corruption Act provided it.

The Prevention of Corruption Act 1916 was passed in the wake of scandals involving the clothing department of the War Office, where viewers and inspectors of merchandise had taken bribes to pass sub-standard clothing. The Act provides that where the transaction is a contract or proposal for a contract with a government department or a public body, the maximum sentence would be raised from two to seven years. The Act also provides that in such cases where a gift has been received by a person in the employment of government or any public body, from someone who has or wishes to obtain a contract from any of those bodies, then that payment will be presumed to have been given and received corruptly.[2] The development of anti-corruption legislation has been characterised not so much by a desire to provide measures that will lead to the prevention or readier detection of corruption, but rather to ensure that once it comes to light, the prosecution process is tightly controlled by the executive through the Attorney-General; that convictions will be easily obtainable where the burden of proof is reversed and that punishment will be severe. Hence there is a strong symbolic element in the criminal law on corruption through which the probity of the system may be asserted through the periodic legal and social anathematisation (to use Clarke's term—Clarke, 1981, p. 5) of corrupt officials and their corruptors.

Opportunities for corruption in local government

The functions of local government have expanded over the last 150 years to the point where, with the exception of social security and medical services, local government has become the principle vehicle of welfare state provision; it also has responsibility for roads and transport facilities, as well as the planning and execution of projects for the development or re-development of land. Some idea of the scale of these activities can be gathered from the breakdown of local

Table 2.1 Capital and non-capital expenditure by service in
England and Wales 1978-9

	Capital expenditure £m.	Other expenditure £m.	Total gross expenditure £m.
Education	400	7,500	7,900
Housing	2,400	2,800	5,200
Local environmental services	500	3,100	3,500
Law, order and protective services	100	1,600	1,700
Roads and transport	400	1,300	1,700
Personal social services	100	1,300	1,400
Other	100	600	700
All services	4,000	18,200	22,000

Source: Local Government Financial Statistics, England and Wales, 1978-9, London, HMSO, 1980.

government expenditure shown in Table 2.1. With the exception of education, social services and policing, these functions are normally carried out by contracting out the work to contractors in the private sector, except in the rare cases of local authorities that have small direct labour departments. Since the election of the 1979 government, contracting out of local government functions to the private sector has been encouraged as an efficiency measure, incidentally creating another area where corruption may arise.

The Salmon Commission (Report 1976, para. 38) felt that one of the most important structural factors leading to corruption was the 'conditions created by Parliament in the field of planning law and in urban and housing development which have put greater strain on a system of locally elected councils whose members may enter public life with little preparation and may find themselves handling matters on a financial scale quite beyond their experience in private life. The power to make decisions which lead to larger capital gains or business profits has given rise to obvious temptations on both sides.'

Local authorities are not only the potential customers of the private sector, but they also exercise controlling functions over areas of business that are potentially lucrative for private entrepreneurs. This control is exercised through the discharge of licensing functions and through the regulation of land use through the exercise of the planning role mentioned above. Licensing of various activities and the granting of planning permission can both create profit and enhance the value of property or a business. As an illustration of the point that market values can be altered, or even created by decisions of a local authority, the Department of the Environment, in their evidence to Salmon, noted that (1976, p. 2): 'A plot is more valuable when it carries planning permission to develop than when it does not. For example, in Spring 1974 prime agricultural land in the outer London Metropolitan area was worth £1,000 or perhaps £1,500. Similar land with planning permission for housing was worth £45,000 an acre'. Thus the exercise of power, sometimes even executive power, within a local authority, by elected representatives can, at the stroke of a pen, turn land of comparatively little value into property that immediately guarantees substantial profits with little or no investment, skill or risk.

The other area providing scope for corrupt activities is that of development or re-development of land. The Local Government, Planning and Land, Act 1980 s.91 gives wide powers to local authorities (subject to the consent of the Secretary of State for the Environment) 'to acquire compulsorily . . . any land which is in their area and which is suitable for, and is required in order to secure the carrying out of one or more of the following activities, namely, development, re-development and improvement'. Many local authorities, including several urban authorities have used equivalent powers to acquire land compulsorily in city centres for the purpose of erecting large shopping and entertainment complexes. The construction of such developments is farmed out to private building companies. Each of the case studies dealt with in the following sections provides an illustration of the way each of these areas can provide opportunities for corrupt activities.

The Redcliffe-Maud Committee and the Salmon Commission

Until the 1970s the prevalent attitude to official corruption in Britain was characterised by a complacent sense that corruption was largely a foreign phenomenon. This attitude was rudely shaken by the Poulson affair, following which a corrupt architect and his leading acolytes in central and local government were jailed, and the Home Secretary at the time, Reginald Maudling, resigned.[3] Tomkinson and Gillard (1980, p. viii) describe the reaction to the affair as follows: 'As a succession of men in public life paraded through the courts and the press to answer charges arising out of their involvement with Poulson, the proceedings seemed more typical of some tiny banana republic or even the United States, than Britain'.

Poulson had recruited a small army of councillors and officials as well as one or two Members of Parliament to his cause. Inducements were offered in return for influencing lucrative public works contracts. In response to the scandalised public reaction, a Royal Commission on Standards of Conduct in Public Life (Salmon, 1976) and a Prime Minister's Committee on Local Government Rules of Conduct (Redcliffe-Maud, 1974) were established. Among the central tasks which these bodies posed for themselves was that of assessing the degree to which the pattern of conduct, which was almost accidentally unearthed in bankruptcy proceedings in Poulson's case, was an isolated occurrence or a manifestation of a more widespread social malaise. This was no easy task to perform reliably: although not a crime without a victim, corruption is a crime with victims who may never know that they are victims. Roads, shopping complexes, houses, and offices get built, despite corrupt practices at the tendering stage, and questions are unlikely to be asked until cracks start to appear, which may be years later. Arrest and conviction figures may therefore be even less likely than usual to present an accurate picture. The Attorney-General, in evidence to Salmon, states that from 1970–5 there were 642 prosecutions for corruption in a number of fields. Because the prosecution statistics were unreliable, both the Salmon and Redcliffe-Maud enquiries were forced to rely largely upon the opinions of those who submitted evidence as to the prevalence of corrupt practices. The Salmon Commission endorsed the view (strenuously advocated by many of the individuals and groups giving evidence) that, as the Attorney-General put it in his evidence (1975), p. 1), 'corruption is fortunately not widespread in public life'. The Conservative Party (Redcliffe-Maud, Vol. 2, p. 70) felt that it was desirable that the whole matter should be 'kept in proper perspective' and the Law Society (ibid., p. 135) could see 'very little evidence of serious abuse'.

The Association of Councillors (Redcliffe-Maud, Vol. 2, pp. 1–4) argued that public concern over corruption was something of a moral panic whipped up by a sensationalist press. The bulk of its evidence consists of an attempt to re-define the problem of corruption as one of unjustified lack of public confidence in local government, recommending more vigorous use of the Press Council by authorities who had been smeared, and the establishment of a body to control television journalists, whom they regard as being 'the true masters of the smear technique'.

Having canvassed the areas of activity of local government in which corrupting might occur, both bodies turned to the features of the system of government that might increase the potential for such practices. Here they were presented with a multiplicity of possible causes, each of which bore the indelible hallmarks of the political perspectives of its proponents. The industrialists' group 'Aims of Industry' felt that the major cause was too much government interference, too many administrative procedures and not enough reliance on the private sector and the operation of market factors. T. Dan Smith, a local politician who had been jailed as a result of his involvements as a key figure in the Poulson affair, felt that local government provided greater opportunities for corruption than central government. In his evidence to Salmon (1976, p. 1) he advanced the view, doubtless based on experience, that 'the councillor dominates the officer in a way that Members of Parliament could never dominate the civil servant'. Corruption was also encouraged, in the opinion of many bodies submitting evidence, by the secrecy of many local authority committees, by the prolonged concentration of power at a local level in the hands of one party, and by the risks attached to investigative journalism in Britain by the stringency of the law of defamation.

The Redcliffe-Maud Committee (para. 75) were anxious to emphasise the different standards of conduct which applied in the public and private sectors: 'It is common practice in the commercial world for the transactions of business to be accompanied by the giving of personal gifts or benefits, ranging from the Christmas bottle of whiskey to more elaborate and lavish provision. Public life requires a standard of its own: and those entertaining in public life should be made aware of this from the outset'. Yet what exactly was demanded by this more rigorous standard was not specified in any detail in the report. The Committee declared that 'the test should always be whether the gift or entertainment is genuinely justifiable in the public interest' (para. 77). Other guidance offered included an exhortation that gifts should be refused unless they were trifling and to refuse would give offence, and that hospitality was best extended from the secure base of local authority premises at local authority expense.

Many bodies giving evidence advocated a cautious approach to legislation, arguing that business people would be deterred from serving in local government (Redcliffe-Maud, Vol. 2, pp. 4 and 62; evidence of the Law Society to Salmon, para. 22). Although they acknowledged this argument (1974, para. 22) the Redcliffe-Maud Committee recommended a statutory register of councillors' interests and tougher penalties for their non-disclosure. At the moment the position remains that councillors have discretion as to whether to declare an interest in a particular matter under consideration, subject of course to prosecution if they have wrongfully withheld information. Two years later the Salmon Commission again recommended that all councillors' interests should be open to public examination, and that the penalty for non-disclosure of an interest should be raised to a maximum of two years' imprisonment. To date none of these recommendations has been implemented. It is worth noting in passing that in the case of Murphy, which is briefly described in the next section, the council had debated Redcliffe-Maud on the very eve of one of his corrupt junkets.

Three recent corruption cases in South Wales

In order to illustrate the different forms that local government corruption may take, I now turn to a consideration of three corruption trials that took place in South Wales in the late 1970s. The first illustrates how corruption over the allocation of contracts can occur. The charges arose out of lavish entertainment received by a former elected council leader (Murphy) and a housing director (Harris), which it was alleged had influenced their conduct in awarding contracts to install central heating systems in council houses in the city of Swansea. A chairperson and a marketing director of two private companies were also charged and convicted. The second case involved the chairperson of the Policy Committee of Swansea city council (Jenkins). His party had achieved resounding success in the local government elections, running on an anti-corruption ticket following the trial of Murphy. He was convicted in March 1979 of conspiracy with a nightclub owner, Bernard George, that the latter should corruptly make and the former should corruptly receive inducements to show favour and use his influence as a member of the council, the licensing planning authority and the South Wales police authority (gifts already received included food, drink, leaflets at elections, transport, carpentry and decoration).

Although the previously ruling Labour group had rejected an application by George to open the nightclub in the city, after the election the plan was re-submitted and passed. In March 1977, an application by George's company to build a complex of shops and a ballroom was approved without any other company having a chance to tender estimates. This latter deal fell through because of the opening of police investigations.

The third case also involves corruption in connection with local government's control functions. Ernest Westwood, the former chairperson of Glamorgan Planning Committee, appeared at Cardiff Crown Court charged with conspiracy with four businessmen, that they should corruptly give and Westwood should corruptly receive gifts and considerations to influence his conduct as chairperson of the Planning Committee, between January 1972 and December 1973. He received travel, accommodation, entertainment and gifts including a tape recorder and a fur coat for his wife from the co-defendants, in return for showing favour to Thistlegrange Properties. Westwood had personally managed the planning applications of this company under a Standing Order of the Council that empowered a committee chairperson to act on behalf of the committee in consultation with the Chief Executive or County Secretary if the matter required immediate attention and there was no time to call a special meeting of the council. After an eighty-eight-day trial, the longest trial ever held in Wales, Westwood was sentenced to four and a half years' imprisonment, and the remaining defendants to three years each. This corrupt relationship, unlike that of Jenkins and George, was not based on pre-existing friendship, but solely upon the entrepreneurial activities of a property company based outside the area, who used a local business person as a 'land scout'.

A number of significant points emerged from the defence put forward in each of these trials. First, it was argued that the allegedly corrupt activities were no more than *common business practice*. The activities were everyday events, and their frequency rendered them acceptable as well as normal. Secondly, it was argued that the sums of money involved were, from the standpoint of the companies concerned, trivial, the implication being that a 'real' bribe would represent a more substantial investment. Alternative motives were offered for these trifling expenditures, namely generosity and kindness. Thirdly, it was pointed out in the first case that other, larger companies engaging in these practices were part of the state system. Parties and gifts given by the Wales Gas Board were cited. The implication here is that association with the state legitimates the activities. For example one of the defence lawyers, Talfyn-Davies QC, told the jury in the Westwood trial:

> In the last decade there have been in Wales desperate attempts by Government . . . and by local authorities, to attract, cajole and persuade industrialists to come to this area. All these bodies have been dancing attendance upon people who might come to invest their finance and their skills in South Wales. Is it to be said that because companies are doing this that there is corruption? Of course it isn't—it is known as public relations. Most companies have a public relations budget.[4]

The extent of this public relations work, hinted at by Talfyn-Davies, was elaborated in much more detail by one of the defendants in the Murphy trial, Douglas Barber. Barber freely admitted not only that he had met and treated Murphy and Harris in London by prior arrangement, but that he 'had done this for many councillors from South Wales'.[5] Referring to such public relations work in the jargon of the business world as 'below the line costs', Barber stated that the other firms with whom he competed and the nationalised concerns, British Gas and the National Coal Board, all lavishly entertained councillors. Barber further stated that he would 'seek out councillors visiting London to take them to lunch to cement relationships' and to sell himself and his firm. 'I offered hospitality and extended business courtesy to clients. My job was to impress upon customers that they were dealing with a company of substance and integrity.'[6] Also in the Murphy trial Walter Lewis, marketing director of the NCB for Wales, revealed that the Board had, between 1970 and 1976, paid £67,000 for Everwarm Homes to be spent on the promotion of solid fuel central heating.

If these statements, made under oath, are true, then it would appear that not only does such activity cover a wide scale, but that it seems to be regarded as familiar and unobjectionable in business circles. In his sentencing speech in the Swansea Crown Court at the Murphy trial, Mr Justice Kenneth Jones referred to Barber as a man who had been 'deceived and carried away by his own professional jargon'.[7] Also the managing director of Smith and Wellstood, A. C. Pritchard, has said that as far as he knew all Barber had done was to follow 'usual commercial rules that operate everywhere'. If corruption or the potential for corruption exists on such a wide scale, then one of the questions that must be asked is what are the factors leading to certain individuals being caught and convicted and others getting away with it?

A number of points emerge from the foregoing brief survey. First of all, what is considered corrupt in a transaction involving public officials and the private sector may not be so considered in a transaction between private individuals. This is a point of which great play is made by defendants in corruption trials, in the vain attempt to have their conduct characterised as normal rather than corrupt. Secondly, corruption is generally perceived and presented in terms of 'scandals' or 'affairs', which leads to a scandalised and somewhat sensationalised portrayal of conduct regarded by many as intrinsic to commercial life. This probably results from the fact that corruption is usually discovered by chance in bankruptcy proceedings, or through carelessness, or through investigatory journalism, and thus the number of cases that come to trial is small. However, once detected and prosecuted, the defendants have only a slim chance of acquittal and can expect a severe sentence. Sentence ranged from two to four and a half years in the cases cited. In combination, these features foster a belief in the 'rotten apple' theory of corruption, which is reinforced in a judicial rhetoric of castigation concerning abuse of positions of trust.[8] The implication is that corruption in the United Kingdom occurs as the result of individual ambition, dishonesty or weakness, and that the institutional structure and its typical practices are fundamentally sound.

On the other hand, both experts' and everyday accounts of corruption in developing nations have implicit in them a more or less elaborate 'blighted orchard' theory, that corruption in such societies is normal and only to be expected, thus illustrating the moral inferiority of such political economies.

Conclusion

The study of corruption has been approached by social scientists from a number of angles, most of which until recently have been dominated by functionalist concerns, examining either the functionality or dysfunctionality of corruption from sociological or economic points of view. The more recent tendency has been to examine the socially constructed nature of corruption as both a legal and a sociological category (e.g. Chibnall and Saunders, 1977; Fennell and Thomas, forthcoming; and Doig, forthcoming). There are two questions to be tackled by researchers into corruption. How far does market competition depend upon promotions and perquisites? Is the current legal framework too much geared towards anathematising the small numbers of defendants who are tried in the courts and not focussing sufficiently on rules which will make corruption harder to engage in and easier to detect?

Notes

1. Lord Randolph Churchill, Hansard H.C. Debs., Ser. 3, Vol. 334 col. 810 (1889).
2. For a more detailed account of the history of the criminal law on corruption see P. Fennell and P. A. Thomas, 'Corruption in Britain: an Historical Analysis', forthcoming in the *International Journal of Law and Sociology*.
3. For an extremely thorough account of the Poulson affair see Tomkinson and Gillard (1980). For provocative discussion of issues raised by this affair see Chibnall and Saunders (1977), and Clarke (1981), *passim*.
4. *Western Mail*, 8 February 1977.

5. *Western Mail*, 1 March 1977.
6. *Western Mail*, 4 May 1977.
7. *Western Mail*, 30 May 1977.
8. *Western Mail*, 7 February 1976.

Bibliography

Chibnall, S. and Saunders, P. (1977), 'Worlds Apart: Notes on the Social Reality of Corruption', *British Journal of Sociology*, **28**, 138–52.
Clarke, M. (1981), *Fallen Idols: Elites and the Search for an Acceptable Face of Capitalism*, London, Junction Books.
Cox, B., Shirley, J. and Short, M. (1977), *The Fall of Scotland Yard*, Harmondsworth, Middx., Penguin.
Dickens, B. M. (1974), 'The Prosecuting Roles of the Attorney-General and the Director of Public Prosecutions', *Public Law*, 50–73.
Edwards, J. Ll. J. (1964), *The Law Officers of the Crown*, London, Sweet and Maxwell.
Morrison, H. (1949), *How London is Governed*, London, People's University Press.
Prime Minister's Committee on Local Government Rules of Conduct (Chairperson: Lord Redcliffe-Maud), Cmnd 5636, London, HMSO, 1974.
Royal Commission on Standards of Conduct in Public Life, 1974–6, *Report* (Chairperson: Lord Salmon), Cmnd 6524, London, HMSO, 1976.
Secret Commissions Committee of the London Chamber of Commerce to the Council of the London Chamber of Commerce, 20 May 1898. Minutes of the London Chamber of Commerce, Ms. 16.643/3, Guildhall Library, London.
Tomkinson, M. and Gillard, M. (1980), *Nothing to Declare: The Political Corruption of John Poulson*, London, John Calder.

The evidence submitted to the Salmon Commission is in boxed copies deposited in copyright libraries. The evidence to the Redcliffe-Maud Committee is contained in Volume 2 of the report.

3 Malpractices in British casino management

DAVID MIERS

This chapter is not concerned to advance any theoretical or analytical examination of the legal or any other definition of corruption; indeed as Heidenheimer has shown, there are many different conceptions of corruption.[1] Notwithstanding this variety in most of the sociological and political literature, corruption typically connotes the abuse of public office for personal gain, which is usually, but by no means always, pecuniary.[2] Set against this characterisation, this chapter's subject matter—the unlawful practices adopted by the management of a number of London casinos during the late seventies to increase their income —may seem to fall outside the standard examples of corrupt practices.[3] Those involved, however, were for the most part directors or other officers of public companies, which, though they are not normally equated in law with public bodies, nevertheless share many of their distinguishing characteristics: most notably in the present context, the conferral of powers and the imposition of duties, the exercise and performance of which are governed by legislation, and by other non-legal rules having legislative effect. In this sense the unlawful behaviour of the director of a public company may be functionally indistinguishable from the corrupt behaviour of an official in local government, or of a policeman.[4] Moreover, the legal definition of corruption is by no means confined to the abuse of public office, though this may be viewed more seriously and be more likely to attract a prosecution. Any employee who corruptly accepts gifts as an inducement for doing or refraining from doing anything in relation to his employer's business affairs commits an offence, as does anyone who corruptly offers or provides such gifts.[5] Although, with one or two exceptions, the practices described here did not give rise to prosecutions under the relevant legislation, this was not necessarily because those practices fell outside the appropriate definitions.[6]

The chapter is divided into three parts. The first describes the conditions under which casino gaming becomes profitable and the circumstances obtaining in the London casino market during the mid-seventies that encouraged greatly increased profits. The second describes the nature of the malpractices adopted by Ladbroke's, Coral and Playboy, the three principals in this account, to attract and to maintain the custom of high-staking punters. The final part discusses some of the implications of these malpractices for the regulation of commercial gaming, in particular where it is conducted by large public companies.

The profitability of casino gaming

Casinos make their money by retaining a fixed percentage of all the money staked on games of unequal chance, which are, in order of popularity, American roulette (which is the same as French roulette, but because it does not entail the rituals of the older version, a faster game), punto banco, blackjack, French roulette, dice and baccarat banque.[7] While the exact figure for any particular club depends to some extent on the combination of games it offers and on the competence of its staff, when run efficiently, a casino reckons to retain about 18–20 per cent of the drop (money exchanged for chips). This amount retained is called the gross gaming yield and represents income before any expenditure. During the seventies, some 125 casinos were operating in Great Britain, twenty-five of them in London. From the relatively healthy figure of £225 million in 1972–3,[8] the total drop increased substantially over the next few years, partly as a result of the fall in the value of the pound. A high proportion of this increase was attributable to the per capita growth in the stakes bet by foreign punters, in particular from the Gulf states, Saudi Arabia and Iran. While there was only a 12 per cent increase in attendances by punters between 1975 and 1976 and a 25 per cent increase in business between 1976 and 1977, the drop went up by 36 per cent and 43 per cent to £477 and £680 million respectively.[9] In 1979–80 the total drop was £960 million; and even allowing for the effects of inflation this represented a real increase of some 80 per cent over the 1972–3 figure.[10] However, the income which these figures represent was not shared equally by all 125 casinos. Until 1979–80, 75 per cent of it was generated in London, although this subsequently fell to 70 per cent.[11] Taking 1979–80 as the peak year for the London casinos, sharing a drop of £661 million, and recalling that casino income is reckoned to be at least 18 per cent of the drop, then, in that year the twenty-five London casinos were generating a gross gaming yield approaching £119 million.

Set against this income are the casino's operating costs. Some of these, such as the fee for the annual renewal of its gaming licence, are relatively small; others, such as its recurrent staff costs and the new gaming duty rates, which mean that the larger clubs are paying 20 per cent of their gross gaming yield in duty, account for a much more significant proportion of the casino's income. It is estimated that 80–90 per cent of a provincial casino's gross gaming yield is consumed by its operating costs, but provincial casinos enjoy nothing like the kind of betting typically to be found in London.[12] Although costs may increase with increases in the *number* of punters, the key characteristic of those who patronised West End casinos during the mid-seventies was that they bet very heavily, and costs do not increase in proportion to the increases in the *amount* bet. Ladbroke's, Coral and Playboy were the public companies having the major share of the London market in the seventies. Ladbroke's and Coral both owned four clubs: the Hertford, the Ladbroke and the Park Tower were operated by a subsidiary of Ladbroke's, Ladup Ltd, and the Park Lane Casino by another of its subsidiaries, Hyde Park Casinos Ltd; Coral owned the Curzon House Club, Crockford's, the International Sporting Club and the Palm Beach Club. Due to some internal difficulties in the early seventies, the Coral group never matched the income achieved by the Ladbroke clubs;[13] nevertheless nearly 50 per cent of both groups' total pre-tax profits in 1979 (their last full year of operation) came from their casino divisions: £24.5 out of £49.2 million declared by Ladbroke's and £11.1 out of £23.6 million declared by Coral.

Playboy owned three casinos in London: the Playboy Club in Park Lane, the Clermont and the Victoria Sporting Club, which it bought in October 1979. The extent of its reliance on its London casinos was, however, appreciably greater than that of its competitors. It is reported that in the year ending 30 June 1981, Playboy Enterprises as a whole made a pre-tax profit of U.S.$25.4 million. During the same period, the group's five British casinos contributed $40,357,000—say £22 million—to the parent company. The inference that may be drawn from these figures is that the casinos subsidised the rest of the group by about $15 million. Moreover, most of this profit appears to have come from two of its London casinos, the Park Lane club and the Clermont. During the licence renewal hearings in October 1981, it was reported that the drop recorded at these two clubs between January 1976 and June 1981 was 'a staggering £660.3 million'.[14] The gross gaming yield of these two clubs over the four years ending 30 June 1980 was £105 million.

Such figures are almost breathtakingly vast; but even though the investigations of, and raids by, the Gaming Board and various divisions of the Metropolitan Police have resulted in the permanent or temporary closure of a number of casinos, the drop in London for 1981-2 was still £702 million,[15] producing a gross gaming yield of £126 million for the survivors, of which Grand Metropolitan was in 1982 the largest single operator with six casinos.[16]

Attracting and retaining the wealthy punter

Given the potential and actual income to be derived from bending the rules, it is hardly surprising that some of these operators succumbed. Casino proprietors do not pay great attention to individual wins and losses; what is important is to cultivate a regular clientele in a highstake bracket, whose routine and predictable losses will even out the casino's profits and cushion it against the occasional heavy loss. The enormous increase in the value of the stakes bet during the mid-seventies posed something of a dilemma for the major casinos. On the one hand they were the happy recipients of millions of pounds' worth of losses: for example in 1975 one Kuwaiti punter lost £1 million in three days at Coral's Curzon House Club, and in 1979 a Jordanian lost £1½ million in four hours of roulette at the Ladbroke Club. In the current more straitened atmosphere an individual loss of £10,000 is considered substantial. During the boom years of 1974-6 such a loss would have been regarded as petty cash: the Salon Privé in the Ladbroke Club was reputed to have a nightly turnover (money actually staked) of £250,000.[17] On the other hand, a punter whose stakes are well above those of the other players is in effect taking on the casino head-to-head, and may of course occasionally win. So long as he is a regular patron of the club the casino will eventually retrieve his winnings, and extract a percentage from him as well, but it cannot afford to see such a punter winning say £1–2 million and then losing them in another club. Moreover, to attract the highstaking punter in the first place, it is necessary to have very high table limits, which of course contributes to the possibility that the casino can lose a large sum of money in a few nights' play to a punter who never returns. Thus it becomes an integral part of casino policy to adopt some strategy to attract and, more importantly, to keep the wealthy punter: these I shall call respectively the external and the internal strategy.

Some of the clubs mentioned above have from time to time adopted practices designed to attract possible punters. These practices typically involve paying taxi drivers and hotel porters and commissionaires to direct potential clients to the casino. A variation on this was the 'hotel porters' scheme' run by Playboy between October 1976 and May 1977. This involved recruiting eight porters at five leading London hotels (the Dorchester, the Inn on the Park, the Intercontinental, the London Hilton and the Londonderry) and making them honorary members of the Playboy Club so that they could introduce hotel guests to the casino as their *bona fide* guests. Although contrary to section 12 of the Gaming Act 1968, this ploy was not regarded as a serious breach of the Act, nor was it very successful.[18]

Altogether more elaborate was the 'Unit Six' operation that Ladbroke's began in late 1976, and which cost the company approximately £500,000.[19] Initially the 'Unit Six' operation involved the standard practices of the external strategy—paying taxi-drivers, and paying commission to club members to introduce new clients; but when some of Ladbroke's highstaking punters, including Adnan Khashoggi, who was reputedly the biggest player in the world, placing a minimum of £20,000 on each coup, stopped playing in 1977, the group lost a significant source of its income. Accordingly, Ladbroke's casino subsidiary, Ladup Ltd, decided on a more aggressive policy to attract players from rival casinos. Likely targets were traced, with the help of a private detective agency, through their car registration numbers for whose details 50p per plate was paid to a police sergeant who had access to the police national computer at Nottingham.[20] The information derived from this impeccable source was then used by Ladup's marketing division who invited likely punters to elaborate dinners or sent them gifts, to persuade them to join one of its clubs.

This operation was conducted well into 1978, when accounts of it began to appear in *Private Eye*, following information received initially from a former Ladup employee who had been sacked by Labroke's. Far more damaging however, and as events have transpired, to both companies, was Ladup's decision to poach players from the Playboy Club. Along with the Gaming Board and the police, Playboy, in the person of Victor Lownes, figured prominently as one of the objectors in the normally routine licence renewal hearings in July 1979. The formal objection to the renewal of the licences for the Hertford, the Ladbroke and the Park Lane casinos contained a large number of specific allegations, some of which Ladbroke's admitted. So far as their Unit Six operation was concerned, no one agreed with Cyril Stein that touting in this way was common practice, and, following the evidence of the Gaming Board, whose advice the courts almost invariably accept, the licensing justices concluded that Ladup was not a fit and proper person to hold a gaming licence, and refused to renew the three licences. Matters became much bleaker in December 1979 when its appeal to the Crown Court, based on the solution recommended by its bankers, Morgan Grenfell, to create a new subsidiary independent of Ladup and with a 'clean' board of directors to hold the licences, was dismissed. Ladup's application for judicial review was also dismissed the following February.[21] City and Provincial Gaming Holdings was wound up in March 1981 at a cost of £209,000, including compensation to its seven directors (one of whom was a former president of the Law Society, Sir Desmond Heap).[22]

Following clear intimations by the Gaming Board that it would investigate all its casino operations, Ladbroke's sold its eleven provincial casinos in May 1980, and did not seek to reopen the three London casinos. The immediate effect was a drop in the group's share value from 242p to 158p, and the more delayed effect, a 34 per cent cut in its pre-tax profit for 1979–80. Nevertheless, the group has survived to see some of the mud, which, at a meeting of the British Casino Association in 1979, Cyril Stein promised would fly if Playboy persisted in its objections to the renewal of Ladup's licences, stick to its target.[23]

Having attracted punters to the casino, the object of the internal strategy is to maintain their custom. One of the principal ways to achieve this is through the provision of credit for gaming, which is specifically prohibited under the Gaming Act. As one writer has put it, credit is the lubricant of gaming,[24] but in enacting the 1968 legislation the Home Office view was that clubs should be given as little opportunity as possible to exploit a punter's desire to continue gambling. Accordingly, section 16(1) of the Act prohibits clubs from allowing credit for gaming in any form: '. . . neither the holder of [a gaming] licence nor any person acting on his behalf or under any arrangement with him shall make any loan or otherwise provide or allow to any person any credit, or release, or discharge on another person's behalf, the whole or any part of any debt— (a) for enabling any person to take part in the gaming, or (b) in respect of any losses incurred by any person in the gaming'.

Notwithstanding these prohibitions, the unlawful provision of credit has been a feature of the managerial practices at some of the London casinos. It was however the evidence gained as a result of the raids on Coral's four casinos carried out at the request of the Gaming Board by the Special Patrol Group, the Serious Crime Squad and 400 uniformed police in November 1979 that disclosed how chronic, systematic and substantial such deviance could be. At the licence renewal hearings in July 1980, it appeared that cheques amounting to more than £10 million had been held over a three-year period in the mid-seventies at Crockford's, while at the Curzon House Club, credit was given to three particularly valued customers by means of a fictitious bank account located at the South Eastern National Bank of Miami. There was evidence of other offences under the Gaming Act, and in September the licences in respect of the Curzon House, the Palm Beach and the International Sporting Club were cancelled.[25] Cancellation is very much more serious than the refusal to renew a gaming licence. It permits the justices to impose a disqualification order prohibiting use of the premises for gaming for a period not exceeding five years.[26] Such an order will of course substantially reduce the market value of those premises, a commercial effect that is discussed in the last section of this chapter.

One aspect of credit gaming which is not specifically proscribed by the Act is the acceptance of further cheques after a punter has written bad ones. Provided that it is not post dated, is exchanged for chips or cash of equal value and is delivered to a bank for payment or collection within two banking days, it is lawful for a casino to accept a cheque to enable the drawer to take part in gaming. Clearly, however, a good deal of credit can be extended to a punter if the casino turns a blind eye to those cheques returned to it by the bank, before requiring full, or even part settlement on some subsequent occasion. It has been argued that the Gaming Act imposes no impediment on how a dishonoured cheque may be dealt with by a casino, provided that when it was drawn the provisions of section were complied with. Nevertheless, the Gaming Board regards the holding, compromise or release of dishonoured cheques as being contrary to the spirit of the Act,[27] and it formed an aspect of the Department of Trade's four-year investigation of the management of the Knightsbridge Sporting Club, and of its owner, Scotia Investments Ltd, which led in turn to the raid on the casino's premises carried out by the Organised Crime Squad in March 1981. The evidence obtained from these operations showed that the casino management regularly ignored the cheques returned to it, in one case permitting a punter to bounce seventy-one cheques totalling £966,000 over a fifteen-month period before settling for £175,000. The Gaming Act allows casinos to provide blank cheque forms for players to use to exchange for cash or chips. They are known as scrip cheques and are commonly used in casinos. The investigation into the Knightsbridge casino revealed a number of discrepancies in these scrip cheques, including some which had had false endorsements entered on them so as to indicate that the two-day banking requirement had been complied with.[28] In November 1981 the licensing justices cancelled the licence and disqualified the premises for three years, and in June 1982 the appeal by the new owners to the Crown Court was dismissed.[29]

It was, however, the revelations at the two Playboy Casinos that attracted most attention during 1981. At about the same time as he was preparing his objections to the renewal of the four Ladbroke licences in order, as he put it, 'for the good name of the [gaming] industry to be restored', Victor Lownes added what must be one of the least well advised invitations to his opponents: 'I am inviting them to hit back at me because I know my house is clean.' Ladbroke's did just that, spending £10,000 simply to obtain information from two former employees at Playboy's Park Lane casino. The result of their efforts, and those of the Metropolitan Police's Club Squad was that the Playboy and Clermont Clubs were raided in February 1981. In April it became apparent that the police would be objecting to the renewal of their licences, and later that month Lownes was sacked. The reason was not so much that he might have connived at breaches of the Gaming Act, but that the parent company wanted a clean image to present to the New Jersey Casino Control Commission in pursuit of a permanent licence to operate its $135 million casino in Atlantic City. It was in pursuit of this goal that Playboy appointed Sir John Treacher, a former Fleet and Allied Commander-in-Chief, Channel and Eastern Atlantic, who, since he resigned from the navy in 1977, had been chief executive of National Car Parks, to be the new chairman of Playboy (UK).

The licence renewal hearings for the Playboy and the Clermont Clubs took place in September 1981. The police and the Gaming Board presented a number of objections, although they did not regard all of them as being equally serious. For example, a good deal of publicity was given to the fact that Clement Freud MP, who was a director of Playboy, had gambled at both clubs. Such behaviour, if it did not constitute an offence under section 12, would be regarded as improper by the Board, but this matter was not regarded as seriously as the substantial provision of credit, and it was this practice which constituted the principal ground of the objections to the renewal of the licences.

There were two ways in which Playboy extended credit to favoured punters. The first, operating from 1975–9, was aptly named the 'no account' scheme. Under this, some thirty big players would, when playing, occasionally be permitted to draw cheques for chips drawn against a bank where they held no account: the bank was Playboy's own. During this time 492 cheques to the total value of £2,962,000 were drawn. In addition, 'RD' cheques, drawn by any one of a group of thirty-seven patrons, which bounced were held for long periods by Playboy while the punters continued to patronise the casino. Cheques to a total value of £12 million were held by Playboy in this way, of which £2 million was owed by one particularly wealthy Middle-Eastern punter. This debt was 'put into context' by Playboy's lawyers who pointed out that the same client had nevertheless written cheques totalling £16 million, all of which had been honoured.

In October the justices refused to renew the two licences. In respect of both clubs, they concluded that the premises had been used for unlawful purposes, and that Playboy was not a fit and proper person to hold a gaming licence. Of somewhat more consequence was the finding that the Playboy Club had been 'habitually used for an unlawful purpose', which conclusion pre-empts the discretion the justices otherwise have under the Act to refuse to renew a licence; in such a case refusal is mandatory.[30]

After the customary talk about appeals, Playboy sold its entire UK operations to Trident Television in November 1981 for £14.6 million. This sum represented a considerable immediate loss for Playboy; while its gaming licences were still intact, it has been estimated that the company could have asked this kind of price for the Park Lane casino alone.[31]

One reason for the hurried disposal of its UK assets was Playboy's concern about its standing with the New Jersey Casino Control Commission, which, as I previously indicated, had been showing an uncomfortable degree of interest in the outcome of the raids earlier in 1981 and the subsequent actions of the police and the Gaming Board. The most important factor, however, was the real possibility that Playboy would have received even less than the £14.6 million had the licences been lost on appeal.

Implications for the regulation of commercial gaming

These malpractices raise a number of issues relating to the implementation and impact of the gaming legislation. A critical issue is what should be the sanction against the licence holder who has been engaging in them?

The Gaming Board's view, which was extensively discussed by the Rothschild Commission a few years ago, is that malpractices in gaming can best be prevented by intensifying the already substantial bureaucratic and administrative control that it exercises over licence holders.[32] To put the matter briefly: to operate a casino, a prospective owner must first apply to the Gaming Board for a certificate of consent. Although there are formal preliminaries, the critical test is whether, in the Board's sole opinion, the applicant is likely to be capable of, and diligent in, complying with the Act. Only when in possession of a consent can a casino owner apply to the licensing justices for a gaming licence.[33]

A certificate of consent remains valid until it is revoked (and this only on limited grounds); it does not expire or need to be renewed. Not surprisingly the Gaming Board regards this as a serious defect in its control mechanisms over casino management. Among other things, the Board wants the Gaming Act to be amended so as to require consents to be renewed at periodic intervals, say every three-five years, which would give the Board additional powers to remove undesirables from casino management. The Rothschild Commission was not moved to recommend such change; it could be justified 'only if the existing means of removing undesirable gaming promoters from the scene were shown in practice to be seriously defective. We do not think that they are'.[34] However, a more important point which emerges from the events of the past two years is not whether the Board has, in its own perception, adequate powers to remove the authors of casino malpractice, but whether such malpractice can be detected. Most of the malpractices which came to light between 1979 and 1981 were being engaged in during the mid-seventies and were well established by the time that the Rothschild Commission gave British casinos a clean bill of health. What happened in the late seventies was that, as a result of the first few reports of malpractice, the Board itself discovered *what* to look for, where and how. These events constituted a lesson in detection.

A controversial issue of considerable financial significance is whether a casino owner should be able to sell his casino at something near market value notwithstanding the unlawful behaviour of its management and the justices' refusal to renew, or cancellation of, the licence, or indeed of their disqualification of the premises.[35] Of the formal sanctions relating to the licence, only disqualification directly affects the market value of the casino, but it would clearly be wrong for a court to impose such an order simply to prevent the licence holder from realising the casino's market value in a subsequent sale. This issue is typically complicated by the fact that between the date of the original decision by the justices (and in the case of Playboy's purchase of the Victoria Sporting Club, some seven months before this) and the hearing of an appeal, during which time the premises may lawfully remain open, the licence holder will have sold the casino. What relevance should the fact that the casino is now in the hands of new management have for the disposition of a licence, or of an appeal against refusal, cancellation or disqualification?

The fact that the former holder was not 'a fit and proper person' can and should have no relevance to the issue of the suitability of any subsequent holder; but is 'a fit and proper' purchaser entitled to expect that simply because he is suitable, he will be successful in the appeal, or if not that he will be granted a fresh licence subsequently? Casino proprietors argue that to dismiss an appeal against the licensing justices' decision to refuse to renew or to cancel a gaming licence or to disqualify the premises, which has been brought by a 'fit' casino, can cause hardship to the innocent employees of both the fit and unfit companies, and can seriously affect share values and hence the interests of innocent investors. This matter is further complicated by the fact that the licensing justices are not obliged to give the reasons why they have concluded that the applicant is not a fit and proper person. Although it is clear from the events of the past few years that commercial and legal integrity form one aspect of such a judgment, and that expertise in casino management probably forms another, the criteria by which applicants are to be judged are by no means explicit. Moreover the role of the Gaming Board and the collective experience of the South Westminster licensing justices and of the Knightsbridge Crown Court were significant factors in the disposition of these cases. These points are illustrated by the outcome of the appeals brought by a number of casino proprietors against adverse decisions.

The arguments outlined above formed part of the Playboy's submissions in its appeal in October 1980 against the decision the previous March by the licensing justices, to cancel the licence and to disqualify for three years the premises of the Victoria Sporting Club, where it was alleged that £1.8 million had been skimmed, and which Playboy subsequently bought for £6 million in October 1979.[36] Playboy was able to convince the Knightsbridge Crown Court (Judge Friend) that the casino was now a 'model' operation and, by analogy to the argument that one does not close down the bank because the manager has been found with his hand in the till, that the company should not be penalised for the bad conduct of the casino's former management.[37]

This decision was something of a personal triumph for Victor Lownes, since it was Judge Friend who had, in November 1979, heard and dismissed Ladbroke's appeal against the cancellation of three of its casino licences, and whose decision was upheld by the Divisional court in March 1980.[38] If the restructuring of the subsidiary holding the licence (City and Provincial Gaming Holdings) affected the court, he said, 'that would simply mean that a limited liability company could breach the law as much as it wished and when the consequences came upon them could alter their structure and in their result say it was someone else. . . .'[39]

Neither the Gaming Board, who opposed Playboy's appeal, nor the Metropolitan Police, who had raided the club in November 1978, were or are persuaded by the arguments put forward by Playboy. Their view is that with the financial rewards being so great and the opportunity for abuse endemic, casino management should be expected to adhere strictly to the rules on pain of being closed down. Moreover, licence holders should not expect to be able to sell the premises at the going market rate. Even where a purchaser acquires the premises at less than the going rate, there is still a commercial risk that the new management will not be able to obtain a licence, a fact which Trident have discovered in their so far unsuccessful attempts to obtain a licence for the former Playboy Club.

Encouraged by Playboy's successful appeal concerning the Victoria Sporting Club, the three purchasers of Coral's London casinos—Lonrho (Metropole Casinos), Grand Metropolitan (Mecca) and John Aspinall—took steps to have the decision of the South Westminster licensing justices in September 1980 to cancel the licences reversed. The appeals were heard in March 1981, like Playboy's, by Judge Friend, and were, somewhat unexpectedly, dismissed. The court was now persuaded of the view it had taken in Ladbroke's appeal, that to allow the appeal 'would mean simply that a casino could be improperly run and then when the licence was cancelled, simply sell it off to someone for as much as you can get. Then the other person says "I am a fit and proper person, everything is all right . . ." The acquisition of shares is something which is a means of obviating the control of the Gaming Act'.[40] However, in June the Divisional Court held that Judge Friend's refusal to take the restructuring of the licence holder into account was an error of law and granted the applications for *certiorari* brought by Lonrho (the International Sporting Club) and Mecca (the Palm Beach).[41]

Following Trident's purchase of the Park Lane and Clermont casinos from Playboy, the Gaming Board made it clear that it would oppose any appeal against the justices' decision not to renew their licences. On the other hand, the Board indicated that it would not object if Trident sought fresh consent certificates and fresh licences. Accordingly, when Trident Casinos' application for licences for these two casinos were heard by the South Westminster licensing justices in May 1982, the Board presented no evidence as to the company's suitability, although it did make representations concerning the supply and demand for gaming facilities in Mayfair, which are discussed below.

It was therefore something of a surprise when one of the reasons the justices gave for refusing to grant a licence to the Park Lane casino was that the applicant was not a fit and proper person. It has been suggested that the involvement of a former Ladbroke casino manager was 'not a plus factor',[42] but a further question concerns the actions of the Gaming Board in this instance: if Trident Casinos was not a fit and proper person to hold a gaming licence, why was no evidence forthcoming from the statutory body whose task it is to vet the suitability of casino management? The application for the Clermont casino was heard a few days later, witnesses from the Board being called to give evidence on the issue of the certificate of consent. However, by the time that Trident's appeal against the refusal to grant a licence for the Park Lane casino was heard in July 1982, the Gaming Board had adopted the view that, in the light of the four licences granted in the meanwhile, there was no justification for any further licences to be granted in the area, and the appeal was dismissed.[43]

While it may be difficult to operationalize, a major principle underlying the Gaming Act is that there should be only sufficient casinos as will satisfy the unstimulated demand for gaming; and, accordingly, if the malpractices revealed in the past three years are evidence of an over-supply of casinos in London chasing a dwindling market, then the purchaser of a casino whose licence is under threat has no reason to expect that the fact of his suitability will be sufficient to remove the threat and restore the licence. The Gaming Board denied that it had 'embarked on a deliberate policy of attacking casinos in London with a view to reducing their number';[44] indeed, in 1981 the Board's Chairman, Lord Allen, said that the industry had been shaken up, 'perhaps more than we could have wished'.[45] However, its view then was that there were sufficient facilities in London, and the Board indicated that it would object to applications for additional licences.[46]

Apart from the formal sanctions provided by the Act, there are, as we have seen, informal sanctions whose impact can, in some instances, be very much more potent than the permanent withdrawal of a gaming licence. In this respect Playboy stood to lose its vast investment in Atlantic City, for until April 1982 its casino was operating under a temporary licence; and the share values of Ladbroke's and Coral were significantly depressed following the outcome of the various licence hearings in 1979 and 1980. Indeed, Ladbroke's announcement in August 1981 of a £25.5 million rights issue was interpreted as an attempt by Cyril Stein to discover whether the group had been rehabilitated within the City following the loss of its licences.[47] In this context it may be observed that although the individual figures that have been quoted in connection with dishonoured cheques are large, they are, as Playboy's counsel noted in the licence hearings, relatively insignificant by comparison with the total drop over this period. Where the granting of credit in this way is unlawful, it discloses only marginal criminality; it may be that the most potent constraint upon such malpractices as have been described in this chapter is the very profitability of legitimate casino management.

Some malpractice is inevitable in gaming, and it may be argued that it is exacerbated by the stringent controls imposed on the activity by the Gaming Act, in particular the prohibitions on credit gaming. These were introduced, it may be recalled, to prevent excessive commercial exploitation of an individual's desire to gamble and indirectly to prevent organised crime from obtaining a foothold in the market as it had done in the sixties. Many of those who patronised the London casinos in the seventies were manifestly of enormous wealth, but the alternative of allowing casino management to give credit to such punters is, in the light of the experience which gave rise to the 1968 Act, a complete non-starter. Nor, acknowledging the fact that 80 per cent of these punters were also from overseas, does current government policy envisage the provision of gaming facilities as an aspect of fiscal policy. In this respect casino development in Great Britain should not be compared with the deliberately expansionist policies which informed the legislation of casino gaming in Nevada in 1931, or, more recently, in Atlantic City.[48] It is highly unlikely that the government would permit relaxation of the controls over casino gaming in order to release some of the pressures that encourage malpractice, although there is at present little sign from the Home Office that these controls are, as the Gaming Board would wish, likely to be further tightened.

Notes

1. A. Heidenheimer (ed.), *Political Corruption—Readings in Comparative Analysis*, New York, Holt, Rinehart & Winston, 1970, Part one.
2. E.g. 'Corruption is political behaviour which deviates from the formal duties of public role because of private-regarding (personal, close-family, private clique) pecuniary or status gains; or violates rules against certain types of private-regarding influence.' J. Nye, 'Corruption and Political Development: A Cost–Benefit Analysis', *American Political Science Review*, 61 (1967), p. 419. This definition is representative of the first of the three classes of contemporary social scientific definitions identified by Heidenheimer, ibid.: those which emphasise deviation from public office; those which emphasise concepts of supply, demand and exchange within markets and those which emphasise the public interest.

3. For the law concerning corruption within public office, or in the conduct of Parliamentary and other elections, see *Halsbury's Laws*, London, Butterworth, 1976 (4th edn.), Vol. 11, paras. 921-37 and Vol. 15, 'Elections', *passim*.

4. On corruption in politics see e.g. J. Gardiner, *The Politics of Corruption*, New York, Russell Sage, 1970 and S. Rose-Ackerman, *Corruption, A Study in Political Economy*, New York, Academic Press, 1978; on corruption in business see e.g. W. Goodman, *All Honourable Men: Corruption and Compromise in American Life*, Boston, Little, Brown, 1963, M. Clinard, *The Black Market*, New York, Holt, Rinehart & Wilson, 1952 and L. Sobel (ed.), *Corruption in Business*, New York, Facts on File, 1977.

5. The Prevention of Corruption Act 1906, s.1(1). See *Halsbury's Laws*, para. 1285.

6. See below, note 20. Some of the practices described below, such as theft and false accounting, were unlawful by virtue of falling within the general criminal law; some were specifically proscribed under the Gaming Act 1968, such as the provision of credit for gaming; and some, while not specifically offensive, constituted the grounds on which the primary and secondary enforcers of the Act—the Gaming Board, the police and the local licensing justices—concluded that the management in question was not a 'fit and proper person' to be the holder of a gaming licence (Gaming Act 1968, s.11 and Schedule 2, para. 20(b)). Some of these practices are best seen in the context of white-collar criminality; see e.g. G. Geis and R. Meier (eds), *White Collar Crime*, New York, Free Press, 1977.

7. American roulette has consistently been the most popular game, taking over 50 per cent of the drop (money exchanged for chips). Blackjack and punto banco (a variety of baccarat) are of approximately equal popularity, together accounting for over 35 per cent of the drop. The other three games are thus relatively insignificant contributors to casino income. See *Report of the Gaming Board for Great Britain 1982*, H.C. 311 1983, para. 29. For a description of casino games and an evaluation of the odds they offer the banker and the players see the Royal Commission on Gambling, 1978, *Report* (Chairman, Lord Rothschild), Cmnd 7200, HMSO, 1978 (hereafter cited as Rothschild) Annex B, 451-62.

8. Home Office, *Gambling Statistics Great Britain 1968-78*, Cmnd 7897, HMSO, 1980, table 2.8, p. 23.

9. See the *Report of the Gaming Board for Great Britain 1976*, H.C. 253, 1977, paras. 46-7 and *1977*, H.C. 278, 1977, para. 26.

10. *Report of the Gaming Board for Great Britain 1980*, H.C. 262, 1981, para. 35. See also, Home Office, op. cit., table 2.8, p. 23, and p. 28. The drop in 1980-1 was also £930 million, which represents in real terms a decrease of about 12 per cent; *Report of the Gaming Board for Great Britain 1981*, H.C. 324, 1982, para. 34.

11. *Report of the Gaming Board for Great Britain 1980*, para. 36 and *1981*, para. 35.

12. The average amount of drop per head of adult population in the south-east, north-west and London during 1979-80 was respectively, £7, £15 and £139; *Report of the Gaming Board for Great Britain 1980*, para. 37.

13. See D. Miers, 'The Mismanagement of Casino Gaming', *British Journal of Criminology*, 21 (1981), 79-86. One of these difficulties was the disappearance in 1975 of one Alan Watts, a senior manager of the casino division, with proceeds alleged to be £340,000 skimmed from the Palm Beach Club. In March 1982 Watts was convicted of a number of offences of theft from the club, at which time he admitted stealing £100,000: *Guardian*, 20 March 1982.

14. See *The Times*, 6 October 1981 and *Guardian*, 25 October 1981.

15. *Report of the Gaming Board for Great Britain 1982*, para. 27. The total drop was £1,007 m., ibid., para. 26.

16. These are: the Casanova, the Ritz, the Sportsman, the Golden Nugget, the Hilton and the Palm Beach: see *Sunday Times*, 2 May 1982.

17. *Sunday Times*, 9 December 1979.

18. *Guardian*, 15 September 1981; *The Times*, 16 September 1981.

19. See the account of this operation and of the action taken against Coral's casinos in Miers, op. cit., and *Sunday Times*, 15 March 1981.

20. These actions were followed by prosecutions under the Prevention of Corruption Act

1906: *Observer*, 20 April 1980 and *Guardian*, 21 April 1980.

21. See *R.* v. *Judge Friend, ex parte Ladup Ltd, New Law Journal,* **130** (1980), p. 414 and *Report of the Gaming Board for Great Britain 1979*, H.C. 561, 1980, para. 10; *1980*, op. cit., para. 9 and *1981*, op. cit., para. 8.

22. *Observer*, 15 March 1981.

23. *New Statesman*, 9 December 1979.

24. John Cunningham in an article 'Has London had its Chips?', *Guardian*, 19 December 1981.

25. *Report of the Gaming Board for Great Britain 1979*, paras. 11 and 129; *1980*, op. cit., paras. 10, 11 and 134 and *1981*, op. cit., paras. 9 and 138. Bernard Coral and Brian Sherley-Dale, the former chairman and managing director of Coral casinos, were committed for trial in June 1980 along with thirty-two other employees. The charge against both of conspiring to pervert the course of justice by concealing the offences committed by Alan Watts in 1975 were dropped in September, and in March 1982 Coral was convicted of conspiring to contravene the Gaming Act and fined £50,000. See *Guardian* 13 June and 24 September 1980, and 20 March 1982.

26. Unlike objections to the annual renewal of a licence, an application to cancel a licence may be made at any time during the year; see the Gaming Act, ss.24 and 25, and Schedule 2, paras. 36–48.

27. The argument concerning the lawfulness of subsequent dealings with cheques is set out in an investigation under s.165(b) of the Companies Act: Department of Trade, Scotia Investment Ltd, Report by L. Bromley QC and J. S. Hillyer (1980), paras. 18.4–18.11. See also Rothschild paras. 18.61–18.67, which recommends that these dealings be made specifically unlawful. Some of these recommendations are given effect by the Court of Appeal's decision in *Marcrest Properties* v. *Gaming Board for Great Britain* (1983) 1 W.L.R. 300.

28. See Department of Trade, ibid., paras. 18.19–18.36.

29. *Report of the Gaming Board for Great Britain 1981*, paras. 15 and 136; and *Guardian*, 9 June 1982. The application for judicial review made by the new owners was dismissed by the Court of Appeal; see note 27.

30. *Report of the Gaming Board for Great Britain 1981*, paras. 13 and 135; *Sunday Times*, 5 April and 20 September 1981; *Guardian*, 16 and 19 April, 9 July, 15, 16, 17, 18, 19 and 22 September 1981.

31. *Sunday Times*, 2 May 1982.

32. Rothschild, paras. 19.6–19.14. See also *Report of the Gaming Board for Great Britain 1979*, paras. 22 and 124–125.

33. Gaming Act 1968, s.11 and Schedule 2, paras. 3–7.

34. Rothschild, para. 19.29.

35. See the unsuccessful attempt by the Gaming Board to penalise the Victoria Sporting Club indirectly by refusing to determine Playboy's application to transfer the club's licence until the outcome of the licence hearings (including any appeals) concerning the Victoria Sporting Club were finally known; *Playboy Club of London Ltd* v. *Gaming Board for Great Britain* (unreported decision of the Queen's Bench Division), 14 July 1980.

36. *Report of the Gaming Board for Great Britain 1978*, H.C.11, 1979, para. 108; *1979*, op. cit., paras. 9 and 127; *1980*, op. cit., paras. 12 and 133; and *1981*, op. cit., para. 134. Four of those involved in the management of the club were prosecuted for conspiracy to defraud, but the judge stopped the case for lack of evidence: *Guardian*, 8 and 30 May 1981. They were, however, unable to stop the licence hearing from being determined prior to the trial, see *Justice of the Peace*, **144** (1980), p. 654.

37. *Report of the Gaming Board for Great Britain 1980*, op. cit., para. 22. Playboy had first to obtain *certiorati* to compel the Board to determine its application to transfer the Victoria Sporting Club's licence to the company, see note 35; and see *Gaming Board for Great Britain* v. *Victoria Sporting Club* (unreported decision of the Knightsbridge Crown Court), 17 October 1980.

38. Above, note 21.

39. Quoted in the *New Statesman*, op. cit. See also Sir David McNee, *Guardian*, 18 February 1981.
40. Quoted in *Sunday Times*, 15 March 1981.
41. *R. v. Knightsbridge Crown Court, ex parte International Sporting Club (London) Ltd and Another* [1982] 1 Q.B. 304. The licence for the International Sporting Club was restored at the subsequent Crown Court rehearing; see *Guardian*, 21 July 1981. Mecca had in the meantime successfully applied for a fresh licence for the Palm Beach casino. See *Report of the Gaming Board for Great Britain 1981*, paras. 9 and 10. John Aspinall did not proceed with the application for judicial review, and so the licence for the Curzon House was cancelled; *Report of the Gaming Board for Great Britain 1981*, para. 11. In 1982 the owner successfully applied for a new licence, but the Gaming Board persuaded the Crown Court to reverse this on the ground of insufficient demand, *Guardian*, 15 October 1982. A fresh application in 1983 was, however, successful; see *The Times*, 6 May 1983.
42. *Observer*, 9 May 1982 (Business Section).
43. On the circumstances surrounding the outcome of Trident Casinos applications see, *Observer*, ibid., and 25 July 1982; *Guardian*, 4, 11, 12 and 14 May, 27 and 30 July 1982; *The Times*, 14 May and 30 July 1982; and *Sunday Times*, 2 May and 25 July 1982. By virtue of the Gaming (Amendment) Act 1982, applications for new licences may now be made on up to four occasions during the year, but Trident have yet to take advantage of this change.
44. *Report of the Gaming Board for Great Britain 1979*, para. 13; *The Times*, 6 October 1980.
45. *Sunday Times*, 15 March 1981.
46. *Report of the Gaming Board for Great Britain 1980*, paras. 13 and 14; *1981*, op. cit., para. 38; this view was subsequently modified, *1982*, op. cit., paras. 34–7.
47. *Guardian*, 7 August 1981.
48. See W. Eadington, 'Regulatory Objectives and the Expansion of Casino Gaming', Bureau of Business and Economic Research, Paper No. 82–11 (1982), University of Nevada, Reno 5–11.

4 The corruption of commercial justice: the case of the private security sector

NIGEL SOUTH

All we are saying here is that the constraints of the rule of law, while accepted by the security industry, do not have the same inexorable and sometimes ironic centrality to its activity as in the case of the police. Hence, there is at least a greater potential for those constraints to be set aside in the course of activities based on entrepreneurial enterprise . . . [Carson and Young, 1976, p. 48].

The post-war period in the United Kingdom has seen the development of a wide range of commercial services that might be described as the private security sector. Such services can range from security-vetted office cleaners, factory guards, store detectives and crime-prevention consultants to private investigators, specialist services of surveillance, protection, personnel-profile compilation and industrial espionage and its countering (cf. Bunyan, 1976; Bowden, 1978; Draper, 1978). But even more striking than its breadth is the spectacular growth of private security. In the 'affluence' of the 1950s it was a relatively small phenomenon compared to the outcome of its 'recession-resistant' growth (Kakalik and Wildhorn, 1972) through the following decades. This growth took advantage of opportunities partially opened up by the changing priorities of the public police service (cf. Scraton, 1982). In this respect it is a particularly important, though relatively neglected, example of the type of commercial enterprise that is not simply sustainable but expansive in recession. Indeed, it is an increasingly prominent feature of modern, western capitalist social organisations to accumulate and store information on the individual citizen and to extend and facilitate surveillance and supervision of the population generally (cf. Foucault, 1977; Giddens, 1981). Its more apparent and conventionally recognised significance, however, is limited to that of its place in the world of crime prevention, but this is a double-edged significance. For present purposes, it is indeed important to emphasise the relationship of the private security sector to 'crime control' concerns such as theft, fraud, occupational deviance, corruption and so on, for the private security sector is often employed on behalf of owners of property to protect that property from such depredations. It is a fact, however, that such a task clearly—to any but the naive or wilfully blinkered—gives rise to a series of circumstances and contradictions conducive to the possible corruption of that task.

Today's private security is, in range and form, unequivocally born of the age of modern capital and it represents capital's own policing of and in its own interests. Such interests can generate considerable conflict with those interests espoused in the name of 'formal' or 'informal' justice. Resolution may be sought through the employment of forms of private security operating within the ethos of 'commercial justice'—means to ends sought in (ideal) terms of efficient expediency and cost-effectiveness; though efficiency in the resolution of a problem may be costly and 'expediency' may take some time—but that can be the price of cost-effectiveness. What such a price may also buy is rule-bending, cutting off corners and the circumscribing or flouting of the law. Additionally, the same structural contradictions that promote private security as a medium for resolution of problems particular to its employers also produce a range of pressures, inclinations and invitations for such rule-bending, corner-cutting and legal deviation to be taken advantage of in varying ways, at levels that may be described as occupational, organisational and structural.

The distinctions drawn here between occupational, organisational and structural levels are merely heuristic and suggested in order to help contextualise various examples of occupational deviancy, sources of corruption, sharp or unethical practice, and private security as an agency of commercial justice. Briefly, by occupational culture I refer to the micro-level of interaction between workers in private security occupations, their engagement in and negotiation of their jobs—its rules, situational and spatial constraints and opportunities for deviation.[1] When I consider the organisational level, my concern is less with the practices of individuals in *occupational* roles, as individuals and members of work groups, and more with examples of widespread practices facilitated by the *organisation* of private security, *per se*. Such practices represent institutionalised channels for the organisationally powerful to utilise in bending rules, giving favours and exploiting the 'gate-keeping' capacities of private security (not simply in keeping doors closed, but also in controlling the flow of information). This conception of the organisational level is similar to that of Gouldner (1954, p. 404) where 'the organisation is conceived as an "instrument"—that is, as a rationally conceived means to the realisation of expressly announced group goals. Its structures are understood as tools deliberately established for the realisation of these group purposes'.

Finally, the identification of a structural level is intended to convey the sense of private security as 'more than the sum of its parts'. Hence, here are identified real and potential sources of abuse and corruption of the avowed ethics of private security.[2] Issues of law, regulation, professionalisation and symbolic and ideological significance are also considered at this level and in the conclusion.

It should be obvious by now that I am not here concerned with the issue of corruption in its classic sense of 'public position being abused in the furtherance of private ends'. The legal offence of corruption, and hence its customary definitional focus, appears principally in connection with the abuse of public office or the management of elections. However, the utility and wider applicability of 'corruption' as an operational concept has meant a useful broadening of its definition and use. Here I am concerned with familiar issues such as the abuse of trust, ethics, personal relationships, privileged information, and so on, but only as they occur within the private sector of public companies. Some of the issues raised and examples given may also indicate corruption in its more formal sense among those who hold or have held positions of public responsibility, but in this case these are only of secondary concern. For present purposes my emphasis is on both the specificity of corruption and occupational deviance within the private security sector, as well as their frequent contiguity with and similarity to corruption and deviance within areas of the public sector, such as local government or the police. Generally, while perhaps analytically vague, it may none the less be helpful to the sociologically or socio-legally orientated to conceive of the definitional context in terms of the sociology of white-collar and blue-collar crime applied to an agency of 'crime-control'.

The occupational culture

'Everybody's at it . . .'

One of the most popular and recurrent images of private security in the media is that of the 'school for crooks'.[3] In both sensational and responsible reports, minor cases of the theft of property, or laxity on the part of private security employees, have been treated with a degree of unwarranted indignation, which might be better focussed on balance sheets lodged at Companies House (or even more importantly those not lodged there). The serious edge to such stories is that they often emphasise the absence of any system of vetting, licensing or regulation for private security. As I shall point out below, the regulation issue is a very serious one, but invoking it in stories of petty pilferage and fiddles potentially undermines that seriousness. For a start it allows private security itself to acknowledge that occasionally it has 'a problem', diverting attention from other and more serious problems.

Obviously those unofficial vetting procedures that do exist vary immensely between security companies of different sizes and with different resources, but even the most developed (for example, those with 'old boy network' access to criminal records) are often unable to identify what press releases describe as employees of 'doubtful character'. Although the standard claim and obvious recommendation of the British Security Industry Association is that no one should be employed and put into a job before their references are fully cleared, in practice, issues of cost and staffing shortages tend to make this impossible for the security companies. Thus most companies have many examples of putting people into situations only to find that, on subsequent checks, 'they shouldn't have been put into such "sensitive opportunity situations" '. However, if the private security sector has to admit to any deficiences then it is precisely such 'difficult circumstances beyond their control' that might most reasonably be confessed. Other sources of tensions and problems, such as low pay, low standards, complicated rules without preparatory training, etc., are obviously best avoided.

Generally anathema to all self-respecting business, to the trade unions and to traditional industrial sociology, the recognition that all occupational cultures seem to incorporate some sort of 'hidden economy' of perks, pilferage and fiddles (cf. South, 1982b, pp. 38–61), is, unsurprisingly, a source of even greater discomfort for the private security sector. But, like the police (if that is any comfort), private security is no less fiddle and perk orientated than any other occupational culture, despite being an occupation with a 'privileged position'. Pilferage, for example, is facilitated by the fact that, not surprisingly, it seems very rare that on-duty security guards will follow standard directives to search other guards to see what they are carrying in their bags and lunch-boxes, despite periodic re-emphasis of this procedure in standing orders. Indeed, joking 'moves' to caution and search a colleague can be a familiar play-act and source of banter within the occupational culture.

In fact it should be no surprise to find such informalised neutralisation of the formal work role in potentially uncomfortable circumstances. Nor should it be any surprise to find that there is little new in the numerous criticisms of private security as attracting criminal or negligent 'low-life' employees who are knowing colluders in an occupational subculture of perks, pilferage and fiddles. The 'metaphorical wink' which Ditton (1977) notes as accompanying many of the transactions of this hidden economy has a long (and 'dishonourable') history. As John Wade wrote of the new office of the police in his *Treatise on the Police and Crimes of the Metropolis* (1829; reprinted in 1972, p. 78), 'the office has fallen into the hands of the lowest class of retailers and costermongers who make up the deficient allowance of their principals by indirect sources of emolument, by winking at offences they ought to prevent'. The 'retailers and costermongers' may be gone, but low pay in the labour intensive areas of private security means that, at their basic grades, recruitment is often from the marginalised, casual and floating labour force. The 'deficient allowance' persists therefore, and so too do the 'indirect sources of emolument'.

Particularly sensitive here is the moral balancing act that even the most conscientious security staff must perform with regard to knowledge of, or participation in, petty pilferage, various fiddles and the take-up of perks. Once accepted into this occupational sub-culture, security personnel occupy a fairly unique position of trust in the wider 'differential structure of opportunity to commit such crime which, in turn, reflects the wider class and occupational system' (Hall and Scraton, 1981, p. 46). For private security workers, a 'dual morality' (Ditton, n.d.) is unquestioningly invoked in their self-regulation of such activity as against their 'professional' *raison d'être* of being socially and economically necessary to control, for example, the hidden economy activities of others.[4]

However, it is this relatively unique position in the 'differential structure of opportunity' that is the factor that must be specifically explored in order to understand, or at least adequately describe, the 'corruption' of the privileged and trusted position in which ordinary private security workers find themselves. Static-site, patrol and armoured-van guards tend to find themselves, at least formally, within the grip of systematised and bureaucratised rules and constraints. They face a particular set of occupational pressures attendant to these jobs: monotony (in some cases livened by potential risk); either loneliness or perhaps cramped proximity; time-tabled schedule demands; the bureaucratic denial of autonomous action in procedures, uncomfortably coupled with the 'professional ideal' of preparedness to deal calmly with emergency and the simple fact that the neurotically safety and security conscious procedures can be so temptingly simplified. One consequence is the development of a sense of frustration and tension.

Thus, at least one major factor in the incidence of occupational deviance among private security workers derives from the various means adopted in attempting to resolve such tension. For many, their structurally constrained and individually isolated, or small-team based, situation places them in a highly fiddle-opting and coverable position.

'Insiders' and 'rotten apples'

In reality, everyone knows that the occasional (or frequent) fiddle goes on, but as long as its evidence and acknowledgement is limited then this is vaguely acceptable. However, because of the placing of security employment within the occupational dimension of 'crime control professions', what is not acceptable to the occupational image and professional ideology is the acknowledgement of serious crime or the possibility of corruption in its popular, sensational sense.

As an occupation, private security is a prime target for corruption through forms of bribery in order to gain information or other assistance in crimes such as robbery, burglary or less definable 'offences' such as industrial espionage. The obverse of this recognition is also related to the discussion above—'Everybody's at it'. What this common and commercial watch-word promotes is a 'don't trust anybody' mentality to which the private security sector responds in a style which classically manipulates such commercial paranoia: 'You may never know if you're being ripped off if you don't hire us to find out—and even if we don't find anything, then that could just mean we're dealing with some pretty clever insiders!' What such sales-orientated promotion of 'problems you didn't know you had' can ultimately bring with it, however, is the demand for or promise of 'results' or 'proof'. This can encourage not only false-reporting but corrupt and criminal practice beyond. In this respect the private security sector is in the business of providing its own 'insiders'. One common example among private investigators is the pseudo-corruption of official positions by the age-old technique of impersonation. The 1972 Younger Committee on Privacy listed examples of private investigators impersonating the police, social security officials, insurance representatives, market researchers, telephone engineers, journalists and so on (cf. Draper, 1978, p. 66). Specific legislation prohibits impersonation of the police or DHSS officials but as Draper (1978, p. 66) points out:

> The drawback in prosecuting these offences lies in the nature of the penalties that can be imposed on conviction—a £50 fine has very little deterrent effect on a private detective who undoubtedly charges highly for his unscrupulous approach to the job, and may even add the amount to his clients' bill at the end of the day.

Such corrupted or corruptible private detectives, and the criminal opportunities the occupation offers to other individuals, were noted by the Association of Chief Police Officers in their own evidence to the Younger Committee. Their submission observed that,

> While many private enquiry agents and other institutions are reputable, it has been suspected from time to time that people with criminal records and intent are employed in the commercial field of investigation and security and that, in some cases, they have taken employment with a view to obtaining and supplying information to their criminal associates.

Even conventionally accepted 'good intentions' seem a reasonable cause for concern in this duplicitous world of undercover and underhand infiltration. With intentional irony, Thompson (1970) observes that one major problem with using undercover private security investigators to seek out sources of pilferage, industrial espionage etc., is how to get the agent out once the leak is discovered without the agent being discovered. Noting one Securicor representative being reported as saying, 'we have even faked arrests to get them out', Thompson goes on to note a case of '. . . a perfectly genuine arrest [which] put an end to the activities of one undercover agent who had been recruited by a security officer . . . in Scotland'. The agent ended up facing a charge of attempting to frame a number of his workmates by planting machinery on their lorries. 'He was found guilty and sent to prison' (Thompson, 1970, p. 148). Because of the very nature of the specialised private security world, and services such as undercover work, it is virtually impossible to assess the extent to which their avowed values, morality and legality are corrupted.

On more familiar grounds, Draper (1978) argues that one of the principal reasons why there should be concern about private detectives and private security generally is that 'their work by its very nature provides for access to industrial premises, cash and high-value goods, and confidential information'. (Draper, 1978, p. 11.) Draper's argument is well illustrated by the experience of the ill-starred Purolator Security Company, which lost out in two major thefts, on both sides of the Atlantic, within two years of each other and both the result of 'inside information'. In October 1974 its Chicago vault and highly sophisticated alarm systems were breached—a former guard was part of the break-in team. Less than two years later Purolator was hit by an even more audacious insider-job, this time at London's Heathrow Airport. In June 1976 two men presented themselves as Purolator Couriers at airport vaults where $3.5 million in various currencies were awaiting collection by representatives of the agency. Having produced the necessary papers and authorisation, the couriers left with the currency in an armoured van. The comfortable ease of such secure routine was rudely disturbed when, two days later, two more Purolator guards arrived to transport the money. This time they were the real guards. Neither the company nor the police were slow to realise that such 'secure routine' is in general 'secure', but, to an insider, it is also 'routine'—and therein lies its vulnerability.

As the most desirable insiders imaginable in the perpetration of a neat crime, 'the protectors' themselves are prime targets for corruption. Intriguingly, this seems a source of concern across a fair range of opinion. A recent article in *Police Review* considered the nature of 'confrontation and co-operation' between the police and private security (Kerr, 1979) and observed that, while the

apparently inadequate set of safeguards has proved pretty effective so far . . . nevertheless, there are [firms] who have no declared allegiance to any code of ethics or practice. In 1974 Sir Douglas Osmond, then Chief Constable of Hampshire, speaking at a fire and security conference, said: 'Some three years ago, in one police region alone, no less than 69 persons with criminal records were identified as working as patrol guards.'

In 1982, the *Daily Mirror* (10 August 1982, p. 6) reiterated its concern— shared at various times by the press of all political shades—that '. . . crooks are setting up their own security companies to help them pull off robberies from the inside—and possibly to make industrial espionage easier'. The same report expressed the concern of Derek Hunter, regional officer of the General and Municipal Workers Union, who stated that 'we know of men who walk out of an employment exchange in the morning and are on duty in security guard uniform in the evening'. It seems reasonable to assume here that the GMWU is not objecting to people finding a job within a day but rather to the impossibility of checking references or providing adequate training or briefing within a day. Both the GMWU and 'the independent Low Pay Unit are pressing the Government to introduce licensing for the security industry'. (*Daily Mirror*, 10 August 1982, p. 6.)

The concern of the Low Pay Unit is, and has been for some years, the low levels of pay in private security; presumably in the context of the *Mirror* report this concern reflects the suspicion that low pay for a job giving access to other people's property leads to temptation. Even the supposed 'rotten apples' who

provoke this unifying moral horror seem to agree with such a proposition:
' "One guard asked to be taken off a cash run because he had a conviction and
had been jailed for robbing a security vehicle", added Mr Hunter' (ibid.).

Some of these points are also recognised by various representatives of the
private security sector. However, such recognition is usually to be found in the
arguments that they have continued to put forward in campaigning for exemption from the provisions of the Rehabilitation of Offenders Act, 1975, concerning the law against disclosure of certain past criminal offences. While maintaining
agreement with the fair and laudable principles of the Act, aspects of the argument for exemption maintain that it is unfair and a misjudgement to allow
ex-offenders to be employed in the private security sector: unfair to customers
and unfair to ex-offenders faced with temptation. Whatever way the weighing-up
of rights and interests comes out (and alone it is the Home Office which appears
simply to ignore this whole issue), it is at least interesting to note that this
peculiar paternalistic concern for the best interests of those employees who
might be tempted to stray has been around for a long time. There is probably
a good example in the Bible, but certainly industrial management in the twentieth
century has repeatedly beat its breast and asked itself rhetorical questions like,
'Are you tempting employees to steal tools?' (cf. Hartshorne, 1922; Friedlander, 1956; Gregory, 1962; South, 1982b, pp. 60–1).

At a potentially more costly level of the 'insider problem'—the easing of
industrial espionage mentioned in the *Mirror* report—the private security
sector is less concerned with such charitable understanding and more with the
weakness of available legal recourse. The British Corruption Act, 1906, provides
one of the very few legal bases for attempting to secure prosecution against
in-house industrial espionage. Insider industrial espionage perpetrated by an
employee is usually untouchable as trespass and if information is copied rather
than being stolen in the form of tangible documentation, then there is no crime
of theft (cf. Draper, 1978, p. 112). However, 'if the company can show that the
source of the leak was a bribed employee . . . the British Corruption Act 1906,
provides for a maximum penalty of £500 fine and/or imprisonment for two
years.' Trespass or breach of contract remain the principal grounds for legal
prosecution in cases of industrial spying, though prosecutions have been brought
employing the breadth of conspiracy law, successfully as 'conspiracy to obtain
confidential information by corrupt and other unlawful means', and unsuccessfully as 'conspiracy to defraud' (Draper, 1978, p. 112).

It is undeniably the case that forms of criminal infiltration and corruption
are well evidenced in various areas of the private security sector, and fairly
liberally sprinkled throughout even its more creditable and reputable representatives. As it is principally from these 'reputable representatives' that the shocked
and morally offended demand for official blessing of self-regulation comes,
it is not surprising that their elitist vantage point leads them to attempt to
preserve a case for the integrity of the 'profession' of security. The result is

reliance on the old 'rotten apple theory' again. This is the explanation invariably trotted out in most conventional discussions of police corruption, and is indeed best summed up in the report of the Knapp Commission (1972) on police corruption in New York: 'According to this theory, which bordered on official departmental doctrine, any policeman found to be corrupt must promptly be denounced as a rotten apple in an otherwise clean barrel. It must never be admitted that his otherwise individual corruption may be symptomatic of an underlying disease.'

Given the peculiar and anomalous sense in which private security/investigator work can be one of the 'fiddle-prone' occupations *par excellence* (especially given the almost universal levels of low pay and low standards of qualification, training and incentive), then the confinement of criminal activity to the single individual who realises that they are 'on to a good way of making a bit (or lot) extra' seems a doubtful proposition. The general acceptance of the rotten apple theory, however, functions in a not dissimilar way for the private security sector as for the police, as an attempt to preserve the public image of the private security sector as a whole (and, by association, the integrity of our 'guardians' in general).

The rotten apple theory is hardly adequate to explain forms of criminal activity within the private security sector, creating as it does an all too easy recourse to scapegoating individuals and token sacrifices. The examples of criminal/deviant 'opportunity structure' examined and referred to so far are by-products not the *raison d'être* of organisational form and commercial policy within the private security sector. The corruption and abuse of operations and facilities at what might be called an organisational level begin to indicate some of the purposive and ideological elements of this *raison d'être*.

The organisational level

'Jobs for the (right) boys'[5]

Private security can act as a mechanism for the exercise of nepotism, political or moral bias through the establishment of guidelines and recommendations concerning personnel appointment, levels of responsibility, access to physical areas, materials and information. Its involvement in vetting and personnel selection can provide a source of real discriminatory power—a corruption of any claims to impartiality. As one security commentator expresses his, perhaps extreme, concern: 'many factors can contribute to a lowering of moral standards; political associations, emotional background, mental instability, drink, sex perversions, drugs, etc. There can be no doubt that political associations play a significant part in influencing the course of actions to be taken by the employee intent on "hitting back" at his employers'. (Slee-Smith, 1970, p. 115.)

Private security staff (in-house and external) and private detectives can provide profiles unbeknown to employees or applicants; other agencies specialise in anti-union information and disinformation. Placing the trade unions among a range of modern social problems, one of the leading theorists of the private security sector argues that: 'At least one can say that the advent of the violent protester, the urban guerrilla, the militant school child, the frenetic female, the campus incendiary, the highwayman trade unionist and all the other overturners of the world, has created a bonanza for the security man and the industry which supports him'. (Hamilton, 1972, pp. 111-12.) In seeking out such dangers private security can act as the commercialised corruption of whatever system of presumed impartiality and appointment on merit that applicants may think is left in the world. As Bunyan (1977, p. 247) suggests, such screening processes are becoming standardised practice:

> The first stage of pre-employment checking on industrial workers is detailed application forms and contact with past employers. Within industries the security or personnel staff of different firms will often know each other or a mutual acquaintance, which helps with the inquiries. A telephone call or a letter will soon find out what previous employers thought of an applicant's work, politics and attitudes.

In fact, for many major companies in the UK it seems that the arduous task of ringing around old contacts in pursuit of the subversives may be a thing of the past, replaced by one call to a private 'subversives record office'. The Economic League was founded in 1919 and by 1925 was emphasising its arrangements for a permanent and private 'clearing house of information in connection with alien organisations and individuals' (Economic League, 5th General Report 1925; cf. *State Research Bulletin*, 1978, 7, pp. 135-45). By 1961 the *Daily Express* could matter of factly report that enquiring firms could 'apply to the League's headquarters . . . to check if a prospective employee is listed as a Communist sympathiser' (*Daily Express*, 12 January 1961). In 1969 the *Observer* reported one major subscriber acknowledging that the League 'does a hell of a lot of security vetting for us on political grounds, this is their sole use to us, and for X pounds a year, it's good value for money' (*Observer*, 16 October 1969). In 1972, 4,500 subscribing firms were getting such value for money (cf. *State Research*, op. cit., pp. 138-9); and in 1978 Peter Linklater, personnel director of Shell, gave the League a further glowing endorsement in terms that neatly summarise the purpose of the private security sectors' involvement in the corruption of ethics regarding the privacy of personal information—in order to ensure that jobs go to the 'right' people. 'They give us pretty good value. . . . We are interested in identifying overt opponents of the system to which we are committed. The last thing we want to do is to have political subversives on our payrolls or on sites in which we have an interest' (*Guardian*, 29 June 1978; cf. Labour Research, 22 July 1978).

'*Networking*'

The euphemism of the 'old-boys network' is a common and cosy metaphorical way of side-stepping issues that can often touch upon the corrupt abuse of personal position and privilege. Of direct concern here is the passage of information between private and official channels of information: the unchecked 'co-operation' between private and public sector—from local private security agencies feeding 'observations' and 'hearsay' to the police at local collator level, through checks run through police criminal records as favours to ex-policemen now in the private security sector, to other outcomes of the familiar pattern of cross-over employment from the police to private security. All of this constitutes a significant system of violation of the security of personal and official information. The existence of the old-boys network also confirms the like-minded world-view shared by police and private security personnel.

As noted below, this can contribute to the former seeking the assistance of the latter in the circumvention of certain rules, for example over phone tapping. The up-market end of the private security sector, dealing in commercial intelligence and industrial espionage, also utilises the advantages of cross-over employment and old contacts and in many cases has some considerable disregard for either the ethics of the profession or the laws of the land, or both (although in some cases, such as computer privacy or telephone tapping, effective laws do not yet exist).

The link between private security and the police at local collator level is of obvious mutual and reciprocal advantage where the police can help out with the vetting of prospective employees, and anyone else of interest, in return for the security companies' own local information gathering. Obviously, such arrangements largely depend upon the willingness of the police to co-operate and indeed they rarely co-operate with very small, inefficient or particularly dubious agencies. Despite the fact that a small firm need not necessarily be justifiably regarded as dubious, nevertheless it could be denied this sort of co-operation, which simply means that in many cases (for there are many small firms) the claimed vetting procedures for hiring staff are either ineffective or non-existent. In the 'big league', however, as long ago as March 1971, J. Phillip Sorenson, managing director of Group 4, acknowledged to *The Times* that 'there is no doubt that there is an old-boy network which helps us to discover whether a man has a criminal record'.

Part of the concern about 'old-boy network' cross-over employment from the police to private security is well summarised in a 1963 parliamentary question in which the Secretary of State for Scotland was asked whether he was 'aware that there is a widespread belief among the public, with some evidence, admittedly very difficult to substantiate, that these officers are employed precisely because of their close associations with the police force, their knowledge of police methods and their informal association with policemen?' (Kerr,

1979, p. 124). The response of the Secretary of State was a, now familiar, sympathetic request for evidence of cases not rumours. Repeated examples in newspaper reports presumably count as repeated rumours. 'And an ex-police officer at another firm explained that one of his jobs was to take lists of names of applicants which he showed to his old police colleagues still working' (*Observer*, 6 December 1970). And those rumours just keep on repeating; eleven years later: 'Two Thames Valley policemen were said today to have leaked information from a highly confidential police computer to an ex-colleague working as a private detective . . . [It was] alleged that for money certain Thames Valley Officers have provided information from police computers about individuals and cars.' (*Evening Standard*, 22 October 1981.)

The commercialisation of access to information supposedly protected by public office is evident in one corrupt aspect of the wider corruption involved in the strategy adopted by Ladbroke's casino subsidiary, Ladup Ltd, to draw custom from the casinos of competitors. As Miers (1982) reports, 'Likely targets were traced, with the help of a private detective agency, through their car registration numbers for whose details 50p per plate was paid to a police sergeant who had access to the police national computer at Nottingham' (Miers, 1982, p. 7). What may seem a relatively trivial example of corruption to the post-Countryman cynic is, in fact, ideally illustrative of corrupt intent in one enterprise initiating corrupt practice elsewhere, in this case involving differentially 'privileged' and 'ethically bound' representatives of the private and public sectors.

It is clear that there are links of personnel and ideology between the specialist private security and public agencies, facilitating movement of skills and personal data. It has in fact become fairly unremarkable even to the average citizen to hear or read of the exposure of such connections. Virtually all that remains remarkable are those occasions when we learn that such connections are under official investigation. One recent report (*State Research Bulletin*, 1981, **24**, 141) sums up the story so far. Apparently, as the result of allegations made in an anonymous memorandum, circulated to Economic League subscribers in the New Year of 1981, New Scotland Yard is believed to have held an investigation into 'reports that four former members of the Special Branch have illegally supplied the right-wing employers' organisation, the Economic League, with details of workers' police records'. The memorandum apparently alleged that the League had bought information from a former Special Branch Officer, bought— in cash or in kind—classified information from other police officers, and sent 'inquiry agents' into people's houses under false pretences (ibid., 141). The *State Research* report however also quotes a 'police spokesperson' as saying any investigation was waiting to be sent some evidence, there presently being 'no evidence of any wrongdoing' (ibid., 142).

'Sealing' and 'shielding'

Private security can not only fulfil its routine and expected function of *discovering* pilferage, fraud, corruption and so on, but can also be employed expressly to *conceal* and/or *contain* discovery, or the ongoing nature of such 'business problems'. Public revelation of such problems can be damaging to a corporate image, cause internal problems in management politics, or be cynically contained to be employed as a bargaining tool in the wage-effort negotiation—invoking paternalistic collusion or the coercive threat of legal or extra-legal reaction on the basis of a 'shocked discovery of what's going on'. On the other hand, there is also some evidence of the prevalence of commercial policy advising that no action be taken in many cases. The purposeful turning of 'blind eyes' is easier within a system of self-controlled, privatised justice (cf. Scraton and South, 1980, 45-7). Between the 'shocked discovery of what's going on' and the retention of control over the ability to 'turn a blind eye', private security provides a latent infrastructural service as an intermediary between employer and employee. Management can disavow knowledge of how information is obtained and of its unprocessed form, can claim 'good faith' in accepting its veracity, but profess shock and distaste at the way in which it was gathered should the occasion necessitate this (South, 1982a, p. 12).

In this and other ways, the anomalous insider/outsider position of private security can be operated to isolate, insulate and seal passages of information. Such a capacity can aid the hierarchical direction of corporate power through the control of information. It can invoke various permutations on the 'need to know' principle or indeed develop its own criteria for the 'need to inform'. In fact, within the parameters of its commercial accountability it can develop a significant degree of autonomy from its employers. This ability of private security to seal itself from interference and overview was illustrated (albeit as a surprise to the researcher) in Rojek's (1979) study of shoplifting data for a sample of retail stores in a US mid-western city. Intrigued by the virtual randomness of the statistics for surveillance, apprehension and arrest of shoplifters, Rojek discovered that security personnel were able to employ their assertion of specialisation and a practice of concealment in order to shield themselves from any efficient overview. A base of autonomy was thus firmly established in practice and formalised by influential input into the development of company rules and regulations. The creation of such autonomous space is not in itself corrupt but it can facilitate any corrupt or deceptive practice that is contemplated.

Competition, cutting corners and sharp practice

The private security sector is heavily competitive. However, there is not the space here to consider the consequences of this across the full range of its activities; instead I can only briefly offer examples of deception and cost-cutting within the largest and most visible area of private security, that of provision of guarding services.

Few business concerns are interested in personally involving their own management in the supervision of the safety of their premises and property outside of normal working hours and are content to leave such matters to the police and private security. Hence, opportunities for (literal) short-service are numerous and are fully exploited by some companies. Some customers will pay for all-night guards, who leave the premises as soon as they are deserted and return shortly before work commences the following day. Visiting patrol services often have such long lists of calls that they are physically impossible to fulfil. On one occasion, one of the directors of a firm in my own research interviews had a case of a guard from a competing company offering a job to one of his staff, saying 'you come on at six, you go home at eight, and you get paid for four hours'; the contract to the company was actually for eight hours' guarding. Obviously such arrangements increase profits for the company, keep wages low, and enable cut-rate charges to be offered to the firms employing the company, obviously an asset in under-cutting private security agencies who genuinely try to fulfil the terms and obligations of their contracts.

The prevalence of cost-cutting practices is substantially dependent on, and partially the reason for, the employment in private security of an abnormally high proportion of part-time and casual staff. Moonlighting from another job or taking on this kind of part-time work while formally unemployed are common in private security and employers knowingly exploit this. Unrecorded work and unrecorded payment are familiar in certain areas of the private security business, and obviously, for the firms themselves, employing on this basis produces considerable savings of outlay on insurance and pension contributions etc., allowing a lower tax-free rate of pay and lower charges in the under-cutting of competition.

The structural level, political and civil liberties concerns

About every social issue there is probably a serious truism which by way of repetition is rendered dangerously close to platitude. It thereby loses its force and its subject matter takes on the comfortable and accommodated status of familiarity. Such is the case with the following accurate but almost tired argument for regulation of the private security sector: 'Today it is still possible to set up a security business with an entry in the Yellow Pages, a guard dog, some old uniforms and some headed notepaper. . . . The only controls on the industry are the consciences of the people running it.' (Kerr, 1979, p. 125.) It may be more politically and legally effective to emphasise the point that the issue of regulation (with all its attractions and dangers) is not simply about creating a toothless watchdog to oversee the activities of a growing area of commercial enterprise. Rather more importantly it is one issue in a wider debate about accountability and the guarantee of civil liberties.

To take up one important angle, Britain is one of the few western nations with no specific laws protecting information about individuals and the use made of it. Private detectives, security-vetting procedures and credit reference agencies are all known to resort to the collection of information on a large scale by impersonating police, DHSS, tax and education officials, and so on. The lack of effective controls over the way in which information may be gathered came out particularly clearly in the Malone telephone tapping case of 1978. The observations of the judge in the case included the comment that not only were there no effective controls over police telephone tapping (with a warrant from the Home Secretary, the police can tap private telephones legally), but there are also no effective sanctions against the private individual resorting to telphone tapping. In this regard, Britain does not yet meet the requirements of the European Human Rights Convention on the right of the individual to privacy.[6] Albeit fraught with difficulties of obtaining documented evidence—after all, security is the name of the game—the trade in (private) information and its technology seems one where a symbiosis of private and public sector security agencies may develop, involving the corruption of ethical and legal practice for both commerce and Crown. For example, the *Sunday Times* (10 February 1980, p. 1) carried a front-page story, reporting that:

> Army officers in Ulster, frustrated by official restrictions placed on telephone tapping, have been buying their own personal tapping equipment so they can carry on their activities unhindered by the law.
> A Sunday Times investigation shows that the officers are among a rapidly expanding number of clients using private security firms to tap telephones.

For private security, accountability is to the market, to customers and shareholders; there is no formal complaints procedure, no obligation to produce regular reports for any public authority and no mechanism to provide for public inspection, enforce standards or deal with corruption and fraudulent practice.

It is clear, and no surprise, that where significant sections of the private security sector (such as its professional associations) are in favour of a system of licensing (as opposed to strict regulation and limitation) it is because the voices raised are overwhelmingly those of the figureheads and public relations departments of the larger companies, who would be happy to take up the slices of the market left by any legislation that pushed the smaller companies out of business. This apparently cynical assessment is well understood by all concerned. The work of Carson (1979) on the history of factory legislation illustrates a similar situation where large companies have, over time, been apparently happy to co-operate with the Factory Inspectorate. Quite simply, such companies can afford to come up to scratch whereas their smaller competitors often cannot. Ironically, the Factory Inspectorate has thus tended to strengthen the monopolistic power of the larger companies as small companies are pushed out of the market by the apparent stringency of conditions that they are unable to meet. In consequence, the potential for abuse of regulations—and for hiding such abuse—can actually increase as the dominant companies grow in age, power and respectability. Proposals for the self-regulation of abuses within the private security sector merely reflect an inclination, and mechanism, for the minimisation of the conflicts and revelations which tend to arise out of the independent enforcement of regulation. The operation of this pseudo-'ombudsman' or 'consumer-protection agency' type of informal institution is well described by Abel (1982, p. 287) as based on 'scapegoating the exceptional enterprise that is totally irresponsible, thereby diverting attention from routine business practices and ensuring that regulation and publicity will have only a very limited general deterrent effect.' The prospect of similar developments within any form of a legislatively controlled private security sector is an issue to be considered very seriously.

Conclusion

> The private hire of police officers, fees, gratuities and rewards were all part of a system in which incentives were indistinguishable from temptations. [Radzinowicz, 1956, p. 307.]

One key source of contradictions for the private security sector in its crime control mode is shared with the police *vis-à-vis* their relation to tensions in the law enforcement and justice provision demands of the vocal middle class (as voting public and as employers of security services). In line with a world-view seeking security in the stability of the status quo, the private security sector and the police are urged to 'guard the gates of the city', to deter wrongdoing and also have the highest regard for procedure, legality, due process, etc. (especially in any dealings that they may have with the middle class). However, the middle class are particularly vocal and instrumentally active in calls for pro-active, aggressive policy and action (public and private) in preventing crime (. . . and immorality, falling standards, young people congregating on street corners, etc.). There is obvious and considerable incompatibility between the two ways of seeing necessary action for crime control (cf. Chambliss and Seidman, 1971, p. 358). The commercial and instrumental nature of the private security sector, employed by sections of society most likely to share the second 'way of seeing' the approach to crime control, makes it particularly prone to operating with and within a self-justified ethos of the necessity of short-cuts, providing 'unconventional' services which have a demand, and eschewing strict procedure and legal form. If attractive commercial expedients fit with a justifying rhetoric of the primacy of prevention—need for urgent action and getting results—then so much the better. It is not however a casual but rather a structurally logical 'coincidence'.

The private security sector fills a structural space between state provision of policing and do-it-yourself vigilantism, which is a contemporary anomaly. That space is exploited by commercial entrepreneurs sharing a conservative ideology, a law and order service sector pragmatism born out of and suborned to the profit motive, and the development of a 'professional' rationale reflected in what might be described as the 'security mentality'. This latter aspect of the private security phenomenon helps explain some of the sources of rationalisation for the corruption of formal legalistic ethics in its practice.

Postscript: The world of the 'Continental Detective Agency'

Editing an anthology of Dashiell Hammett's stories about an operative for the 'Continental Detective Agency' ('the Continental Op'), Steven Marcus (1975) draws attention to the Op's operational pragmatism; 'Detecting is a hard business', says the Op, 'and you use whatever tools come to hand'. As Marcus elaborates, there is in Hammett's description of the Op's world 'a paradoxical tension and unceasing interplay . . . between means and ends . . .' (1975, xxvii).[7] Such an example of the instability and contradiction in relations between the practice of the private security sector and its consequences in the social world leads Marcus to consider a remark from Weber in his essay 'Politics as a Vocation'. In so far as the private security sector deals actively in a world of politics and power, the remark is as apposite here as it is to Hammett's world:

> The world is governed by demons, and he who lets himself in for . . . power and force as means, contracts with diabolic powers, and for his action it is *not* true that good can follow only from good and evil only from evil, but that often the opposite is true. Anyone who fails to see this is, indeed, a political infant.

Notes

1. This section draws upon my own ethnographic, observational and interview research with private security workers, and also on private communications from several informants, who, as agreed, should consider themselves most gratefully acknowledged while remaining anonymous. This observational research originated from a post-'New Criminology' concern with the 'power, social structure and social control' relationship, but also from my feeling that the 'New Criminology' school wasn't actually looking at the top and bottom of the relationship; i.e. having resurrected the central importance of power and social structure to genuine criminological endeavour (cf. Chambliss, 1982; Sutherland, 1949; Merton, 1968), it neglected the importance of power, structure, ideology and interaction at 'middle' and 'micro-range' levels. So, while part of a larger project on the historical and structural significance of the private security sector, the research drew on approaches to occupational sociology such as those exemplified by Everett Hughes and Donald Roy.
2. Clearly what is absent from this brief examination of the private security sector at these

levels and with this particular focus, is a more theorised, structural account and analysis. I have attempted to begin developing such an analysis elsewhere (South, 1982a).

3. The research reported here is not centrally concerned with media images of the private security sector, but in addition to covering documentary and magazine reports, I have also checked through the cuttings libraries and back issues of examples of the leading popular Sunday and quality daily press.

4. Such unfortunate invidiousness is not of course wholly unique: respondents in Henry's (1978) research on the hidden economy drew his attention to the hypocrisy of members of the police force whose professional function might be to trace stolen goods, but who were themselves often the most eager to buy something that had 'fallen off the back of a lorry'.

5. *Sic.* The private security sector seems typified at all levels by rather traditional values, a law and order conservatism and sexism. Proportionately, the number of women employed is small, generally confined to secretarial, wage-packeting or other office-type jobs, or store-detective work. Some companies have also employed women in the back of their cash-holding vans, partially because, according to one company, they're not given to heroics and because they have clear radio voices! Operational practice, priorities and attitudes generally reflect a concern with 'jobs for conservative minded males'.

6. Recent government proposals may remedy this, though the reasons for such a move may not represent a straightforward concern for civil liberties. Certainly appearing at last to step in line with the European Convention is part of the motivation.

7. While many know of Hammett as a figure of the American left—refusing to testify before the McCarthy Committee in the 1950s having been called as a witness because he was a trustee of a fund that supplied bail for Communists and others on trial—his earlier life seems less well known. Equally interesting is that from 1914 until the early 1920s (except for a year's war service and some illness) he was a very successful investigator for the Pinkertons' private detective agency, fist in Baltimore and later in San Francisco.

Bibliography

Abel, P. (1982), 'The Contradictions of Informal Justice' in Abel, R. (ed.), *The Politics of Informal Justice*, New York, Academic Press.

Bowden, T. (1978), *Beyond the Limits of the Law*, Harmondsworth, Middx., Penguin.

Bunyan, T. (1976), *The History and Practice of the Political Police in Britain*, London, Quartet.

Carson, W. (1979), 'The Conventionalisation of Early Factory Crime', *International Journal of the Sociology of Law*, 7, No. 1, February.

Carson, W. and Young, P. (1976), 'Sociological Aspects of Major Property Crime' in Young, P. (ed.), *Major Property Crime in the United Kingdom: Some Aspects of Law Enforcement*, Edinburgh, School of Criminology, University of Edinburgh.

Chambliss, W. (1982), 'Critical Criminology and the Study of Corruption', paper to Conference on Corruption, University of Birmingham, 4–6 June.

Chambliss, W. and Seidman, R. (1971), *Law, Order and Power*, Reading, Mass., Addison-Wesley.

Daily Express (1961), Report on the Economic League, 12 January.

Daily Mirror (1982), 'Crooks get into uniform', 10 August, p. 6.

Ditton, J. (1977), *Part Time Crime: Ethnography of Fiddling and Pilferage*, London, Macmillan.

— (n.d.), 'The Dual Morality in the Control of Fiddles', paper to the Outer Circle Policy Group, Hidden Economy Working Party, unpublished.

Draper, H. (1978), *Private Police*, Harmondsworth, Middx., Penguin.

Economic League (1925), *5th General Report*, London, The Economic League.

Evening Standard (1981), 'Policemen "leaked computer secrets" ', 22 October.

Foucault, M. (1977), *Discipline and Punish*, London, Allen Lane.

Friedlander, M. (1956), 'Profile of a Plant Thief', *Personnel Journal*, 37, 170–3.

Guardian (1978), Report on the Economic League, 29 June.
Giddens, A. (1981), *A Contemporary Critique of Historical Materialism*, London, Macmillan.
Gouldner, A. (1954), *Patterns of Industrial Bureaucracy*, New York, Free Press.
Gregory, A. (1962), 'Why Workers Steal', *Saturday Evening Post*, **235**, 68–71.
Hall, S. and Scraton, P. (1981), 'Law, Class and Control' in Fitzgerald, M., McLennan, G. and Pawson, J. (eds), *Crime and Society*, London, Routledge and Kegan Paul.
Hamilton, P. (1972), *Computer Security*, London, Associated Business Programmes.
Hartshorne, J. (1922), 'Are you Tempting Employees to Steal Tools? *Industrial Management*, January, 41–2.
Henry, S. (1978), *The Hidden Economy*, Oxford, Martin Robertson.
Kakalik, J. and Wildhorn, S. (1972), *Private Police in the United States: Findings and Recommendations*, volume 1, Rand Corporation Study for U.S. Department of Justice, Washington, D.C., Government Printing Office.
Kerr, M. (1979), 'Confrontation or Co-operation', *Police Review*, 26 January.
Knapp Commission (1972), Report by the Commission to investigate allegations of police corruption in New York City (Whitman Knapp, Chairman), 3 August 1972. Reprinted in Chambliss, W. (ed.) (1975), *Criminal Law in Action*, Santa Barbara, Hamilton, 137–44.
Labour Research (1978), 'Economic League Blacklists Revealed', *Labour Research Department Fact Service*, **40**, No. 28, 22 July, 113.
Marcus, S. (ed.) (1975), *Dashiell Hammett, the Continental Op.*, London, Macmillan.
Merton, R. (1968), *Social Theory and Social Structure*, New York, Free Press.
Miers, D. (1982), 'Casino Corruption', paper to Conference on Corruption, University of Birmingham, 4–6 June.
Observer (1969), Report on the Economic League, 16 October.
Observer (1970), Report on private security, 6 December.
Radzinowicz, L. (1956), *A History of English Criminal Law and its Administration from 1750*, volume II, London, Stevens and Sons.
Rojek, D. (1979), 'Private Justice Systems and Crime Reporting', *Criminology*, **17**, No. 1, May, 100–11.
Scraton, P. (1982), *Policing Society; Policing Crime*, Issues in Crime and Society Course, Block 2, Part 6, Milton Keynes, Open University Press.
Scraton, P. and South, N. (1981), *Capitalist Discipline, Private Justice and the Hidden Economy*, Occasional Papers in Sociology and Criminology, No. 2, Enfield, Middlesex Polytechnic.
Slee-Smith, P. (1970), *Industrial Intelligence and Espionage*, London, Business Books.
Spitzer, S. and Scull, A. (1978), 'Privatisation and Capitalist Development', *Social Problems*, **25**, 1.
South, N. (1982a), *'Private Policing', Private Security and Social Control*, Occasional Papers in Sociology and Criminology, No. 7, Enfield, Middlesex Polytechnic.
— (1982b), 'The Informal Economy and Local Labour Markets' in Laite, J. (ed.), *Bibliographies on Local Labour Markets and the Informal Economies*, London, Social Science Research Council.
State Research (1978), 'Background paper: The Economic League', *State Research Bulletin*, **7**, August–September, 135–45.
State Research (1981), Report on the Economic League, *State Research Bulletin*, **24**, June–July, 141.
Sunday Times (1980), 'Army Men Enlist the "Pirate" Tappers', 10 February.
Sutherland, E. (1949), *White Collar Crime*, New York, Dryden Press.
Thompson, A. (1970), *Big Brother in Britain Today*, London, Michael Joseph.
Times, The (1971), J. Phillip-Sorenson in report on private security, 11 March.
Wade, J. (1829), *A Treatise on the Police and Crimes of the Metropolis*, reprinted 1972, Montclair, NJ, Patterson Smith.
Younger Committee on Privacy (1972), Cmnd 5012. Report of the Committee on Privacy, July, HMSO.

5 Journalistic investigation of corruption

DAVID MURPHY

One of the justifications for a free news medium put forward by journalists and proprietors is its role as a watchdog. This implies that the news media as a matter of routine scrutinise the activities of government from a variety of standpoints. Important among these is that the press and the broadcasting organisations are among several institutions which expose and control corruption. It is this aspect of journalism which I wish to examine in this chapter.

The evidence on which I shall draw is a number of cases I have examined as a participant and an observer. They have all been successful for the journalist concerned in that the story has been published, although the study of failed endeavours would be an equally interesting study. In order to analyse the journalistic treatment of corruption I shall deal mainly with the work organisation of journalists in terms of their relationship with individuals involved in the processes of 'newsgathering'. This requires that we examine both their conceptual organisation of the world of events they describe and the organisation of the news-processing enterprise as a collective system of production.

Studies of the police,[1] psychiatrists,[2] and lawyers[3] have drawn attention to important aspects of work in which a description of the world is central. First, the routines which workers adopt help to determine the outcomes of their activities. Police reports have to be formulated around police procedures for arrest and prosecution; psychiatrists may construct their reports to meet the demands of the hospital bureaucracy; courts produce accounts of events that depend on the adversarial nature of court procedure, in which prosecution and defence may negotiate to ignore events related to a case if they embarrass either side, perhaps on a tit-for-tat basis.

Secondly, in those occupations, workers are dealing primarily with groups who would conventionally be regarded as deviant. Indeed the definition of the subjects of such occupations as in some way special is implicit in the justification for the job. However, David Sudnow[4] in identifying the notion of 'normal crime' draws attention to an important effect of the routinisation of work. When an actor is engaged in the organised construction of reality he or she proceeds by routine, and in order to make sense of reasons for events it is necessary to fit these events to a model of a 'normal' version of the particular form of deviance—insanity or crime.

From these two tendencies it is possible to infer how particular professional routines and assumptions depict society and these who deviate from it. Such an inferential exercise from the implicit nature of work routines is often sustained by more directly observed data. The explicit statements of, say, police federation spokesmen or the debates about the reform of psychiatric treatment reveal how the workers in these areas depict the relationship between the normal and the deviant, the ethical relationship between power and punishment, individuals' responsibility for their own actions.

In journalism also the production of news proceeds by routines. It relies on a conceptual and interactional organisation of the world. Conceptually, versions of events are related to depiction of the socially normal; interaction between the journalist and lay persons or among journalists is organised to produce versions of events that can be organised as news within the ambit of this conceptual organisation.

News concerns deviation from the 'ordinary' rather than the norm. All news stories have to be propounded on the basis that they are worth recording in relation to some assumption about the normal. Sometimes this may relate to normative deviation, at other times to an unusual mixture of actor and deed; at others the deed and the doer may be appropriately combined but the event may be special. For instance in the first type of news a burglar stealing jewellery of modest value from a house may be perfectly 'normal' behaviour for a criminal but the very deviance will make it news. On the other hand if the burglar happens to be, say, a judge or a bishop, then the second definition of news intensifies the story's newsworthiness, in that the intrinsic deviance of the deed is overlaid by the disruption of social expectations based upon a depiction of both normal bishops and judges (that they are not criminal) and of burglars (that they are not normally from white-collar backgrounds, especially the 'liberal professions'). On the other hand when two people marry, this may be normal in the sense of the moral or psychological states of the participants. However, given the relationship between audience and actors, the fact that such a ceremony has special ritual significance will make it news. In a village any couple's wedding is news to its inhabitants; at a national level the weddings of the heroes and heroines of public dramas are conceived of as news.

The work of the journalist is to make depictions of events identifiable as deviating from the run-of-the-mill daily routines of social life. In addition to the special nature of the events described, it is also necessary that they are seen as being relevant to the audience at whom they are directed.

News is organised conceptually by journalists around the notion of an audience unified by a common interest in certain events—which makes them a community. In order to gain access to this world of events, journalists develop a system of interaction with contacts who provide them with information. This information is considered to be relevant to readers as members of a community and is acquired from actors who are considered to be 'gatekeepers'[5] in the communications network. They are considered to be 'in the know' because of the position they occupy in the system of interaction of the community.

These contacts at local or national level tend to be those of high status, or with some 'official' function. They may be policemen, politicians, headmasters, heads of business, officials of political parties, secretaries of gardening clubs, clergymen. The characteristic that they have in common is that their status gives them access to knowledge of events that are organised as being done in the name of a community or some collective part of it. Documents such as Hansard, the Family Expenditure Survey or Congleton Borough Council Minutes have the same force. They are official accounts of matters deemed to be communally relevant by those with authority.

These sources are seen by journalists as having the force of 'spokesmen': they speak authoritatively as representatives of some collectivity. Statements of fact about their area of responsibility can be reported as true without checking them. That is not to say that journalists believe them, but for the purposes of creating news they behave as if they do. Similarly, when high ranking officials such as the Chief Constable of Manchester express opinions about their own area of responsibility, these are by definition newsworthy. And this newsworthiness can be a self-fulfilling prophecy so that in the end such an official's opinions on subjects as various as dieting, the socialisation of children or religion come to be regarded as news.

The organisational advantage of using the spokesman as a source of this information is that the process is self-validating. Because the person's status defines what is said as authoritative there is no need to check it. If some other authoritative voice disagrees, then that becomes a story in itself. All the newspaper has to do is to provide an accurate account of what is said. For instance police crime figures will be published as facts: 'Crime Wave Hits City'. If challenged by a prominent criminologist or statistician, the paper then reports that authoritative challenge: 'Police Statistics Inaccurate—Professor'.

In either case the authoritative source is accepted at face value; conflicts over veracity are simply reported—not checked or judged. The relationship between the organisation of concepts, interaction and of the ordering of resources briefly works as follows. The traditional journalistic conception is of a readership or audience drawn together by some common identity—e.g. they are residents of Birmingham, the UK or Congleton and news comprises stories about events relevant at the level of that communal identity. This is seen as the means by which newspapers are sold. There is an identity between the market and the community because the audience's interest in buying papers is seen as emerging from membership of the community. The contacts giving access to this community are defined by the fact that they can speak authoritatively about communal events. The most poignant example of this process is the parliamentary lobby system analysed by Jeremy Tunstall,[6] where the press provides the powerful with the means to promulgate to the public descriptions of their own deeds.

The allocation of journalistic resources reflects this state of affairs. In the local press reporters engaged in the production of local political news either simply paraphrase local government documents or interview one or two authority figures—the chairman of the housing committee or the borough engineer, for instance. The fact that, as a matter of routine, spokesmen's versions of events can be used without checking means that the output of stories per worker is consequently the greater.

In the national popular press the number of reporters as a proportion of journalists is generally less than a third of the total. The majority of journalists are engaged not in the observing of events or the questioning of participants but in the presentational and organisational aspects of newspaper production. They are copy-tasters who decide whether submitted items are worth including; sub-editors who re-write, correct for grammar, write headlines, lay out pages; chief subs; depty editors of news or features, etc.; (day and night) editors-in-chief. Their work is to fit the contents and display of the paper to their perception of their readership's demands.

The process is thus circular. The readers are seen as having a common set of interests that are represented in the news produced: Manchester news for Mancunians. In order to 'get at' these stories reporters obtain information from spokesmen who are seen as gatekeepers to those sections of the community where they have power or official status. Treating them as spokesmen—self-validating sources of information—solves the reporter's problems of how to get reliable information quickly and on a regular basis in order to fulfil his work routines. And every time this process is undertaken it confirms the spokesman as a 'good contact', and, if quoted by name, as a reliable authority figure for the reading public. Thus, the contact's reputation, the quality of the news and the reputation of the journalist are intimately intertwined. The information is then recreated as news stories in a form which is perceived by journalists as most saleable to their readers, access to whom having dictated that choice of contacts in the first place.

The above is a very truncated account of the traditional journalistic process which I have dealt with elsewhere.[7] In this process validation, the choice of contacts, the structure of stories, and the assumption that there is an identity between the formal authority structure and the local community are taken for granted. They are all dealt with by routines that enable news to be produced as a regular organised activity.

In the investigation of corruption these taken-for-granted aspects of normal journalism are all problematic. This is because the validation of factual statements has to be accomplished explicitly as part of the activity of preparing the data and writing the story. The investigation of corruption involves an inversion of the role of the spokesman. Whereas in normal journalism the spokesman is both an informant and a source of empirical validation for the investigation, here the spokesman is the target of an ideologically subversive activity. The initial information will almost certainly come from an informant who is not a spokesman.

In normal journalism the news story is perceived as relevant to the audience because it concerns the community and agencies who define their activities as relevant at the societal level. In investigative journalism news is also about agencies and individuals who define themselves and their activities as relevant to the community. The object, however, is to show that these agencies are not behaving according to the norms they themselves publicly avow.[8]

The actors who in normal journalism validate stories, and whose prestige is enhanced by them, are under attack by the subversive investigative journalists. And the more a spokesman is built up by normal journalism, the wider becomes the possible definition of corruption in his case. He becomes a bigger and more desirable target. When an informant provides a piece of information, the journalist needs to be able to do two things to accomplish a viable story: (i) he or she has to be able to validate the story; (ii) he or she needs to demonstrate signification.

The first is done classically by making the spokesmen or their apparatus inform against themselves either through a public 'confession', or through the publication of documents to whose composition they have contributed, or by making them lie demonstrably in public. The second requires that the information concerns the 'community', especially when it involves a public figure acting in some way relevant to the exercise of economic, political or legal power. Signification and confession may well be alike and achieved by obliging a spokesman to make an expressly public statement in the role that makes him a spokesman. An official enquiry or court case into the events concerned, by involving the legitimate agencies of the community or the state, may also confirm for the investigator that what is being revealed is significant at the societal level—not in an absolute sense but as a matter of social accomplishment. Because these processes are not taken for granted, they require more time, more person power and cost more money than routine journalism. The consequence is that just as the interaction between reporter and contact is more complex than in routine journalism, the relationship between reporter and editor or other executive journalist is equally complex. The contact's reliability is always more open to question, as is that of the reporter. 'Moral characters' in this context are constantly open to question.[9] By taking a number of cases as examples, I hope to show how the journalist solves the problems of empirical validation and signification in dealing with informants and spokesmen, and how, in writing and publishing the news story, social control agencies make investigative journalism a marginal or deviant activity.

I wish to commence by a consideration of two investigations concerning the popular Chief Constable of Manchester, James Anderton. From any normal moral assessment the first case is trivial and the second serious. The importance of this difference is to show how the journalist's skill manifested itself in provoking a reaction by the police chief that acknowledged the first case as being of sufficient significance to warrant his taking official action. Thus, signification is shown to be an accomplishment by the journalist in obtaining an acknow-ledgement that what has been done is subject to the rules that define public morality and is worthy of executive action.

The first story is the case of the Iranian whisky. It began around Christmas 1978 when, according to the contact of a reporter (whose work I was observing as the fieldwork for my doctoral thesis), the Iranian *chargé d'affairs* in Man-chester had sent two crates of very expensive Crawford's de luxe whisky to named high-ranking Manchester police officers. The informant told the journalist, who worked for the *New Manchester Review*, an 'alternative' fortnightly run by a workers' co-operative, that a legation limousine complete with CD plates had drawn up outside the police headquarters and a lackey had delivered the whisky into the building.

The parcels bore the names of individual officers: all were above the rank of inspector and they included the Chief Constable, James Anderton, who had been given a crate all to himself, the informant claimed. A simple enough inci-dent in itself, but what made it a story for the journalists were three factors:

(1) The police disciplinary code forbidding officers to accept gifts from mem-bers of the public or drinking on duty is severely applied in Manchester. Uniformed police officers are frequently disciplined for drinking on duty or accepting drinks while in uniform.

(2) Manchester police had previously been called to the Iranian legation to clear out an infestation of revolutionary students against whom public order charges were brought. Clearly, gifts from the Shah's representative could be seen as implying a compromisingly close relationship with British bobbies. Was it a case of services in return for whiskies rendered?

(3) Anderton was then, and is even more so now, so much a public advocate of the 'driven snow' version of morality that even the slightest stain on his character would be enlarged by the magnifying glass of his own publicity mania and preoccupation with the minutiae of rectitude into a king-sized blot on his personal escutcheon—or so the informant and the journalist thought.

The journalist's task was therefore to prove adequately for his own profes-sional needs that the whisky had been delivered and that this fact constituted an issue of public morality. A straightforward confrontation with the police public relations department would have been unsatisfactory, he judged, for two reasons. First, it might have exposed the contact through an internal investiga-tion of the leak. Secondly, the authorities might organise a cover-up and simply deny everything.

In order to avert such a simple blank denial in the whisky story, the journalist decided to entrap the Iranian consul into an admission that he had sent the whisky. To do this we arranged to visit him at the consulate (as chance had it, on the day the Shah left Iran for his final holiday abroad). The purported reason for the visit was that we were journalists writing an article on the difficulties facing Iranians in Manchester at a time of such turmoil, and on how the local 'Iranian community' were 'coping with this time of danger for their nation etc.'. Our scheme was simple: to engage him in talk about the differences between Islamic and western customs, such as present-giving at Christmas and then arrive at a jovial statement of the sort, 'By the way, the lads down at the police headquarters were really pleased with the whisky you sent them . . .' in order to obtain an acknowledgement that he indeed had sent the whisky.

During the interview the consul plied us with cigarettes and tea. As I am a non-smoker, my journalist-companion was given two at a time and for considerable periods sat with two cigarettes placed behind his ears while furiously smoking a third in order to get through the supply. A further absurdity was generated by the diplomat's weak English, which actually helped him to avoid the rather puerile traps we set him, since he found it difficult to grasp what we were saying.

After three attempts the Iranian grasped what the journalist was saying and took the bait. He acknowledged that he had sent five bottles of whisky to the police headquarters and, despite the understatement of the amount, this was a sufficient confession for the journalist's purpose. If subsequently questioned by police authorities, the consul would have to acknowledge that he had mentioned the whisky. He showed no awareness that the whisky had any significance. His only concern was that we should not publish anything he had said about Iranian politics since he feared reprisals by whoever came out on top at home. The reporter made our farewells more or less as soon as the diplomat made his confession and we left. He then rang up the police PRO saying that he had been interviewing the Iranian consul who had 'mentioned' having sent whisky as gifts to the police. He asked if this was a breach of the rule about gifts from members of the public to the police. The PRO said he would look into it, and the following day issued a statement which read:

> It appears that, unknown to the Chief Constable of Greater Manchester, a parcel containing intoxicating liquor from the Iranian consulate in Manchester may have been delivered to a Manchester police station before Christmas. The matter is now being investigated. A further parcel addressed to the Chief Constable and Mrs Anderton from the Consul General of Iran in Manchester and his wife was delivered at the same time to the Chief Constable's office. The benefit of this gift was passed on to the Northern Police Convalescent Home at Harrogate, since it is the Chief Constable's policy that personal gifts should not be retained.

The statement fulfilled the journalistic requirements for the corruption story in that it acknowledged: (a) the factual basis of the allegation; (b) that symbolic action at the societal level had to take place in the form of an official inquiry. In other words, the spokesmen in the police hierarchy and at the consulate were being made to say through a spokesman publicly what the informant had told the journalist. The police authorities were also being obliged to act officially as an institution and this action could be reported as a fact at the level of the community. In doing this the journalist was also able to refer to the other data such as the interview with the consul, which were made relevant by the official acknowledgement implicit in the statement and the inquiry.

The story appeared in the *New Manchester Review* under the headline 'Police Probe Case for Prosecution' under the rather provocative strapline 'Corruption'. The story was 'nosed' on the inquiry. It was then followed up by the *Observer, Daily Mirror* and *Manchester Evening News*. These papers followed the line of the fact that a statement had been issued and an inquiry started.

While this case may be regarded as lightweight on moral issues, and in the realms of comedy rather than drama, it illustrates the fundamental requirements for the journalist in carrying out investigations of corruption. It illustrates the way in which the authority figure, the spokesman or the institution, have to condemn themselves in terms of empirical validation and signification.

These necessities underlie the second case I wish to consider. This concerns two incidents at a police training college in North Manchester. During March 1982, a sixteen-year-old male police cadet at the college was raped allegedly by three Saudi Arabian police officers training at the college. They were said to be members of King Khaled's bodyguard and among forty Saudi police students there. About a week later an anonymous contact telephoned the northern offices of the *Daily Mirror* and the *Daily Telegraph* in Manchester, and stories appeared the following day referring to the incident, indicating an internal police inquiry was under way. The *Manchester Evening News* followed up the national dailies. The stories all speculated that court procedures might not follow because of possible 'diplomatic pressures'. A week later a contact of a BBC 'Nationwide' reporter told him that there had been an even worse case earlier. In 1981, a woman cleaner at the college had complained to the police that three Saudi officers had raped her, but they had pressured her to withdraw her complaint and she acquiesced. Three months later she committed suicide. At the inquest, reference was made to the allegation of rape, but the police witness said that he could not go into detail because the matter was *sub judice*.

The three suspects in the earlier case were never charged and were allowed to return home. In the case of the homosexual assault the alleged assailants were about to be spirited away. The allegations of rape were not in themselves the issue. The story for the BBC journalist was that the police authorities had deliberately covered them up and that in doing so at various points had either lied, omitted to tell the truth or had been partial in applying the law. Further, in doing so they were in some way succumbing to diplomatic pressure because of the relationship between the British Foreign Office and the Saudi Government. Finally, the aim was to show that the cover-up occurred at the highest level: that the person who made the decision was the puritanical, garrulous Chief Constable James Anderton.

The relatives of the female victim were located and were willing to be interviewed on film. The woman's brothers and sister-in-law stated that she had said she was pressured by the police to withdraw the complaint. They produced a letter from the investigatory officer saying that the matter of the rape had been 'fully investigated'.

The journalist now had two police statements to be checked: one was the statement at the inquest that the matter was *sub judice*, the second was that the matter had been fully investigated. The first was to be checked by the method of making the spokesman condemn himself. The police were asked if there were ever plans to prosecute the three assailants. The second was checked by asking the neighbours of the woman whether they had ever been interviewed by the police about the rape. Given that the rape was supposed to have occurred late at night in her terraced house, a full investigation, it is reasonable to assume, would have included interviews with the immediate neighbours. They were interviewed and said on film that they were not interviewed about the rape. The police stated that they had not brought charges against the three. The matter had never been fully investigated; the matter had not been *sub judice*. Inference: the police were covering up. The question was then how high was the source of the cover-up.

The journalist posed the question to the police public relations department: what action was to be taken over the second rape; and on whose decision was this and the earlier action taken? The reply was that no action was to be taken. The case was reviewed by James Anderton, whose final decision it was not to proceed.

Again the journalist is faced with two problems: the establishment of the facts; the accomplishment of the public acknowledgement of the significance of the factual state of affairs as a public, moral issue. In one sense, the task was easier than in the case of the whisky. The first rape and suicide were already referred to in the transactions of the inquest. In the second case the whistle was already blown on the homosexual rape, and the police had already acknowledged the fact and the issue by admitting they had instituted an inquiry.

In another sense the task was more complex. The substantive claim was that there had been a cover-up. The higher up the hierarchy the cover-up could be located, the more self-evidently it could be seen as involving an issue of public morality, and therefore as involving an implicit statement about the corruptibility of the system. The decisions not to prosecute either trio of assailants, along with the use of the false claim of *sub judice* to gag any discussion of the rape at the inquest were conveyed in the TV film to indicate the cover-up. Equally, the evidence to show that the police had not thoroughly investigated the rape, combined with an official letter, shown and read out in the broadcast, was further used to show police bad faith in their dealings with the family, and to indicate that they had prejudged the issue in favour of inaction. Finally, the statement by the police PR department laid the responsibility for the decisions at the door of Mr Anderton. In both of these cases the role of the contact is vital since it is his or her information that provokes considerable expenditure of time by the journalist investigating the story. When the journalist decides to take up the issue he or she is already convinced that the story is true; investigation is not discovery of truth, but a matter of making out the case. If the story proves untrue, then the reputation of the contact may have to be re-worked, a new 'biography' may have to be created.

The traditional notion of corruption is the misuse of political authority or financial knowledge for personal gain. In the investigation of such matters the same sort of constraints and methods apply. There are the same necessities to prove the factual basis of the story and to show the significance of what is derived.

I shall now refer to two stories in order to show how the process of manufacturing this type of story works. In both cases working with another journalist I took an active part in investigating the allegations of corruption.

The first case is the more recent and concerns the operation of Crest International, a company engaged in property dealing. While working on another story with a journalist as part of my research, I was approached by a Manchester businessman who told me that a deal had taken place which involved a company using questionable property valuations in order to overvalue its assets to the tune of several million pounds. The significance of these dubious practices was that they had taken place within the framework of the Unlisted Securities Market (USM), a recent innovation in Stock Exchange dealings, which relieved newly formed companies of the normal stringent requirements for listed companies imposed by the Stock Market Committee. The USM could be seen as part of the new, freemarket, Thatcher-style capitalism, and Crest International could be seen as the first 'scandal' on this new market. During the period from January to October 1981 their shares had nearly doubled in price, and they were one of two leading shares on the market, much praised by the *Stock Exchange Gazette*.

The bare bones of the scheme were as follows. The company had been formed by two businessmen, Tom Farmer and Walter Alec Stenson, both directors of Kwikfit Exhausts. Tom Farmer transferred the assets of his own firm Tom Farmer Limited (TFL) into Crest in exchange for just over £900,000 worth of shares. These assets were a portfolio of thirty-three automobile safety centres—buildings designed for brake, tyre and exhaust fitting. In 1979 TFL had acquired the garages. They were bought for and valued at £1.5 million, a valuation of about six years' purchase.[10] At the inception of Crest into the USM one and a half years later these garages had increased in value to £2.4 million, a valuation of ten years' purchase.

The rents on the buildings had hardly increased—about 4 per cent over the period. The allegation made to me was that the 66 per cent valuation increase was for the purpose of increasing the company's asset value and thus increasing its share ratios and the market price of these shares. Along with the auto centres the company's other real property and balances (which stood at £350,000) had a book value of around £3 million. The directors held shares totalling £1.15 million in value and £1.4 million's worth of shares were authorised by the Stock Exchange for sale to the public. That is to say £2.55 million in shares were dependent on the various properties and balances. But if the automotive centres were overvalued, as my informant alleged, to the value of around £1 million, the shares issued exceeded the market value of the assets by at least £1 million.

To this overvaluation it was alleged a second advantageous valuation was added. Tootal House, a listed historic building and the Manchester headquarters of the Tootal Company was sold by Tootal to Crest on 20 July 1982 for £2.05 million. Four days later the building was valued at £2.8 million, a gain of £750,000 in four days. Tootal rented back the building on a five-year lease, and this lease could have accounted for the increase in valuation which was supposed to be a market value. Two arguments could be put against this: (i) the lease back and the sale took place at the same time; therefore, Tootal sold the land with the leaseback and the original price of £2.05 million included that factor; (ii) the lease absolved Tootal of responsibility for structural repairs and normally a full maintenance lease, which *would* increase the value, would lay this duty on the tenants. Since the actual lease laid it on the landlords, Crest, the value could not be increased.

Part of the price for Tootal House was paid for by five million 10p shares accepted at their market value of $16\frac{1}{2}$p in consideration of £825,000. These shares were a new issue. The official asset value of the company went up to 19p. The total market value of the company's issued shares was therefore now just under £6 million. If the book value of the properties and the balances were added together this market price would be an accurate reflection of the company's worth. If my informant's allegations were accurate, and both the auto centre's portfolio and Tootal were overvalued as he said, the real value of the company would be only a little over £4 million.

The alleged overvaluation was greatly to Tom Farmer's advantage. He had raised two loans on behalf of TFL to buy the auto centres for the original price of £1.5 million. When he transferred the portfolio to Crest, the TFL debts went with them and he took over £900,000 of shares at par value. When the market price of the shares rose to 19p his personal stake then became worth about £1.8 million without actually having to risk any substantial amount of his own money.

In order to substantiate this story with the detail I have now included it was necessary to seek the documents issued by Crest at the launch and at the purchase of Tootal House. In order to acquaint ourselves with the Unlisted Securities Market we studied the *Financial Times* and *Stock Exchange Gazette*. The documents relating to Crest we obtained from Extel Statistical Services, the company's registered office (the registry department of a commercial bank) and a stockbroker. From these documents we pieced together the above account—the informant gave us no details, but directed us through the welter of documents we acquired. Although the figures showed the sudden increases in valuations, this did not prove that there was anything untoward in the business, merely that some surprising increases in value had taken place. When we showed our informant the papers, he remembered a story from a friend in property valuation that some of the valuations of the auto centres were really strange, and that the valuers had not even seen all the buildings in the portfolio.

We therefore decided to check out the centres. The Extel Services documents gave the addresses. Where we could visit we did so, but in other cases we used the telephone. By chance we were lucky early. In the documents issued by the valuers 187/189 Oxford Street, Swansea was valued at £100,000 and described as a 'modern, purpose-built, single-storey building, 6,000 sq ft, limited car parking space, 'Freehold'.

The company renting the building was Autoparts Ltd and their subsidiary Autella. This was an Autella building. I rang up the garage claiming I was on my way into Swansea and had a broken exhaust pipe. I said I wanted directions. The manager explained how to get there. I asked: 'It's a modern single-storey building, isn't it?' He replied that I must have the wrong place. It was the old two-storey building next to National Tyre centre. The valuation certificate by the valuers stated 'we inspected and carefully considered the 33 properties owned by Tom Farmer Limited . . .'. They had clearly not even visited the Swansea site. This was the factual indication that the valuations were suspect.

We wrote two stories for a local, now defunct, newspaper, an attempt at a hybrid of *Time Out* with the *New Musical Express—The Manchester Flash*. The first story was an account of how Tom Farmer was £1.8 million better off as a consequence of the bank loans and two extraordinary valuations. It did not allege any corrupt deals.

The second story appeared three weeks later and was 'nosed' on the wrong valuation. After consultation with lawyers, the story again highlighted the strange increases in value and referred specifically to the Swansea site. Without being experts in valuation ourselves we wondered how a valuer could mistake a two-storey building for a single-storey building.

I contacted the *Sunday Times* and told them the story. They sent a photographer to Swansea and ran a story on the front page of their business section with a large picture of the Swansea garage. The story related the occurrences at Crest to the difficulties being experienced by Mr Farmer in his other company, Kwikfit Exhausts.

This story was much more complicated in its content and less dramatic in the events to which it referred than the alleged rape cover-ups. Yet someone was getting very rich, and someone else had not been to Swansea and the two were related. A series of other allegations about individuals and buildings were put to me which I was not able to substantiate. The signification was achieved in Manchester by reference to the large sums of money, the unlisted securities market as something new and significant and the large, historic landmark, Tootal House. For the *Sunday Times* the story's significance lay in the USM angle and the relation of Crest to a big company in trouble at the time— Kwikfit—in the form of Tom Farmer. Kwikfit is now prospering.

The documentation made necessary by company law provided the evidence by which the spokesmen (company officials in this case) condemned themselves. And as in the case of the police claim to have investigated the rape, a simple piece of investigation established the basis for implying an untruth.

The final case I wish to examine resulted in an abortive libel case. It concerned the then Manchester councillor, Harold Tucker, now the Tory group leader, who was an estate agent and a secretary of a number of housing associations. Briefly, the story was as follows. In 1972 Tucker (the ex-councillor) and a solicitor colleague bought a house from a man who was retiring and leaving Manchester. Previous owners had applied on several occasions for permission to knock down the house and redevelop the site with a block of flats. On each occasion the applications had been turned down by the Planning Committee on the grounds that the land was required for a school playing field by the Education Committee.

Within a week of finanalising the deal to buy the house the ex-councillor, Tucker, had obtained the acquiescence of the Education Committee to drop its demand for the future compulsory purchase of the land. The ex-councillor's wife was also a councillor and a member of the Education Committee. (She was not at the Education Committee meetings but did attend the full Council meeting and did not declare an interest when the education minutes were passed.)

Especially interesting were Tucker's means of negotiating with the Education Committee. He wrote to them as Secretary of the Greater Manchester and District Housing Society saying that they intended to buy the site to develop it as flats rented on a non-profit making basis to needy tenants such as pensioners, nurses, students etc. The present owner was retiring and leaving Manchester, and a decision was needed so that he could move to his new home. No mention was made by the writer of the fact that he, Tucker, was negotiating to buy the land had had actually become part-owner before the Council approved the Education Committee's minutes. After the planning situation changed, the land, held in a private property company solely owned by the estate agent, his councillor wife, the solicitor and the solicitor's wife, was then sold by them to the Housing Society at a profit of around 170 per cent, with the conveyancing work paid for by the Housing Society done by the aforementioned solicitor.

The story was told to me a year later by an angry citizen who had himself been negotiating for the sale of that house at a price of £7,000 and was gazumped by the estate agent who offered £7,900. The angry citizen had made application for outline planning permission to redevelop the site with flats and had been turned down. When he heard about the ex-councillor's subsequent success in this venture he was naturally extremely hurt and alleged that 'something was going on'. He had taken the matter to another councillor who had obtained copies of the correspondence, minutes and planning applications. I contacted the former owner who, regretting having sold his house to someone who had made such a large profit, was willing to provide details of the deal, including copies of the land registry documents. Although the price the property speculators received from the housing association was in excess of £20,000 we were unable to discover the exact amount.

I asked the chairman of the Planning Committee why the change in planning status had taken place and he instituted a Town Hall enquiry. The Town Clerk received all of the correspondence and reports—most of which we knew already—and called in the estate agent, Tucker, who by now had been re-elected to the Council, and asked him how much he had received for the land. He refused to answer.

A reporter at Granada Television, with whom I was working, managed to obtain a copy of the Town Clerk's confidential report from a contact in the Town Hall, and Granada broadcast a twelve-minute item in their local news programme based on this report along the lines of 'questions remaining unanswered'. The chairman of the Planning Committee was interviewed and he expressed doubts about the deal.

The estate agent issued a writ for libel against Granada and against the Planning Committee chairman. This writ was the subject of protracted out-of-court legal wrangling for nine years before it was finally dropped. During that period Granada spent several thousands of pounds in legal fees on the case, although there was never any finding against the company. But the effect of the writ was to silence any coverage of the issue until it was a deadletter.

Towards the end of this nine-year period the matter was resurrected in the local alternative press in the form of the now defunct *New Manchester Review*. Inquiries through a contact in the Housing Corporation, the government agency controlling housing associations, revealed that the two businessmen had done much better out of the deal than we had originally suspected. They had paid £7,900 for the land, as we knew, and sold it for £22,000. The solicitor had received legal fees, the estate agent management fees. The redevelopment was made up of three sites: the house in question, a house that was purchased from the council and a third house bought from a builder. The builder had paid £2,300 for this property in 1968 and received £22,900 for it in 1973. Furthermore, the builder, an old business associate of the other two, was given the contract for the redevelopment, without tendering, at a price of £145,000. An architect who was also a member of the Housing Society management committee took the contract to design the building. All of the money came in the form of loans from the Housing Corporation. So no private capital was ever at risk. When this information was published it was six years old and no writs for libel were received. The Housing Corporation subsequently required the re-organisation of the Housing Society.

Again official documents and enquiries are seen as the necessary means of proving the existence of the data and demonstrating its significance. In this instance conflict of public and private interests was the theme. In each of these cases I have looked at the existence of corruption is not something provided for the journalist in the way that a court case, or a council meeting, or even a fire, or a ceremonial event or a strike is. In all of these cases the paper is simply reflecting the signification accorded to *events* organised by others. In the *investigation of* corruption the journalist has to formulate his or her own construction of events. A case has to be made.

This is a time-consuming activity. Each of these investigations took in excess of three weeks to accomplish from the first information being received to the final position of writing the story. The financial stories are time-consuming in coming to terms with what the documents mean and learning new terms such as, say, the meaning of 'year's purchase'. And with each conclusion drawn it is necessary to go back to one's source. In attempting to provoke authorities into holding inquiries, similarly, one is dependent on the speed of those being manipulated, who are, incidentally, normally one's opponents.

Normal newspapers, especially local ones, and television news programmes are not geared to this time scale or this level of expenditure per news item. The last story was undertaken by me as a research student and the television reporter in his spare time. The police rape story was broadcast in a specialist 'investigation' slot in a television news programme. With newspaper investigative journalism the reporter spends considerable time in selling the story to editors. Where this is done on a freelance basis the rate of return per hours of work makes investigation of corruption a marginal occupation: rather like growing grapes in the Falkland Islands.

The threat of libel actions is also constricting. It is not the actual libel case which is so fearsome. I have no direct experience of this ever occurring. Writs, however, are cheap to issue and even to serve. And, whatever their legal significance, their actual effect on editors is to silence them. This means that a heavy investment in digging out a story may be wasted because it becomes unusable after one crack of the whip. Gagging writs are an especial difficulty of this operation, preventing any publication.

The major shortcoming of investigative reporting is, however, more profound and intrinsic to its practice in the context of business, governmental and media organisations. Because of government and business secrecy, investigation only takes place where either someone with information complains, or an inside informant 'blows the whistle' on the operation of a government or business bureaucracy. This means that the tighter and more ruthless the control, or the more dedicated the members of a bureaucracy, the less likely is it to be investigated. In this sense it seems most likely that the most potentially corrupt and dangerous organisations are impregnable to investigation.

The relationship between contact and journalist is also fraught with difficulties. In each of the above cases the contact had an axe to grind. A policeman who was the victim of draconian controls, a relative of a wronged individual, a gazumped house purchaser. All that the journalist can do is to check the truth of the contact's story. His own identity becomes involved in showing what an amazing story it is, and the secrecy of his contact becomes like a property right. The possibility that the writer is being manipulated is one that is therefore pushed to the back of his mind. But in a real sense the journalist remains in the final analysis someone who is acted on rather than an initiator, and the process by which an injustice or a corrupt act is brought to light remains fundamentally random.

Notes

1. Sacks, H., 'Notes on Police Assessment of Moral Character', in David Sudman (ed.), *Studies in Social Interaction*, New York, Free Press, 1972.
2. Garfinkel, H., ' "Good" Bureaucratic Reasons for "Bad" Psychiatric Records' in H. Garfinkel (ed.), *Studies in Ethnomethodology*, Englewood Cliffs, N.J., Prentice-Hall, 1967.
3. Sudnow, D., 'Normal Crimes' in E. Rubington and M. S. Weinberg (eds), *Deviance, the Interactionist Perspective*, New York, Macmillan, 1972.
4. Ibid.
5. There is a whole series of studies which examines the role of the 'gatekeeper' in the work of the journalist. The references for these studies appear in L. H. Dexter and D. M. White (eds), *People, Society and Mass Communication*, New York, Free Press, 1963. This reader includes White's own 'The Gatekeeper, A Case Study in the Selection of News', pp. 163-70. I have argued elsewhere (doctoral thesis, University of Manchester, 1981) that the definition of an actor as a gatekeeper is the outcome of journalists' work practices, not of the intrinsic nature of the actors' socially nodal location.
6. Tunstall, J., *The Westminster Lobby Correspondents*, London, Routledge and Kegan Paul, 1970.
7. Murphy, David, *The Silent Watchdog*, London, Constable, 1976.
8. See Gunther Walraff, *The Undesirable Journalist*, London, Pluto, 1978, for an example of this approach using an impressive array of subversive strategies.
9. As in the case of Sacks's 'moral characters', see note 1.
10. A year's purchase is the theoretical income a piece of land or property would raise in a year. Values are assessed as multiples of this figure. A piece of property with a specific usage might have a low value—say six years' purchase while an adaptable, well-placed piece of property might be valued at, say, ten or twelve years' purchase.

6 'You publish at your peril!' The restraints on investigatory journalism

ALAN DOIG

Indispensable to the health and honesty of politics

Police Officer: Now listen, mind you I've got a bit worried as things have gone on . . . Listen to me, let's get one thing fuckin' straight. In all this trouble you've fuckin' got on here, you've got one fuckin' friend, you have.

Club Owner: Who is it?

Police Officer: Me, one fuckin' f riend. All your chief superintendents, your fuckin' Eddie Washbournes, the fuckin' lot of them have done fuck all for you . . .

Unfortunately for Detective Constable Alan Gray, Rob Rohrer, then a freelance journalist, had spoken to the club owner (Michael Kountis) on Saturday, 19 April 1975, about the demands for a bribe to fix the latter's appeal against a four months' prison sentence for assault following a police raid on his club in December 1974. Rohrer had returned on the 21st with two tape recorders, one of which recorded the conversation that led, in October 1976, to publication of the conversation in the *Sunday Times* and to court in December 1977. The bribe of £100 was never handed over and it was never suggested anyone else was involved or that the evidence for the appeal was fixed. In May 1975, however, Kountis changed his appeal against the conviction to an appeal against the sentence and had the latter reduced to a £75 fine. Gray was convicted largely on voice identification and sentenced to twenty-one months' imprisonment for corruptly agreeing to accept a gift of £100 inducement to show favour to the club owner.

A modest tale of opportunist extortion as the Gray case may have been, the fact that the club owner had already been to the police to complain ('He gave me so many versions,' said Eddie Washbourne, then the head of the Regional Crime Squad. 'Quite honestly I said to Michael, "look, if you want to make this complaint you must go and make it official". He's a likeable rogue is Michael.')[1] highlights the role of the press as an alternative medium for the investigation of corruption, a role they often enthusiastically embrace. 'Parliamentary privilege', reproved the *Sunday Times* in 1980 after Jeff Rooker, MP had unreservedly apologised to a Rolls Royce executive for alleging in Parliament in June of that year that he had been bribed by an Italian firm to give them contracts, 'will be the more carefully used now that Mr. Jeffrey Rooker has come such a condign cropper . . . In general, MPs would do better to bring their doubts to the press for due investigation.'[2] Putting aside the press's own assessment of its investigatory role, however, it is clear that, given the limitations and difficulties of the various formal means and agencies for enforcing standards of conduct and investigating allegations of corruption and misconduct, the media have an important watchdog role, a role recognised by the two public inquiries that have looked at standards of conduct in British politics. The 1974 Redcliffe-Maud Report stated:

> the aim should be to keep the total quantity of confidential business as small as possible, and to ensure that initially confidential business which is eventually to become public should do so at the earliest, not the latest, practicable stage. An atmosphere of unnecessary secrecy not only makes misconduct easier to hide; it also encourages public suspicion and mistrust, to which the new authorities may in any case be more liable than the old because of their greater size and consequently greater apparent remoteness and anonymity. . . . A successful policy of communication with the public requires as one of its foundations a sound relationship with the local press, and with local radio and television . . . the initiative lies first with the local authority, as the originator of policies and the source of information. The flow of facts should be as free, copious and clear as possible. . . . Genuinely critical reporting and comment are indispensable to the health and honesty of local government, as of other institutions, however uncomfortable this may sometimes be for those subjected to criticism. . . .[3]

In her addendum in the 1976 Royal Commission on Standards of Conduct in Public Life Mrs Audrey Ward-Jackson, a Commission member, stated:

> Almost all the investigations that have led to prosecutions have been sparked off either by *Private Eye* or by commercial television or by other branches of the media or by other unofficial bodies or individuals. They have not been initiated from any official source. Furthermore, since the police (not surprisingly) take the view that it is no part of their duties to seek out evidence of malpractice but only to start inquiries after information indicating corruption has been provided to them, the conversion of public uneasiness or suspicions into successful prosecutions has depended, in some cases, on some individual courageous enough and public-spirited enough to expose himself to severe unpopularity (or even the destruction of his own career) by trying to bridge the gap between suspicion and evidence.[4]

The right of the public to know the deeds—and misdeeds—of government has been an integral part of the history of reporting and the battleground over which the media have long waved the banner of press freedom. Yet few of the major cases of corruption or misconduct in British politics during the twentieth century originally emerged as a result of media investigations. Indeed there is plenty of evidence during the scandals of the 1960s and 1970s from within the media to suggest that the media's investigatory role was often fortuitous rather than a result of well developed investigatory techniques and approaches. It was the *Sunday Times* Insight team that impetuously announced in 1972 at the onset of the Poulson bankruptcy hearings that 'revelations at the bankruptcy hearing . . . have followed a simple journalistic rule: "scandals" in public life, once scented, grow in complexity according to the number of journalists investigating them. Yet the Poulson affair is, in fact, straightforward'.[5] Paul Foot, then a journalist on the magazine *Private Eye*, was more direct on the impact of his first reports on Poulson's political relationships: 'It was the first time we had devoted three whole pages to one subject but it fell with a sickening thud. I did not get one single reaction to it.'[6]

Two other journalists, Martia Bailey and Bernard Rivers, who were instrumental in bringing to public attention the British government's role in the sanction-breaking oil shipments to Rhodesia, also expressed their concern at the general indifference to their story when they were doorstopping editors for support to pursue their leads. The story, they said later, 'only came out through an extraordinary chain of circumstances. Looking back, the chances of anything emerging were minimal . . . what we wonder is, how many more of these sort of things are happening, and who has the time or the money in our society to investigate them?'[7] To understand why investigatory journalism has not always been as widely or as successfully practised as the media claim or others hope is important, particularly in view of the variety and number of cases of corruption or misconduct that have occurred in recent years.

Order, harmony and packaging the news

The limits on the investigatory role of the media are various, overlapping, and both internally and externally generated. They essentially cover three broad areas: collecting the information, publishing the information and integrating the benefits of that publication with the primary objectives of the organisation concerned. The media themselves are well aware of the implications of all three. The editor of the *Guardian*, Alaistair Hetherington, warned that, on the question of how far a newspaper had to go to get a story:

> it must go to the point at which the newspaper possesses hard evidence even if some risks have to be taken in getting that far. To stop short of that is to be left with only flimsy suspicions, unsupported and unsubstantiated. You have neither a story nor solid evidence. And nobody will take much notice. Why should they? But the minute you set about collecting evidence you may be in trouble . . .[8]

The decision to publish is also one beset with difficulties and painful consequences, as Lord Goodman warned when chairman of the Newspapers Publishers Association:

> A great newspaper, if it believes that some villainy ought to be exposed, should expose it without hestitation and without regard to the law of libel. If the editor, his reporters and advisers are men of judgement and sense, they are unlikely to go wrong; but if they do go wrong, the principle of publish and be damned is a valiant and sensible one for a newspaper and it should bear this reponsibility.[9]

Finally there is the question of whether newspapers have the capacity as well as the capability to undertake controversial investigations. As the Newspaper Publishers Association told the 1977 Royal Commission on the Press: 'a newspaper is still a piece of private property with public responsibilities and the issue at the heart of the present inquiry is whether such a hybrid can survive under modern conditions. Is a press which is run on strictly commercial lines now capable of discharging its public functions?'[10]

This final question has become increasingly prominent in discussions on the future of the media and in particularly in relation to the press. The problems of Fleet Street are well documented.[11] The conflicts between owners, management and unions over the issues of overmanning and new technologies have overtaken any debate on contents, prompted the inevitable misuse of the principle of 'press freedom' and attracted formal recognition through the establishment of Royal Commissions. Fleet Street's turmoils are, however, only reflecting what has been happening in the provinces for the past few decades where, caught between the news output of the national media and the variety of local outlets, the provincial press have been primarily concerned to protect their commercial existence—and selling newspapers is not necessarily synonymous with selling news—and to guarantee the security of regular, lucrative advertising revenue. Closures and amalgamations following the steady escalation of costs in a labour- and material-intensive industry meant that by 1974 10 per cent of publishers controlled nearly 81 per cent of provincial evening papers' circulation, with four companies owning forty titles and 49.6 per cent of the total UK circulation, with strong local monopolies and groupings of local weeklies. The percentage share accruing to such monopolies include, for example, Thomson's 34 per cent share in Wales, SUITS' 24 per cent share in Scotland, Eastern Counties Newspapers' 53 per cent share in East Anglia and the Iliffe family interests' 41 per cent share in the West Midlands. Some newspaper groups have a tight grip on other newspapers in their area—the Liverpool Post and Echo group owns 60 per cent of Merseyside's weeklies' circulation—while others have built up national groupings: the Westminster Press owns nineteen Northern weeklies, seventeen Southern counties' weeklies and sixteen weeklies in Greater London.[12] Nearly all urban areas are now served by only one local daily evening newspaper, and where there is a local morning newspaper both are invariably owned by the same company. These developments, together with the tendency of provincial newspapers to belong either to large groupings or companies with other interests, have encouraged the rise of the company accountant and the primacy of cash-flow, turnover, market-share and product image. This is hardly surprising when the biggest single cost is production and the biggest share of income comes from advertising. In the 1977 Royal Commission of the Press the survey of provincial newspapers listed the average income (in pence at 1975 prices) as: net circulation revenue (3.6), net advertising revenue (6.6), other (0.7). Average costs were: newsprint/ink (2.2), production (2.3), editorial (1.6), distribution (0.7), advertising (0.6), staff/administration (1.9), other (0.4). Protection of advertising and the standardisation and regularity of the package has dictated the space and often the flavour of their news and features content. In another survey for the Royal Commission of eleven morning and twelve evening provincial papers the percentage distribution between editorial space and advertising was 60/40 and 45/55 respectively. Within editorial space the distribution of news material was:

> *morning*: 37.6 per cent news (33.7 per cent national; 49.7 per cent provincial) and 11.8 per cent features (44 per cent non-local and 56 per cent provincial). Some 20 per cent of news and 9 per cent of features related to political, social or economic matters.
> *evening*: 25.3 per cent news (23.5 per cent national; 67 per cent provincial) and 10.4 per cent features (47 per cent non-local and 53 per cent provincial). Some 20 per cent of news and 10 per cent of features related to political, social or economic matters.[13]

Monopoly positions and the search for commercial security have been complemented by editorial policies, which have reflected a shift away from the partisan and combative stances of earlier days. Provincial and local newspapers in particular see themselves as part of the local establishment where 'a sense of responsibility to local authorities assists in defining the local newspapers' value system', which in turn reinforces its 'sense of community identity and cohesion'.[14] This view was confirmed by the Morgan and Cox study of the press on Merseyside, where the widely read evening newspaper saw itself as part of and defender of the corporate identity and public image of the city and its institutions.[15]

Thus what general political reporting there is tends toward a simplified source of record, focussing on personalities and ceremonial or easily identifiable issues that fall within the editorially perceived knowledge and interests of the readership. Campaigns or inquiries are normally promoted within those parameters because 'campaigns do not work in isolation. They can only work if there is already a body of opinion in favour of the campaign.'[16] The routine reporting must furthermore be regular, relevant and tailored for available space. To that end journalists tend to 'position themselves so that they have access to institutions which generate a useful volume of reportable activity at useful intervals'.[17]

Political sources, councillors and officials, tend to be wary of the media and often accuse it of sensationalism, misinterpretation or bias and critical coverage is a sure way to end the 'useful volume'. The Morgan Cox study of the Merseyside press noted that many councillors of all political persuasions claimed to see distortion, lack of knowledge and reporting of trivia in the local media. The politicians' attitude 'clearly indicated their disregard for the local press as a serious source of reliable fact or opinion, though there was ample testimony to its capacity for mischievous use of both'.[18] Other studies have found similar mistrust. In Wolverhampton the coverage of local politics by the *Express & Star* was considered 'sparse, sometimes inaccurate and usually dull'.[19] In Birmingham a majority of councillors 'felt that the papers covered local political news adequately, although many criticised them for being sensational or journalistic'.[20] Politicians' and officials' co-operation is also necessary to sift the 'reportable' terms from the vast output of information and compensate for the poor training of reporters. The Association of Metropolitan Authorities told the 1977 Royal Commission on the Press that 'there is only a limited number of journalists with the specialist interest and knowledge now needed to report accurately the complexities of local government affairs'; for example, the *Sunderland Echo* staff were said to be faced with over a hundred local authority committees within its readership area to be covered by a handful of reporters.

Despite such difficulties, however, the local media become defensive when it is suggested they are less than successful at investigatory journalism. When criticised for 'missing' the Poulson story J. D. Evans, editor of the *Northern Echo*, wrote to the *Guardian*:

> Both Harold Evans (now editor of the *Sunday Times*), my predecessor as editor, and I detached reporters for long periods to investigate corruption in County Durham. In my case one of my best reporters was detached from most of his normal duties for three months to investigate Alderman Cunningham. He discovered a lot of smoke but not fire. Newspapers cannot afford to report smoke if they are unable later to exhibit in court the fire that produced it. It took the Poulson bankruptcy hearing to reveal the fire.[21]

While it may be wondered what is the journalistic distinction between 'normal duties' and investigative reporting, editors may not be enthusiastic about stories that are too fragmented or divorced from the knowledge of the readership. They see a danger of those stories ending 'not with the bang of resolution and information but with the whimper of low follow up or, after, deafening silence'.[22]

The emergence of commercial radio worried local papers, not as an alternative news source but a drain on advertising revenue; the *Liverpool Post and Echo* proposed to the 1962 Royal Commission on the Press that 'provincial papers should have priority when licences are granted in order to avoid widespread closures'. It is hardly surprising that the local press have bought their way into commercial radio, and even less surprising that the stations should follow the local press's example and influence by packaging their advertising revenue securely, in their case within 'the easy inevitability of the basic pop formula wrapped up with local ribbons of news and chat'. The ratings game and audience profiles have further developed a 'homogenised and trivialised' format, which has ensured that political journalism is not a core activity. Anthony Wright's analysis of local radio has cogently argued from surveys of stations that:

> the great majority of stations, both BBC and ILR, have no local government specialist at all, despite the fact that today's local government and its environment is a complex system and requires someone with a sure grasp of the issues, institutions and personalities involved to make it intelligible and accessible to the ordinary listener. The paucity of local government specialists has been judged to be a major deficiency of the local press . . . yet their absence is even more conspicuous (and the consequences of their absence more apparent) in local radio. The broadcasting organizations and the individual stations must surely address themselves to this matter urgently if the proclaimed role for local radio in fostering local democracy is to be taken seriously. . . . Many local broadcasters are less than enthusiastic about political coverage in general and local government coverage in particular. To them it represents, in a recurring phrase, 'the great switch-off' . . . In fact, local broadcasters are often found to exhibit some of the same attitudes towards local government matters as those which were identified as characteristic of the local press: for example, an attitude towards local government coverage that is at best dutiful rather than enthusiastic, and an emphasis on the unity of the local 'community' that carries with it a distaste for local conflicts and disagreements. Many stations deliberately and vigorously fly the integrative flag of 'community' (the ethos of stations and the remarks of broadcasters testify to this) and in doing so overlook the fact that communities are rooted in conflict as well as in consensus.[23]

In such circumstances it is difficult to see how investigatory journalism can flourish in the local media where, as Gyford states: 'its bland and not overly informative picture of local government, its commitment to the notion of "the good of the town" and to the idea of order and harmony prevent it from analysing or exploiting sectional disagreements and grievances; and its lack of resources prevent it from developing analytical and investigatory journalism. If the local press is a public watchdog on the town hall it is a singularly accommodating animal, with no bite and a rather muffled bark.'[24]

The trouble with collecting the evidence

Nevertheless for editorial policy to switch toward a more critical and inquisitorial approach to politics would require a reassessment of the media's role in the local community and of their dependence on their sources. The considerable extent of the reassessment that is needed is demonstrable by politicians' belief in their capacity to determine and supervise their own standards and activities, and their displays of secrecy, resentment or hostility to investigation (or, to them, ill-informed interference) in their affairs. 'You publish at your peril', one Blackpool councillor told the *Sunday Times* investigating property deals there in 1978; 'I think what puts me in an invidious position is this kind of interview where I'm singled out for some reason for these questions', James Stewart told 'World In Action'; 'the publication of the substance of the report will do nothing to assist the proper resolution of the matter', said the Chairman of the Lancashire Police Committee on the publication of the Osmond report by the *Lancashire Evening Post*. It may ultimately lead to the hypocritical disregard for the media, which in 1969 led Fred Smith, Labour leader of Blyth Borough Council in Northumberland, and a majority of councillors (who all happened to be Labour councillors) to vote against the press being admitted to council meetings. Fred Smith resented hostile reporting, proclaiming 'it is unjust, incorrect and untrue to suggest that either there is anything to hide or that the public are demanding to know more than that with which they are at present provided . . .'.[25] Fred Smith, however, held many public positions (chairman of the Blyth Constituency Labour Party, Labour leader of the council, chairman of the Housing Committee, chairman of the Town Centre Redevelopment Committee, member of the Harbour Commissioners) in a town T. Dan Smith himself in 1974 was to describe as 'basically a corrupt constituency in every sense—politically, in business, in its dealings with people, my impression of it was precisely that'.[26]

Trapped between the structural restraints and the threat of offending crucial sources of information, reporting, particularly in the local media, can easily become a matter of organisation and selection. As David Murphy explains:

The local journalist—editor or reporter—has to produce a given amount of news every week or every evening. The determining factor in the size of a newspaper is the amount of advertising: and the amount of news expands and contracts proportionately to match the fluctuations in this quantity . . . The written material in the council minutes and the meetings themselves provide the journalist with a supply of news material which can be processed by paraphrase, summary and amplification. The journalists I observed went through a process known as 'checking' on stories in the minutes or 'digging' or 'lobbying'. However, this did not mean that the journalist checked to see if a version of events with which he was presented was true according to a set of evidential rules. What it did mean was that a reporter would ring up a contact, or approach one after a council meeting either for information or a quote about some issue, and would stop when he came to the first contact who could give him the information. . . .

The council then provides the newspaper with a series of events organisationally constructed within given boundaries, and all that the journalist has to do is to follow the leads provided, selecting those items which are seen as having the strongest appeal possible to the audience at which the paper is aiming. But the chief element in the organisation of events in time in the newspaper office is the office diary. The events of each day that are revealed by the mail coming into the office or as a result of a reporter's calls on contacts are entered into the diary and allocated to a reporter and/or a photographer. The expected outcome of this news-gathering activity is then used by the editor to plan his paper.[27]

The corollary to this approach to newsgathering is that anything unusual such as the possibility of an investigation into misconduct or corruption offers a countervailing demand on the routine functioning of the journalist, and may force him into a position of conflict with those with whom he normally enjoys a reciprocal and privileged relationship and threaten the flow of information at that time and in the future. David Murphy quotes the example of a local government reporter approached by neighbours of the property belonging to an ex-councillor (see Chapter 5), in an attempt to get the press to take up the story. 'The local government reporter they approached had had a long working relationship with officials and councillors, although not the councillor involved, and was not predisposed to believe that officials or council members were anything but honest and regular in their dealings.'[28]

Similar conflict has also been found in the national press. For example, a year after *The Times* advertised for a former burglar to help on a house-protection article, the ex-burglar brought 'a distressed young friend' to the newspaper. The friend, Michael Perry, a car dealer with a string of previous convictions and the threat of a frame-up hanging over him, led *The Times'* reporters to the 1969 clandestine recording and photographing of his meetings with two detectives from Scotland Yard and one from Camberwell. While the former collected thirteen years between them (the latter, Det. Sgt. Symonds, fled abroad but returned in 1981 and was imprisoned), the Metropolitan police began its protracted and controversial campaign to root out corruption in the force. The decision not to tell the police of the story because of the uncertainty about the extent of the 'firm' of corrupt officers provoked an angry reaction at the newspaper's failure to play the game, not the least from crime reporters whose perceptions of such investigations are clearly, as Steve Chibnall's study of crime reporting demonstrates, influenced by the need to protect their sources of information:

We burnt our fingers bad over the bribery case. We don't want to do more stories like that, we want to live it down—it brought us into a direct head-on-clash with the police [crime specialist on *The Times*].

If I know a copper who's bent, it depends on how bent he is. If it came to my notice that one of my contacts was really bent I would feel obliged to do something about it, I wouldn't write about it in the paper, I'd talk to my mates in the police force [crime correspondent].

I, probably more than anybody else on this paper, have quite a number of police contacts and it would completely destroy my role to have my by-line on a story knocking the police [Sunday paper reporter].[29]

Publishing and being damned

For those sections of the media with a propensity to investigate there are a variety of restraints on the collection and publication of 'hard' evidence, of which the most important concern confidentiality, privacy and official secrecy, contempt and libel. What concerned one writer about the restraints on access to official information was their cosmic coverage. Whatever the position may be in practice, the government is legally in a position to enforce a total blackout on public affairs. A second prominent feature is the antiquarian nature of some of the laws, not just in the sense of their ill comportance with modern democracy but also in the dependence on ancient customs and conventions'.[30] Open government and the public's 'right to know' may be publicly held tenets of politicians—and some civil servants—but the practice tends toward a general protection of information that may expose the workings—and *real-politik*— of the political and administrative processes. An official secret is any official information, irrespective of its nature, and the legal means to keep such information so applies to all public employees and can be used against those who receive ·as well as those who hand it over. Official secrecy affects three categories of people. Firstly there are those who wish to conceal the activities of government and Sections 1 and 2 of the 1911 Official Secrets Act provide a comprehensive means to do so. Their very nature, however, means that what comprises an official secret is the government's choice and, as Jonathan Aitken said after his 1970 prosecution (and acquittal) for publishing a diplomat's report on the Biafran war, the Act

> fails to draw a clear distinction between espionage and leakage and between those disclosures which compromise national security and those which merely embarrass the government of the day . . . the same legal teeth that in 1911 were sharpened to prevent information on the movement of the Royal Navy's battleships falling into the hands of enemy agents are today being used merely to prevent embarrassing gossip about maladministration of the welfare services from falling into the hands of national newspapers.[31]

Indeed the diversity of the newspapers, journals, etc. under investigation may confirm that public knowledge rather than state secrets are behind such investigation:

> . . . [a] bizarre use of the Official Secrets Act took place when the *Sunday Times* published a railway policy document, drafted inside the Transport Ministry, proposing major closures of railway lines as part of wide-ranging reorganisation. Scotland Yard raided the offices of the *Railway Gazette*, suspected as the initial channel of the leak, and then attempted to intimidate Harold Evans, editor of the *Sunday Times*, and Richard Hope, editor of the *Railway Gazette*, in the hope of discovering how the document reached them. The fact that the subject had nothing remotely to do with State security, foreign spies or military secrets, confirms the eccentric use for which the Act can be invoked.[32]

The second group concerns those officials who feel that disclosure of information outweighs both secrecy and organisational pressure to stay silent. Those on the inside who leak information do so for various reasons, but are all aware of the promotion or career consequences of so doing. Many leakers do talk to the media because they feel that impartiality or integrity are not prominent in the activities of their organisations. One Foreign Office 'mole' felt that the 'Foreign Office was providing the basis for debate, which the newspapers accepted as the basis for debate, when in fact the Office and the civil servants were thinking on quite different lines. The public were being grossly misled. I felt furious at times when I picked up a morning newspaper and saw what was being put out . . .'. Another who helped reveal the existence of the government's secret phone-tapping centre in Chelsea described his actions as 'redressing the balance' and deciding 'enough's enough'. Accused of 'sneaking' he retorted that 'that's a bit preposterous, and public schoolboy language too. The only people who've reacted that way are people with a vested interest—you know the sort—the quiet-life, no-bother, the I'm-only-doing-my-job brigade, the quietest, the politically lazy supporters of the status quo, bunch of wallies and wankers'.[33]

Be that as it may, bureaucracies thrive on such people, and they may make a substantial effort to warn them to stay as such by relentless pursuit of those who break ranks. Leslie Chapman was asked to be 'gentlemanly and sportsman-like' and let the Civil Service see his book on efficiency in the Property Services Agency. Following the leak of Cabinet papers on child benefit Roger Cook reported that 'top political advisers inside and outside the Department were finger-printed, a process which we've now confirmed went as far as David Ennals, the Secretary of State responsible—and a member of the Cabinet'.[34] The British Steel Corporation hunted its mole (who provided documents to Granada TV's 'World in Action' suggesting poor management and inefficiency at a time when the Corporation was engaged in a strike over a low pay offer to its workers) through the courts. While the BSC argued that the mole was in breach of contract, there was a strong feeling at the time that the expensive route taken by the BSC was to warn off any future mole from similar activities.

The third group affected by such secrecy are those journalists who receive information. Again the decision to publish from privileged information must be offset against the possible damage to, often, a monopoly supplier of information. Thus lobby journalists, who operate inside Parliament, have been guided by their own 'code' of practice, which included such suggestions as:

It is the lobby correspondent's primary duty to protect his informants, and care must be taken not to reveal anything that could lead to their identification . . . Sometimes it may be right to protect your informant to the extent of not using a story at all. This has often been done in the past, and it forms one of the foundations of the good and confidential relationship between the lobby and members of all parties . . . Keep in mind that: (1) while you have complete freedom to get your own stories in your own way, and while there are no restrictions of any kind on personal initiative, you have a duty to the lobby as a whole; (2) you should do nothing to prejudice the communal life of the lobby, or the relations with the two Houses and the authorities; (3) this in your interest and that of your office, as well as in the general interest of the lobby.[35]

Other journalists have also come across the need for caution. A *Times* journalist noted that, 'as a defence correspondent you could be denied all Ministry of Defence facilities, such as visits to military establishments, transport in service aircraft, and most important of all, off-the-record talks in Whitehall. Without these facilities most correspondents would find it extremely hard to do their job.'[36] Indeed such threats, if not always successful, to the conventional reciprocity when the supplier of information feels the other side has stopped playing the game and is presenting them in less than a favourable light require a determined rejection. As James Margach illustrated:

A similar incident centred on Noyes Thomas of the *News of the World* who confidently forecast in his paper that Marcia Williams, political secretary to the Prime Minister, Harold Wilson, was about to be created a life peer and made a Minister in the Wilson Government. Wilson was so incensed that he immediately demanded that his Press Secretary, Joe Haines, should denounce the report as a lie and then instructed Haines not to give press briefings to lobby meetings attended by Thomas. This attempt to blackball Thomas, if successful, would have prevented him from earning his living (though Haines told Wilson he could not stop his attending lobby meetings as demanded). The lobby repudiated the implication that it should blacklist a colleague in response to a diktat from Downing Street, and in due course Thomas's forecast was vindicated.[37]

The British Steel case concerned another area of conflict, that of confidentiality and contract; the documents supplied to Granada TV were, said the Corporation's counsel, stolen. Furthermore the defence of the right of access to information of public concern was quickly put aside by the courts. In May 1980 the High Court decided that Granada TV had 'behaved so badly that they have forfeited the protection which the law normally gives to newspapers', after which the Lords ruled the television company must name their informant. The *Sunday Times* ran into difficulties over its thalidomide story because, as Harold Evans later said, 'a judge has ruled that the Distillers' thalidomide documents can never be published in Britain, even if they disclose negligence, because of the company's property rights in the information'.[38] In two other more successful court cases involving newspapers the *Sunday Times* successfully fought off attempts to protect confidentiality. In September 1968 the newspaper approached Maurice Fraser, a public relations man, about a report he had prepared for his clients, the Greek Junta. This report, the grandly named 'Fifth Report on Public Relations Programme in Europe', followed on his various proposals to the Greek Colonels, based on the principle that 'PR is not just a question of disseminating favourable news and withholding unfavourable views. It has a positive role to play in policy decisions, and it is an essential adjunct to government. There is no dividing line between PR and politics.' Fraser's intended campaign included an Anglo-Greek Association 'sponsored by government supporters in London, but not apparently so', a contemporary history of Greece written by a respectable historian, teach-ins 'packed with supporters', favourable media coverage and 'a full-time lobbyist to maintain a constant vigil on Anglo-Greek parliamentary activities and to create a strong lobby on your behalf'. The Fifth Report itself made claims of contacts with foreign governments and their media but what made the Report controversial was a claim that Fraser's PR office had a British MP working 'behind the scenes in order to influence other British MPs [whose identity] we have to protect . . . otherwise he would be exposed'. Fraser's response to the *Sunday Times'* approach was to obtain an injunction restraining publication.[39] It was later lifted by the High Court on the grounds that Fraser's confidence had not been breached because the newspaper had obtained the material after the report had been submitted. This qualified success was repeated when injunctions against the *Sunday Times* and Jonathan Cape Ltd in 1974 for publishing extracts from the Crossman diaries were dismissed on the grounds that their publication did not reflect any evidence of continuing confidentiality or 'inhibit free and open discussion in the Cabinet hereafter'.

In 1981 the Contempt of Court Act stated that 'no court may require a person to disclose, nor is any person guilty of contempt of court for refusing to disclose, the source of information contained in a publication for which he is responsible, unless it is established to the satisfaction of the court that disclosure is necessary in the interests of justice or national security or for the prevention of disorder or crime'. This would not, if extant at that time, have affected the *BSC* v. *Granada* dispute. The Act itself attempted to bring order to a chaotic area in which 'imminent' proceedings could force newspapers not to print information and risk prosecution for contempt in threatening to prejudice the outcome of court cases. The Act tried to indicate the nature of contempt by defining it as publication done consciously, done publicly, and as a substantial risk to the course of justice in proceedings in question when those proceedings are live, and the publication is not a fair and accurate record of those proceedings. Publication made in good faith on matters of public affairs or of a general public interest is not in contempt if the risk of prejudice or impediment is incidental to that publication. Proceedings are active in criminal proceedings from an arrest, or, in the case of other proceedings, from the time when arrangements for the hearing are made. Nevertheless the Act has come under attack for allowing judges to restrict the reporting of criminal trials, particularly when such cases involve wider issues of principle where the media should be bringing the facts before the public.[40]

The most controversial restraint on the media is, however, that of libel. An accepted definition may be summarised as follows:

> Statements may be defamatory which tend to lower a person in the estimation of right thinking members of society generally or which tend to make him shunned and avoided or which bring him into hatred, ridicule or contempt or which tend to discredit him in his profession or trade. The plaintiff need show only that the statement complained of *tends* to defame him, he does not have to prove that persons to whom it was published in fact think the less of him; indeed a person may be defamed even though those to whom the statement was published know it to be untrue.[41]

The plaintiff has to show that the words refer to him, are published and are defamatory or capable of being defamatory; the defence can argue public interests, truth, fair comment, privilege or unintentional defamation. For comment on public figures and activities the important aspects for the media concern truth, fair comment and public interest. The problem with truth (or justification) is that fact offers both an inferential as well as a literal interpretation. The standard textbook on libel offers a clearcut example from 1946:

> The following case illustrates the danger of not being able to prove the truth of defamatory inference although the facts be justified. In that case a newspaper reporter was informed that of two houses which had suffered similar war damage one, which belonged to a local councillor, was being repaired extensively whilst the other, which belonged to someone who was not on the council, had been very scantily repaired. The reporter checked carefully the information he had received and inspected both houses. He found that what he had been told was true.

At about the same time a number of vacant houses in the neighbourhood were requisitioned, including that belonging to the councillor, but immediately after the requisitioning notice was served in respect of the councillor's house it was withdrawn.

The facts clearly indicated preferential treatment of the councillor.

The newspaper published a factual article, one paragraph drawing attention to the repairs, another to the de-requisitioning. Following this the councillor brought proceedings claiming damages for libel against the proprietors of the newspaper alleging that the article clearly imputed that he had improperly *secured* for himself preferential treatment. The newspaper proprietors proved:
  (i) that the councillor's house had received much better treatment than the adjoining house, precisely as alleged in the article;
 (ii) that the councillor's property had been de-requisitioned immediately after requisitioning, again precisely as alleged in the article, and
(iii) that he had therefore *received* preferential treatment.

It was, however, held that the article carried with it the imputation that the councillor had *secured* preferential treatment for himself and, as this charge had not been proved, the councillor succeeded. He was awarded £100 damages.[42]

On the question of public interest, criticism of a public figure's private behaviour must be such as to show that that behaviour has a bearing on 'his ability or qualification' for public office. The textbook again refers to two cases in 1862 and 1920:

Where the plaintiff, a QC and a Member of Parliament, was Recorder of an important town it was held that his private conduct was open to criticism if it tended to show that he was destitute and devoid of such qualities as integrity, honesty, and honour which were essential for a man in his public position. So too where it was alleged that events in the plaintiff's private life made him an unsuitable person to be elected to Parliament it was said in the course of interlocutory proceedings that 'The private life of a member of Parliament may be material to his fitness to occupy his public office. His private life may be such as to show that he is quite unfit to exercise any public functions or to occupy any public office.'[43]

Finally on the question of fair comment, that comment is acceptable only where it is supported by the facts and where hostile criticism is not overtaken by the imputation of 'corrupt, dishonest and wicked motives'. Thus, when the editor of the *Bolton Evening News* took offence in 1948 at the behaviour of opposition MPs during the report stage of the Transport Bill—some leaving the Chamber, one dancing a jig, and several moving over to the opposite benches —he felt compelled to write a leader denouncing the MPs' performance as 'nauseating, a sorry degradation of democratic government by discussion, the nadir, let us fervently hope, of this Parliament.' Sued by Bessie Braddock—who allegedly danced the jig in the House—he won because the jury felt his leader was fair comment upon a matter of public interest.

Nevertheless political service in this country is a part-time occupation and many councillors and politicians continue their private business and other interests while in office. Thus conflict of interest has been an ever-present problem, only recently—and partially—corrected by attempts to tighten up on the requirements of disclosure in Parliament and to warn councillors through a National Code of Conduct to avoid situations where a conflict might arise or appear to arise. Nevertheless the imputation or inference that might arise from drawing attention to such interests in certain contexts or to the possible existence of a conflict of interest has invariably found the media in court and invariably paying out damages.

In May 1967 Barry Arnold Payton, solicitor and former Peterborough councillor, was awarded £500 damages for libel in a 1965 *Daily Sketch* article entitled 'The empty flats that nobody wants'. The article concerned the St. Mary's Court flats in Peterborough, a luxury development built by the Mitchell construction group whose solicitor was Payton. Although Payton had nothing to do with the planning permission since he had not yet been elected, had declared his interest in the firm on his election and the firm's tender was in any case the lowest, the article suggested he was in a position where he could 'hardly escape misplaced suggestions of partiality'. Payton sued on the grounds the article implied he had 'dishonestly, corruptly and improperly' used his position as a councillor and prominence in the local Labour Party to obtain advantages for the firm. Judge Swanwick considered the press had the liberty to comment freely on matters of public interest but not to permit that liberty to degenerate into a licence to attack the character and reputation of private individuals unfairly. The journalist who investigated the story was found not liable as he had not approved publication, had not written all of it and was not responsible for 'its sting'.

Also in May 1967 £5,000 was awarded to William Pope, former mayor of Chichester, for a 1965 article in the *People* headed 'A City Gossips—and No Wonder'. The court felt that in suggesting he had bought a granary at a lower price than its true value by using information available to him in his public office (the article stated he should not have continued to sit at Council meetings while negotiating the purchase) the newspaper was imputing dishonest or dishonourable conduct. Defence counsel claimed that the article simply meant he was guilty of 'an appalling indiscretion' by sitting; the jury chose Pope's interpretation of the article.

More recently the late Reginald Maudling won undisclosed substantial damages in 1978 from the *Observer* 'to compensate him for any damage which they may, unintentionally have done to his reputation'. In October 1976 the newspaper, alerted to the end of Poulson prosecutions, had drawn attention to the position of the MPs involved with him under the heading 'Corruption: Three MPs Escape Prosecution—Exclusive'. His counsel said that although the newspaper specifically stated in the article he was not one of the three MPs referred to in the headline, 'some readers of the *Observer* might have inferred from the presence of his photograph and the caption to it that he was one of the two unnamed Members of Parliament or was in a similar category'.

One further aspect to libel concerns the 1974 Rehabilitation of Offenders Act. Offences for which the defendant received any prison sentence of up to two and a half years (excluding remission), fines or any lesser punishment are 'spent' after certain periods of time: after ten years for prison between six months and two and a half years; after seven years up to six months; and after five years for fines. After these periods the offence no longer 'exists' in the eyes of the law. This is of particular relevance to the question of bribery and disclosure of interest. Under the 1889 and 1906 Prevention of Corruption Acts the maximum sentence is two years' imprisonment and/or an unlimited fine. Only under the 1916 Prevention of Corruption Act, relating to bribery over contracts, does the period of imprisonment extend to seven years. The punishment for failing to disclose an interest under the 1972 Local Government Act is a fine. Thus in some 220 major cases between 1970 and 1980 involving political or public-sector corruption the majority received sentences of two years or less, and sometimes large fines were used, one suspects, as an alternative to the limited imprisonment the courts could impose. Furthermore, since 1977, the courts have been unable to use the unlimited period of sentence available under a 'conspiracy to corrupt' charge and are now required only to impose that sentence that the offence itself would attract if it were the basis of the charge. The Rehabilitation of Offenders Act does not prohibit the media publishing details of spent convictions but it does give those with such convictions the opportunity to sue for defamation. On the other hand the plaintiff has to prove that publication was primarily motivated by a desire to injure his reputation. This motive—malice, in which publication stemmed from spite, ill-will, or other wrong or improper motive—is not, however, one that any plaintiff will necessarily find easy to prove in court. Nevertheless a 'reformed' politician with a spent corruption conviction may use the Act to discourage reference to that offence by the media.

Other external restraints on the media include public inquiries, the Press Council and the Independent Broadcasting Authority. Set up in 1953 as the General Council of the Press and reconstituted as the Press Council with some lay members and an independent chairman in 1962, the Press Council is intended, *inter alia*, to protect the established freedom of the press, maintain the character of the press in accordance with the highest professional and commercial standards, consider complaints about the conduct of the press and keep under review developments likely to restrict the supply of information of public interest and importance. The Press Council has no effective sanction other than the publication in the press of its adjudication on complaints but that in itself can influence some newspapers in carrying out their functions. In 1980 the Council defended the *Northern Echo* when Wear Valley District Council complained that the newspaper had been unnecessarily sensationalistic and contained misleading information and innuendos implying impropriety by one of its officers, his department and the council generally. The newspaper had written a series of articles about a council official who had purchased a cottage earlier condemned by his department and about the council's later, secret inquiry, which concluded that all the procedures had been observed but the official's decision to buy had been ill-considered. The Council considered that it was the council, not the newspaper, that created and perpetuated the affair that stemmed from the conduct of one of its officials, and that the newspaper had performed a valuable function, part of the proper role of a newspaper.[44]

On the other hand the Press Council with its self-determined standards in its role as an adjudicator can often misunderstand the function of investigatory journalism and those who regularly pursue it. In 1981 the Council censured the *New Statesman* for a breach of journalistic ethics and for failing to publish an adjudication upholding a complaint against it. That complaint came from the Civil Service Union after criticism of its conduct toward some of its members —and the misconduct of many others of its members—who worked for the secret electronic eavesdropping and spy facilities in Britain and abroad, particularly at GCHQ, Cheltenham, and its Hong Kong listening base. The publication of the allegations by the *New Statesman* the previous year was the culmination of the efforts of one official to have government pay attention to allegations of lax security, fiddling, inefficiency and corruption. The Council considered that the *New Statesman* should have allowed the union a reasonable space for reply and regretted the editor's lack of co-operation particularly as the complaint concerned 'an obligation so generally accepted' as the right of reply to a published attack. Not unnaturally the adjudication was published elsewhere, which could be seen as suggesting that the complaint and the failure to reply were significant to the contents of the story or that the story itself might be flawed, when the Council might have been better employed investigating the difficulties, including the phone-tapping of journalists and the lack of official co-operation the magazine faced in putting together a story in an area of continuing public interest.

Public inquiries into the press have also been used to turn specific examples of reporting into condemnation of investigatory journalism in general because of the uses to which that journalism was, on those occasions, put. Thus Harold Macmillan's 1962 establishment of the Radcliffe inquiry effectively ended the myriad rumours surrounding the Vassall affair. The damning report held the press up to contempt, in many cases correctly, but it also had two more serious consequences:

The Radcliffe exposures stoked the anti-Press feelings in Parliament and in the country and helped to push back overdue reforms by a generation. But the most significant aspect of the whole affair passed unnoticed. The appointment of the Tribunal proved a master-stroke in the hate–hate relations between Downing Street and Fleet Street. Harold Macmillan, as ever a shrewd and subtle pastmaster in the exercise of power, succeeded nobly in turning the inquiry into a show trial of the Press and its method, with the Press humiliated in the dock. As a result, scant attention was ever given in public to Whitehall's responsibility for allowing a foreign spy service to operate with ease at the heart of Britain's defence system. . . .

But there was an ironic twist to the Vassall affair: it appeared to give the Prime Minister a false sense of security. When the much more compulsive Profumo scandal burst on the national scene, he believed that the newspapers were once more engaged merely on an irresponsible campaign to denigrate Ministers and other public figures—and at the same time to wipe off the old Radcliffe score. It was to prove a grievous miscalculation.[45]

A more recent example was the decision of the 1977 Royal Commission on the Press to pick, negatively, on one example of investigatory journalism and elevate it to official censure following an enquiry 'from the present Prime Minister' on the 'issues of principle' the story raised. The *Daily Mail* splashed its 'World-Wide Bribery Web by Leyland' headline in May 1977. The newspaper alleged the firm had a multi-million pound fund to pay bribes and undercover commissions to win overseas orders.

The *Daily Mail*, however, chose to place these allegations in a political context, suggesting that the Labour Cabinet created the atmosphere for this type of behaviour. It attempted to skewer the Government, the National Enterprise Board, British Leyland, the Bank of England and the Department of Industry with a forged letter from the former chairman of NEB, Lord Ryder, to Alex Park, British Leyland's former Chief executive, alleging Ministerial (Eric Varley) and Bank of England approval for the commission arrangement, claiming 'the stench of humbug in high places is beyond words'.

Two days later the *Daily Mail* had the nightmare privilege of scooping the forgery story, but paid heavily in the end (some £200,000 in libel costs to the various forgery victims) and attracted almost venomous media and political criticism for irresponsibility and bias. It also had to suffer the delighted contempt of the rest of Fleet Street. The *Observer* summarised the press response: 'the *Daily Mirror* castigated "a great and once distinguished newspaper" for an error of such magnitude as to encourage the enemies of newspapers and dismay their friends. The *Evening Standard* said the mistake was gargantuan by any standards. *The Times* said the whole affair was a sorry episode, and the weekly *Spectator*, less subdued, accused the *Mail* of having been "blinded by lust for a scoop" '.[46] The *New Statesman* went one stage further and denounced the *Daily Mail* for using the documents, irrespective of their veracity, in the same irresponsible way and for the same political ends as it did with the Zinoviev letter in 1924. The former BL executive, Graham Barton, was found guilty of forging the NEB letter and another from the Bank of England, and received two years' imprisonment. Only after the trial did the serious newspapers pick up the details of the story, the *Sunday Times* warning that 'some of Britain's most prestigious firms regularly pay bribes to win contracts. And if the British Government or Parliament really starts to inquire into the ramifications of the British Leyland affair, the result could rival the Lockheed–Northrop scandal'.[47] The *Daily Mail* had successfully killed off that possibility with not a little help from their colleagues. Instead of discussing the difficulties of investigating those ramifications or of governments' reluctance to pursue such allegations to establish the truth, the Royal Commission chose to use the slant of the story as the basis for criticism:

> it is certainly the case that some newspapers of the right persistently seek for discreditable material which can be used to damage the reputation of Labour Ministers or those connected with the Party or with trade unions. The 'slush money' story is a lamentable example. Nevertheless, it is not new evidence that the *Daily Mail* is a polemical and politically partisan newspaper, for it has been that for a long time. What is novel is the extreme lengths to which the newspaper was prepared to go in an attack on the Government based on inadequately-checked information. . . .

> . . . there is no escape from the truth that a free society which expects responsible conduct must be prepared to tolerate some irresponsibility as part of the price of liberty. It is also true that cases of irresponsible conduct such as the *Daily Mail*'s behaviour over British Leyland must imperil the freedom of the press by encouraging cynicism and political hostility towards newspapers which could give rise to pressures for restrictive legislation.[48]

Finally, Ray Fitzwalter's clear and concise explanation of the reaction of the Independent Broadcasting Authority to his 'World In Action' programme in 1973 on Poulson is a set-piece of the establishment's search for the easiest route to inertia and procrastination:

> At the last moment, before transmission in January 1973 the Independent Broadcasting Authority prohibited the 'World in Action' programme on the Poulson affair. This hour-long documentary, 'The Friends and Influence of John L. Poulson', . . . was scheduled for transmission on the night of Poulson's eighth bankruptcy hearing. The programme consisted of a careful assembly of the known facts about the case. It was banned by the Authority without its members reading the script, or seeing the film itself, and, moreover, after Granada's solicitors had advised that there was no legal impediment to transmission.

This hasty and unwise decision caused dismay in the television industry particularly when it was known that an eminent barrister acting for Granada and the IBA had also given the programme a clean bill of health. Granada was unable to discover the reason for the ban which the Authority said was 'permanent' and 'irreversible'.

In so far as the IBA action could be analysed, it seemed like the response of a group of worried people who believed the Poulson affair was undermining the very fabric of society. Some members were concerned that innocent people could be smeared by allegations made in the bankruptcy court, which might be reported; others were afraid that the programme would destroy public confidence in local government and some feared that Granada's intention to recreate excerpts from the hearing using actors to read the words amounted to a trial on television. . . . Far from stilling doubts and silencing rumours, this act of censorship, which involved replacing the programme with a repeat showing of 'The Flight of the Snow Goose', only served to increase the doubts and amplify the rumours. The press came up with a theory relating various members of the IBA with prominent figures in the Poulson drama. Baroness Sharp, for example, had been Dan Smith's only character witness at his Old Bailey corruption trial and she was also a director of Bovis. Another IBA member, Sir Frederick Hayday, was a friend of Andy Cunningham and a colleague in the GMWU. Baroness McLeod was a close friend of Mr Maudling while the IBA's chairman, Lord Aylestone, had been Chief Whip and Leader of the House of Commons when Dan Smith's influence in the Labour government had been at its zenith. It was at this point, too, that news of Smith's recent resignation from the board of Tyne-Tees Television leaked out—a move prompted by the making of the programme. The public were also told that the prominent city solicitors, Allen and Overy, were advising the IBA on Poulson while continuing to advise Mr Maudling, who was referred to in the programme on the same subject.

These relationships were neither sinister nor surprising. The IBA was one of those British institutions on which it was thought to be an honour to serve, a patronage of the great and the good. But the situation which had arisen left some IBA members ill-equipped to rebut the suggestion that, although well intentioned, their professional or public interests had played upon their subconscious in the secret process of their decision. Certainly there was little to indicate any positive intention to fulfil their duty to inform the public of what was going on in the Poulson affair.[49]

News you're not supposed to know

The investigatory function of the media has been and is under threat both internally and externally. The successful inquiries of the sixties and seventies are all the more praiseworthy because they were often published in spite of rather than because of the structure of the media or the restraints of the laws that govern its activities. There are, furthermore, signs that such a function is likely to diminish as newspapers battle for circulation by pandering to readerships with titillation, voyeurism and sensationalism or as television is ordered to reflect tenets of impartiality and moderation. On the other hand investigatory journalism is both possible and essential, given the right journalistic skills, the right editorial leadership and the willingness of companies specifically to promote such investigations. Three cases illustrate all too clearly that such ingredients do exist. Uncluttered by the more conventional media's structural, editorial and external restraints the activity of investigatory journalism is an acquired skill that was most noticeable in the seventies with the rise of small radical publications. Any excuse of time, numbers of staff, expertise or availability of stories was amply contradicted when journalists decided in the 1960s to publish their own spiked stories and exploit the techniques of cheap publishing.

The *Liverpool Free Press* emerged from three earlier attempts by young local journalists to find an outlet for investigatory stories. Exploiting their own deductive skills and their local sources of information, the handful of journalists began with the premise of publishing 'news you're not supposed to know' and ran a series of secret reports or inside stories on local housing shortages, grandiose civic centre plans, MPs' interests, conmen, property speculators, corrupt councillors and officials and police brutality that initiated council rows, a Commons Select Committee of Privilege's Report, DPP inquiries and criminal convictions. The significance of their investigations, however, is not only that a handful of journalists with local knowledge and sufficient time could provide a crucial aspect of local accountability but also that the investigations they carried out were often not small-town fiddles but large-scale corruption resulting from irresponsible or unaccountable political leadership, quiescent administrations, a moribund local media and increasing public expenditure. The local media were either unaware of or unwilling to tackle such stories, while the national media were too London-orientated to have someone on the spot for months trying to substantiate, if they ever heard them, the rumours of corruption.

In September 1974 the *Free Press* ran a story about a £114,000 ski slope built in Kirkby, a modern town on the fringe of Merseyside. It was built against expert advice, the wrong way round, without technical drawings or bills of quantity, a proper tender or planning permission, over the water mains to the local industrial estate, on land the council did not own, to use up money before local government reorganisation, by a local firm, Leatherbarrows, under the twin approval of the council architect, Eric Stevenson, and the local council boss, Dave Tempest. Using conventional and some highly unconventional investigative methods two journalists, Steve Scott and Chris Oxley, pieced together over several months a long-running corrupt conspiracy. In his book *News Ltd* another former *Free Press* journalist, Brian Whittaker, detailed the exploitation of those methods:

> Steve began his inquiries by approaching councillors. He talked to several opposition Liberal councillors and one or two on the Labour side who had the reputation of being honest. But they knew nothing and suspected nothing. He spent the next two weeks in Kirkby library, going through old council minutes. From his notes, we compiled a list of contractors who had worked for Kirkby council and we ran company checks. Two things in particular stood out. One was that most of the building contracts—about £10 million-worth—had gone to George Leatherbarrow, while the big national firms which usually won contracts from neighbouring councils, scarcely got a look in. The other was that whenever anything odd happened, the council's architect, Eric Spencer Stevenson, was in the thick of it.
>
> The council minutes also gave the names of people who might be willing to talk: the Personnel Committee minutes included names of officials who had left the council. Steve tried to track them down and eventually found one who was co-operative, but warned that he would never get another job in local government if it became known that he had talked. Steve went to see him. Actually he knew very little about Leatherbarrow, but suggested several other lines of inquiry. . . . Through a tenants' organisation we found someone who had been a shop steward at Leatherbarrow's. He gave us the names of other workers, and they told us there had been something called the Star Gang—a group of privileged workers who went round doing 'special' jobs. We got their names and Steve and Chris went to see them. By that time Leatherbarrow knew we were asking questions and the Star Gang were reluctant to talk. Steve recalls the visits to one of them: 'We must have been there five times. We just kept turning up on his doorstep and each time he kept adding a bit more. He was the driver who had delivered some of the materials and he kept denying it.'
>
> Eventually the Star Gang revealed that Leatherbarrow had built a kitchen extension for Stevenson and a much larger extension to Tempest's house. Materials for both these jobs had been taken from the site in Kirkby where Leatherbarrow was building council houses.
>
> Meanwhile, Chris had traced a former manager of Kirkby Stadium, the council-run sports centre. The manager had lost his job when he was jailed for obtaining £2,000 by deception. In court he had explained that high living while he worked for Kirkby council had led him to crime. He had told the court of lavish entertainment and trips to Europe paid for by contractors. He gave us details of these trips and mentioned one to London paid for by George Leatherbarrow. Among the party had been Tempest and Stevenson.

Then he dropped a bombshell: he said Stevenson had a car that was known as 'Leatherbarrow's car'.

More details of the car came from another source. George Leatherbarrow had been divorced and re-married. His first wife told us the car was a maroon Alfa Romeo, and gave the rough date when Leatherbarrow bought it. And she put the friendship between Leatherbarrow and Stevenson in a new light. She said the best man at Leatherbarrow's second wedding had been Stevenson.

On proving who paid for the London trip they resorted to subterfuge:

First we tried the hotel where they were supposed to have stayed, without any luck. Then we got the name of the travel agent where Leatherbarrow had booked the train tickets. Chris decided to try subterfuge. He phoned the travel agent, posing as Leatherbarrow's accountant. He said he needed to know the cost of the tickets and would hang on while they checked. Certainly, they said. They would have a look. There was a long, tense pause. Then the answer came. £114.90—and the bill had been sent to Mr Leatherbarrow, marked "Personal". Fortunately, the party had travelled in style, by Pullman. And Pullman tickets carry the names of passengers. Among the seven names were Leatherbarrow, Tempest and Stevenson.[50]

Their investigation turned up a long-running saga of how a one-time small firm, a corrupt councillor and a corrupt council official were able to run roughshod over contract procedures and win the firm the largest public works contract (over £7 million) awarded anywhere in Europe at that time. Selling the story for a cheap £250 for a 'Nationwide' programme brought a producer who proved the link of the car between the builder and architect. The BBC asking questions prompted the council to call in the police, who had to wait for the *Free Press* issue and the TV programme for all the detail which formed the basis of allegations against the builder, George Leatherbarrow, the council architect, Eric Stevenson, and two councillors, David Tempest and William Marshall. At the end of the nine-week trial in June 1978 Marshall was acquitted and the other three got four-, three- and one-year terms of imprisonment respectively for a conspiracy between 1967 and 1974 corruptly to give and take gifts and considerations as inducements or rewards in relation to contracts.

The bribes were small, the all-important personal friendships and power-broking crucial. The court proceedings attracted only modest attention from the national media, despite the size of the contract. The cost to the council, however, has been substantial, with the long-term penalty of interest charges and the substandard quality of some of the housing. The firm itself was placed in the hands of the receiver in 1978. The ski slope, found to contain brick ash, sand and wood dumped on the site and resulting in an unusable surface, was abandoned in September 1975 and ultimately demolished.

Brian Whittaker said later: 'It would, however, be wrong to suggest that investigations like ours at Kirkby were beyond the pocket of the national Press. They are not. National newspapers frequently spend thousands of pounds on stories—as the *Express* did in finding escaped train robber Ronald Biggs. But the difference is this: while there is little value for readers in knowing the whereabouts of Ronald Biggs, there is enormous value for a newspaper in being able to tell them.'[51] Of the Kirkby story itself the *LFP* said: 'But the real justification for our story is this: it's true, it happened, it affects the people of Kirkby, and they have a right to know about it. Kirkby people will be paying for Tower Hill, the ski slope and all the rest for years. And our story put the record straight.'

Great editorial courage

After a formal complaint, over the way firearms certificates were issued, from a Blackpool CID sergeant to an HM Inspector of Constabulary on his annual inspection in July 1976, the Lancashire Police Committee, on the Home Office's suggestion, commissioned an inquiry by Sir Douglas Osmond, Hampshire's Chief Constable, into 'certain matters which are within the personal jurisdiction of the Chief Constable'. Beginning in September Osmond took two months to complete his report, which went to the DPP and then to the Police Committee in January 1977. The *Lancashire Evening Post*, a Preston-based evening paper with circulation of over 100,000, had pieced together the contents of the report and independently verified them through the separate contacts of the three journalists on the story: Barry Askew the editor, Bob Satchwell the news editor and David Graham the chief reporter. Askew decided that the allegations warranted their trying to obtain the report itself. By 8 February their story was ready to run, but after some hestitation and much persuasion one of Satchwell's contacts agreed to let them see his copy of the report because he was afraid that secrecy and committee politics might bury it. Satchwell borrowed a 35mm. camera from the paper's chief photographer and, on the bathroom floor of a hotel room, painstakingly photographed the report. The journalists secretly typed it up, destroyed the film, cleared the story with company lawyers and printed it on 25 February 1977, under the banner headline: 'Why Lancs Police Chief Must Go'.

Osmond's findings were splashed over four pages, concerning allegations of interventions by the Chief Constable over various offences; favouritism towards firms or individuals, misuse of official resources and unwise friendships. 'The story as a whole', concluded Osmond, 'indicates a lack of judgement on the part of the Chief Constable, a failure to communicate, and a lack of concern at the impression he was creating, all of which are most unusual in a senior officer.'

The publication of the story attracted extensive media coverage and furious reaction from the Police Committee, which had played down the Osmond Report prior to publication, but which then decided there was a case to answer.

After accepting many of Parr's explanations it considered others were unsatis-factory at its March meeting, when it suspended him and set up an independent tribunal under discipline regulations. The tribunal found twenty-six charges proved (five involved intervention on behalf of or for friends, three of whom were councillors or ex-councillors, while the remainder concerned the use of police cars for various purposes), with eleven not proved.

Locally the paper was heavily criticised: 'I wish to say in the strongest pos-sible terms how much I deplore the irresponsible and totally unauthorised publication', said Frank Lofthouse, Chairman of the Police Committee, which tried and failed to have the paper prosecuted under the Official Secrets Act and censured by the Press Council. In March 1978 prospective Conservative candidate (elected as MP for Preston North in 1979) Robert Atkins attacked parts of the Osmond Report for being based on innuendo and gossip. More surprisingly, in February 1977, *West Lancs Evening Gazette*, the Blackpool-based sister paper of the *LEP*, reported on being out-scooped that 'our readers may say that this attitude is a case of sour grapes on our part. Not so, not so at all. The *Evening Gazette* took advice from the highest legal source available about the publication of this secret report. We were told, not surprisingly, that there would be grave legal risks involved . . . Apart from legal risks, which may or may not be involved, there was the question of fair play. And we do not think that up to now Mr Stanley Parr has had fair play. . . .' Two months later the *Morecambe Guardian*, another sister paper to the *LEP*, argued that 'many people thought some of the allegations trivial, others preferred to wait until Mr Parr had the opportunity to answer them, but nearly everybody felt a certain amount of sadness that it all should have happened'.

All three journalists—and especially Satchwell, when it was learned that he was the source of the story—were subtly and sometimes not so subtly pumped for information and pressurised. Askew, the editor, was, however, an aggressive journalist with a penchant for investigative journalism and an understanding of the use of the media for a reforming as opposed to a sensationalistic campaign. He was astute enough to accept the limitations of the *LEP* in tackling the wider questions raised by the report, including those concerning the accountability and adjudication of police misconduct. Accordingly he pushed his demands for a wider investigation by providing information for local MPs to keep the matter before the Commons and the pressure on the Home Secretary. The journalists provided a fifty-page dossier on allegations of corruption, which they developed from leads in the Osmond Report and passed on to trusted officers in the Lancs force and thence to the Nottingham police ordered in by the DPP. The inquiries paved the way for a larger team from the Surrey police and the Metropolitan Fraud Squad.

While there were no prosecutions from the thirteen reports submitted—only one case came to court (both defendants were acquitted after the first round of inquiries)—and the newspaper lost or settled three libel actions, the newspaper's fight to publish the story demonstrated both the strength of local establishment preference not to break ranks and the newspaper's clever use of its limitations to promote external inquiries. The editor accepted that this type of story could be a jolt to the newspaper's position in the local government structure and to its flow of routine news, but more revealing than the formal accolade of the top award of the 1977 British Press 'Journalist of the Year' Award to the three journalists was the North West Region of the Guild of British Newspaper Editor's approval of Askew's decision to publish with the rider that, 'in our view, he showed great editorial courage at a time when it would have been far easier to do nothing'.[52]

An abuse of justice

Dundee enthusiastically embraced urban redevelopment during the 1960s with new housing estates and tower blocks, a new city centre development, schools, libraries, etc., and one of the most expensive hospitals in the country. A Scottish building firm, Crudens Ltd, collected contracts worth over £62 million. The steady rise of certain councillors, however, to positions where they were both business men directly involved in the massive redevelopment and key councillors on the relevant committees resulted in allegations of conflict of interest as early as the mid-sixties. A two-year police inquiry begun in 1964 and inquiries by the Town Clerk, from which a dossier went to the Lord Advocate, both achieved nothing. Complaints by the Dundee Ratepayers Association about the speed with which some council business was transacted, by local business men on the close links between certain companies and some councillors, and by Labour councillors on the need to disclose relevant interests similarly fell on deaf ears. By the beginning of the 1970s the back of local protest was effectively broken; 'there's no doubt credibility has gone down and . . . people in Dundee have become most apathetic about it', said one Labour councillor although Dundee Council had, on paper, a substantial political opposition.

In July 1973 the *Sunday Times* was making up for lost time after the Poulson hearings. It planned to do a story on alleged misconduct in three local authorities, focussed on Dundee, before finally reporting on Tom Moore, a jute mill clerk who had risen to become Labour Lord Provost, chief magistrate and Lord Lieutenant of Dundee. Through his plant hire and property companies Moore was both a major council contractor and property developer. Moore claimed his land sales were 'good deals' and argued that 'I have always been the first to publicly condemn land speculation. However, when you are in business you have to make as much profit as you can.' Other Labour councillors were less impressed. An expulsion motion at a private executive meeting of the local party, however, failed while a decision by the Scottish Executive of the Labour Party to hold a private inquiry resulted in an inconclusive one-day visit by a three-man delegation.

About August 1974 Ray Fitzwalter of 'World in Action' received word of the continuing disquiet from a source in London and another in Dundee who had seen the WIA 'Business in Gozo' programme and felt WIA capable of undertaking a similar investigation which, coincidentally, WIA were looking for. The inquiry, which took seven months, involved analysing vast amounts of documents, locating all the deals and interviewing dozens of people in Dundee, Edinburgh and London after persuading them to talk for a programme that was originally envisaged to take in more than building contracts. From the outset it was apparent that there were grounds for concern, and the failure of local means of accountability was encouraging behaviour sufficiently public and verifiable to the point that there was a reasonable chance of meshing the evidence necessary for the programme. Fitzwalter went through seventeen years of council records in the public library, piecing together each contract, the related committee membership and the voting patterns, and through property records (only open to the public in Scotland), which showed who bought and sold what, when and at what price. His research centred on the multi-million public building programme begun in 1959, and certain three Labour councillors including Moore and James Stewart (an ex-factory worker who became leader of the Labour Party group).

When Fleet Street heard the programme was ready for transmission they all asked to see the script; when they learned it concerned Dundee all but one lost interest. The national Scottish newspapers gave the programme good coverage but the local newspaper did not. One local MP claimed the programme was an abuse of justice amounting to trial by television, while Willie Ross, the Labour Secretary of State for Scotland, announced that rather than sensationalising the evidence it should have been sent to the Procurator Fiscal or the police. While police inquiries (they already had most of the necessary documentation before the programme went out) got under way, three councillors were precipitately sacked from the Party, then reinstated on procedural grounds by another Labour Party inquiry that was unwilling to inquire too deeply into the programme's allegations, partly to avoid bad publicity and partly not to fuel the left–right split in the local party.

In 1980 the trial of Stewart, Moore and Maxwell (a business colleague of Moore's), which had been postponed because of the latter's ill health since 1976, ended with the three being found guilty of corruptly soliciting and receiving rewards as inducements for Stewart and Moore to use their council influence to ensure that a £5 million shopping development went to a client of a London estate agent and that it was built by Crudens. Stewart was found guilty of asking for sub-contracts for his electrical firm in return for using his influence to get some £16 million worth of contracts through the council for Crudens and of receiving £30 for a trip to London. He was also convicted of soliciting money from a partner of the estate agents and from the chairman of Crudens at a meeting in the North British Hotel in Edinburgh. Maxwell was found guilty of soliciting and receiving £6,320 for himself and Moore from the estate agents to award the contract to their client. All three got five years. In June 1980, however, Moore's and Maxwell's convictions were set aside on appeal and both were freed. Stewart's conviction and sentence remained unchanged.

Conclusion: for whom the bell tolls

The media as an independent source of investigation have been formally applauded for exposing indefensible public behaviour, as in exposing the activities of John Stonehouse's British Bangladesh Trust or the Crown Agents' money merry-go-round, or in forcing public and official reassessment of such behaviour. Thus the convictions resulting from *The Times*' 1969 police corruption relevations did much 'to legitimise a much greater consciousness of police corruption. It was forcing a previously impervious public to absorb the fact that many London policemen were very probably "bent".'[53] Nevertheless politicians are only too aware of the political disadvantage or public mistrust that may be generated by investigations that demonstrate public behaviour is less than solely governed by the tenets of public service and personal disinterestedness.

It is probably this fear of a truly independent press with financial security and few legal restraints that keeps governments and parties from doing more than paying lip-service to the freedom of the press or recommending another Royal Commission. As long as they continue to struggle with commercial viability, regularity of news input and the ever-present threat of some costly or embarrassing legal action, the media are unlikely to expand investigatory journalism. Indeed to watch the development of newspapers or television programmes with investigatory pretensions over the past few years is to see, with a few notable exceptions, a move away from the hard-edged stories that named 'the guilty men', toward a softer, analytical/comment format on general current affairs. On the other side, governments are unlikely to move toward more public awareness of their activities or those of the civil service, partly because of the traditional secrecy that has surrounded the decision-making processes, and particularly because what political parties say in public and do as governments are not always compatible or possible. Furthermore, while politicians may applaud the actions of *The Times*' story of Metropolitan Police corruption or *The Times* and *Guardian* articles on the Crown Agents they cannot but be aware of the long, controversial investigations that have followed, often with a less than satisfactory outcome, but also with a good deal of criticism and lingering suspicion. Real-world politics acknowledges the existence of corruption at all levels and it would appear that such levels, as long as they are not shown to be too entrenched or too pervasive, are to be tolerated. Media that are too intrusive, from the point of view of politicians, could well generate a demand for reform that would also be intrusive or restrictive on current practices.

Acceptance of a degree of corruption or an acceptance that corruption is nothing more than an occasional individual aberration—the rotten apple syndrome, without inquisitive media to upset the applecart—does more than simply avoid even the modest reforms proposed by the 1976 Royal Commission on Standards of Conduct in Public Life to deal with corruption. Consideration of the restraints on investigatory journalism must inevitably lead to thoughts about the purpose and structure of the media in general. That is an exercise most governments are not enthusiastic to undertake. Similarly, relaxing the restraints would have much wider consequences than simply easing the work of journalists and editors, and would require extensive revision of the law and current practices. Nevertheless the importance of investigatory journalism must not be allowed to be devalued or diluted. The media do not have a good track record in uncovering the cases of corruption of misconduct during the 1970s—not that any other agency with a responsibility for enforcing standards of conduct was any better, but for every British Leyland disaster there were the Metropolitan Police, the Crown Agents, Kirkby and Blackpool successes. Investigatory journalism may be impalatable medicine to many politicians and public servants but it is indispensable to the health of democratic government.

Notes

1. *Sunday Times*, 31 October 1976.
2. *Sunday Times*, 6 July 1980.
3. *Report of the Prime Minister's Committee on Local Government Rules of Conduct*, 1974, Vol. I, paras 135 and 142.
4. *Report of the Royal Commission on Standards of Conduct in Public Life*, HMSO 1976, Cmnd. 6524, p. 110.
5. *Sunday Times*, 9 July 1972.
6. *Sunday Times*, 5 May 1974.
7. *The Times*, 31 August 1978.
8. *Guardian*, 20 November 1973.
9. Quoted in Robin Callander Smith, *Press Law*, London, Sweet & Maxwell, 1978, p. 45.
10. *Royal Commission on the Press*, Final Report, HMSO 1977, Cmnd. 6810, p. 11.
11. For a general discussion, see Graham Cleverley, *The Fleet Street Disaster*, London, Constable, 1976, and for a specific example, see Eric Jacobs, *Stop Press*, London, Andre Deutsch, 1980.
12. See 'Concentration of Ownership of the Provincial Press', Research Series 5, Royal Commission on the Press, Cmnd. 6810-5.
13. See 'Analysis of Newspaper Content', Research Series 4, Royal Commission on the Press, Cmnd. 6810-4.
14. See I. Jackson, *The Provincial Press and The Community*, Manchester, Manchester University Press, 1971.
15. See Harvey Cox and David Morgan, *City Politics and The Press*, Cambridge, Cambridge University Press, 1973.
16. C. Wintour, *Pressures on the Press*, London, Andre Deutsch, 1972, p. 30.
17. Paul Rock, 'News as Eternal Recurrence' in S. Cohen and J. Young (eds), *The Manufacture of News*, London, Constable, 1973, p. 77.
18. Cox and Morgan, op. cit., p. 127.
19. G. W. Jones, *Borough Politics*, London, Macmillan, 1964, p. 15.

20. Ken Newton, *Second City Politics*, Oxford, Oxford University Press, 1976, p. 188.
21. *Guardian*, 7 May 1974.
22. Cox and Morgan, op. cit., p. 115.
23. Anthony Wright, 'Local Broadcasting And The Local Authority', *Public Administration*, **60**, Number 3 (1982), pp. 316–17.
24. J. Gyford, *Local Politics in Britain*, London, Croom Helm, 1976, p. 122.
25. Roger Burke, *The Murky Cloak*, London, Charles Knight & Co., 1970, p. 38.
26. Chris Hitchens, 'Labour and the North-East', *New Statesman*, 17 May 1974.
27. Dave Murphy, 'Control without Censorship' in James Curran (ed.), *The British Press: a Manifesto*, London, Macmillan, 1978, p. 178.
28. Ibid., p. 185.
29. Steve Chibnall, *Law-And-Order News*, London, Tavistock Publications, 1977, p. 164, pp. 158–9.
30. Anthony S. Matthews, *The Darkest Reaches of Government*, Berkeley, University of California Press, 1978, p. 130.
31. H.C. Deb., Vol. 951, C.1299–1300.
32. James Margach, *The Abuse of Power*, London, Star Books, 1979, p. 10.
33. 'Decent Exposure', Reel Evidence, BBC Radio 4, 3 June 1980.
34. Ibid.
35. Jeremy Tunstall, *The Westminster Lobby Correspondents*, London, Routledge & Kegan Paul, 1970, p. 125.
36. Quoted in Brian Whittaker, *News Ltd.*, London, Minority Press Group, 1981, pp. 71–2.
37. James Margach, op. cit., p. 6.
38. *Sunday Times*, 11 May 1980.
39. See *Sunday Times*, 6 October 1968.
40. See *Daily Telegraph*, 30 October 1982.
41. Peter F. Carter-Ruck, *Libel and Slander*, London, Faber and Faber, 1972, p. 53.
42. Ibid., p. 111.
43. Ibid., p. 119.
44. See *Daily Telegraph*, 27 October 1980.
45. James Margach, op. cit., pp. 9–10, 123.
46. *Observer*, 29 May 1977.
47. *Sunday Times*, 22 May 1977.
48. *Royal Commission on the Press*, 1977, op. cit., addendum to Chapter 10, paras 7 and 11.
49. Ray Fitzwalter and David Taylor, *Web of Corruption*, London, Granada, 1981, pp. 216–18.
50. See Brian Whittaker, op. cit., pp. 114–16.
51. Ibid., p. 120.
52. *UK Press Gazette*, 14 March 1977.
53. Barry Cox, John Shirley and Martin Short, *The Fall of Scotland Yard*, Harmondsworth, Middx., Penguin Books, 1977, p. 87.

7 When the wheel comes off: reactions to police deviance in Amsterdam

MAURICE PUNCH*

Introduction

Corruption scandals rocked three metropolitan police forces in the seventies—in New York, London, and Amsterdam. Examination of these cases convinces one not only that corruption is a complex phenomenon covering a range of activities but also that police organisations have great difficulty in policing themselves (Punch, 1983a). This leads, first, to the need for a measure of conceptual clarification in focussing on the nature of corruption and, second, to a scrutiny of how policemen react when they are faced with scandal, exposure, labelling, and strident calls to put their house in order. The seventies was also an unprecedented period for exposing governmental and corporate deviance (Ermann and Lundman, 1982), but many large business organisations defended themselves vigorously and scarcely seem harmed by the critical light shed on their systematic deviance (Clinard and Yeager, 1980).

Police organisations are different and, when they are faced with external control and 'the wheel comes off', they may encounter both considerable external hostility and strong internal resistance to labelling. A control agency which is itself corrupt excites particular condemnation for the breach of public trust involved and must often make a dramatic and public showing of reform (Sherman, 1978). This house-cleaning may be bought at the cost of some extreme institutional upheaval because policemen are forced to police themselves and this betrays the powerful, informal code based on secrecy and solidarity (Westley, 1970). This painful process and its consequences have been covered in some detail for New York and London but far less is known about the Amsterdam case. I was already engaged in research with the Amsterdam Police when the scandal broke and was in the fortunate position of being able to follow the developments closely from within the force while I also had access to documents and to a wide range of policemen concerned in the affair for interviews (Punch, 1979 and forthcoming). This chapter, then, is an attempt to examine the nature of police corruption as a preliminary to analysing Amsterdam as a case-study of police reactions to scandal and investigation.

*This is a revised version of the paper 'Heroin, Whores and Handouts: Police Deviance in Amsterdam' which was presented at the Conference on Corruption, University of Birmingham, June 1982.

Police deviance and corruption

When considering the nature of police corruption, it is plain that there is no unanimity on defining it and, moreover, there is a paucity of good, analytical material on the subject. The indispensable sources are Sherman (1974 and 1978), the review of the literature by Simpson (1977) and the accompanying bibliographical guide of Duchaine (1979), and the typology of Barker and Roebuck (1973). Simpson (1977:4-6), for instance, states that 'no functional definition of corruption has yet been agreed upon' but that 'secrecy may be a definitive characteristic of the phenomenon'. Most studies support the view that corruption is endemic, if not near universal, in police departments. Comparative research, for example, is said to document it 'not as a unique pathology, but as a given feature of every police system in the world' (Sherman, 1974:73) while, given that Americans tend to confuse America with the world, it is perhaps safer to assert more parochially that, 'virtually every urban police department in the United States has experienced both organised corruption and a major scandal over that corruption (Sherman, 1978:xxiii). The latter statement certainly does not hold for Great Britain and The Netherlands although that says nothing about the actual incidence of corruption, which remains unknown and probably unknowable. Indeed, there is very little agreement on the meaning of the concept so that definitions and interpretations can vary widely between cultures and over time.

A major problem, then, revolves around the fact that the concept has different meanings in different contexts and the term is used differently in everyday language, in social science, and in law. Heidenheimer (1970:3-9), for instance, classifies definitions around three elements: misuse of authority for personal gain, patterning bureaucracy on the characteristics of the free market (the official 'regards his public office as a business, the income of which he will . . . seek to maximise') and behaviour related to 'violations of the common interest for special advantage'. The first view is fairly widely held and Sherman (1978:30) adopts it when he defines police corruption as 'an illegal use of organisational power for personal gain'. The difficulty here is that legal definitions of corruption incorporating this element are generally very wide (and in practice suffer from considerable problems with evidence and proof), that the word 'personal' suggests individual deviance and that personal gain tends to be seen largely in pecuniary terms. Indeed, some authors virtually equate corruption with bribery involving money or material reward (Barker, 1977:356). In these terms, a policeman who accepts a cup of tea or a cigarette for overlooking a minor parking infraction is 'corrupt' although the incident would be regarded as relatively innocent and harmless by most observers. But what if the parking infraction was perpetrated by a known criminal? The behaviour is the same but its significance is altered. There is always a difficulty in interpreting the motives and intentions of people.

Precisely what deviance consists of in the police world, then, requires some clarification here because general police deviance could include an extremely broad range of practices, from sleeping on duty to breaking open a safe.[1] One widely used typology of police corruption is that of Barker and Roebuck (1973) and I wish to extend it while agreeing basically with their position that

> (1) police corruption is best understood as organizational deviance and not as the exclusive behavior of individual officers; (2) police officers engage in certain types of corrupt practices in accordance with a temporization process among four sets of uncomplementary norms, viz., formal and informal norms of the police organization, legal norms, and situational meanings and rules; (3) there is not one but many analytical types of police corruption; (4) police corrupt behavior is a dynamic and progressive form of deviant behavior (pp. 48-9).

In their typology, Barker and Roebuck take into account five factors—act and actors involved, norms violated, support from peer group, organisation content, and departments' reactions—and elucidate eight categories of 'corruption'. I shall reproduce the categories here with a brief explanation of them and then proceed to modify the typology.

(1) *Corruption of authority*: free meals and services, and discounts, which are seen as informal rewards, as not criminal and the man who refuses is considered 'deviant'.

(2) *Kickbacks*: from towing companies, bondsmen, undertakers, lawyers, for providing them with business. Seen as clean money.

(3) *Opportunistic theft*: often at the scene of a crime where insurance coverage may replace missing items and, within limits, it is seen as clean. There is no corruptor.

(4) *Shakedowns*: payments to officers to prevent prosecution following apprehension usually for a minor offence, and normally the victim does not complain. Money from certain criminals may be considered 'dirty'.

(5) *Protection of illegal activities*: often in relation to so-called 'victimless crimes' and can be for legitimate or illegitimate enterprises acting illegally.

(6) *The fix*: direct intervention in procedure of justice—by quashing prosecution, disposing of parking tickets, softening evidence to facilitate bail or influence sentencing—and done for friends, family, or criminals.

(7) *Direct criminal activities*: premeditated burglary and robbery, with no corruptor and generally considered 'dirty'.

(8) *Internal payoffs*: involves police officers exclusively and is related to work assignments and promotions.

All of these are illicit, being infringements of the criminal law and/or departmental regulations, but they cover very different types of activity. If, for the moment, we think of corruption as essentially concerning a *relationship* between a corruptor and a corruptee and involving some reciprocation in return for some form of reward (material or otherwise) then 1, 2, 4, 5, 6 and 8 imply corruption but 4, 5 and 6 are generally perceived as the core practices because of their potential seriousness in undermining the administration of justice. This is a useful classification that helps to clarify the range of deviant activities that policemen engage in but it requires amplification in two directions. Firstly, I would prefer to put more emphasis on a broader orientation to police occupational deviance (which was plainly not Barker and Roebuck's intention) and, secondly, I consider it necessary to examine the *intention* of corrupt practices more closely because Barker and Roebuck do neglect an important category of offences, such as 'flaking' and 'padding', which are designed to enhance the effectiveness of law enforcement. This approach is adopted in order to emphasise the spectrum from ordinary, normal, day-to-day deviance—which may also involve lying, deception, and management of appearances—to the criminal activities which, not unnaturally, tend to dominate the literature.

In this respect, I would add to the above classification the following categories:

A. *Work avoidance and work manipulation*: 'cooping' (sleeping on the job), 'easing' (getting time off to attend band practice), 'cushy numbers' (easy jobs inside). These forms of activity are designed to make work or working conditions more comfortable and acceptable. They are found in all organisations, at all levels, and are rarely seen as serious. In police circles, they may even be seen as partially condoned ways of avoiding the rigours of patrol work or of keeping the personnel happy (Cain, 1973).

B. *Employee deviance: against the organisation*: pilfering, sabotage, absenteeism, leaking information, neglect. These are ways for employees to subvert organisational ends and to hit back at the organisation for various reasons. They are often confined to lower levels of the organisation, but not exclusively, and are seen as negative and damaging by management.[2]

C. *Employee deviance: for the organisation*: bending rules to achieve quotas, cutting administrative corners, informal deals to circumvent formal blockages. In short, these activities consist of the countless ways in which people try to get their jobs done, frequently with the intention of promoting organisational ends, but which deviate from formal rules and regulations. Often these deviations are seen as minor and as unavoidable, although they can be rarely acknowledged as such formally, but they may involve the development of an informal system that fosters neglect, inefficiency, incompetence, conspiracy and even crime.[3]

D. *Informal rewards*: perks, pilfering, private telephone calls, tipping, discounts, services, presents. This covers a potentially huge range of ways in which organisations provide for, or condone, informal rewards that may increase in sophistication as one moves up the organisation (where it may extend to variations in offices, carpets, secretaries, cars, expenses, trips, entertaining, and so on). These rewards may be widespread but rarely acknowledged, such as informally permitting certain levels of employee theft, and in certain service industries may be part of the way of life.

The four categories mentioned above simply acknowledge the many practices in daily, organisational life that are virtually universal and which, in many ways, are accepted and even condoned (this is less true of B, which one expects to find particularly in polarised or divisive organisations). If we turn more specifically to the police and to corruption then I assume that all four of the above categories are also to be found in police organisations but that most public concern is with relatively serious offences.

E. *Police misconduct and crime*: brutality, discrimination, sexual harassment, intimidation, illicit use of weapons. These are disciplinary and legal infringements related to citizens, suspects and criminals where policemen, individually or in groups, opportunistically or systematically, abuse their authority in ways (not principally aimed at personal gain) that are considered externally to be illegitimate and improper. This includes categories 2 and 7 of Barker and Roebuck's typology. In essence, all deviant police activities fall under this heading, but I wish to reserve it for the relatively serious abuses that are police initiated and not related to organised crime or political control (except in marginal or tenuous ways).

Corruption is one facet of police crime, being by definition criminal, but there is an ambivalence in our use and understanding of the word, for it is used to cover both profiting in some way from abuse of power and the abuse of power itself. In the former case, there is an exchange implicit or explicit, in that something is done or not done in return for some reward or advantage, whereas in the second the relationship is not simply one of mutual advantage and may even be one of antagonism.

F. *Straightforward corruption*: something is done or not done for some form of reward. This is most people's understanding of the word and covers 1, 2, 4, 5 and 8 of Barker and Roebuck's classification. Frequently, the relationship is stable, predictable and may allow for token raids and arrests. The work-load may be low and can lead to idleness and inefficiency.[4]

G. *Strategic corruption (predatory)*: the police stimulate crime, extort money and actively organise graft.[5] In 2, I am assuming a mutual accommodation between, say, organised crime and the police where, in essence, the former 'buy off' the latter. But when does soliciting a bribe move into extortion? Here the police are in the driving seat and become 'meat-eaters', who exploit legitimate and illegitimate enterprises for pursuing illicit ends. Numbers 2, 4, 5, 6 and 8 in the typology could be based on this largely 'predatory' relationship.

H. *Strategic corruption (combative)*: 'flaking', 'padding', falsifying testimony, 'verbals', intimidating witnesses, buying and selling drugs, 'scoring' or burning informants, and paying informants with illegally obtained drugs.[6] Most of these practices are involved in 'building a case' (Manning, 1980:85f) in which the major goal is to make arrests, obtain convictions, confiscate drugs, and get long sentences for criminals. It may involve accommodations with criminals and informants but it is posited on using illicit means for organisationally and socially approved ends. Numbers 4, 5 and 6 of the typology could be part of the set-up—shaking down criminals as a form of informal 'fine', protecting some establishments in exchange for information about others and softening prosecution for informants while hardening it for target criminals. This is generally found in specialised detective units. Barker and Roebuck scarcely consider this form.

I. *Corruption as perversion of justice*: lying under oath, intimidating witnesses, planting evidence on a suspect, and so on. In F and G of my classification the relationship is one of some mutual advantage, although the power imbalance and the directional 'flow' of corruption vary, while in H the purpose is to make the law work effectively. But here the motive is to use one's power and position to ensure that justice does or does not get done for reasons that are not mercenary and not 'idealistic'. I am thinking of a policeman or group of policemen who conspire to take revenge on someone or to avoid prosecution themselves for motives other than those mentioned above. The activity is police-initiated and involves a serious breach of trust and misuse of authority. An example would be where a policeman shoots an unarmed suspect and then, to cover himself, plants a weapon on the body, falsifies his report, lies in court and persuades colleagues to corroborate his version of the incident. It may appear to overlap considerably with H but the motivation of the policemen is the distinguishing quality. It involves the perversion or 'corruption of justice' largely in order to avoid the consequences of behaviour in my category E. Again, Barker and Roebuck do not cover this style of deviation.

In terms of motivation—and, needless to say, motives can be mixed (a lucrative shakedown can also be seen as an informal fine)[7]—the nature of the 'gain' involved in corruption is important. By focussing predominantly on bribery, many authors have emphasised pecuniary gain and mercenary motives whereas there are umpteen ways that people can gain advantage individually and institutionally from deviance. But here it is obvious that in the two separate classifications above we are concerned with malfeasance (commission of a forbidden act), misfeasance (improper exercise of legitimate power) and nonfeasance (failure to enforce a law). Building on this I wish to adapt McMullan's definition of corruption (1961) by extending it and by amplifying the gain from merely pecuniary advantage. For me, then, corruption is when an official gains, receives or is promised significant advantage or reward (personal, group or organisational, and material or non-material) for doing something that he is under a duty to do anyway, that he is under a duty not to do, for exercising a legitimate discretion for improper reasons and for employing illegal means to achieve approved goals.

This attempt at conceptual clarification has been considered necessary here because the word corruption is imprecise and is used to cover a large number of practices. The spectrum of police deviance goes from perks (free meals, cigarettes, newspapers) to 'clean' money from victimless crimes, to 'dirty' money from narcotics scores and police burglaries, to pure criminal involvement in blackmail, extortion, murder, planning burglaries and robberies with criminals, and in actively promoting crime in order to profit from it.[8] These offences (penal or disciplinary) vary enormously in terms of level of organisation involved, visibility, internal legitimacy and external disapproval and yet, when the wheel comes off (or as Americans would say more graphically 'when the shit hits the fan'), all of them tend to be dubbed corruption and an investigation will stigmatise and label as deviant behaviour internally perceived as widespread, harmless and legitimate, or probably as rather 'dicey' but justified in order to get the job done. Now clearly this opens up a minefield of rationalisations, accounts, motives, lies and double-think, but it is important to take this perspective into consideration when viewing how policemen themselves react to the role reversal of being suspects under investigation.

The Amsterdam corruption scandal

The build-up to the scandal

When the corruption cases within the Amsterdam Police became public knowledge they excited intense press coverage as this level of police corruption was unprecedented in the Netherlands (Punch, 1982).

The cases unfolded in four phases. First there was the origin of the cases internally and the early attention of the press. In terms of publicity the breakthrough came in early 1977 with the publication in *Nieuwe Revue*, a rather sensationalist weekly, of an interview with an ex-policeman, who implicated his former colleagues in corrupt practices. The second phase concerned the arrest of eight policemen on suspicion of corruption. Then there was something of a lull until the third phase when, again surrounded by wide press coverage, the cases came to trial. Because the court did not impose sentences, which would have entailed automatic dismissal from the force, the focus shifted to an internal disciplinary enquiry. In this fourth phase, attention was turned on the functioning of the force, and in particular the Drugs Squad, the accusations of some of the suspects against their superiors and the relationship between the force and the city council in terms of disciplinary sanctions that might be taken against local government employees (which is the official status of city policemen in the Netherlands while the mayor is the head of the local police).

The Warmoesstraat station (the research station in the Amsterdam inner-city) has never been short of publicity. Generally this has centred on accusations of undue force and racial discrimination (Punch, 1979a). During the first phase of my research with patrolmen in 1974–6 corruption was not evident and was never mentioned as a serious issue. However, in the spring of 1976 an internal enquiry within the Warmoesstraat was opened that eventually brought the whole issue to a head. Only after this enquiry had been transferred to the Internal Affairs Department at police headquarters did news of it leak out. Rumours circulated but did not touch off public debate about the issue of corruption. What really did catch the limelight, and brought the affair to a wide public, was the interview with an ex-policeman, Jac. Zijlstra, in *Nieuwe Revue* (28 January 1977, 'Police Succumb to Money').

For the first time, illicit practices were explicitly spelled out and were given seemingly irrefutable authenticity by the ex-policeman's words. Zijlstra made several accusations against his former colleagues. Heroin was used to pay informants, money was stolen from suspects and from drunks, goods were stolen at the scene of burglaries on the understanding that the insurance would pay for it anyway and Chinese criminals were forewarned about forthcoming raids.

Jac. Zijlstra estimated that twenty or more of his colleagues were bent and that detectives, members of the PCS (the Plain Clothes Squad) and some uniformed men were involved. A man, who had worked for the Chinese, asserted that members of the Aliens Police arranged residence permits for Chinese in return for gifts of gold Rolex watches (these policemen allegedly became known as 'the Rolex men') and green jade jewellery. He went on to say that such practices were to be found in the 'top' of the police organisation and not just among the ordinary beat-men, and that Chung Mon (once the leading figure in the Chinese community) had sent large baskets, containing turkeys and envelopes with 2–3,000 guilders in them, to several policemen and also to a number of Public Prosecutors. In essence, these accusations were to be reiterated time and again throughout the affair and formed the core of the cases. *Nieuwe Revue* had dramatically put corruption in the public eye.

The arrests

The *Nieuwe Revue* article generated an enormous amount of copy about corruption, which culminated in the spring of 1977 with the publicity surrounding the arrest of the eight policemen.

At this stage, virtually every daily paper and weekly magazine turned their attention to the issue of corruption within the Amsterdam Police. The *Haagse Post* had the advantage that Ton van Dijk had moved from *Nieuwe Revue* to them and brought his tapes of the interview with Zijlstra along with him. Furthermore, he had contacts in the inner-city and also within the police organisation. From early on he displayed a good deal of inside knowledge and he particularly tried to show that the publicised cases were only the tip of an iceberg. In trying to associate criminals with officers, for instance, he reported rumours that 'Commissioner Litjens' has been on holiday in the Canaries with Chung Mon, that his daughter went riding with Chung Mon's daughter, and that his wife had borne Chung Mon's child. His reporting also swiftly focussed on the dubious methods used in the investigation by policemen and on the unrest generated internally between lower and higher ranks.

Van Dikj had got hold of the reverberations caused internally by the fact that the senior officers in the Warmoesstraat had opened the investigation on their own initiative.

> The internal investigation has caused a lot of bad blood. The gentlemen officers screwed the ordinary copper, who's not allowed to go out on the town within his own district and who mustn't accept drinks, while they're eating copiously with Chung Mon's successor, 'Mao', on the day that he was riddled with bullets as part of the power struggle surrounding the heroin trade. 'Van Thiel' [Chief Inspector in Warmoesstraat] is even said to have declared 17.50 guilders for the meal although the Chinese offered it gratis. . . . The Warmoesstraat complains long and loud about the rummaging, highly placed gentlemen, who have Chinese meals for five guilders fetched for them and then declare more, while they crack down on the ordinary copper for less serious matters. (*Haagse Post*, 30 April 1977.)

The trial

The third phase was characterised by an initial falling off of interest following the spectacular news of the arrests (spectacular, that is, by Dutch standards). The investigation proved long drawn-out and some of the suspects, hoping presumably to influence their cases, began to give interviews and to leak documents (rules of *sub judice* are not enforced in the Netherlands). So much was leaked that the trial came almost as an anticlimax although, inevitably, it was widely covered. When the cases came to court, roughly one year after the arrests, two weeklies had managed to get their hands on the 350-page dossier (which named around thirty policemen) containing statements of witnesses and they published extracts from these. Although these were more vivid and authentic than previous leaks they did not in essence add much to the pre-trial revelations.

Some of the key elements of the cases—Chinese paydays, lucky money, fruit-baskets, a cash-book recording payments to the police—emerged in this phase and entered Amsterdam folklore. Charley Yan Tim Lee of the Wah Yong gambling house on the Geldersekade emerged as a crucial character in the affair. He had been a disciple of Chung Mon and, after his death, took up on his own account. Charley was on good terms with the police and had even borrowed 1,000 guilders from a policeman; he had obtained his red Mercedes via a detective; the cash-book in Chinese of his Club No One recorded payments of 400–600 guilders a time to the police; he sent bulging fruit-baskets to policemen at New Year; he paid sums of 100–200 guilders to policemen on the 2nd and 16th of the month, which were 'paydays' for shareholders in his gambling house. Chinese who won at the gambling-table distributed 'lucky-money' to people in the vicinity and some policemen used this money to gamble. The book-keeper of the club, Lui Hang Ki, never saw money passed because the policemen went to the office to shake hands with the other boss, Li Pak H. One of the suspects (known to the Chinese as Lo So Tsai or 'Little Mouse' and as Lao Tsji Tsy or 'Quick Running Mouse') was said to have regularly taken lucky-money worth 20–50 guilders from Charley, which he then placed on the gambling-table, and might leave with 200 guilders (roughly £40 or $70).

A major facet typical of the sparring match prior to the trials was the attempt to shift blame from the suspects to a number of senior officers. Two of the suspects had themselves demanded a new investigation that would include scrutinising the performance of the force leadership (*De Volkskrant*, 3 December 1977). One of the officers in the Warmoesstraat was said to have accepted sherry from a local business (as did everyone else in the station). That the officers in the Warmoesstraat were aware of the irregular use of drugs by their subordinates was said to be evident in a notice posted in the station, which called for an end to 'messing around with drugs for informants'. The unpopularity of the officers who had initiated the whole investigation was depicted by a constable who allegedly threatened Chief Inspector van Thiel with the words, 'You broke your leg once at football, but if it goes on like this I'll break both your legs' (*Haagse Post*, 8 October 1977). In the same article, one of the suspended policemen was reported as saying, 'If I have to show my backside [he means in the search following arrest] then go ahead. But you can be assured that I'll start talking and then you'll see that my backside is a lot whiter than a whole lot of others, and that includes bosses'.

The defence lawyers more or less portrayed the cases as a storm in a teacup because the men had to behave as they did in order to do their work and never considered such practices to be corrupt. There were headlines reflecting this last theme such as 'Refusal of Money Detrimental for Contacts' (*De Volkskrant*, 18 May 1978) and 'Money Not Seen as Corruption' (*Het Parool*, 10 May 1978).

The refrain at the trial was 'we couldn't refuse because otherwise our contacts would have been ruined'. The suspects all confessed to accepting money or gifts but hotly denied corruption. The four members of the PCS were said to have accepted sums of between 50–100 guilders at a time to a maximum of 1,600 guilders. One of them saw his trip to Paris with a Chinese couple as a private affair in his free time and claimed that the policemen paid for the hotel and the petrol. Finally, he claimed to have been influenced by the atmosphere and style of work current at that time and, with others, to have collectively slipped off the correct path.

The Public Prosecutor launched a strong plea for stiff sentences ('No Pardon for "Corrupt Policemen" ', *De Telegraaf*, 1 June 1978). These prison sentences would have meant the automatic sacking from the force of all six policemen who came to trial. But when the judges met to pass sentence two weeks later they were lenient and reduced the Prosecutor's demand. Their decision was as follows: three men were fined, two were released on a technicality (to be retried later and fined) and one was set free. They suggested that an internal disciplinary investigation be mounted as soon as possible (*De Volkskrant*, 15 June 1978).

In effect they neatly returned the hot potato into the reluctant lap of the Chief Constable. In place of a decision that would have rid him of the six suspects he was faced with eight suspended policemen whose behaviour had to be rescrutinised in terms of force discipline. Suddenly the attention switched away from fruit-baskets, lucky-money, and the ritual of the court-room and towards the internal functioning of the Amsterdam police. In anticipation of the end of this phase one article endeavoured to sum up the lessons. The piece focussed on the lackadaisical attitude within the police force where constables were sent out on the street with the casual comment, 'have a look around and sort it out for yourself'. It commented critically on the vacillating policies in relation to the Chinese gambling-houses, on superiors who let subordinates sink or swim and on the faulty policy of the city council. The theme, which was to dominate the fourth phase, of looking for scapegoats and of distributing blame (if possible, high up the hierarchy) was clearly spelt out (see 'The Lessons of the Amsterdam "Police Corruption Case" ', *Elsevier's Magazine*, 27 May 1978):

> It is obvious that in the so-called Amsterdam 'police corruption scandal' it has not been the highest trees which have been ruffled by the wind. Rather it was the small bushes who were left in the lurch by their superiors, suffocated in a mass of work, and continually having to reach compromises without the benefit of an elementary handbook or even of simple instructions.

Reverberations

If the first three phases tended to be dominated by the errant members of the PCS in the Warmoesstraat and their contacts with suspects, dealers, and Chinese underworld figures, then the fourth phase saw a shift in emphasis to headquarters, to internal rivalries and tensions, and particularly to the functioning of the Drugs Squad. Rather than detailing with relish the deviant antics of a number of low-level policemen, the press now turned its attention full square on the internal functioning of the force, on the methods used by the Drugs Squad in combating crime, on the disciplinary inquiry and on four key figures. If van Thiel and Maartens, the Chief Inspectors in the Warmoesstraat, had been the 'villains' of the piece earlier then now the headlines were captured by

Commissioner Litjens, Chief Inspector van Rossum, and the two 'Chinese experts', Hoogland and Lighthart.

With the elevation of Amsterdam to a world drugs centre the Drugs Squad was first seen to be inadequate but, strongly reinforced and primed by the DEA (the American Drug Enforcement Agency), gradually became the dramatic and even romantic pivot around which the whole Amsterdam detective force seemed to revolve. Everyone—senior officers, press men, and even constables on the beat—became practically mesmerised by drugs. In the mid-seventies the Drugs Squad was always good copy and its head at that time, Litjens, was not shy to grasp the publicity. He was promoted to head of Serious Crimes, of which the Drugs Squad was one part. There his successor was Chief Inspector van Rossum who also did not shy away from publicity but who was more systematic and managerially orientated than Litjens. Under his leadership, the Drugs Squad went on to attain even more success. Initially, the two Chinese experts had played a vital role in all this. As detectives in the Warmoesstraat they had specialised in the Chinese community, had learned elementary Chinese and were instrumental in solving a number of cases in that criminal world. Hoogland (known as Kau Foe or 'Godfather' to the Chinese and also as 'Baldy' or 'Egg-roll') had begun to focus on the Chinese community in the inner-city from 1969, and had been joined in 1973 by Lighthart (known as Tai Loo or 'Big Brother' and more colloquially as 'Tom Jones'). Because of their special knowledge they were moved, under Litjens's patronage, to headquarters where they were members of the CID (the Criminal Intelligence Branch) but where they worked exclusively on the Chinese scene. When arrested they steadfastly denied everything and the cases against them were dropped in November 1977. But they remained suspended pending a disciplinary inquiry. Unlike some of the other suspects they did not seek publicity and refused all interviews with the press. Towards the end of 1978, however, it became common knowledge that, on the basis of the disciplinary inquiry, the Chief Constable was recommending their dismissal to the mayor. The Chinese experts decided to talk. Earlier it had been the Warmoesstraat which had taken most of the flak. Now the same imagery was used to depict the symptoms of decay and disarray at headquarters. The magazine *Extra* asked 'Is the Capital's Drug Squad Rotten to the Core?' (29 December 1978) while *Panorama* (26 January 1979) promised to reveal 'a ruthless x-ray of a mortally ill police apparatus that is suffering from frustration, prejudice, jealousy, and especially the thrusting imperialism of the puppet-master of the CIA's drugs department, the Drugs Enforcement Agency'. The basic material for the new turn in the corruption affair was undoubtedly the interviews which the two Chinese experts gave to the press. These two detectives had been extremely active policemen and had gained a lot of sympathy for their plight. Now they had to face the prospect of possible dismissal from the force and they decided to open their mouths and their hearts to the press. The two Chinese experts set out both to elicit sympathy for their predicament and also to turn the spotlight on the rivalry between van Rossum and Litjens, of which they had allegedly become the victims. That a well-known policeman of the rank of Commissioner was involved in a scandal, however marginally and however much by insinuation, was unprecedented. Now the two detectives spoke out in graphic terms, 'They're embittered, feel they've been sacrificed, and have made counter-accusations' (*Extra*, 29 December 1978). One of them, Lighthart, elaborated on this:

> All of a sudden I was picked up. Even my wife wasn't allowed to know where I was. I was put away for a couple of days and my wife wasn't even given the chance to fetch my dirty underpants. We were treated like pigs. In comparison with us Litjens has had VIP treatment, but then he's a commissioner and we're only a couple of street cops. Damn it, now we're treated as crooks but I swear to you we never took a thing. Maybe now and then an egg-roll but you have to go along with the Chinese. Give and take, win their confidence . . . otherwise you won't get a shred of information. We were Litjens' experts, his Chinese boys. Now he's in the shit himself but he'll get out of it alright. But not us . . . we did the work and Litjens sold it to the press. But in the end we got the brush-off as thanks. When we needed him he said he was not at home.

They then launched into a whole series of serious accusations against their former bosses, van Rossum and Litjens. They objected to the fact of being caught between rival bosses who demanded to be informed of everything in case the rival gained an advantage. They claimed that the Drugs Squad and the Warmoesstraat resented their successes and their close contacts with the Chinese. They claimed, further, that Chinese contacts complained to them that they lost money during police searches; that they objected about a detective who kept 425 guilders after searching a Chinese suspect and that Lighthart once wrote 1,400 guilders in the register after a search of a Chinese suspect but the Chinese found only 400 guilders in the envelope at the moment he was deported from Schiphol Airport. Van Rossum was said to have signed blank search warrants to cover the period when he was on a course in the USA, to have kept a collection of keys to houses owned by Chinese people and to have 'stolen' opium pipes after a raid on an opium den. They mentioned a case where an informant had been promised 6,000 guilders by the Drugs Squad for information but, although the money was signed for and issued, it never reached the informant. Another informant provided information leading to the confiscation of two and a half kilos of heroin, which entitled him to 2,500 guilders reward, but he only received 500 guilders from Litjens. Litjens also damaged their relations in the Chinese community, where they had been initiated into some of the secret practices of the triads, by publishing details of the triads on his return from the Far East. Furthermore, a number of informants were allegedly brought into danger and perhaps even murdered because Litjens and van Rossum talked too much to the press in order to get publicity and this endangered informants. 'The informant must always be protected, if necessary from colleagues and bosses. That's why we've always made sure that nobody could identify the informant from any of the papers'. The Drugs Squad may even have betrayed some informants to the underworld.

But all this was used to suggest that much of the 'truth' had not come to the surface and that, if told, it would reveal a good deal that was fundamentally wrong inside the central detective branch of the Amsterdam Police. 'Litjens was literally supposed to have been the tip of an iceberg of corruption that covered the whole of the Amsterdam Police. The whole of the capital's detective apparatus was said to stink, from top to toe' (*Extra*, 29 December 1978). The finale to this fourth phase, with its internal bickering and mutual accusations, reached a climax in January 1979 when Litjens was moved from headquarters to a district station. This was, in effect, a humiliating demotion for an internationally renowned detective. *De Telegraaf*, which had close relations with Litjens, took his side and presented him as the victim of an intrigue in which his jealous arch-rival, van Rossum, was the major culprit. Since the previous summer a secret internal investigation had been conducted which had pointed in Litjens's direction, and this had led van Rossum to 'spy' on his boss. When Litjens was away on a business trip to Cairo, van Rossum, on the orders of the Chief Constable, opened his safe and apparently discovered drugs and weapons but no prosecution was ever brought against Litjens.

But, in effect, the corruption affair was petering out. Few people believed that anything serious could or would be proved against Litjens. In a last effort to extract copy from the case and to throw in their lot with Litjens, the reporters of *De Telegraaf* claimed that there was a crisis of confidence in the personal leadership of the Chief Constable, that he had isolated himself with his close acolytes and refused all communication with his opponents and that he had twice suggested that he might retire early. The Chief Constable appeared on television to refute these allegations. But really these were the last shots in a dying battle because the 'crisis' failed to materialise and public attention waned. After four years of turmoil the Amsterdam Police returned to an uneasy peace and the press saw little copy any more in the corruption case.

Conclusion: police reactions to scandal and investigation

It's like handling a pot of shit. I can take off the lid and start stirring around in the shit but then some of it might stick to my fingers. [Policeman responsible for investigating corruption in Amsterdam.]

The Amsterdam affair lasted some four years and documented a pronounced 'leniency pattern' (Gouldner, 1954) with regard to low-level deviant practices. Although the courts could not prove 'corruption', no one doubts that 'straightforward' corruption existed although this was confined to plainclothes men and detectives working with vice, drugs and/or aliens in the inner-city. There seems to have been a pattern of 'predatory strategic corruption' (scoring, stealing, extorting, etc.) and even of 'corruption of justice' (blackmail, intimidation, illegal telephone tapping, etc.). But, when the wheel came off, the deviant practices were justified (and only the mildest forms were admitted) in terms of 'combative strategic corruption'; in other words, accounts were couched in positive terms of doing the job, cutting corners, getting arrests, building up necessary contacts with informants, essential reciprocal hospitality with criminals and carrying out what were considered to be activities condoned by senior officers. Furthermore, the investigation—with which no one was satisfied —unleashed turmoil, bitterness, and recriminatory accusations within the force (Punch, 1983b). What, then, are some of the lessons from this case study?

As in London and New York, drugs seemed to have a considerable impact on changing police work in Amsterdam, where the picture was further complicated by its concentration in the ethnically impenetrable Chinese syndicates. The drug scene is reputed to be unpredictable and dangerous, dealers frequently face stiff sentences if caught (this is less true in the Netherlands than elsewhere), and quantities of drugs and large sums of money are frequently present at the time of arrest or raid (allowing policemen to 'score' the criminals for money and/or drugs in return for freedom). The Chinese criminals also brought with them a culture of gifts and meals as hospitality, which could prove difficult to refuse but which may also have been a deliberate attempt to compromise officials.

The press did not bring the scandal to light, as was the case in both London and New York (Burnham, 1976), but they did latch on to the affair in a big way and, fed by internal leaks, they managed to keep the issue on the boil over a number of years. The suspects collaborated with the press to suggest continually that senior officers were also involved.

The investigation began as an internal inquiry in the Warmoesstraat, was handed over to state detectives when it was clear that crimes were involved and ended as a disciplinary investigation within the force. Corruption was never proved, no senior officers were ever prosecuted and the investigation was universally seen as ham-fisted and amateuristic, while the state detectives worked purely reactively and were handicapped by language problems, by witnesses recanting their testimony, by problems of evidence and proof and by witnesses being unavailable for interview.

Policemen set out to hunt other policemen, and the methods they used were precisely those used against ordinary criminals (surveillance with binoculars, interviewing witnesses, attempting to identify suspects, etc.) and this process set up extraordinary tensions inside the organisation. In particular, senior officers tend to dominate formal enquiries and to focus downwards where the lower ranks, feeling that they are being made scapegoats, fight back with resistance and hostility. The case led to a deep divisiveness between officers and men (Punch, 1983b).

The lower ranks hit back with leaks to the press, informal social control against investigating officers (ostracism, threats, illegal telephone tapping), leaking of documents and information to the suspects, collusion with the suspects and sanctions against colleagues who appeared to co-operate with the investigation.

There developed a counter-mythology that the suspects were excellent policemen, that 'bosses' were also implicated but were sacrificing the small fry to save their own necks and that suspects and witnesses were put under illegitimate pressure to confess.[9]

What clearly emerged was the rivalry, competition, hostility and non-co-operation between units who were jealous of information and territory and who all sought juicy arrests and interesting cases. The ends justified the means and led to paying informants with heroin, 'padding' and 'flaking', and 'fishing with live bait' (i.e. using lower-level dealers to get at criminals superior in the hierarchy).

Another feature of the cases was that policemen enjoyed friendly relationships with criminals and could become ensnared by the elements of risk and excitement involved in gambling, sexual favours, trips abroad and drinking in night clubs. To a certain extent, corruption was fun, exciting and easy (working with steady informants and criminals could bring in good, predictable, 'easy' arrests).[10]

From the point of view of most policemen you had to cut corners, had to use informants, had to cultivate relationships with criminals and had to bend rules. This was seen against a background of a lenient penal and judicial system (and a tolerant society) that seemed incapable of tackling rising crime and the drugs problem. With no substantial buying, no conspiracy laws, and no tradition of undercover work (all staples of DEA methods), the Dutch policemen were handicapped in making cases. The creation of the normative ghetto in the city centre of Amsterdam—where prostitution, gambling, drugs, illegal aliens, and porn shops could all flourish with some degree of official blessing from judicial and municipal authorities (Punch, 1979a)—created a corruptive environment where laws were not meant to be enforced.

This sponsored an opportunity structure of selective enforcement condoned by the 'bosses' (senior police officers, politicians, and judicial representatives). Many of the deviant practices uncovered involved low-level, occupational deviancy such as perks and gifts but also stretched to serious offences. An investigation exposes immediately the 'normal', everyday, informal rewards and behaviour of occupational deviance but often finds it difficult to break through to the more insidious forms of criminal deviance. The bitterness and resentment arises because the lower ranks believe that such practices are universal and legitimate—in fact you would be deviant *not* to indulge in them[11]—and are perhaps even more pronounced among senior officers. Even the more 'dodgy' practices, such as 'planting', may be considered appropriate as informal punishment in a weak justice system. Above all, the men feel that the practices were either actively condoned by bosses pushing for results or passively accepted by officers who protected themselves from guilty knowledge. In essence, a police investigation of corruption involves betrayal at three levels: the 'public', as represented by watchdogs, hypocritically imposes standards which it does not itself follow; senior officers abandon the lower ranks and point the inquiry inexorably downwards; and, most crucially, policemen themselves are forced to break the powerful norms of secrecy and solidarity by hunting other policemen and by breaking the rule of silence in implicating others to save their own necks. All these self-justificatory rationalisations and bitter feelings of betrayal were present in Amsterdam and also form the core of Leuci's bitter and tragic story of betrayal in New York (Daley, 1979).

New York (Murphy and Plate, 1977) and London (Mark, 1978; Cox *et al.*, 1977) were cases that led to visible reform and apparent decline in corruption. Sherman (1978) sees New York, alongside Oakland and Newburgh, as a successful attempt at reform[12] accompanied by house-cleaning, rotation of personnel, proactive anti-corruption enforcement, new enforcement-patterns, a reduction in autonomy for the detective branch and a new public policy of decentralisation and accountability (Kennedy School, 1–4:1977). Mark instituted in the Metropolitan Police a new department to investigate cases, put the detective branch under control of the uniform branch, rotated personnel continually in sensitive areas and employed disciplinary procedures ruthlessly to force out scores of policemen who could not be brought to trial. In Amsterdam no senior heads rolled, none of the suspects was removed and no significant alteration in the way police work, including anti-corruption activities, was structured took place. In effect, the scandal may have had a salutary effect but it did not lead to substantial institutional reform.

This review of the Amsterdam corruption affair has endeavoured to accentuate the complexity of the case and to look at it from the point of view of those involved. The perspective underpinning this chapter is that police corruption needs to be understood in terms of the occupational and organisational deviance that is partly unique to the police and partly held in common with other organisations and professions. I would argue that we need a range of case studies, cross-culturally and cross-nationally, to examine this complex phenomenon. In part, for instance, the trauma caused by the Amsterdam corruption scandal can be explained by the fact that until then the Dutch police had scarcely ever been involved in a comparable affair. Thus, although it was only a mild case of corruption (Punch, 1979b) in comparison to the cases in New York and London, it caused unprecedented turmoil within the organisation. The press had a field-day, personal disputes and mutual incriminations were relayed direct to the papers, some units were almost paralysed with dissent, officers were threatened and were shadowed by their own men, two deaths were ascribed to the affair, there were crises of confidence between lower ranks and senior officers in the Warmoesstraat and between young officers and the top ranks, there was virtually a sit-down strike in the Warmoesstraat where near mutinous patrolmen refused to go out on the streets and there were sympathy demonstrations for Amsterdam by many other units of the Dutch police.

My research in Amsterdam, with its accent on the micro-processes of institutional life, does not portray the police organisation as a harmonious, integrated entity with a comforting consensus and with unbreachable defences against internal investigation and outside enquiry (Punch, 1983a). On the contrary, it conveys a deeply divided pattern of semi-autonomous and conficting units, a picture of policemen facing the practical dilemmas and contradictions of police work on the streets, and a portrait of an ambivalent and even irrational occupational culture based on the primitive, almost tribal, norms of a continually threatened group who must engage in morally vulnerable work. Above all, then, police corruption needs to be understood in terms of how police work actually gets done and how policemen view their occupational reality with all its perks, rewards, risks and pitfalls (Manning, 1977). Lies, deception, and falsification may simply become part of the job[13]—and be perceived as normal, legitimate and even essential—until, that is, the wheel comes off.

Notes

1. 'The Denver police burglars in the early 1960s were professional safecrackers. They were so proficient at safecracking that one safe job was completed in seventeen minutes start to finish. The three principal members of the group were probably the most experienced safecrackers in the nation at that time; they were able to crack a supposedly burglar proof safe, a Diebold 10 with three inch thick steel walls.' (Ralph L. Smith, *The Tarnished Badge*, pp. 14–31, quoted in Barker and Roebuck (1973, 36).)
2. Cf. Ditton (1977) on fiddling and pilfering in a bakery, and Rubinstein (1973) for deviant practices among policemen in Philadelphia designed to undermine supervisory control.
3. Here I have in mind Dalton's (1959) work on managers.
4. Serpico (Maas, 1973) gives a graphic account of how plainclothesmen in New York made an occasional arrest but spent a lot of their time at the cinema, swimming at home and playing cards or pool; their energy went into maintaining the 'pad' (the collection of graft money from gamblers), but not into police work. This can be compared with Leuci's picture of the SIU (Special Investigating Unit) as consisting of hard-working, highly competent, strongly motivated detectives—who just happened to be corrupt (Daley, 1979).
5. Commenting on the Chicago affair, Brashler (Beigel and Beigel, 1977:x) spoke of 'illegal, aggressive police activities in the areas of bribery, extortion, conspiracy, and perjury. Cops became bullies, demanding "dirty" money totalling hundreds of thousands of dollars'.
6. 'Flaking' refers to planting evidence on a suspect; 'padding' means adding to drugs to strengthen a case; 'verbals' is used in Britain to indicate where words attributed to a suspect are invented by policemen to incriminate him; 'scoring' (as a verb or as a noun 'the score') concerns 'shakedowns' where police take money, drugs or goods from their victims. The terms 'clean' and 'dirty' money are worth mentioning here. Clean money refers to straight graft from, say, gambling whereas the proceeds of drugs and police burglaries are often considered dirty. Also the Knapp Commission in New York (1972)

popularised the dichotomy between 'grass-eaters' (passive recipients of graft) and 'meat-eaters' (who actively sought out opportunities for organising graft).

7. A good source for examining this ambivalent motivation is Daley (1979) who describes SIU detectives who believed they were fining, punishing and deporting wealthy foreign dealers who would otherwise wriggle out of any sanctions. This seems less specious if one considers that the rest of the justice system is corrupt and that lawyers, DAs and judges can be bought. In Chicago, for instance, a policeman recalled how 'business' might be conducted, even in the courtroom, on throwing a case (Beigel and Beigel, 1977:254). Indeed, Leuci's ostensible motivation in going undercover to work against some of his own colleagues was that it would lead to arrests of corrupt lawyers. The fact that inquiries tend to halt, or run out of funds, when they reach these levels only reinforces policemen in their view that they are used as scapegoats for the rest of the system. Serpico too hoped that his revelations might lead to sanctions against senior officers: 'Serpico thought of the real culprits—the superior officers, the "bosses"—who allowed corruption to thrive in the department and who would escape untouched. He told Roberts that he, and everyone else in the room, could go to hell. The whole thing was a farce. He had come forward under the illusion that this action would result in a broad investigation to clean up the Police Department. "So what happens?" he said. "All they get is some flunky cops, and I end up the schmuck. The bosses must really be having a laugh over this one".' (Maas, 1974:176.)

8. Fogelson (1977) gives historical examples for a number of American cities while Beigel and Beigel (1977:69) mention a case in Chicago where police moved prostitutes and drug addicts into a black area where community projects were threatening to clean up the neighbourhood.

9. The American Civil Liberties Union felt moved to condemn the methods used by the Knapp Commission against corrupt policemen (Sherman, 1974).

10. Holdaway (personal communication) has emphasised this point to me, which reflects his own insights into the hedonistic features of the police subculture (Holdaway, 1980). Reisman (1979:126) examines the social and personal implications of bribery, which may have little to do with economic motives; some people may derive a 'deep psychological gratification' from the act of bribery, outweighing material benefits, and he asserts further that, 'the moral aspects of bribing or evaluating particular bribes may be very complex, requiring exploration not only of the transaction but of the phenomenal world of the actors as well'.

11. Cf. Stoddard (1968), where he discusses the 'code' regulating informal police practices and socialisation into deviancy: policemen might be told of newcomers—'you've got to watch him, because *he's honest!*'—while others would go along with leniency in return for services, say for meals, because not to do so would 'be goofing up their [other officers] meal ticket . . . it was the normal accepted thing to do. I'd have been more ashamed, and I'd have kept it quiet if I'd stopped such a man as this [He is discussing a restaurant owner who offers policemen free meals and who consequently enjoys virtual immunity from prosecution], because I'd have felt like some kind of an oddball. I would have been bucking the tide, I'd been out of step.'

12. Sherman (1978) has written the major book on police corruption but, as his main interest is the administrative cycle of 'scandal and reform', he tends to jump from scandal to reform whereas I focus on the institutional upheaval in between. His work on organisational deviance (Sherman, 1979) is also relevant in this context as is Reiss's (1983) article on compliance and control in organisations.

13. Cf. Manning (1978). In some of the accounts of deviance there is an element of 'drift', which erodes the significance of the act over time: 'then before you know it, you're up to your ears. I can't even remember where the money was coming from. You know, taking money is like getting laid. You remember the first time with a broad; after that it's a blur.' (Statement of police witness before the Knapp Commission, Schecter and Phillips, 1973:87–8.) Similar statements, if not so colourful, were forthcoming from businessmen in relation to dubious payments and lavish hospitality; in the heavy electrical equipment anti-trust case of 1961, witnesses claimed that price-fixing had become a 'way of life' and was so common that 'I think we lost sight of

124   *Maurice Punch*

the fact that it was illegal' (Geiss, 1967:144). See also Reisman (1979) and Clinard and Yeager (1980).

Select bibliography

Barker, T. (1977), 'Peer Group Support for Police Occupational Deviance', *Criminology*, 15, No. 3, 353–66.

Barker, T. and Roebuck, J. B. (1973), *An Empirical Typology of Police Corruption: A Study in Organizational Deviance*, Springfield, Ill., Thomas.

Beigel, H. and Beigel, A. (1977), *Beneath The Badge: A Story of Police Corruption*, New York, Harper and Row.

Bracey, D. H. (1976), *A Functional Approach to Police Corruption*, New York, John Jay Press.

Burnham, D. (1976), *The Role of the Media in Controlling Corruption*, New York, John Jay Press.

Cain, M. (1973), *Society and the Policeman's Role*, London, Routledge.

Chatterton, M. R. (1975), *Organizational Relationships and Processes in Police Work*, unpublished doctoral thesis, University of Manchester.

Clinard, M. B. and Yeager, P. C. (1980), *Corporate Crime*, New York, The Free Press.

Cox, B., J. Shirley and M. Short (1977), *The Fall of Scotland Yard*, Harmondsworth, Middx., Penguin.

Daley, R. (1979), *Prince of the City*, London, Panther.

Dalton, M. (1959), *Men Who Manage*, New York, Wiley.

Ditton, J. (1977). *Part-Time Crime*, London, Macmillan.

Duchaine, N. (1979), *The Literature of Police Corruption: Vol. 2, A Selected, Annotated Bibliography*, New York, John Jay Press.

Elsevier's Magazine (1978), 'De Lessen van de Amsterdamse Politie Corruptiezaak', 27 May.
— (1980), 'De Commissaris Slaat Terug', 23 February.

Extra (1978), 'Exclusive Onderzoek: Corruptie Schandaal bij de Amsterdamse Politie', 29 December.

Fogelson, R. M. (1977), *Big-City Police*, Cambridge, Mass., Harvard University Press.

Gardiner, J. A. (1970), *The Politics of Corruption*, New York, Sage.

Geis, G. (1967), 'White Collar Crime: The Heavy Electrical Equipment Antitrust Case of 1961' in M. B. Clinard and R. Quinney (eds), *Criminal Behaviour Systems: A Typology*, New York, Holt, Rinehart and Winston.

Goldstein, H. (1975), *Police Corruption: A Perspective on Its Nature and Control*, Washington, D.C., Police Foundation.

Gouldner, A. (1954), *Patterns of Industrial Bureaucracy*, New York, Free Press.

Haagse Post (1976), 'Is de Amsterdamse Politie Corrupt?', 4 October.
— (1977), 'Dossier Corruptie—1', 30 April.
— (1977), 'Dossier Corruptie—2', 14 May.
— (1978), 'Politie Special', 13 May.
— (1978), 'Pieter Menten's Staatsgeheim', 25 November.
— (1979), 'De Dienst Bouw- en Woningtoezicht', 3, 17 and 31 March; 14 April.

Heidenheimer, A. J. (ed.) (1970), *Political Corruption: Readings in Comparative Analysis*, New York, Holt, Rinehart and Winston.

Holdaway, S. (1980), *The Occupational Culture of Urban Policing*, unpublished doctoral thesis, University of Sheffield.

Kennedy School of Government (1977), 1. 'Note on Police Corruption in New York in 1970'; 2. 'The Knapp Commission and Patrick Murphy (A)'; 3. 'The Knapp Commission and Patrick Murphy (B)'; 4. 'The Knapp Commission and Patrick Murphy: Sequel'; unpublished documents, Cambridge, Mass., Harvard University.

Knapp *et al.* (1972), *Report of the Commission to Investigate Alleged Police Corruption*, New York, Braziller.

Lundman, R. (1979), 'Police Misconduct as Organizational Deviance', *Law and Policy Quarterly*, 1, No. 1, 18–100.
Lundman, R. J. and Ermann, M. D. (1982), *Corporate Deviance*, New York, Holt, Rinehart and Winston.
Maas, P. (1974), *Serpico*, London, Fontana.
Manning, P. K. (1974), 'Police Lying', *Urban Life and Culture*, 3, No. 3, 283–305.
— (1977), *Police Work*, Cambridge, Mass., Massachusetts Institute of Technology Press.
Mark, R. (1978), *In the Office of Constable*, London, Collins.
Murphy, P. V. and Plate, T. (1977), *Commissioner: A View from the Top of American Law Enforcement*, New York, Simon and Schuster.
Nieuwe Revue (1977), 'Politie Bezwijkt Voor Geld', 28 January.
Panorama (1979), 'Dossier Amsterdamse Politie', 26 January, 2 and 9 February.
Het Parool (1978), 'Van Corruptie Verdachte Amsterdamse Politiemannen: "Geld Niet Beschouwd als Omkoping" ', 18 May.
Punch, M. (1976), 'Front-line Amsterdam', *British Journal of Law and Society*, 3, No. 2, 218–32.
— (1978), 'Backstage: Observing Police Work in Amsterdam', *Urban Life*, 7, No. 3, 309–35.
— (1979a), *Policing the Inner City*, London, Macmillan.
— (1979b), 'A Mild Case of Corruption: Police Reactions in Amsterdam to Internal Deviance', *British Journal of Law and Society*, 2, 243–53.
— (1981), *Management and control of organizations: occupational deviance, responsibility and accountability*, inaugural lecture, Nijenrode, The Netherlands School of Business, Leiden, Stenfert Kroese.
— (ed.) (1983a), *Control in the Police Organization*, Cambridge, Mass., Massachusetts Institute of Technology Press.
— (1983b), 'Officers and Men: Occupational Culture, Inter-Rank Antagonism, and the Investigation of Corruption', in M. Punch (ed.), op. cit.
— (in preparation), *Everything but Temptation: Police Occupational and Organizational Deviance*.
Reiss Jr., A. J. (1983), 'The Policing of Organizational Life', in M. Punch (ed.), op. cit.
Riesman, M. (1979), *Folded Lies*, New York, Free Press.
Rubinstein, J. (1973), *City Police*, New York, Farrar, Strauss and Giroux.
Shearing, C. D. (ed.) (1981), *Organizational Police Deviance: Its Structure and Control*, Toronto/Vancouver, Butterworth.
Schecter, L. and Phillips, W. (1974), *On the Pad*, New York, Putnams.
Sherman, L. W. (1974), *Police Corruption*, New York, Doubleday.
— (1978), *Scandal and Reform: Controlling Police Corruption*, Berkeley, University of California Press.
— (1980), 'Three Models of Organizational Corruption in Agencies of Social Control', *Social Problems*, 27, 478–91.
Simpson, A. E. (1979), *The Literature of Police Corruption*, London, McGraw-Hill.
Stoddard, E. R. (1968), 'The Informal Code of Police Deviancy: A Group Approach to Blue Coat Crime', *Journal of Criminal Law, Criminology and Police Science*, 59, June, 201–13.
Telegraaf, De (1978), 'Geen Pardon: "Corrupte" Politieman', 1 June.
— (1978), '1978: Het Jaar van de Corruptie', 23 December.
— (1979), 'Narcotica Expert op Zijspoor', 29 January.
— (1979), 'Undercover Agent Dringt Door in Onderwereld', 17 March.
Volkskrant, De (1978), 'Van Corruptie Verdachte Agenten: Weigeren van Bedragen Nadelig voor Contacten', 18 May.
— (1978), 'Omkoping door Onderwereld: Celstraffen Geëist Tegen Zes Agenten', 1 June.
— (1978), 'Andere Onbestraft: Drie Agenten Beboet voor Aannemen Giften', 15 June.
— (1978), 'Weer Beschuldigingen Tegen de Politie', 9 October.
— (1979), 'Verdachte Beschuldigt: Politie Betrokken bij Heroine-handel', 24 January.
— (1979), 'Bij Opsporing Narcotica: Hof Acht Gebruik Infiltranten Legaal', 3 February.
— (1979), 'Undercover Agent Scherp Controleren', 3 February.
— (1979), 'Heroine-Handelaar Weer Vrijgelaten', 22 February.

Volkskrant, De (1979), 'Schorsing Twee Rechercheurs Opgegeven', 5 March.
—— (1980), ' "Litjens" Vrijuit na studie Wiegel', 29 February.
Vrij Nederland (1978), 'De Overheidsdeelneming aan de Drughandel', 14 October.
Westley, W. A. (1970), *Violence and the Police*, Cambridge, Mass., Massachusetts Institute
    of Technology Press.

8 Classes, clients and corruption in Sicily

NICK SMART

Introduction

During a recent holiday in Italy I got involved in a rather nasty argument in a bank. I had tried to change a £50 traveller's cheque, but was told by the clerk that as my passport and cheque signatures were dissimilar, doubts about my identity forced him to refuse to accept the cheque. Being short of cash and temper I asked to see the manager. He and the clerk conferred, then he came round the counter to speak. He apologised for the inconvenience, but added that he had to support the clerk's judgement. I might try elsewhere, he said, but would encounter problems as the cheque was already signed and, as it was, my face and passport photograph did not correspond too closely. Feeling rather glum I turned to go, but as I did so the manager made me an offer. As a gesture of good faith, he stated in the most generous tones, the bank would accept the cheque, but not at the official rate. He confided in me that as I was a risk, the bank had to seek some security.

In something of a rage I left the bank and went to another close by. I explained that as I was ignorant of these things I had signed the cheque out of sequence, and offered to supply as many specimen signatures as the teller thought necessary. The teller shrugged, accepted the cheque at the official rate and wished me good morning. I could not resist returning to the former bank, and there vented my spleen on the clerk (the manager was unobtainable). I gave a little speech on unethical conduct, disgraceful behaviour towards tourists and minor corruption. Then, after abusing the Italian banking system generally, I left.

I suppose that seasoned travellers to Italy would say that this kind of confrontation is fairly typical, an almost everyday occurrence. If it is not the bank, then it will be the police or any public servant. All over the place, they might say, there exists this disposition to depart slightly from the rules, to make little deals outside the confines of established procedures, and to personalise what would otherwise be bureaucratic matters. It may be irritating sometimes, but it does not pay to get too uptight. After all, if Italians were to forget their minor corruptions, what would happen to their warmth and charm?

At a guess, most people in Britain would say there is more corruption going on in Italy than there is here. They might cite the climate, the Latin temperament or the diet as contributory factors. They would probably add that the culture, generally, is conducive to corruption, great and small. For their part, Italians might hold different views on temperament, diet and culture, but many would agree that corruption is very rife in Italian society. The honest politician or bureaucrat is regarded as a rare bird. Similarly, the institutions of the law, which are many and various, are held to disprove daily the legend which adorns every courthouse: that everybody is equal before the law. Among Italians, quasi-ethnic explanations of corruption are commonplace. If things are bad in Milan, they are supposed to be so much worse south of Rome. Southerners might be charming on occasion, but there lies their danger, for they are the biggest crooks. While for the northerner money is the key to status, it is power which attracts the southerner, and power tends to corrupt. When all is said and done, it is the corruptness of southerners which lies at the root of the *Questione Meridionale*, the problem of the south. When people speak of the 'meriodionalisa-tion of the state' they are not talking of a few isolated scandals, but of a systematic takeover of the state apparatus by corrupt southerners.

I lived for two years in Sicily, the largest and southernmost of Italy's *regioni*. I was not there specifically to study corruption, but was, I suppose, in a position to see at close quarters something of the corruption that was going on. The label 'corrupt' is as often ascribed as it is achieved, but as I was interested in the behaviour of politicians and bureaucrats, I was keen to find out whether the behaviour of public administrators conformed to some 'hidden structure' which was at odds with the codified procedural rules laid down by centralised authority. In other words, I wanted to find out whether there was a real system that somehow supplanted or by-passed the official system; and if there was, I wanted to find out what the relationship was between the two.

The city I lived in was dotted with impressive-looking public buildings, and in accordance with its provincial capital status, a sizeable proportion of the working population was engaged in public administration (15 per cent in 1971). The solid nineteenth-century *prefettura* and *municipio* were flanked by the Fascist-style post office and *Questura*. The modern plate glass and concrete *palazzo della provincia* dominated the city's *centro storico*. It occurred to me then that there was something suspect about such a conspicuous state presence, as if an attempt was being made to cow an unco-operative, or even unruly, population into submission. People I spoke to regarded the buildings and what they stood for with a mixture of indifference and scorn. Nobody it seemed had much faith in public administrators, and any status they were afforded derived from their good fortune in landing a state job rather than from any consideration of worth. Just as everyone laughed at my literal translation of the term 'civil servant', nobody believed that any common code was practised, or that the same procedural rules were applied to cases of the same category.

It was difficult at first to reconcile this popular view of a corrupt public administration with the conspicuous presence of such a large number of state institutions, yet when I became more familiar with some of the offices and their staffs, I could see why a reputation for corruption could be made to stick. In one of the larger social security offices, the *Istituto Nazionale per la Previdenza Sociale*, dog-eared bundles of records were stacked haphazardly in open cabinets and shelves. There they stayed, I found out, *in giacenza*, or like a corpse laid out in a coffin, until someone came along to give them a *spinto*, a shove. In order for individual forms to be processed, the special *spinto* is necessary, as nothing moves through the system by itself or through consistent bureaucratic practice. Facing the visual appearance of such a system, and familiar with its reputation, the individual is convinced that unless his forms receive a shove in the right direction, his interests will be lost for ever among the dog-eared stacks.

While experience of public administration seemed to conform all too closely with the popular image of an over-paid, over-staffed and corrupt bureaucracy, it was apparent that the persistence of the 'real' system was not due merely to on the spot improvisation, inefficiency or lack of facilities, but was part of a much wider social, economic and cultural environment. Perhaps Sicilians get the bureaucracy they deserve. After all, what would commonly be regarded as corrupt in Britain might be normatively sanctioned or even mandatory in an island society.

Sicilian society, it seemed to me, was in a curious position. On the one hand there was much which anthropologists would call 'traditional', while on the other hand, there was much that was 'modern'. Just as the economy is usually described as if it exists in a pre-capitalist, or certainly pre-take-off, phase, investigators usually emphasise the importance of primary rather than secondary groups in social structure. Yet on top of this there exists a form of political and bureaucratic organisation which, in theory at least, owes more to institutional than personal inspiration. Put at its crudest, a *Gemeinschaft*-type social formation has, grafted on to it, the norms, values and codified rules of the *Gesellschaft*.

Furbi 'and fessi

It seems reasonable, if a little feeble, to describe Sicilian society in terms of the break-up of one social formation, and the non-emergence of the other, so that although elements of both are present, neither is predominant. We might expect all sorts of apparent anomalies and inconsistencies to arise in such a situation, but would have some difficulty in categorising. After all, how does a centrally instituted bureaucracy operate when it is set in a vertically integrated 'traditional' society?

Yet this position is rather feeble because it assumes either that the institutions of civil and political society have no relationship with each other, or that through some process of super-adaptiveness, the individualistic requirements of people (nepotism, favouritism, particularism in our language) can be accommodated within a bureaucratic system that leaves the 'public good' unaffected.

If all the claims and cases need a *spinto*, and the only way to *sprigare* (hurry things along) is to seek a personal *raccomondazione*, it seems inconceivable that all individuals are in a position to ensure that their interests are properly looked after.

My initial impression of a commendably anarchic people basically ignoring the regulations of a comic opera bureaucracy became a bit blurred. After all, if rules only exist to be bent, then one's capacity to bend them and have access to the 'real' system must depend on social position and, more to the point, on inside connections. Perhaps the real consequence of the break-up of one social formation and the non-emergence of the other is not the differentiation between 'real' and 'official', but that between the *furbi* (the cunning ones) and the *fessi* (the mugs). To be a *furbo*, I learned, is to enjoy particularly high status in Sicilian society. A *furbo* is a particular kind of person, one who is skilled in the art of *arrangiarsi* (of getting by in adverse economic circumstances) and whose success depends upon preying on the weaknesses of *fessi*. In terms of public administration, the *furbo* knows that there is a 'real' and an 'official' system, but his cunning extends to knowing how to use the 'official' system and make it work so that he can fulfil his 'real' requirements. In other words, where *furbi* and *fessi* are concerned, there is no alternative bureaucracy that covers for the inadequacies of the 'official' system, nor is there a parallel administration which, in by-passing official channels, conforms to the requirements of a 'traditional' society. Instead, *furbi* only exist inasmuch as they can use the 'official' system for their purposes. Just as the *fesso* cannot actively differentiate between 'real' and 'official', the *furbo* has an interest in keeping the distinction blurred.

A *furbo* public official would, presumably, know how to go by the book, but he would also know when it would be advantageous to bend the rules and grant the special favour to the anxious applicant. He might act in a spirit of disinterested magnanimity, or perform kindly deeds in the name of friendship, but every *furbo* knows that in granting the special favour he is laying the basis for a particular kind of relationship, one where the recipient is obliged to him, and where a kind of reciprocity (perhaps delayed) can be expected. If the official says that he is not in a position to intervene personally, then he is, in effect, making a pronouncement that the matter cannot be dealt with, the licence issued or the claim for an invalidity pension seen to. In the knowledge that successful dealings with bureaucracies depend upon inside contacts, the claimant is forced to cultivate friendships with officials in order to ensure that a personal interest is taken in his affairs. Not all posts offer the *furbo* official free rein, but those in positions of authority have the power that derives from their offices' considerable (and perhaps deliberate) disorganisation to freeze some cases in *giacenza* and to push others through as if 'red tape' never existed.

If, as I suspect, the qualities of *furberia* and *fesseria* are distributed fairly evenly throughout the world, why is it that the differentiation should be so marked in a society like Sicily? Similarly, if there is a line of demarcation between 'real' and 'official' systems everywhere, why is it that in Sicily the 'real' system is so predominant that its usage is known as *regolare amministrazione*? What is it that elevates the Neapolitan phrase *'cca nisciun e fesso'* (nobody's a mug here) to the status of a popular adage throughout the south, when any number of *furbi* must require a goodly number of *fessi* to prey upon?

What appears so overt in Sicily might, of course, exist in more covert form elsewhere, but the organisation of Sicilian society is such that the positions to which high social status are attached are those which require *furberia* in their attainment. If it is a characteristic of the Sicilian social and economic environment for each individual to assume that he or she is a *furbo*, then each individual will seek to maximise personal advantage, believing that others will be doing the same. If it is believed that an act of disinterested altruism is either eccentric *fesseria*, or a more sophisticated form of *furberia*, then the ground on which the seeds of rationally created universalistic rules are thrown will be very stony indeed.

To some observers of the Italian south, the widespread belief in the importance of *furberia* is a typical illustration of a vertically integrated society's individualistic consciousness that seeks to adapt, on its own terms, to forms of authority imposed from outside and that derive from horizontally integrated societies. *Furberia* is often linked to the famous thesis of 'amoral familism' introduced by Banfield over twenty years ago, which attempted to explain the lack of civic consciousness shown by southern Italians.[1] Yet though *furberia* and a presumed ethos of 'amoral familism' appear consistent with or conducive to forms of corruption, and can be used to explain a process of adaptiveness, corruption, as we understand it, is something rather different. A corrupt social order has already, we imagine, entered its terminal phase, and is well on its way to oblivion, whereas the society which supports *furbi* and *fessi* seems well suited to cope with 'state-led modernisation'. Similarly, if a *furbo* is to employ a 'real' system, then there must be its 'official' equivalent close enough at hand to make the difference indiscernible enough to pass for *regolare amministrazione*.

For these reasons, it seems to me that any analysis of corruption in Sicily has to embrace a larger environment than that of politicians and bureaucrats. The distinction between *furbi* and *fessi* is a useful beginning but is too clumsy, and the notions of 'individualism' or 'amoral familism' unfalsifiable. Therefore, it seems better to construct a model which incorporates these ideas, but has a closer relationship to mainstream Mediterranean studies. The most productive course seems to be to employ the notion of clientelism.

Clientelism

To talk about corruption through using the terminology of clientelism or the patron–client relationship might appear an obvious piece of subterfuge, especially as clientelism has been rendered one of those residual catch-all terms that is both 'a jack of all trades . . .' and a 'concept which has been pushed too far and too fast beyond the realms of reasonable conceptual rigour'. While those who have used the term clientelism as a concept for all seasons have provided sceptics with plentiful ammunition, we can, if we are careful with definition and usage, build a conceptual framework that will help us to explain corruption in contemporary Sicily.[2]

It is, perhaps, unfortunate that there is no general agreement on what the terms clientelism, patron–client ties and patronage mean. Because of this there is still less agreement on the types of society to which clientelist analysis may be applied. Yet, despite the confusion which surrounds the terms and their usage, there are, I think, two broad approaches to clientelism that have some bearing on corruption. The first of these is a close derivative of classicial social anthropology, while the second is closely linked to the neo-Marxist thesis of capitalist underdevelopment. It is worth spending some time outlining these two approaches before pronouncing on corruption or mere adaptiveness in Sicily.

Clientelism, as envisaged by classical social anthropologists, describes a kind of *sui generis*, autonomous type of social organisation that has little to do with the social relationship of class. By contrast, when neo-Marxist anthropologists employ the term they emphasise the social cleavages that enable powerful patrons to patronise a wider society of atomised clients. Because the two approaches are so different, they employ two distinct models. The classical model will be summarised first, then the neo-Marxist model, which I shall term the 'revisionist' critique, will be presented and commented on.

Classical clientelism

At first glance, the classical model of clientelism is better fitted to incorporate notions of corruption in southern Italy. Put very simply, corruption will be the likely short-term occurrence when a traditional society is put through the modernisation mill. Accordingly, corruption is not a natural consequence of 'traditionalism', but an unfortunate, though probably inevitable, consequence of modernisation. Thus, in identifying the state with legality Wolf states that 'the patron offers the client economic aid and protection against legal and illegal exactions of authority'.[3] The greater the cultural clash, the more economically and socially convulsive the effects of change are; and the more local elites have to be appeased, then the greater the scope for the corrupt. In addition, as modernisation does not work comprehensively, and does not affect all areas of society at the same rate, residues will be left which will exert corrupting influences. This incidentally, is the classical explanation of the survival of that most famous of Sicilian institutions, the Mafia. On the one hand, the Mafia is regarded as a defensive cultural institution, a sort of collective Robin Hood that enables peasant communities to resist change. On the other hand, the

Mafia is seen as an enduring but fundamentally parasitic organisation that has slipped into areas where the state's presence is weak, and has 'gone public'.[4]

The patron–client relationship is seen by classical clientelism analysts as conducive to, rather than necessary for, the survival of the Mafia. For the Mafia obsession with *omertá* (of being a man and not running and squealing to the authorities) is regarded as involving such a level of threatening coercion that it is only a mutant relative, even a corrupt derivative, of the voluntary relationship of patron and client. In stressing the face-to-face, dyadic context of patron–client ties, classical anthropologists do impose fairly strict 'type of society' criteria before they work their model. Peripheral communities are different, and should be expected to be so, because of their remoteness from the centre. Naturally, sub-cultural defence mechanisms will be invoked when the traditional way of life is being challenged. Clientelism then is the typical social organisation of traditional pre-capitalist societies cut off by distance, geography or language from developed centres. Those living in these isolated regions will have inherited a distinct set of values that encourage them to view the world in a particular way. Just as their lives are hard, then so are their perceptions of people and abstract ideas, which have very little relevance to their everyday lives. Foreign invaders have come and gone, and Italian regimes that have promised much have been replaced by others whose promises have turned out to be equally empty. The world is regarded as a hostile and dangerous place, and the idea of wholesale change for the good has little currency among people who have experienced the folly of idealism. Just as God is said only to give nuts to those who have no teeth, it is small wonder that the people of these isolated communities should put their trust in those who are demonstrably *furbi* and who have the means to protect them. Naturally the people of these communities will see problems as individual afflictions that require individual solutions, for friendship and trust can only exist on a personal, face-to-face basis. As the popular saying goes, 'a group needs an odd number of people, but three is too many and one is too few'. Their whole attitude to prayer tells them that as little people they cannot expect to talk directly to God, but must go through inter-mediary saints. In life too, as the saying goes, everybody needs a saint.[5]

The number of studies that purport to describe the dynamics of these isolated communities which, 'cut off through time and reason', conform to some peculiar structure of social organisation, is legion. Very often these snapshots of times past are written as if to remind us what peripheral Europe can teach us about our pasts. Emphasis is placed on the practical value of patron–client relation-ships, their adaptiveness, and on how patron–client fact-to-face contact welds the component parts of a community together into a harmoniously integrated unit. Yet however sympathetic and observant these clientelistic snapshots are, there is general agreement that, in the short term at least, modernisation will bring with it several unsavoury and corrupting side effects. Graft is an obvious one, for when public rather than private resources constitute the basis of patron–client exchanges, the paternalism of the old style patron will be replaced by the calculating intensity of the entrepreneurial *furbo*. New generations of parvenu, 'get-rich-quick' opportunists, will pervert the time-honoured role of the patron (viz. the character of Don Fabrizio in Lampedusa's classic novel *Il Gattopardo*), and as the emphasis shifts from the ownership of land to the control of public resources, humble clients will be easily confused by the transition. Still we find the pathetic instance of the peasant woman taking her tray of cakes to the official who processes her insurance contributions, and who, in providing a service, expects some show of respect from his clients. She is merely following the practice of her forbears who, as a gesture of respect, would take a basket of eggs to the landlord's house. For his part, the landlord would reciprocate such gestures of loyalty by taking a paternal interest in the affairs of his tenants and acting as their patron and adviser in their dealings with the outside world. Then, the relationship was not vulgarly material. The patron looked after his clients as a father cares for his children. He observed his duty before God and his fellow men to serve the meek and the humble. If his services ran to acts of *furberia* (e.g. helping clients to evade military service) then an external, and essentially abstract, collectivity would suffer rather than the local community.

Just as the utility of exchange was founded on the practicalities of everyday life, frequent contact helped them endure over time, and even span several generations. Now, the peasant lady with her cakes is obliged to carry on a ritual with the institutions of authority that are immediate rather than distant. She has no choice but to personalise her relationship with public power, and to regard the services of an institution as a favour from one person of high status to another of low status. To spurn the friendship of the official would be to deny his importance, and run the real risk of denying herself her civic rights.

Thus the process of modernisation, and the blend of continuity and change, will carry with it such corrupt side-effects. As bureaucracies expand and recruit, people are elevated to positions of public authority who are self-interested, and whose notions of respect extend only to private rather than public service. It would be difficult for the Sicilian official not to help relatives or friends in a public *concorso* (an open examination for state posts) for to do so would be to offend the 'real' as opposed to the 'official' system. It would be equally difficult to refuse the gifts of those who sought to befriend him. For owners and tillers of the land, patron–client ties were both natural and mutually beneficial, whereas now, the qualities of respect and affection can so easily be confused with the personalisation of functionality, and the pseudo-authority that derives from control.

As the 'revisionist' model of clientelism stems, largely, from a critique of the classical approach, it should be possible to criticise the classical model and its incorporation of notions of corruption while laying the basis for introducing the 'revisionist' critique. It is hardly possible in an article of this length to mount a thoroughgoing criticism of such a large body of social anthropological study, but there are three main areas relevant to corruption that the 'revisionist' critique addresses.

The first of these areas concerns the tendency of patron–client relationships to perpetuate themselves. The classical model attempts to show how patrons provide their clients with an individual means of coping with the unfair, hostile, impersonal or just plain inconvenient load of external pressures. As it is frequently observed that reciprocity rarely involves a specific 'cut' for the patron, classical anthropologists seem to believe that respect, loyalty, friendship and kinship are the important conditioning elements of patron–client exchanges. It is thus a cosy little world which they portray, devoid of conflict and envy. What is ignored is the extent to which patrons have an interest in keeping 'official' systems unfair, hostile, impersonal and inefficient. Just as 'real' systems operate within rather than parallel to 'official' systems, the patron must make sure that official institutionalised power is so misused that the would-be beneficiaries of public services become his low-status clients. In addition, the patron's operation of (both) systems ensures that adaptation to external pressures is kept to an individual level, and does not become group, or even political, activity.

While it is true that many classical anthropologists see the potential for exploitation and manipulation within patron–client exchanges, there is a common tendency to assume a harmony about clientelistic relationships which, if not so evident now, was a feature of former times. It seems to me that any relationship that is characterised by 'lop-sidedness', 'asymmetry of status', 'differential access to resources', and 'exclusivism' is as likely to lead to antagonism and conflict as it is to social harmony, whatever the historical epoch.[6]

The second area of criticism is that which refers to the classical social anthropologists' insistence that clientelism is a distinctive *sui generis* type of social organisation. Stress on kinship, godparenthood and friendship is all very well, but if we accept that patrons have a vested interest in perpetuating the inadequacies of official systems, we begin to see patrons and clients interacting in a somewhat less than cosy light. Respect and loyalty might be commodities unfamiliar to any codification of the social relationship of class, but to concentrate on these non-material constituents of exchange is to forget the power the patron has to affect the economic livelihood of his clients. It may well be that outward shows of respect and affection (supposedly the hallmark of patron–client exchanges) are no more than legitimising camouflage for a form of class domination.

To change tack slightly: it is, I suppose, natural that classical social anthropologists should discern a close historical link between the clientelism they observe today (social security claimant and public office holder) and that pure form that existed before the peripheral community became so closely integrated into the modern state (landowner and tenant). In this way, they emphasise the link of continuity rather than the stress of change in describing contemporary patron–client relationships. Yet even though this historical/cultural link is often very eloquently portrayed, there are good grounds for questioning its validity. Gestures of respect and loyalty might well have characterised the exchange relationships that existed between landlords and tenants, but landlords and tenants have an economic relationship which, even in pre-capitalist economies, is one of class rather than status. In other words, if the landlord takes an interest in the affairs of his tenants, his ownership of the land the tenant works is his qualification, and not any especial quality of *furberia*. Perhaps paternalism is a better way to describe such a relationship, and if so it rather disqualifies the notion of clientelism.[7]

To question the historical basis of the classical model of clientelism is not to argue that clientelistic relationships have always contained their economic element, but rather to suggest that contemporary clientelism is as much a product of modernising influences as it is a stubborn residue of traditionalism. To say this is also to suggest that the classicalist conception of a (clientelist) state of endogenous social harmony being destabilised only by exogenous influences is faulty. It is a common enough idea to put the blame for the current corruptions of 'traditional' societies or to pernicious 'modernisation' programmes, but in the Sicilian case it is like saying that the corrupt official is the blameless victim of the corrupting influence of change.

It is, I think, one of the more serious flaws in the classicalist model that their conception of contemporary clientelism is founded on an inappropriate historical analogy. The course they choose does allow them to ignore class analysis, but in doing so they also tend to ignore the fundamental principles patrons and clients must adhere to if clientelism is to exist. While I am not quite sure that definitions of clientelism couched in terms of 'structurally unequal exchange relationships' clearly differentiate clientelism from other forms of direct and indirect exchange (if only because such relationships are not necessarily conspicuous for their quality of 'equalness'), it does seem that some participants in patron–client exchanges benefit more equally than others. Just as patrons seek to perpetuate the inadequacies of 'official' systems, they will not conduct exchange that will make them lesser patrons or their clients lesser clients. If, through his favours the patron were to help his client towards a position of independence, so that he could become a free citizen in a free society, then there is no longer a patron, nor is there any longer a client. In other words, no matter how generous he is, and no matter how many favours he dispenses, the patron cannot afford to expend all his patronage capital in the name of friendship. To give a favour, to expend patronage capital, is to make an investment for the future; that is, it is only done when the return, the reciprocated exchange, will add to the stock of patronage capital's value. The public-spirited patron is, very often, the darling of classical social anthropologists, but the public-spirited patron cannot, by definition, exist.

The third area of criticism relates to the classicalists' use of the terms 'traditional' and 'modern'. Of course, nobody believes that ideal types are anything more than heuristic devices, but in this case, they are distinctly unhelpful ones. In addition, when these ideal types are spanned by the term 'transitional', the continuum is positively dangerous. The commonplace that transitional phases tend to last longer than their supposed pre- and post-positions is one that many Marxist, as well as these very non-Marxist, scholars might bear in mind, but here the problem for the classicalists is not merely that of creating a timetable for the transition from 'traditionalism' to 'modernity'. Instead, the problem is defining what the transition consists of. As I have already deemed the 'pure' agrarian clientelism beloved of classicalists, paternalism, it becomes rather difficult to see contemporary clientelism as the transitional bridge to developed modernity. One of the consequences of this confusion of historical epochs is that the logic of the classicalist argument becomes rather circular. This is especially so in relation to corruption. Corruption, which to classicalists is no more than a side-effect of change, becomes a physical demonstration that the transition to modernity is taking place. When corruption has ended, and the 'official' system becomes the 'real' system, we will be able to say that the transition process has been completed.

The revisionist critique

The time taken to outline these three areas of criticism of the classicalist approach serves as a way of introducing the 'revisionist' model of clientelism. Revisionists do point to the tendency of patrons to seek to preserve their positions as monopolistic exponents of 'real' systems, just as they question whether the relationship of landlord and tenant can be described properly as one of patron and client. Yet the most distinctive aspect of the model is that clientelism is seen, primarily, as a social relationship embracing much more than status. The model's basic starting point is that clientelism only exists in that it serves the interests of the dominant class. In other words, according to 'revisionists', clientelism is far too systematic a feature of the Italian south to permit a certain amount of corruption. It is systematic in that it forms an integral part of developed Italy's relationship with the underdeveloped periphery.

In so far as 'revisionists' view clientelism as a functioning product of a structured centre-periphery relationship, patron–client ties are not regarded as stubborn survivors of 'traditionalism', nor are they seen as a symptom of the society's distance from some abstract modernity. Instead, clientelism is seen as the social and political expression of the south's subordinate integration into the national economy. Accordingly, patrons and clients are not part of a locally generated ideology of backwardness, nor are they locked in the idiocy of rural life. On the contrary, they exist in a much wider social, economic and political context with the institution of clientelism enabling the centre to keep tabs on the periphery.

'Revisionists' are particularly interested in explaining the political conservatism of the south in terms of licensed patrons manipulating subordinate social strata through state patronage, and the 'maintenance of an electoral consensus' is usually regarded as the prime function of contemporary clientelism. Their stress on the political importance of clientelism is itself a reaction to the conscious neutralism of the classicalists. Political conservatism is, to classicalists, the natural political expression of 'traditional' societies, which patrons might enhance by acting as 'brokers', but which is still a product of political culture rather than manipulation. 'Revisionists' explain conservatism in very different ways, and cite 'new' or 'mass' clientelism as the consensus creating agent. They argue that it is through clientelistically organised state agencies that the importance of the south in national politics is underlined, and maintain that the social relationship of patron and client is foisted on the Italian south by that class whose interests the state apparatus serves. The functionality of clientelism rests, according to the model, on its being able to preserve the south as the centre's economic and political 'strategic reserve'.[8]

What 'revisionists' call 'mass' clientelism is, of course, regarded by classicalists as not much more than a side-effect of the transition to modernity, a corrupt derivative of the 'pure' agrarian patron–client relationship. These instances of the privatisation of public resources are likened by classicalists to the bossism of nineteenth-century seaboard America; the distributive politics of the Tammany Hall type political machine. Yet here too, 'revisionists' argue the inappropriateness of this historical analogy. The distributive politics of nineteenth-century America developed among immigrant communities and, of more importance, before the age of bureaucracy. By contrast, the politics of distribution in post-war Italy developed in the context of, and helped to expand, an enormously inflated bureaucracy that profited by the profligacy of successive (Christian Democrat dominated) governments. In other words, while Tammany Hall-type systems were, in their time, as 'official' as they were 'real', the scope for operating 'real' systems in Sicily has been allowed to grow in proportion to the introduction of 'official' systems.[9]

While the 'revisionist' model has a lot to say about social relations, consensus creation, and the subordinate integration of peripheral regions into the national economy, it has less to say explicitly about corruption. This is so, I suspect, because in common with a good deal of neo-Marxist writing, 'revisionists' are more interested in uncovering major antagonisms and contradictions than they are in minor dysfunctions like corruption. Liberal democracy is not, in Marxist eyes, a corrupt sham which exists only because a false consciousness is perpetrated, but is the logical ideology of the bourgeoisie. If clientelism is part of this hegemonic structure then, warts and all, it must be so for some reason, and must be, ultimately, functional to the bourgeoisie's requirements. Marxists hardly regard themselves as the consultants of bourgeois governments, so are not likely to advise on how good government can be achieved without altering the economic basis of the society. If corruption is sanctioned by clientelism, then no standard has been breached because clientelism does what it is supposed to do. As a system of social control, clientelism ensures a political consensus for the party of government and, at the same time, affords northern oligopolistic capital a free run of the underdeveloped periphery.

As the 'revisionist' model of clientelism is so closely linked to the neo-Marxist thesis of capitalist underdevelopment, it becomes rather difficult to criticise the 'revisionists' without taking on the 'underdevelopmentalist' edifice. By the same token, to focus on capitalist underdevelopment might reveal something of the economic relationship between developed and underdeveloped Italy but would, inevitably, involve a lengthy digression away from corruption in Sicily. Yet what I propose to do is to use the 'revisionist' model as a basis for examining clientelism and corruption in post-war Sicily. In sticking to the 'revisionist' terminology, I am implicitly saying that I think them more right on clientelism than the classicalists, but I shall also argue that, in their terms, clientelism is dysfunctional as well as corrupt. Put very simply, it seems to me that the system of 'mass' clientelism the 'revisionists' identify involves the breaking of too many eggs to produce a very unsatisfactory omelette. Modern 'mass' clientelism, in the form of party-directed patronage, might be an identifiable system of 'privatising' public power, but it is one which is more dysfunctional than functional to the interests of the nationally dominant class. By the same token, southern underdevelopment is more a millstone around the neck of productive capital than a 'strategic reserve' bolt hole for northern oligopolies.

Of course, the 'revisionist' model is linked to the thesis of capitalist underdevelopment in the sense that 'mass' clientelism is envisaged as the political arm of a strategy of economic colonisation, the complement to the requirements of the capitalist market. Clientelism's utility lies in the capacity of patrons to keep people in order, oblige them to vote properly at election times and distribute a few welfare crumbs in the form of personalised favours. As a system, clientelism is cheap to run because favours are denied rather than lavished on clients, it gives little political trouble and keeps the southern economy in its necessary state of dependent underdevelopment. If, occasionally, scandals break out which reflect badly on Christian Democrat politicians, then a bit of adverse publicity is a small price to pay for the services clientelism performs, and for the consensus clientelism maintains.[10]

Regarded individually there are, I think, several inconsistencies in the underdevelopmentalist thesis and the 'revisionist' model. Taken together, and combined to form a theory of class domination there are several large holes.

Clientelism and underdevelopment

According to the joint 'revisionist-underdevelopmentalist' argument, the role allotted to the south during the years of the 'economic miracle' was to provide a pool of cheap labour for northern industry, and, at the same time, suffer the capital-intensive attentions of the public industrial sector. Yet now, northern industry is shedding rather than employing labour and the public and para-public sector is in great difficulties. In addition, as small- and medium-scale private concerns have remained indifferent to the incentives offered by the state's southern development programmes (the concern of the famous *Cassa per il Mezzogiorno*) and as unemployment increases, the political need to underwrite the public sector's unproductive southern commitments grows rather than diminishes.

As it is, the south remains a region of flagging demand and low consumption. The labour reserve army (which occupies such a prominent place in under-developmentalist literature) is now on the dole, or is working in the tax haven of the 'black economy'. In other words, the south does not produce very much, and is still too poor to consume the surplus production of northern industry. In the social security and welfare fields, public expenditure has risen enormously this past decade, and transfer payments to the south have been drastically increased in both absolute and relative terms.[11] Yet with inflation running into double figures, and with government cutbacks in capital expenditure, the south promises to play little part in any forthcoming economic recovery. All in all, it seems very difficult to justify the underdevelopmentalist label 'strategic reserve'. This past decade especially, public expenditure in the south has been cited as one of the major causes of the state's fiscal 'crisis', and according to a view widely put about in business circles, makes a nonsense of government's intention to impose austerity measures as a prelude to recovery.

Considering that clientelism is supposed to be a supremely cost-efficient system of social control, which produces the goods for that class whose interests the state apparatus serves, it becomes rather difficult to see how clientelism contributes to the state's fiscal 'crisis'. In their attempt to explain how something is both functional and dysfunctional, 'revisionists' tend to smuggle in a differentiation between political and economic power under the general heading 'the relative autonomy of the state'. The phrase is a bit of a nonsense in that, in the usual way, something is either autonomous or it is not, but it does offer neo-Marxists a way of explaining how motives of power rather than profit have determined the shape of southern development policies. Accordingly, it seems, the northern bourgeoisie (the nationally dominant class) has always been prepared to write off much of the capital invested in the south as part of its political strategy to contain the Communist threat. To have left the region to its natural poverty and *miseria* would have been to invite the Communists to exploit the land hunger of peasants and the bitterness of the urban poor. Therefore, capital had to be diverted from productive sectors in order to keep the lid on social tensions and institute a system of social control that would produce votes for the party of government on the basis of an obliged rather than merely grateful electorate. Naturally, local elites had to be recruited to run such a system, and if they were to be maintained as a subaltern class (the *'classe dirigente'* or the *'classe dominante'*) it was better that their access to public resources should be sanctioned by the centralised apparatus of Christian Democracy.

In making a distinction between economic and political power, 'revisionists' are able to stress the functionality of maintaining a system of 'mass' clientelism through party-directed patronage. At the same time though, they are also re-defining the purpose of southern development and the role of the dominant class in shaping it. In differentiating between political and economic criteria, 'revisionists' are also inadvertently hinting that the 'maintenance of a con-sensus' might involve policies that would be antagonistic to the interests of capital.

From the relative autonomy of the state to the relative autonomy of patrons

Even though the purpose of this 'revisionist' argument is to account for the utility of clientelism through elevating Christian Democracy to a position of relative autonomy from big business, such relativism boomerangs slightly in that it has an equal bearing on the role of southern patrons. Now it seems, southern patrons are not the gatekeepers of northern industry, but the local custodians of a political party. What is their relationship to this political party? Do they wield local power under licence and, as such, act as subordinate middlemen? Or do they constitute a bloc, an interest, which has a direct exchange relation-ship with government?

Thoroughgoing 'revisionists' would, I think, plump for the former explana-tion, arguing that as local patrons' main function is to provide blocks of votes for the party of government, their reward is the minimal one of being allowed to pillage local administrations in a more or less corrupt way. It seems to me though, that the contemporary scene in Sicily and throughout southern Italy is not one of a subaltern class doing the donkey work for its political masters, but is instead one of constant renegotiation of the exchange value of votes for public resources. According to 'revisionists', local patrons exist to provide votes, but as far as they themselves are concerned, local patrons do not provide their services to the party of government as a matter of course. It is in their interests as political entrepreneurs to strike as hard a bargain with government as they can, and furnish votes only after the government has released resources which they can put to personal use. As their local power is dependent on their stock of patronage capital, they are hardly likely to sell those votes they con-trol cheaply. Patrons in the locality understand the behavioural principles of clientelism, and it would be unnatural for them not to employ the same prin-ciples when conducting exchanges with central government.[12]

The term patronage capital is general enough to comprise those areas where a patron can so 'privatise' public resources that he can induce lop-sided exchanges with obliged clients. In this sense, public administration is a more profitable area of operation than public enterprise because there are no business managers to contend with, no board to answer to and nothing concrete to produce. Yet just as the field of public administration has expanded during this past decade, so has the scope of the *furbo* patron. If he can control access to public benefits then many more citizens will become the patron's obliged clients. The more clients he recruits the more votes he controls, and, so positioned, the better able the patron is to blackmail government into letting him run local affairs on an ever-expanding public resource base. In that the size of his *clientela* increases his bargaining power with government, the patron uses his new resources to oblige more clients to him. It is they who have been most responsible for the dramatic increases in state transfer payments in the region, and it is they who have come to determine the main part of southern development policy. Far from being a subaltern class, the autonomy with which southern patrons have been able to operate in the 1970s has made them resemble what 'revisionists' conceive of as the 'dominant class'.

This suggestion appears rather alarming, for while nobody contends that the south as a whole is not a vitally important Christian Democrat stronghold, few have argued that the strategic importance of the region affords southern patrons much leverage over party leaders, government ministers and the captains of Italian industry. It does seem strange, admittedly, to label a bunch of non-productive parasites, who emerge only occasionally from the provincial sticks, the 'dominant class'.

Southern patrons might have been subject to party discipline in the days when the party itself was administered by a coherent majority, and when a peace was preserved between the factions. Indeed, the entrepreneurial tendencies of southern political bosses were kept in check by Fanfani's party reforms of the 1950s, and through the decade of the *dorotei*. But when the dorotean majority broke up, as it did in 1969, and when factional conflict reached levels that made the creation of a new acceptable majority impossible, southern patrons could behave much more like their old-style notable predecessors, and demand more for the essential political services they performed. The 1970s was a golden period for *furbo* southern politicians. Inside the Christian Democrat party, faction leaders could be forced (through fear of defection) to pay a higher price for the loyalty of their provincial supporters, and government ministers could be made to devote special attention to the particular problems of the patron's locality. At no other time was the value of being a nuisance so clearly emphasised.[13]

In political terms, an atmosphere of 'crisis' is the patron's best friend. The shakier the governing coalition, and the more discredited the Christian Democrats' image, the more ominous the Communist threat. In such circumstances, the political significance of the south and how its electors would vote would be greater, and the protestations of local patrons about the especial needs of their localities would be heeded. The only way patrons could be made to promise to deliver the vote at the appropriate times would be for government to inject resources into their fiefs, effectively allowing them to add to their stock of patronage capital.

Political patrons and corruption

Political entrepreneurs flourish or perish according to the quantities of public resources they control (material goods and services) and the way they use their resources. Yet the patron has always to maintain the edge between possession and expenditure of the resources he controls. In other words, he must conserve more than he gives away in the form of personalised favours. He must interrupt or divert the flow of resources from state agencies to private citizens. Thus, transfer payments which are subject to the patron's controls cannot be paid out in full, nor can all those classes or categories of claimants receive the benefits that are their due. What might appear corrupt is no more than a logical consequence of the behavioural principles to which patrons and clients conform, and the changed nature of the relationship between local politicians and their notional leaders.

To talk of institutionalised corruption might sound vaguely paradoxical in that we normally associate clientelistic systems with an environment of severe resource restraint instead of abundance. Yet patrons do not necessarily preside over communities that are starved of resources. Instead, they exist on the basis of performing a balancing, or rather imbalancing, act of maximising their acquisition of resources and minimising their expenditure. If the debit-credit balance were equalised, and if resources were distributed in full to their designated areas through an 'official' system, there would be no patrons and there would be no clients.

The power of patrons, and hence the importance of clientelism has risen in this past decade as a result of the break-up of the majority within the Christian Democrat party. One of the more obvious manifestations of this power is the increase in state transfer expenditure in the southern regions. Payments to citizens are, of course, administered by local agencies whose personnel are not so much Christian Democrat men as the personal placemen of the local patron. Most obviously, the patron can quietly launder funds that come his way (he can send the money to Switzerland, or speculate in property at home and abroad), but his corruption does not stop at personal graft. Instead, he must so control public resources as to maintain himself as the indispensible link man between the citizen and public power. While he is perhaps to be credited with a good deal of entrepreneurial sense and drive, the patron is none the less a corrupt figure. On the one hand he deprives the community he serves of the benefits which are its due. On the other hand, he subverts the purpose of state transfer payments by conducting lop-sided exchanges with government and state agencies.

Politically, he renders his fief a less certain electoral 'blue chip' for the party of government, and economically, he imposes a strain on the productive sector's capacity to subsidise unproductive sectors.

Inasmuch as patrons must maintain a difference between 'real' and 'official' systems of administration, they have an interest in keeping the southern regions underdeveloped and dependent. Their achievement over this past decade has not been merely to keep the south in a state of poverty, but to make government dependent on them for their political services. What is corrupt about clientelism is, principally, that a parasitic class which 'skims off' a self-decided level of surplus should, by its actions, contradict the interests of the nationally dominant class. The fact that they perform no recognisable productive or reproductive function is, perhaps, neither here nor there, but southern patrons show no sign of succumbing to the process of modernisation. Ironically, the power of patrons will remain for as long as the Communist party is the only alternative governing party to Christian Democracy, and for as long as southerners persist in believing that they are all *furbi*.

Notes and references

1. See Edward Banfield, *The Moral Basis of a Backward Society*, Glencoe, Ill., Free Press, 1958.
2. These qualifying comments are talked through in the introduction to S. N. Eisenstadt and René Lemarchand's reader, *Political Clientelism, Patronage and Development*, Contemporary Political Sociology Vol. 3, Beverly Hills, Calif., Sage, 1981.
3. See E. R. Wolf, *Peasants*, Englewood Cliffs, N.J., Prentice-Hall, 1966.
4. The literature on the Mafia is extensive, but not much of what is published is very analytic (e.g. M. Pantaleone, *Mafia and Politics*, London, Chatto and Windus, 1966 and Norman Lewis, *The Honoured Society: The Mafia Conspiracy Observed*, London, Collins, 1964); Henner Hess, *Mafia and Mafiosi*, Lexington, Mass., Saxon House, 1970 is analytic, if rather pedestrian. Perhaps the best study of all is Anton Blok, *The Mafia of a Sicilian Village*, Oxford, Basil Blackwell, 1974.
5. The first two of these phrases are extracted from Anne Anfossi, *Ragusa: Communita in Transizione*, Turin, Taylor, 1959. The last idea is from J. Boissevain's 'Patronage in Sicily', *Man* (NS), I (1966), 18–33.
6. These, some of the earliest definitional terms given to patron–client ties were coined by J. K. Campbell, *Honour, Family and Patronage*, Oxford, Clarendon Press, 1964; J. A. Pitt-Rivers, *People of the Sierra*, Chicago, Phoenix Books, 1966; and M. Kenny in J. G. Peristiany (ed.), *Acts of the Mediterranean Sociological Conference*, The Hague, Mouton, 1963.
7. This idea comes from P. Littlewood, 'Patrons, Ideology and Reproduction', *Critique of Anthropology*, 4, No. 15 (1980), 29–47.
8. The term 'strategic reserve' has acquired such a wide currency that it is difficult to attribute it to any one original source. Percy Allum uses it widely in his chapter 'La Ricostruzione del Sistema Meridionale' in *L'Italia: tra crisi e emergenze*, Naples, Guida, 1979.
9. See S. Tarrow, 'The political economy of stagnation: Communism in Southern Italy: 1960-1970', *Journal of Politics*, 34, 1972.
10. The clearest exposition of this thesis is written by E. Mingione in his preface to Nella Ginatempo, *La Citta del Sud: Territorio e classi sociali*, Milan, Mazzotta, 1976.
11. See Robert Wade, 'Fast Growth and Slow Development', in D. Seers, B. Schaffer and M-L. Kiljunen (eds), *Underdeveloped Europe*, Brighton, Sussex, Harvester Press, 1979.

12. Of course, all this rather clouds the issue of who is the patron and who is the client. Judith Chubb, 'The Social Bases of an Urban Political Machine', in Eisenstadt and Lemarchand (op. cit.) talks of clients being able to blackmail their patrons on occasion, but hedges on the question of whether clients can, over a protracted period, impose their demands on patrons. In another context, Joseph LaPalombara, *Interest Groups in Italian Politics*, Princeton, Princeton University Press, 1964, introduces the same idea when he talks of *clientela* and *parentela*. As he says, it is sometimes better for a group to be in a *clientela* relationship with a government ministry (e.g. Confindustria and the Ministry of Industry) than it is to be in a *parentela* relationship (e.g. the Church and the government). The notion that patrons might also be clients is a useful one in that it underlines the mutability of patron–client exchanges over time.
13. See Percy Allum, *Politics and Society in Post-war Naples*, Cambridge, Cambridge University Press, 1973, for a chapter on the careers of Lauro and Gava.

Further reading

Abercrombie, N. and Hill, S., 'Paternalism and Patronage', *British Journal of Sociology*, 27, No. 4, 1976.
Ammassari, P., 'Classes and Class Relationships in Contemporary Italian Society', *Il Politico*, 44, No. I, 1979.
Bailey, F. G. (ed.), *Gifts and Poisons: The Politics of Reputation*, Oxford, Basil Blackwell, 1971, especially 'What are Signori' by F. G. Bailey.
Boissevain, J., *Friends of Friends*, Oxford, Basil Blackwell, 1974.
Brogger, J., *Montaverese: A study of Peasant Society and Culture in Southern Italy*, Bergen-Oslo-Tromso, Universitet Forlaget, 1971.
Cancian, F., 'The Southern Italian Peasant: World View and Political Behaviour', *Anthropology Quarterly*, 34, 1961.
Chapman, G., 'Development and Underdevelopment in Southern Italy', *Reading Geographical Papers*, No. 41, Reading University Geography Dept., 1976.
Colclough, N. T., 'Social Mobility and Social Control in a Southern Italian Village' in F. G. Bailey (ed.), *Gifts and Poisons*, op. cit.
Cronin, C., *The Sting of Change*, Chicago, Chicago University Press, 1970.
Davis, J., *People of the Mediterranean*, Library of Man series, London, Routledge and Kegan Paul, 1977.
Flynn, P., 'Class, Clientelism and Coercion: Some Mechanisms of Internal Dependency and Control', *Journal of Commonwealth and Comparative Studies*, 12, No. 2, 1974.
Galt, A., 'Rethinking Patron–Client Relationships: The Real System and the Official System in Southern Italy', *Anthropology Quarterly*, 47, 1974.
Glasser, R., *The Net and the Quest: Patterns of Community and How They Can Survive Progress*, London, Temple Smith, 1977.
Graziani, A., 'The Mezzogiorno and the Italian Economy', *Cambridge Journal of Economics*, 2, 1978.
Graziano, L., 'A Conceptual Framework for the Study of Clientelistic Relationships', *European Journal of Political Research*, 14, No. 2, 1976.
Pizzorno, A., 'Amoral Familism and Historic Marginality', *International Revue of Community Development*, 15, No. 16, 1966.
Schneider, J. and P., *Culture and Political Economy in Western Sicily*, New York, Academic Press, 1976.
Tarrow, S., *Peasant Communism in Southern Italy*, New Haven, Yale University Press, 1967.
Weingrod, A., 'Patrons, Patronage and Political Parties', *Comparative Studies in Society and History*, No. 10, 1968.

9 On presidential graft: the Latin American evidence

LAURENCE WHITEHEAD

Why focus on presidential graft?

To focus on the way heads of state use their office for illicit personal (or family) enrichment may seem to trivialise and sensationalise the much more serious and widespread phenomenon of political corruption. A critic might object that whether or not an individual president was personally venal must be quite accidental—what matters for the country as a whole is whether or not the political machine under his care operates to any significant extent under the incentives of graft. It is not difficult to find examples of personally incorruptible rulers who select and manipulate their subordinates by appealing to their greed —after all, to become a president normally requires great dedication and single-mindedness, so that the selection process can be expected to favour those with an appetite for power rather than merely a lust for money. Forced to choose between the certainty of future wealth and the possibility of continued power, most heads of state are likely to opt for the latter (although one or two apparent exceptions, such as Batista in 1958, have occasionally clouded this generalisation). Surely, a chapter on political corruption, which narrows the focus to purely presidential graft, leaves out too much and reduces the subject to the level of mere anecdote and journalistic polemic?

Certainly if one consults the standard academic reader on *Political Corruption* (an excellent compilation edited by Arnold J. Heidenheimer) only six of the fifty-eight articles included therein encompass presidential graft as part of their subject matter, and even these mostly concentrate on the more elusive and diffuse topic of 'low-level corruption'. Although many of these articles are informative and suggestive, such an approach raises many difficulties which need not arise in the discussion of presidential graft. For example, with 'low-level corruption' there is the problem of encountering a suitable objective definition—some writers shuddered at the thought that they might be imposing values derived from Western industrial society on conduct which was perceived quite differently in a 'non-Western' context. However, in the case of flagrant personal enrichment by Latin American rulers, this problem does not arise to the same extent; those not enjoying the spoils are just as likely to resent the illicit privileges of their top leaders in Latin America as people in the United States of America, even though their opportunities for protest and redress may be fewer. Of course at the margin there are still problems of definition about what constitutes abuse of office, but I am little troubled by this objection since so few of the individuals discussed in this chapter operated anywhere near the margin. I would also claim that in the case of presidential graft the problem of marshalling reliable and representative evidence, although substantial, is more manageable than in the case of low-level corruption. Furthermore, the causes and consequences of, and the alternatives to, political corruption (generally nebulous and uncertain in the literature on the low-level variant) seem clearer and more specific in the case of presidential graft.

But is the evidence on presidential graft really sufficiently accurate and comprehensive to justify such claims? There are obvious motives both for exaggerating and understating the scale of graft committed by any individual president, and where possible both a high and a low estimate are given. Most of the argument would hold just as well whether the numbers were halved or doubled. The most likely source of inaccuracy would be if a large number of presidents had engaged in extensive peculation without yet being discovered or denounced. Fortunately there is detailed information on enough cases to show that the phenomenon is widespread and involves huge sums, and to explain how it operates. Likewise it may seem an omission to exclude personally honest presidents who tolerate corruption among their subordinates, but even without cases of this kind (which are, of course, difficult to interpret objectively), there is enough material to work on.

But how can one be sure that the slanderous accusations so frequently made against Latin American ex-presidents are not partisan fabrications? It is, in all probability, this fear of taking gossip for fact (and thereby insulting named individuals who may still have a large political following) which to a large extent explains why academics have focussed chiefly on low-level generalised corruption, rather than on presidential graft. Imperfect though they may be, the sources used here are sufficiently varied, serious and specific to uphold a fairly substantial general argument. Naming names on the basis of second-hand reports has obvious drawbacks but also some compensating advantages. By *personalising* corruption one can clarify motives and bring into sharper focus the usually inconclusive debate about consequences and alternatives. Unlike imprecise forms of low-level corruption, for example, it cannot be claimed that presidential graft is good for society because it 'softens the rigidities of the bureaucracy' for poor citizens, or represents socially desirable 'speed money' for circumventing red tape. Even in their general form such arguments evade the likelihood that a bureaucracy which profits from rigidity and red tape will tend to reinforce these characteristics. If the president chooses to profit from rather than curtailing them, there can be little ambiguity about the case of these social ills or the possibility of an alternative to them.

In fact in Latin America the office of the presidency generally concentrates so much power and responsibility in the person of a single leader that an accurate analysis of political corruption must personalise and must devote special attention to the Chief Executive. Indeed, in a significant number of extreme cases, the head of state has harnessed the whole apparatus of state power to the task of advancing his own personal enrichment until it seems as though the first aim of political activity in certain countries (especially around the Caribbean area) is to facilitate the systematic 'extraction of surplus' on his behalf. The massive implications such an abuse of office can have for the distribution of property, level of investment and overall economic policy of certain relatively small poor economies should be made apparent below. Such cases can provide an unusually clear demonstration of the ultimate supremacy of politics over economics that is possible in determining the allocation of resources when no internal checks and balances are left in operation. Fortunately Somoza's Nicaragua is not typical of Latin America as a whole, and there are other republics in which well established institutions and procedures regulate the interaction between political and economic elites. But even in the most advanced republics, institutional defences against high-level corruption are characteristically weak, and hence Somoza-like practices intermittently arise in privileged enclaves of the state bureaucracy. Limited corruption can always occur despite presidential vigilance, of course, but on a large-scale systematic basis it normally must require at least his tacit acquiescence and, more likely, his personal supervision.[1]

The incidence of presidential graft

Not all presidential graft is hidden from the public. Some rulers have chosen to be quite brazen about what they were doing. For example, after President Trujillo, the 'benefactor' of the Dominican Republic (1930–61), took over the country's only shoe factory there was no secret about the ensuing decree forbidding anyone in the capital from going barefoot. Visiting American journalists reported with enthusiasm that the country was less poverty-stricken than they had expected—e.g. everyone wore shoes—but domestic opinion cannot have been deceived. Likewise President Zayas of Cuba (1921–5) made no secret of his attitude towards the National Lottery: 'his wife notoriously always drew the first prize and his daughter the second—both without shame' (Braden, *Diplomats and Demagogues*, p. 292). For every one such instance, of course, there are a dozen uncheckable rumours. Excluding such instances for lack of evidence, how many heads of state either paraded their corruption, like Zayas (who in 1925 signed a $2.7 million government contract with the statement that he had 300,000 good reasons for doing so (Thomas, *Cuba: The Pursuit of Freedom*, p. 572)) or were effectively exposed? Table 9.1 (referring to the twenty-one republics of the Western hemisphere, including the USA) gives my provisional estimate.

A significant proportion of Western hemisphere republics seem to be involved and this tentative estimate indicates no tendency for the number of countries

Table 9.1   Strong Evidence of Presidential Graft

1932	1952	1972
5	6	6

involved to fall. Only Nicaragua appears in all three periods, however; Cuba and Venezuela, both of which appear in 1932 and 1952, are not included in 1972, and the reverse is true for the USA. Table 9.1 is, however, a very crude indicator of the incidence of presidential graft, for it puts Richard Nixon's alleged $576,000 tax fraud on the same basis as Rafael Leonidas Trujillo's grandiose achievements, which his biographer values at $500 million.[2] An alternative indicator of the probable scale of president corruption is given in Table 9.2, which is drawn from evidence about the twenty Latin American republics in the decade before the Alliance for Progress. This time the USA is omitted, since its economy is so much larger and the scale of its political graft is so relatively small. It presents figures for the reported fortunes of five presidents ousted between 1952 and 1961. Even the most well grounded of these estimates (that concerning Trujillo) is subject to a large margin of error. In addition there is a more serious source of distortion in the cases of Aleman and Peron. In the first case the figures refer to the amounts allegedly 'deposited in foreign banks' by Aleman 'and the high officials of his administration' between 1946 and 1952 (*New York Times*, as reported in Lieuwen, *Arms and Politics in Latin America*, p. 150); and although Lieuwen's figure of $700 million for Peron supposedly refers to the amount he 'escaped with' in 1955 (ibid., p. 149), if it is accurate it must surely include the funds appropriated by his subordinates over the preceding decade.[3] But if these two items tend to overstate the total value of strictly presidential graft in the period, Table 9.2 suffers from an offsetting distortion, which may well exert an equally powerful effect on the total, in the opposite direction. It makes no allowance for the personal fortunes of at least five other presidents who were ousted over the same period and who are sometimes alleged to have enriched themselves on a substantial scale in the process. Balancing up these considerations it is not unlikely that the presidential fortunes which 'matured' in Latin America over the 1952–61 decade totalled somewhere around $2,000 million. If Trujillo, with over one-third of his money in foreign banks, was representative[4] then, on fairly cautious assumptions, capital flight attributable to presidential graft would have totalled around $700 million. This bears comparison with the $795 million received by Latin America as a whole over the same decade in the form of much publicised 'official grants' to promote the economic development of the continent. It can also be compared with the size of the external public debt of the republic in question at the date of the ouster (see the last column in Table 9.2), which indicates the macro-economic significance of this degree of presidential graft.[5]

Table 9.2   Reported Fortunes of Some Presidents Ousted Between
1952 and 1961

Ousted	Name	Country	Estimated fortune ($m.)	Comments	External public debt ($m.)
1952	Aleman	Mexico	500–800	includes top cronies	509 (1950)
1955	Peron	Argentina	500–700	least documented	442
1958	Perez Jimenez	Venezuela	over 250	add $100m. for his ordinance chief	227
1958	Batista	Cuba	100–300	higher figure more likely	about 800
1961	Trujillo	Dominican Republic	500		6
Total			1,850–2,650		

Sources: Lieuwen, *Arms and Politics in Latin America*, pp. 149–50, for Aleman, Peron and Perez Jimenez, also allegations against Arbenz, Magloire and Rojas Pinilla, all 'gleaned from a variety of newspaper reports'. (Lieuwen probably also had access to confidential US government sources.) On Aleman's personal fortune, see below. Thomas, op. cit., p. 1027, quotes Batista's ex-press secretary as estimating his master's personal fortune in 1958 at $300 million (Batista was a sergeant when he first entered politics in 1933). See also Crassweller, *Trujillo*, p. 279. For corruption under Kubitshek see Gerassi, *The Great Fear in Latin America*, p. 385, according to whom the governor of one state (Governor Lupion of Parana) was accused of embezzling over $100 million. Sir George Bolton estimated that by 1963 the Latin American capital invested outside the continent exceeded $5,000 million in total (*Annual Review of BOLSA*, 1962–3, quoted by Thomas, p. 1184).

If we take a longer time horizon can we identify any trend in the incidence of presidential graft? Certainly if we follow Samuel P. Huntington's analysis of the correlates of political corruption in general we should expect its incidence to fluctuate over time. He considers that: 'Corruption may be more prevalent in some cultures than in others but in most cultures it seems to be most prevalent during the most intense phase of modernisation' (Heidenheimer, p. 492). In the context of twentieth-century Latin America it is not easy to give these categories such as modernisation a clear empirical content. When were the basic values of, say, Mexican or Venezuelan society 'traditional'? When did Brazil or Cuba undergo their 'most intense phase of modernisation'? The onus must rest with the modernisation theorists to demonstrate the applicability of their categories. There is, however, sufficient information about purely presidential graft in twentieth-century Cuba, Mexico and Venezuela to demonstrate that it persisted on a large scale for at least half a century. Indeed it could be encountered in a variety of different contexts including the fast-rising prosperity of Cuba (up to 1925); the economic and social stagnation or retrogression of the same island from 1925 to 1958; the political and economic disaster that was

Mexico for a generation after 1910; the essentially peasant society that was Venezuela under Gomez and the sophisticated urban society of Brazil in the 1950s.

Consider the record of presidential graft in *Cuba, 1909–58* extracted from *Cuba: The Pursuit of Freedom* by Hugh Thomas (which gives exhaustive further details).

President Gomez 1909–13: 'known as the Shark . . . he ended his Presidency a millionaire after having entered it quite poor' (p. 504).

President Menocal 1913–21: 'was understood to have possessed $1 million in 1913 when he became President; when he left in 1921 he had perhaps $40 million' (p. 524).

President Zayas 1921–5: in 1923 '14 members of his family obtained advantageous or strategic positions. Not only the rest of the loan [a foreign loan of $50 million] but in addition the annual revenue of $81 million was used up before further employees could be paid, and bogus bridges were once again provided for in lavish maintenance grants, as in Menocal's day' (p. 555).

President Machado 1925–33: 'the President and his friends absorbed a graft equivalent to a fifth of the national product [Thomas must mean national budget] or $10 million a year' (p. 581).

Fulgencio Bastista, strongman 1933–40, President 1940–4: in 1953 Fidel Castro denounced Batista (newly returned to power) as 'not content with the $40 million that crowned his first regime' (p. 489). Obviously such an estimate by Castro may be considered suspect, but deals of specific rakeoffs to Batista identified by Sprille Braden, US Ambassador to Cuba 1942–5, confirm its plausibility. One instance of a $2 million bribe, of which Batista received $400,000, is quoted in Braden's memoirs, *Diplomats and Demagogues*, p. 293.

President Grau 1944–8: in February 1949 the ex-president 'was forced to appear before the courts, accused by the government of having misappropriated $174 million' (p. 761). However 'on July 4th 1949 the court in which his case was being heard was broken into by six masked men who . . . stole 35 files of documents relating to the proceedings' (p. 764). Eventually in March 1951 'Grau was finally indicted with ten of his ex-ministers (two existing congressmen among them) for the theft of $40 million' (p. 768).

President Prio 1948–52: on 10 March 1953 President Batista publicly 'accused Prio and his brother of stealing $20 million from the Treasury: they replied from Mexico that it had been lent to them' (p. 801).

President Batista 1952–8: 'it is of course obscure to what extent Batista enriched himself. His press secretary in exilé and one who was for a time youth leader of his party estimated his fortune in 1958 as $300 million, mostly invested abroad in Switzerland, Florida, New York or Mexico (p. 1027, which also contains a footnote giving the more modest alternative of more than $100 million).[6] If intense 'modernisation' was going on in Cuba over this fifty-year period, it was surely proceeding in slow motion. But, it might be objected, Cuba was a notorious exception, distorted by the overpowering US influence in the island since 1898. (The only other major country with a comparable history of such protracted US predominance is the Philippines, where by many accounts even more lavish political graft has flourished for an even longer period.) How about the trend in *Venezuela* over the same half century?

President Gomez 1910-35: 'it seemed as though the only beneficiaries of the Gomez system, besides the oil firms, were himself, his family, the military officers, and his Tachira friends in high government positions. Gomez ran the nation as the private preserve of his own family and the army. Through various kinds of graft, particularly peculation in dealing with oil concessions, and through confiscating the property of his opponents, he became the nation's largest landholder. His accumulated fortune in cattle, coffee plantations, industrial plant, and real estate was estimated at over $200 million' (Lieuwen, *Venezuela*, p. 49).

President Lopez Contreras 1935-41 and President Medina Angarita 1941-5: 'each during his term of office made off with about $13 million, then following the 1945 revolution retired in New York' (Andreski, *Parasitism and Subversion: The Case of Latin America*, p. 76).

President Perez Jimenez 1952-8: 'Perez Jimenez is estimated to have accumulated a fortune of over $250 million during his entire tenure of office, his ordinance chief Colonel Palido Barreto over $100 million (largely through transportation and parking meter concessions), while lesser officials made away with additional millions' (Lieuwen, op. cit., p. 98).

The evidence of these two countries and similar evidence of presidential graft in Mexico over the first half of the twentieth century, which I shall omit for reasons of space, might cast doubt on the precision with which any meaningful indicator of 'intense modernisation' can be expected to correlate with gross presidential graft in Latin America. However, the passage quoted by Huntington also hinted at an alternative explanation of the distribution of corruption, which might seem to fit the record better. 'Corruption may be more prevalent in some cultures than in others', he wrote, and further on he expands this line of argument (drawing on the authority of Needler, *Political Development in Latin America*, Ch. 6) as follows:

In the 'mulatto' countries (Panama, Cuba, Venezuela, Dominican Republic and Haiti) of Latin America 'there appears to be greater social equality and much less rigidity in the social structure' than in the Indian (Mexico, Ecuador, Guatemala, Peru, Bolivia) or *mestizo* (Chile, Colombia, El Salvador, Honduras, Nicaragua, Paraguay) countries. Correspondingly, however, the relative 'absence of an entrenched upper class means also the absence of a governing class ethic with its sense of *noblesse oblige*' and hence 'there seems little doubt that it is countries in this socio-racial category in which political graft reaches its most flagrant heights'. [Heidenheimer, op. cit., p. 496.]

There are, in fact, no grounds whatsoever for the supposition that political graft has been less flagrant in 'Indian' Mexico under Miguel Aleman (1946–52) or 'Indian' Bolivia under General Rene Barrientos (1964–8), nor that these countries could be characterised by a governing class with a sense of *noblesse oblige*. It might be countered, however, that these two regimes both arose in countries where a social revolution had shattered the old ruling class and, in any case, perhaps the generalisation is more well grounded in the case of the countries Needler has rather oddly classified as *mestizo*? General Anastasio Somoza (effective ruler of Nicaragua 1932–56) completed his education in Philadelphia in the twenties, while General Alfredo Stroessner of Paraguay (1954–present) still cherishes relatives in Hof, Bavaria. These two rulers are neither mulattos nor revolutionary upstarts and may indeed pride themselves in their sense of *noblesse oblige*. But for all that, the higher forms of political corruption are integral to their systems of government (which have sometimes been labelled 'sultanistic').

Consider Stroessner's regime. 'Since the early sixties the contraband traffic has replaced the public sector as the major source of finance for the purchase of equipment by the Paraguayan armed forces', a journalist report in *Latin America Newsletter*, 19 November 1971. This report continued:

Arms for the armoured divisions, which were previously paid for by siphoning funds from the state alcohol monopoly (APAL), are now financed out of the profits from the traffic in contraband cigarettes, which is controlled by the chief of the *Caballarria*—General Andres Rodriguez. Traffic in scotch whisky has likewise replaced funds from the state water board (CORPOSANA) in the case of Stroessner's own crack *Regimiento Escolta*. And the traffic in heroin has replaced the customs department as the major financial support for the counter-insurgency Regimiento group—RI14—whose chief, General Patricio Colman, is one of the organizers of the heroin smuggling.[7] General Rodriguez handles re-export by air with old DC-4's belonging to the government, and also his own private fleet of Cessnas. River borne contraband is handled by Rear-Admiral Hugo Gonzalez.

It is on this basis that President Stroessner has retained the backing of the Paraguayan military for his almost thirty years of personal dictatorship.

The evidence is clear that presidential graft in Latin America is widespread, has persisted over long periods of time and can often involve very large magnitudes in relation to the scale of overall economic activity. A more detailed review of the literature would demonstrate that its occurrence is not confined to the smallest republics, nor to the poorest republics, nor to dictatorships,

nor to countries where the population has any particular racial or social characteristics, nor is it limited to the 'intense phase of modernisation', whatever
that may be; nor to highly regulated economies. Perhaps these may seem rather
obvious and negative findings, but they do contradict some common assertions
and they serve to indicate that presidential graft is an important phenomenon
in its own right, not to be subsumed under vague culturally defined notions of
a diffuse propensity towards corruption.

This section has provided some concrete descriptions of important instances
of corrupt behaviour, which are necessary before one can realistically assess the
consequences of political corruption, or the alternatives to it. These are the
questions to be considered below.

Consequences and alternatives

Most of the explicit discussion of the consequences of political corruption
has been by American political scientists. Although there is, of course, no
consensus, these writers have tended to adopt what might be termed a *real-
politik* stance on the issue, determined not to condemn the phenomenon
out of hand, in a way which would once have been instinctive to all right-
thinking liberals. A conscious effort is made to avoid such 'moralism' and
instead to draw up a balance sheet showing the social costs and benefits of
political corruption. In some societies, at some stages in their history, it would
seem political corruption is a lesser social evil than the alternatives.[8]

In this section I shall briefly assess two of the main types of social benefit,
which, it is sometimes suggested,[9] could justify some forms of political corruption. In the light of my evidence limited to presidential graft in Latin America,
this concluding section assesses one economic argument (that it may be good
for efficiency, the rate of accumulation and therefore the rate of growth); and
one political argument (that it provides a way of resolving political disputes
and integrating disaffected groups, which substitute for violence and upheaval).
Since no assessment of either of these supposed benefits can be made without
also implying some opinion about the alternatives available, this section also
considers one major alternative to gross presidential corruption that has been
potentially available in Latin America.

It will be apparent that this alternative is one which successive US governments (and some prominent US wealth-holders with Latin American connections) have consistently considered even less desirable than political corruption.
Their reasons, however, have been quite different from those proposed by the
realpolitik school of American political scientists.

First let us consider the alleged economic benefits that some forms of political
corruption may bestow. The 'speed money' argument, as we saw earlier, only
works (if at all) for low-level corruption; Latin American presidents generally
have alternative methods of corruption at their disposal if they wish to rush

specific measures through the bureaucratic machine. It is thus the 'accumulation' argument on which the supposed economic benefits must depend, and to make this clear Nye distinguished between insecure corrupt rulers (who will tend to send their money to Swiss banks) and secure corrupt rulers (who may reinvest the surplus they have illegally extracted from consumers, in which case presidential graft might accelerate the rate of economic growth).[10] Nye writes:

> Too great insecurity means that any capital formed by corruption will tend to be exported rather than invested at home. In Nicaragua, for instance, it is argued that the sense of security of the Somoza family encouraged them in internal investments in economic projects and the strengthening of their political party, which led to impressive economic growth and diminished direct reliance on the army. [Heidenheimer, op. cit., p. 574.]

So let us examine the example of Nicaragua. General Anastasio Somoza (senior) became head of the National Guard in 1932, while US Marines still occupied the country.[11] According to the *Financial Times*, 12 May 1972, after forty years of family rule, the current Somoza's business interests, variously estimated to be worth between 150 and 200 million dollars, stretch into the national airlines, LANICA, the country's only shipping line, MAMENIC, cattle and meat packing, fishing, rum and beer, hotels, banking, cement, radio, television and newspapers. And the president is also the local agent for Mercedes Benz. (Nicaragua's GNP was 800 million dollars, to be divided among a population of two million.) Then on 23 December 1972 an earthquake caused damage estimated by the same newspaper (10 May 1973) at $845 million, and left 250,000 homeless. The *Latin American Newsletter* reported on 9 February 1973 that 'because of the now desperate shortage of foreign exchange, there will for some time be few imports of expensive cars, liquor, cigarettes and luxury goods, whose passage round the customs posts was so beneficial to national guard officers. Another lucrative prize, especially for officers just before retirement, has been control of brothels, bars and gambling houses; but of course in Managua these are now mostly rubble, and provincial cities are heavily engaged in looking after refugees.'
When offers of help and emergency supplies poured in,

> From the very first, General Somoza demanded that all food and medical supplies should be made over to his government for distribution through the canton or neighbourhood system, which is virtually identified with his Nationalist Liberal Party . . . A senior member of the Spanish embassy saw his relief supplies pilfered by the authorities at Managua airport and was insulted when he protested (etc.) . . . Last week in Managua a reliable foreign eyewitness recounted to me how at Christmas he had seen senior officials, charged with the suppression of looting, dividing among themselves goods looted from the damaged stores in the disaster zone . . . General Somoza, as

he told me himself last Friday, has no worries at all about getting all the money he needs from the US. The US embassy, fearful of any change in the government . . . is likely to spend $100 million a year for the next two years on aid to the government . . . [Yet] as one relief worker in Managua remarked, the Somoza family, which with 22,000 employees is a larger employer than the state, could afford to pay all the damage itself, and still not be poor. [*Financial Times*, 10 May 1973.]

Thus the Nicaraguan example appears to confirm that, given sufficient political security, it is possible in a small country to found a dynasty based on presidential graft and so reinvest the surplus thereby extracted that the economy as a whole can eventually be converted into a personally owned fiefdom. Whether or not this produces a socially optimal level and pattern of investments is more debatable, since even from a narrowly economic point of view this degree of monopoly power can be expected to distort all the supposedly normal market mechanisms. If the definition of social welfare is broadened to include such variables as the distribution of income and wealth, the case becomes still weaker; and 'moralistic' though it may seem, many observers might hesitate to classify economic growth policies that require the systematic subjugation and even degradation of an entire population group in the interests of an all-powerful dynasty as socially desirable.

The other supposedly beneficial consequence of political corruption concerns its possible contribution to the non-violent resolution of social conflicts. In what follows, two strands of this argument are identified and two relevant case studies considered. Firstly, if a country seems threatened by violent conflicts, can its people opt for an appropriate amount of presidential graft, just sufficient to stifle the violence and no more? The Dominican Republic example is considered. Secondly, where extensive presidential graft has become established, can it be relied upon to substitute for violent conflict, or may it in fact generate further violence? Batista's Cuba provides a suitable case study. This example brings us naturally enough to the question of whether there is a connection between political corruption and social revolution, and if so, of what kind.

Two opposing hypotheses have been proposed concerning the connection between corruption and political instability: *The Economist* has suggested that the average costs of corruption may diminish over the life of a regime as it becomes more secure, whereas a Singapore Minister of Foreign Affairs has re-stated the old maxim that 'l'appétit vient en mangeant', *The Economist* of 15 June 1957 quoted a comment about one South American dictator as follows: 'it is cheaper for the country that he should be president for life, because he has made his fortune and is satisfied. When we changed presidents every few years the cost of presidential fortunes used to ruin us' (in Heidenheimer, op. cit., p. 491). The Foreign Minister of Singapore put the opposite view:

it is, I think, in the very nature of kleptocracy to progressively increase the size of its loot. For one thing, the kleptocrat can stay in power only by bringing more and more supporters to his side, and this means that the size of his loot must increase. As the years go by he must win over all the instruments of state power—the army, the police, the entrepreneurs, and the bureaucracy. If he must loot then he must allow his subordinates from the permanent secretary to the office boy to join in the game. [Ibid., p. 548.]

Generalissimo Rafael Leonidas Trujillo holds the record as the longest-lasting life president in twentieth-century Latin America. This self-styled 'benefactor' ruled the Dominican Republic for thirty-one years, so his case provides a suitable test of these rival contentions. His biographer tells us that as early in his career as 1939 'estimates of family income ran to more than $2,000,000 annually. A more heady estimate, from a bank source in this same year, put Trujillo's personal income as high as $200,000 a month.' But it seems his acquisitiveness was never dimmed by satiation, and indeed by the 1950s he had proceeded to take over much of the republic's sugar industry, where he reportedly 'made every technical mistake in the operation of this industry that it was possible to make, and on a cash-flow basis the entire operation lost money' (Crassweller, p. 259). Even at this stage he was still keenly interested in adding to his assets, as Harry Kantor's account makes clear:

On practically every transaction by the government Trujillo got a ten per cent cut. This was brought into the open in 1957 when a committee of the US Senate was investigating a corporation that deducted a $1.8 million bribe to Trujillo as a legitimate expense from its taxable income. The US Internal Revenue Commissioner, justifying the allowance of the deduction, states 'Bribes are an ordinary and necessary business expense to do work in the Dominican Republic' [Kantor, *Patterns of Politics and Political Systems in Latin America*, p. 320].[12]

Thus the Dominican Republic example runs counter to the hypothesis suggested by *The Economist*. On the contrary it would seem that, given long enough, an unrestrained system of presidential graft can expand far beyond the limits that could possibly be justified by terms of the supposed need for corruption in order to 'resolve conflicts' without upheaval.

This brings us to a final aspect of the argument that corruption can be socially desirable—namely, the claim that in some circumstances and in suitable amounts it can be an alternative to large-scale violence, rather than an extra source of social upheaval. However, in the words of the Singapore Foreign Minister quoted above, the successful kleptocrat will always need to protect his position. Furthermore, most of the benefits of such high-level graft accrue to a rather small number of highly visible public functionaries, while almost invariably the costs are borne by a far larger number of people who would therefore be very likely to turn against the rulers if they had the information and the opportunity. Hence large-scale kleptocrats, like those named above, are obliged to use extensive violence in order to deny their subjects such information and such opportunities. To demonstrate that presidential graft is a substitute for violence, it is not sufficient to show that in the short run it averts political upheaval. For thirty-one years there was no political upheaval in the Dominican Republic, yet in a single notorious episode of Trujillo's rule (October 1937) he ordered a massacre in which, according to his biographer, a 'reasonable estimate' of the deaths would be 15–20,000 (Crassweller, p. 156). Far fewer died in the 'political upheaval' of 1961 which followed the dictator's assassination and even the tragic 'civil war' of 1965 (itself in many ways a delayed reaction to the legacy of Trujillo's corruption) was less bloody than that year of kleptocratic 'political stability', 1937. Nor is it sufficient to claim that the country would have been just as violent under an incorruptible president: the claim that presidential graft is socially desirable requires that in its absence there would have been even more violent conflict and/or that the violence would be more futile. Considering the amount of violence usually associated with presidential graft, this would be a difficult claim to establish at all convincingly.

Pre-revolutionary Cuba provides an appropriate conclusion to this discussion both of political violence and of presidential graft. This extreme case demonstrates that at least in some circumstances these two social evils can get entirely out of hand, and feed on each other. Taken in conjunction with the recent experience of Nicaragua, the Cuban example strongly suggests that such 'sultanistic' regimes may have extreme difficulty in curbing their excesses or in preserving a minimum basis of social support. Consequently they may be highly vulnerable to challenges from revolutionary partisans, and if they collapse the resulting scope for drastic social changes may be unusually large.

Despite Nye's general scepticism on the subject,[13] the Cuban example in fact suggests that large-scale corruption may well be a major factor contributing to the outbreak of social revolution. Here is the interpretation given by James O'Connor:

Under Batista's last government, the corruption system was extended and more elaborate, and elevated to an everyday system of business. A confidential business report service described the system: 'The "Collector" is an important man on the island. Everybody doing business, from the cabbie to a hole-in-the-wall shop must pay to the regime's and the machine's ambulatory cash register. Veritable scales have been set for anything from street vendors to big businessmen . . . [graft] probably has never risen to such heights (or dropped to such depths), nor has it ever been so efficient, as under Batista . . . In the years preceding the revolution, the average amount of graft in public works (alone) cost as much as the works themselves. About three-fifths of the budget of the Public Health Ministry was stolen, and about one-third of the Education Ministry budget . . . it was common for teachers and school inspectors to sell their positions for one half or less of their salaries. Successive regimes failed to clean up the education racket, graft in the ministries . . . and the systematic corruption in the armed forces. These interests, particularly the latter, had to be respected in order to maintain the consensus. Thus . . . segments of all classes profited by the system, yet at the same time the system thwarted the aspirations and plans of all classes' [quoted in Bonachea and Valdés (eds), *Cuba in Revolution*, pp. 71–3].

O'Connor therefore argues that 'Cuba's system of corruption and bribery was at once one way in which Batista maintained a consensus of support, and one source of his downfall; its inequities, irrationalities, and hardships helped to win for Castro's 26th of July movement allies in all layers of society' (ibid., p. 70). Confirmation of this judgement can be found in the work of Mesa-Lago, who argues that the anti-corruption theme in Castro's campaign caused many rival property owners to welcome his triumph, and that in early 1959 even urban capitalists willingly paid back taxes on a massive scale in the hope that under an honest regime there could be a return to economic expansion. Even among such wealthy groups, he claims, the confiscation of property from Batista's henchmen was not disliked (*Revolutionary Change in Cuba*, pp. 357–8 and 364–6).

In short, at least in Cuba gross corruption engendered additional violence and political alienation, and indeed paved the way for a sweeping and puritanical social revolution. To say this is not to romanticise the Cuban revolution (which has uprooted at least half a million Cubans), but merely to state that it offers an alternative to the types of political corruption discussed above. Obviously the alternative is more attractive to some groups and interests than to others, but since those who attempt a cost benefit analysis of political corruption are bound to make counter-factual assumptions, they would do better to consider at least one of the alternatives to political corruption that has in fact now been adopted in two Latin republics formerly plagued by presidential graft (Cuba and Nicaragua). Naming these two instances may indicate why Washington policymakers so often regard political corruption a 'lesser of evils'. It also suggests what the *realpolitik* school of political scientists were really about (perhaps unwittingly) when they stamped an imprimatur of academic respectability on the notion of 'socially beneficial forms of corruption'.

Notes

1. In the largest republics, state governors may exercise a substantial degree of autonomy, at least on routine matters, and the central executive may decide to tolerate a corrupt

state governor because the political costs of overturning him may seem too high. Various states within the Brazilian and Mexican federal structure are larger and potentially more lucrative to govern than many Caribbean republics.

Consider a couple of Mexican examples drawn from the notoriously vice-ridden states which border on the USA and attract huge influxes of 'tourism'. President Aleman (1946–52) sponsored Governor Montones of Chihuahua (1950–5), who was finally forced out by a vast protest movement. 'Many people asserted that the governor controlled prostitution in Ciudad Juarez and that the money collected from medical inspections and licensing of prostitutes was being siphoned into his personal accounts rather than into the public treasury', D'Antonio and Form, *Influentials in Two Border Cities: A Study in Community Decision-Making* [sic], p. 164.

President Ruiz Cortines (1952–8) appointed Governor Maldonado Sandez of Baja California (1953–8). He too was forced out after scandal concerning prostitution in Tijuana 'where more than eight thousand whores were exploited for the profit of the governor and his friends, and which helped to pay for a front organisation called the Committee for Destitute Children that was headed by the governor's own wife' ('Por Que?' quoted in Johnson, *Mexican Democracy: A Critical View*, pp. 134–5).

In the last few years the state oil monopoly, PEMEX, has acquired a reputation for corruption that could only occur with presidential acquiescence.

2. On 8 November 1974 a Mr Edward Morgan pleaded guilty before the US Special Prosecutor of 'wilfully and knowingly' preparing affidavits for Nixon, which officially donated his Vice-Presidential papers to the US National Archives. 'The law that would have enabled the former President to claim tax deduction for his gifts was abolished in July 1969: Mr Morgan, it transpired today, made up, and had the President sign, affidavits a year later, but then had them backdated so as to appear they were filed before the expiry of the law.' The effect of this was to swindle the Internal Revenue service of $576,000. One journalist has asserted that 'since Mr Morgan acted solely on Mr Nixon's behalf, it is almost inconceivable that the former President could have failed to know about the backdating' (*Guardian*, 9 November 1974). According to Crassweller (*Trujillo: Life and Times of a Caribbean Dictator*, p. 279), by the 1950s the income of the Trujillo family . . . 'as estimated by a competent source, was approximately equal to the combined national expenditure for education, public health, labour, social security and public works. The factories owned by him in one way or another now employed about 60,000 workers. The value of his sugar interests could be estimated at $150 million. Another $100 to $200 million had been invested or secreted abroad, mostly in New York . . . If one were to venture a rough guess as to the total value of Trujillo's holdings in the Dominican Republic and abroad, $500 million would be as plausible a figure as any.'

3. The low ($500 million) estimate for Peron's 'loot' comes from *Time*, 3 June 1957 (quoting 'an authoritative source'). The information about Peron is much more open to doubt than the rest.

4. Aleman seems to have ploughed back most of his wealth into Mexico, but few ex-presidents feel that secure from retaliation. Unlike Trujillo, all the other ousted presidents had sufficient advance notice to make their dispositions.

5. In the light of these comparisons it is rather puzzling to read Andreski's assertion that: 'Like their American counterparts, the upstart Latin American politicians usually try to make fortunes rapidly, but they cannot squeeze very much out of the powerful hereditary rich. As the latter, moreover, in their capacity of landlords and financiers appropriate the greater part of what can be squeezed out of ordinary people . . . the proportion of wealth which remains available for embezzlement . . . must be smaller in Latin America than in tropical Africa'. (Quoted in Heidenheimer, op. cit., p. 356.)

If Andreski were right, the wealth of tropical African rulers would be very great. But the figures given by First, *The Barrel of a Gun*, pp. 101–4, are not large by Latin American standards. For example, Sir Albert Margai of Sierra Leone was apparently asked to repay £771,037 after his fall from power and ex-President Maurice Yameogo of Upper Volta was charged with embezzling £1,212,000. These are small, poor countries of course. But are the magnitudes involved in Nigeria, Zaïre or Kenya really sufficient to uphold Andreski's argument?

6. Totting up the total of these eight rulers it seems not unlikely that this cumulative personal theft from the Cuban state over forty years reached $400 million, which would make an average of $10 million a year. Very crudely this would approximate to $2 per capita of the Cuban population each year, in a country where the average income per head over most of the period was around $500 (with many living at only a fraction of that level).

7. In a later number the same newsletter added (25 August 1972) the following obituary of Colman which indicates the personal wealth of this particular general: 'Stroessner originally granted Colman his smuggling franchise (restricted to cigarettes and whisky in those days) in 1960 after the general had led a successful campaign of repression against FULNA guerrillas . . . He later expanded his activities to channel heroin through from Europe to its destination in North America . . . His personal rule extended over vast tracts of Paraguay and he operated private airstrips for smuggling on his private cattle ranches in strategic spots such as Pilar and Santa Helena . . .'.

8. In principle this hypothesis must imply that even in the United States and even in the present and in the future the same might be true, but curiously this is not an aspect of their position that such writers have been inclined to stress, at least up to now.

9. Writing in the *American Political Science Review* in 1967, J. S. Nye provided a clear example of the cost benefit approach and concluded that: 'it is probable that the costs of corruption in less developed countries will exceed its benefits except for top level corruption involving modern inducements and marginal deviations and except for situations where corruption provides the only solution to an important obstacle to development' (quoted in Heidenheimer, op. cit., p. 578).

10. One example of a country in which this principle has been consciously applied is Mexico. After the excesses of the Aleman period mentioned above, President Ruiz Cortines inherited the task of rehabilitating the economy (including devaluing the peso) while preserving political stability. According to Frank Brandenberg he 'informed *alemanistas* who had pilfered the public treasury that exchanging any more of their "investments" into dollars for purposes of taking capital out of Mexico would prove extremely unwise; this capital was to remain in Mexico and to contribute to economic developments'. (*The Making of Modern Mexico*, p. 111.)

11. 'The English he had learned . . . in Philadelphia enabled him to become one of the interpreters between the Nicaraguan officials and the military and civilian Officials of the US occupying forces. . . . [The Marines withdrew in 1933 and in June 1934 a US arms salesman wrote to Mr Monaghan, export manager of the Remington Arms Co. He] suggested that Monaghan communicate with Mr Nichols of Colt's and tell him to write to General Somoza offering to sell direct to him. "I would suggest that in this quotation he should include a 10 per cent commission for General Somoza." Remington was naturally anxious to have Colt's supply the guns, for which they could then supply the ammunition. The guns had to come first. It takes only a few deals like this before one has enough money to start buying up plantations, airlines etc., which in their turn pour more money into the bank. Somoza's income was estimated at $1 million a year and his assets at about $100 million . . . Somoza put every relative he had on the public payroll; soon after his grandson was born, the baby was made a captain in the army with full pay and privileges.' (Kantor, *Patterns of Politics and Political Systems in Latin America*, p. 167.)

12. As a result, after Trujillo's assassination in 1961, 'official sources revealed that Trujillo's share of the national wealth had amounted to the following: bank deposits 22%; money in circulation 25%; sugar production 63%; cement 63%; paper 73%; paint 86%; cigarettes 71%; milk 89%; wheat and flour 68%; plus the nation's only airline, its leading newspapers, and the three principal radio and television stations. According to the Swiss daily (Basle) *National Zeitung*, the Trujillo family had deposited no less than $200 million in Swiss banks . . . [Also] the dictator owned 10% of the productive land and 10% of the cattle industry; 45% of the Nation's active manpower was employed directly in Trujillo enterprises; a further 35% was engaged

in the Armed Forces and the government-operated banking, hotel and electricity systems' ('Hispanic American Report' quoted in Horowitz *et al.* (eds), *Latin American Radicalism*, p. 254).
13. Nye wrote that 'it is not clear that corruption of the old regime is a primary cause of social revolution. Such revolutions are comparatively rare and often depend heavily on catalytic events (such as external wars)' (Heidenheimer, op. cit., p. 571).

References

Andreski, Stanislav, *Parasitism and Subversion: The Case of Latin America*, London, Weidenfeld & Nicolson, 1966.

Bolton, Sir George, *Annual Review of BOLSA*, London, Bank of London and South America, 1962–3.

Bonachea, Rolando E. and Valdés, Nelson T. (eds), *Cuba in Revolution*, New York, Doubleday, 1972.

Braden, Spruille, *Diplomats and Demagogues*, New York, Arlington House, 1971.

Brandenburg, Frank, *The Making of Modern Mexico*, Englewood Cliffs, N.J., Prentice-Hall, 1964.

Crassweller, Robert D., *Trujillo: Life and Times of a Caribbean Dictator*, New York, Macmillan, 1966.

D'Antonio, William V. and Form, William H., *Influential in Two Border Cities: A Study in Community Decision-Making*, Notre Dame, Indiana University Press, 1965.

First, Ruth, *The Barrel of a Gun*, Harmondsworth, Middx., Penguin, 1970.

Gerassi, John, *The Great Fear in Latin America*, New York, Macmillan, 1963.

Heidenheimer, Arnold J., *Political Corruption: Readings in Comparative Analysis*, New York, Holt, Rhinehart and Winston, 1970.

Horowitz, Irving Lewis *et al.* (eds), *Latin American Radicalism*, London, Cape, 1969.

Johnson, Kenneth F., *Mexican Democracy: A Critical View*, New York, Praeger, revised edn. 1978.

Kantor, Harry, *Patterns and Politics of Political Systems in Latin America*, Chicago, Rand-McNally, 1969.

Lieuwen, Edwin, *Arms and Politics in Latin America*, New York, Praeger, 1961.

— *Venezuela*, Oxford, Oxford University Press, 1961.

Mesa-Lago, Carmelo, *Revolutionary Change in Cuba*, Pittsburg, Penn., University of Pittsburg Press, 1971.

Needler, Martin C., *Political Development in Latin America*, New York, Random House, 1968.

Nye, J. S., *American Political Science Review*, **61** (1967), 417–27.

Thomas, Hugh, *Cuba: The Pursuit of Freedom*, London, Eyre & Spottiswoode, 1971.

10 Corruption and the spoils system in Zambia

MORRIS SZEFTEL

This chapter is concerned with corruption in Zambia, its place in the political process and its contribution to class formation. At the outset it must be stressed that corruption cannot be understood in isolation, as a discrete phenomenon, but must be located within a wider pattern of socio-political behaviour whereby state resources are diverted from public to private and group ends. This process can be characterised as a 'spoils system'.[1] Corruption constitutes only one way in which public wealth and influence is appropriated and accumulated by individuals with access to public office or to public officers. As such, it is much less typical of Zambian politics than clientelism and patronage and, in any case, is so intimately bound up with them that the two forms of behaviour overlap. If corruption appears to be fairly common in Zambia, it is not yet endemic and the frequency with which it is discovered and punished indicates that it remains a risky undertaking. While it is an important problem for administrative practice and policing, its social and political significance lies more in its character as one way in which individuals appropriate the spoils of office or, more generally, of access to the state.

The importance and pervasiveness of the spoils system is a reflection of the centrality of the state and the resources it commands, particularly in an under-developed economy. In Zambia this underdevelopment is part of a legacy of racial discrimination during the colonial period when Africans were systematically excluded from wealth and power. Economic domination by multinational mining companies and by white settlers precluded the formation of a significant African bourgeoisie, or even petit bourgeoisie, and created a vast, under-privileged peasantry often forced to migrate to the towns for work. In this context the state became the primary focus for African aspirations, both for what it could do to redress the grievances of the population as a whole and (more significantly for the purposes of this chapter) as a resource in itself, a means of livelihood, an avenue of upward mobility and, not least, a source of wealth for entry into the private sector.[2] Corruption provides a useful point of entry for any examination of the political process developing out of this legacy, but it is only one of several.

The concept—and some difficulties

Definitions of corruption generally focus on one of several aspects of the pheno-menon.[3] Some are what has been termed 'public-interest-centred', regarding corruption to be in some way injurious to or destructive of the public interest.[4] Others are 'market-centred', suggesting that the norms governing the exercise of public office have shifted from a 'mandatory-pricing model to a free-market model',[5] especially in circumstances where such governing norms are unclear or nonexistent—as in new states. A third set of definitions is 'public-office-centred', stressing that public office has been misused by incumbents for private gain. Still other studies employ what might be termed 'public-opinion-centred' definitions, emphasising the perspectives of public opinion, or sections of it, about the conduct of government and the probity of officials.[6] All such approaches are, clearly, partial in their perspective. In addition, all are beset by problems of operationalisation; Scott, for instance, notes the problems inherent in determining the rules and norms which govern public interest, behaviour and authority and so suggests a fifth approach—that corruption should be treated purely in terms of legal criteria.[7]

The difficulties surrounding the criteria on which any definition rests are clear. While there is probably a range of actions that might be termed corrupt in most societies, the concept tends to blur at the margins and to shade into other forms of activity. Most obviously, there are problems associated with *a priori* assumptions of the injurious consequences of corruption or of the corrupt character of actions injurious to the state. Nor is it clear what the public interest is in most cases. And the market model assumption of 'normlessness' suffers from debatable (and ethnocentric) presumptions about the nature of third world politics that are common to modernisation theory. There is little evidence that corruption is tolerated more in Zambia than in, say, the United States or that office holders have a weaker understanding of the rules and obligations surrounding the exercise of office in the former than in the latter. There is even some evidence that the opposite might be the case. Nor is all corruption trans-actional; auto-corruption (where a public official appropriates state resources for personal enrichment without the involvement of a third party) would con-stitute a significant proportion of corrupt behaviour. The problem of agreeing on and defining what constitutes public opinion seems so enormous as to leave such an approach, where not tied to one of the others, extremely questionable. (For all that, it must not be forgotten that people often come to regard their governments as more or less 'corrupt' and that such an ideological climate is fundamentally important to the legitimacy of a regime.) And the problems inherent in identifying the rules and norms regulating the conduct of public office are also difficult to overcome.

Yet to narrow corruption to purely legal criteria in order to escape from these difficulties seems equally problematic. Official responsibilities and duties are likely to extend beyond the range of legally defined felonies. Administrative practice and political assumptions about honesty and sharp practice also influence the parameters of official behaviour. It would seem almost inevitable that there would be, in most polities, a hierarchy of actions which would be regarded as improper in some way but which would not always be legally prohibited—or which might only subsequently be prohibited. As Brooks has noted: 'The sanctions of positive law are applied only to those more flagrant practices which past experience has shown to be so pernicious that sentiment has crystallized into statutory prohibitions and adverse judicial decisions.'[8]

In addition, it is clear that statute and administrative rules distinguish different forms of what might be regarded as corruption under a number of rubrics; in addition to 'corruption', terms such as 'theft', 'theft by public servant', 'extortion', 'discrimination' and 'abuse of power' (the last only in some of its forms) abound.[9] Regimes which exhibited a high degree of any of these practices would be considered corrupt by many, if not most, observers, whatever the technical status of these activities. Thus, while legality is clearly an important element in understanding corruption, it should not be allowed to obscure the patterns of social behaviour identified by the other approaches mentioned. The study of political corruption must extend beyond legal forms to comprehend the social significance of a wider body of behaviour. No judgment is therefore made here about the legality or otherwise of the actions discussed.

Whatever the problems surrounding the definition and treatment of the concept, it would seem clear that all approaches, despite their varying emphasis, regard corruption as involving some form of misuse of a public office or public authority. It is the appropriation for individual gain of a public role or duty that is regarded as in some way injurious to the public interest, or as involving a shift to market pricing criteria, or as occasioning allegations of corruption (or even as requiring legal censure). It would seem, then, that unless some form of delegated authority is employed for individual enrichment in a manner regarded as contrary to the obligations of that authority, we cannot speak of corruption at all.[10] The essence of the subject is thus closest to 'public-office' approaches, albeit broadened to include special cases where public authority is involved though no office is held—such as election or appointment to public positions governed by such rules and norms.[11]

A working definition that might permit us to explore corruption in Zambian politics might thus be: corruption is behaviour which deviates from the norms, rules and duties governing the exercise of a public role or office for purposes of private gain; it may do this by ignoring prohibitions against certain acts, or by fulfilling obligations to act or by exercising legitimate discretion to act, as long as it does so for private advantage or for private-regarding motives.[12] Although the problem of defining such norms and rules remains and is inherent in the concept, the definition has merit on several grounds: it makes no *a priori* assumptions about the consequences of corruption for society; it is not tied to a discussion of only those forms of behaviour deemed illegal; it requires that there be some sort of delegated power or authority to be corrupted; it requires that such actions involve some form of personal or private gain as an end and so excludes inefficiency; and, finally, it underlines the inherent element of discrimination or arbitrariness that corruption infuses into the exercise of public authority.

Yet the limitations of such a definition (or any of the others, for that matter) become apparent the moment we cease to consider corruption as a discrete variable and begin to contrast it with political clientelism and the use of patronage. Patronage involves personal relationships of exchange characterised by inequality, reciprocity and personal contacts.[13] In the political context it involves payoffs for favours and support. If we consider a classic case of patronage, in which a public official obtains a job or loan for a political supporter, or for an acquaintance of a supporter or of a patron, by using his or her influence to procure the service, then it is clear that such an action involves the exercise of public office for private gain and that it violates rules or norms prohibiting the use of office for private-regarding gain. Is patronage then a form of corruption? In the strictest sense, the answer would seem to be affirmative (and in legal terms many instances would incur heavy penalties). But such a conclusion would necessarily label a substantial proportion of political activity as corrupt. It is likely that many people in a polity would regard patronage from which they benefited as right and proper and that from which their opponents benefited as corrupt. But it is also likely that most poeple would draw some fairly vague distinction between corruption and payoffs for political support.

While both might be labelled as corrupt, there seems to be, in many people's minds, some difference between using clientelist links to obtain state contracts or public office or using knowledge of urban planning to obtain valuable land, on the one hand, and stealing government funds or taking bribes, on the other. The distinction which George Washington Plunkett drew between 'honest graft' and 'dishonest graft' contains an element of truth in addition to its irony.[14] While 'honest graft' may often be as illegal as the 'dishonest' form (insider trading on the stock exchange, for example) and may be impossible to effect without occasional resort to the latter, it is often regarded as less reprehensible, less 'criminal', by public opinion. If not many politicians would openly admit with Plunkett that 'I seen my opportunities and I took 'em', it is nevertheless true that official position offers many perks and privileges. Those without similar access are likely to resent such activities, but it is also possible that many will consider them a due reward for political support and part of the spoils of office. Other activities, on the other hand, will not find a similar legitimation through the patronage system; there is likely to be a more general public rejection of 'dishonest graft'.

It is clearly important to try to distinguish between corruption and patronage, despite their manifest relationship. It might perhaps be useful to employ the term 'patronage' to denote activities involving the dispensing of state resources to third parties in return for political support of some kind, while 'corruption' would be confined to activities involving the use of state resources so as to ensure personal benefit directly for the officials involved. But such a distinction is likely to be difficult to preserve in practice and many instances are likely to exhibit characteristics of both forms of activity. Thus, while it is necessary and valuable to keep the two conceptually distinct, their close relationship must be stressed. In Zambia both are elements of a broader clientelist form of politics. They are therefore not so much discrete phenomena with an existence of their own as manifestations of a political process through which individuals win access to the state and subsequently appropriate the spoils afforded by such access. While our focus here is on corruption, its place in the Zambian political system can be more readily grasped if it is understood as one element on a continuum of social behaviour. At one end of the continuum, public officials might fully utilise the perks, privileges and 'technical' advantages afforded by office while obeying the rules surrounding that office. At the other end of the continuum might be located activities which involve clear criminal behaviour, such as the theft of resources by officials. In between these poles would be found such activities as patronage, nepotism, improper use of state resources, the abuse of power for individual enrichment and the levying of charges for undertaking services already incumbent on the official.

Here, then, my concern is with the accumulation of rewards permitted by access to the state apparatus, specifically those acquired outside formally approved procedures or outside the framework of officially sanctioned practices. It is hoped that such instances will illuminate the spoils system in general. In the next section a number of cases will be examined to indicate the nature of political corruption in Zambia, its forms and its place in the spoils system.[15] In the final sections the implications of such behaviour for the Zambian state, for the nature of factional conflict within the political system, and for the emerging class structure will be considered.

Some case studies

Although numerous instances of misuse of public office could be cited, a number of important cases have been fairly well documented in official reports and in the press. Since these cases had a particularly important impact on the political process, and since they provide valuable evidence of the operation of the spoils system in Zambia, I have chosen to concentrate attention on them here. While their political significance does not make them typical,[16] they nevertheless exemplify many of the ways in which state resources can be diverted to private hands. They are therefore particularly useful indicators of the wider political relevance of corruption.

The 1968 Lusaka City Council inquiry

In 1968 a Commission headed by the Chief Justice of Zambia presented a report of its investigations into the affairs of the Lusaka City Council.[17] The Blagden Report constitutes the only systematic consideration of the conduct of public office since Independence in 1964 and is therefore worth considering at some length. It is also of interest in that it examines the behaviour in office of the first generation of Zambian local-level politicians and officials during a transitional period in the Council's history, when the senior officers were still white expatriates and when expatriate civil servants provided the expert research and reports for the Commission. The Report therefore assesses the conduct of local government in terms of the inherited norms and values of the colonial administration and in contrast to the pressures on many politicians to make political payoffs to supporters and to advance themselves. Thus the Report is itself an indicator of the degree of divergence between officially sanctioned rules of conduct and the practicalities of the spoils system.

The Commission's Report claims to have found little evidence of actual corruption and some evidence that it had been resisted by members of the Council. Nevertheless, if few instances of illegal activities are recorded, the Report comprises a chronicle of official impropriety made all the more impressive by the fact that no attempt was made to provide an exhaustive account of such behaviour.[18] But the cross-section of activity that is described illuminates the variety of ways in which spoils can be extracted from public office. Two major categories of such expropriation can be identified, indicating both the wide range of forms and their interrelationship with patronage practices.

The first category comprises a number of activities through which individuals used office or access to officials in order to advance personal wealth or position. One such instance was found in the allocation of Council housing. The rapid growth of Lusaka's population after 1964 (as a result of migration from the rural areas to the capital it increased by 80.8 per cent between 1963 and 1969[19] and peripheral shanty towns mushroomed everywhere) made housing very scarce and expensive and placed great pressure on Council resources. The Commission found a number of instances where housing had been allocated as a result of special representations by city councillors, MPs and businesses. There was also a massive increase in the proportion of house rents in arrears. The Commission accepted that many of the problems surrounding housing were the result of inefficiency and lack of capacity, but it also was clear that other irregularities arose from the use of influence: an unusual number of houses went to prominent people for reasons which could not be explained.[20]

A much greater degree of irregularity was found in the allocation of trading stands and food-stall sites. Fifteen per cent of such properties allocated over the 1965–7 period went to councillors (in one of these cases to the wife of a councillor) and another plot went to a person who later became a councillor. This represented a very high rate of success for this group, given that there were 592 applications for forty-five allocations. It transpired that the procedure in committee was for a councillor to suggest a name of a suitable applicant on the list and for this proposal then to be seconded and agreed; there were no records of debate or counter-proposals. The Report, somewhat ingenuously, considered that this 'could easily lend itself to corruption'.[21] Despite the inquiry, this pattern of behaviour appears to have continued throughout its investigation. In February 1968, for instance, the Council's Estates Committee considered 392 applications for twelve trading stands. In every case there were candidates better qualified in terms of experience, skill and financial standing than those who finally obtained plots. A query about this eventually obtained the observation that 'sometimes Councillors would personally know some of the people who were doing very well . . . and therefore might be given more to do'.[22] This pattern of behaviour appears to have reached its zenith with the reservation of 103 residential plots for possible purchase by the Mayor in 1967—before any of them had been advertised for sale. For some ten weeks prospective buyers were put off or refused the plots. Thereafter, following public queries —especially from the Bank of Zambia, which wanted thirteen of the plots— the properties were released for public purchase; but later ten of them (including two already allocated to the Bank) were again reserved for the Mayor for a further thirty days. The Commissioners considered that the Mayor had 'brought undue pressure to bear upon members of Council staff'.[23] It was also held that the Mayor had obtained advantage from the Council in the case of two other properties: he had obtained a waiver of policy in order to gain permission to sell liquor on land where he had built a bar; and he was allowed to transfer his interest in one site to an interest in another (without the second being advertised) as a result of a special resolution by an appropriate committee.[24] There appear, therefore, to have been a number of possibilities to use the decision-making machinery of local government for private gain.

A second category of practices involves the use of the local government apparatus to advance members of the ruling party, UNIP, and also to penalise members of the opposition ANC.[25] There were, for instance, several cases where membership of UNIP seems to have influenced appointments to Council posts. During the period from 1964 to the inquiry, there had been 454 new officers entering an establishment of 685 and there were also 234 promotions.[26] Opportunities and temptations in this area must therefore have been great and the Commissioners describe instances where qualified candidates were over-looked in favour of others with privileged political access. The Personnel Officer had been appointed over five others with equal qualifications and the Report implies that his distinguished role in nationalist politics probably tipped the scales in his favour. Others seemed rather more fortunate to have obtained their jobs. A Chief Administrative Officer was appointed over five others with superior qualifications; he had been a UNIP Regional Secretary. In the appointment of a Marketing Officer eight interviewees had inferior qualifications to those of seven applicants not interviewed. Another Marketing Officer was appointed after the Personnel Officer had received a letter from UNIP National Headquarters introducing him as 'our comrade for the post as arranged yesterday'. The Personnel Officer had then entered this candidate's name on the list of applicants previously interviewed and written against his name 'appointed by the Chairman for urgency purposes'.[27] The Commission considered this a corrupt appointment[28] but it does not seem substantively different from others discussed and, indeed, its motivation seems to have been to promote political supporters rather than to obtain some individual pecuniary gain.

A particularly blatant political appointment was that of a man as Assistant Swimming Pool Superintendent although the City Engineer considered him the least qualified of the four interviewed. The successful candidate could not express himself well in English, found the technicalities of operating the filtration plant difficult to grasp and could not swim, the last being the primary qualification for the job. The Assistant Personnel Officer, a former full-time party official, strongly recommended him, arguing that the candidate's previous political background gave him important experience in managing people of different races and this offset his other handicaps. The appointment was made despite criticism from the City Engineer, political credentials, superseding technical qualifications. In the event, the man had to be relieved of the job when it was discovered that he attended work irregularly, was uninterested in the job and refused to learn to swim.[29] Nor were these the only instances.

Council powers appear also to have been abused in order to attack members of the opposition ANC. In one case an application for permission to extend business premises owned by an ANC member was delayed for about sixteen months because the applicant had been denounced by local UNIP officials and because one councillor had urged the eviction of the man from the property. 'We entertain no doubt that the improper deferment of Mr M's application was due to political considerations', says the Report.[30] In another case, a decision to allocate a plot to a former councillor who was an ANC member was reversed and his application to construct business premises was refused. The chairman of the Town Planning Committee noted that the individual was 'not popular in the district'.[31] In contrast, a respected former UNIP councillor was given every consideration after contravening statutory limitations on construction on a particular property—even though he had been warned to desist and had ignored the warning. Here the Council appealed to central government, asking the Minister to rezone the area in order to regularise this one breach of the rules.[32]

Party considerations seem to have been important in a struggle for control of Lusaka's marketplaces—market stalls being a much desired prize for a host of petty traders. From 1956, the city's three markets were run by one co-operative society but this dissolved in 1964 as a result of political conflict between members. Thereafter, two markets were controlled by a society whose members were all in UNIP (and whose leader was a councillor at the time of the inquiry) while the third was run by a society of ANC members. By 1967 there were six markets, four of them administered by the UNIP society, which was permitted to acquire control of two more markets despite the fact that its rent arrears stretched back over eighteen months. The ANC society, although not in arrears, had its market taken over by the Council in October 1965. The Commissioners considered this pattern of behaviour to be discriminatory and a dereliction of official duty in the unduly unfavourable treatment accorded the UNIP marketeers.[33]

The Land Act controversy

In 1977 President Kaunda dismissed the Minister of Lands for what he termed activities 'tantamount to abuse of office'.[34] A Land Act had been passed in August 1975 with the intention of curbing land speculation and, by regulating the property market, providing an opportunity for more Zambians to acquire valuable commercial land previously monopolised by expatriates and the wealthiest Zambians. It also allowed the state to acquire undeveloped and abandoned land compulsorily. To these ends, the Act required government approval for transfers of state land (as distinct from land being held under customary, communal tenure) and gave the Minister wide discretionary powers to approve individual transfers and the price at which such transfers occurred. This implicitly gave officials the power to override even agreements between the contracting parties.[35] And, not surprisingly, there soon followed allegations that attempts were being made to circumvent the intentions of the Act—one MP, for instance, alleging that political leaders and top officials were acquiring many of the affected properties.[36]

There were also rumours of improper influence at the Ministry, in one instance prompting the Minister to defend the leasing of land to a Greek national by saying 'he did not bribe me and he did not corrupt me in any way because I am not corrupt. . . . Allocation of this land was done as it should be and there is nothing scandalous about it.'[37] The Minister's comments also included criticism of certain 'lawyers of fortune' who, he claimed, bent the law for their own benefit. This, in turn, drew criticism from the Law Association (including comments on perceived inadequacies in the law and on the insecurity it produced) and from the Commercial Farmers' Bureau (an overwhelmingly expatriate interest group).[38] The Minister reacted in turn to what he called a capitalist clique, which he regarded as seeking to restore freehold tenure and speculative prices.[39] The controversy escalated even further when the chairman of the Law Association, a prominent Zambian lawyer, questioned the Minister's exercise of his discretionary powers. He alleged that the Minister had personally intervened in one transaction (involving the sale of an engineering company) to lower the agreed price and to direct the company's lawyers to sell to a specified individual (not the agreed purchaser) and to no other. He also claimed that in one case where consent had actually been given, an official intervened to halve the price agreed. In other cases, he said, different prices had been assigned to identical housing units, a builder had been ordered to sell a house below cost and, in one housing area, consent to alienate had been given for some new houses and refused for others. He concluded by claiming that 'this appears to be a prima facie case of abuse of power'.[40] As a result, the Minister was suspended pending an investigation. Subsequently, he was dismissed although the dismissal was not connected officially to the controversy.

Public office as a private business

Thus far we have observed cases where public office can be used to obtain preferential access to state resources and services. There are also cases where officials act to appropriate funds and property by turning their offices into businesses.[41] The use of government vehicles for haulage or as private taxis, the sale of driving licences to members of the public or of state land to residents seeking plots for housing where such land has not been demarcated for alienation (as undertaken by some party officials in one Copperbelt town, seemingly with the assistance of some members of the police) are all possible.[42] Also possible is the acquisition of government property at low prices or through indefinite loans. The reports of the Auditor-General are particularly instructive about such practices: in June 1970, for instance, when police were instructed to auction off five vehicles stolen from Zambia and later recovered in neighbouring Zaïre. The auction took place at the Zambian consulate in Lubumbashi without the services of an auctioneer. Consulate staff 'outbid others at the auction and subsequently disposed of the vehicles to themselves and acquaintances at nominal prices, ranging from approximately K28 to K50'.[43]

Even in offices where the pickings would appear to be meagre, there have been examples of much ingenuity in plundering resources. For instance, the practice evolved from colonial times that the office of the District Secretary would receive funds from individuals for collection by third parties—often the beneficiaries of deceased estates—thus easing the problem of transmitting money to the remotest parts of the rural areas. Pending collection, such sums were kept in suspense accounts under a separate serial coding to ensure that they remained distinct from office funds. Clearly these suspense accounts could show a credit or zero, but never a debit, balance. Assisted by incompetent checking and lack of supervision, cases have occurred where clerical officers have appropriated large sums from government by inflating the amount held in such accounts on statement copies and drawing the fictitious excess against the name of the beneficiary of the file. In 1972, for example, an accounts clerk obtained K35,123 in this way over a six-month period; investigations later revealed that he had acquired K4,916 at his previous posting in the same way.[44] The paying of wages to fictitious employees was another method used to collect public funds—the provincial office of one ministry having K78,697 in wages, overtime and allowances paid to non-existent officials in 1973.[45]

Perhaps the most famous case in which public office was seemingly used as a private business involved the prosecution of two Permanent Secretaries for the alleged sale of citizenship to resident expatriates. Economic reforms introduced by the government between 1968 and 1971 had excluded non-citizens from trading in specified economic sectors and from specified geographic areas. There was therefore a high premium placed on Zambian citizenship by those who stood to lose their livelihoods and, at the same time, pressure by Zambians hoping to take over such businesses, demanding that the state prevent the reforms from being frustrated by new 'economic citizens'. Certainly citizenship applications took an extremely long time to be processed and many applicants believed that this was deliberate policy designed to facilitate the reforms. The Asian petit bourgeoisie was particularly affected and vulnerable.

The trials of the Permanent Secretaries followed an investigation ordered by the Minister of Home Affairs after allegations by a party official that some expatriates were obtaining citizenship to which they were not entitled. Both were charged with various offences including corruption and were convicted on some counts; both appealed unsuccessfully in 1976. During one of the trials, a witness alleged that in three cases of which he knew, citizenship had been granted after applications had been turned down by the Minister.[46] A number of Asian businessmen further testified that they had paid large sums in cash, furniture, electrical equipment and appliances and motor vehicles in return for citizenship.[47]

Public office could be, and was, used, therefore, to accumulate resources from both public and private sectors. In the vast majority of cases, it seems clear that it has involved the lower levels of the bureaucracy. And, despite government readiness to prosecute and even to make examples of senior people, it does not appear to have diminished. The Public Service Commission Report noted that some 198 officials were dismissed from the civil service in 1971 for misappropriation of public funds.[48] In 1976, the Prime Minister, answering a question in the National Assembly, stated that in 1974 fourteen officers had been convicted of offences relating to corrupt practices, sixty-eight of corruption and more than a thousand of theft by public servant. The increase between the two years must reflect improved methods of detection, as the Prime Minister clearly thought: anyone who had escaped apprehension was 'just lucky', he said.[49] But the figures may also indicate an increase in the incidence of such practices; such optimism, for instance, was less evident in 1982, when the acting Chief Justice, as head of a new 'anti-corruption commission', indicated that it was becoming increasingly difficult to investigate cases of corruption because of inadequate resources—despite the fact that the new commission had been inundated with allegations concerning various parts of the public services.[50]

The African Farming Improvement Funds scandals of 1970

The close relationship between the use of state resources for individual advancement and enrichment, on the one hand, and patronage, on the other, is clear in a case of central importance to the political process in Zambia. Under the African Farming Improvement Fund Ordinance of 1958 the colonial government set up African Farming Improvement Funds in Eastern, Central (CPAFIF) and Southern (SPAFIF) Provinces to promote 'better conditions for African farmers through improved farming and marketing of agricultural produce and the conservation of natural resources'.[51] Each fund was designed to improve African farming within its respective province and was administered by a Board with powers to use funds and make loans to African farmers within its province of jurisdiction. This legal and administrative structure was inherited by the independent Zambian government in 1964. It must be stressed that the funds which the Boards used were contributed by peasant and 'improved' farmers through levies on maize surpluses which these farmers sold on the state-controlled market. Money came from the surplus produced by these farmers and was supposed to provide the infrastructure and loan assistance necessary to permit them to expand and, perhaps, become commercial farmers. When the Credit Organization of Zambia (COZ) was created soon after Independence, the funds ceased to make loans and were used solely for infrastructural development. This was the situation in 1968.

In that year, the Minister of State for the Central Province, Henry Shamabanse, was moved to Southern Province in the same capacity and thus became chairman of the SPAFIF Board *ex officio*. He had previously headed the CPAFIF Board. In November 1968 he informed the SPAFIF Board that he and the Minister of Agriculture, Munu Sipalo, had consulted the Attorney-General and been advised that the Board could make loans 'as and when and to whom it thought merited them', though the Ordinance did not permit such a discretion.[52] Subsequent events have been summarised as follows:

> Mr Shamabanse initiated what we can describe as an orgy of granting loans. In the first instance, loans were granted on Mr Shamabanse's sole authority without reference to the Board, though the Board was subsequently asked to ratify. This, of course, was completely irregular as it was for the Board to grant loans. It is perhaps significant that in the minutes . . . the following appears:

> 'The Chairman warned members that it was not intended that the Fund should reassume its former role of making loans to farmers, which function has now been taken over by [COZ]. In order that farmers should not be misled in this way, it would be as well if no publicity was given to this exercise otherwise the Board would be overloaded with applications for loans.'

> This warning was so well observed that even the members of the Board, as

a whole, were not aware of what loans were being made until the middle of 1969 when they were asked to ratify them. Later, however, the Board did carry out the function of granting loans. By the early part of 1970 loans amounting to K312,533 had been issued of which only . . . K390 had been repaid . . . The manner in which loans were granted . . . was extraordinary. The outstanding feature of the procedure was that loans were made without any inquiry as to how far arrangements had been made for the purchase of the properties concerned, without any inquiry as to whether the persons concerned were African farmers, whether they were farming in the province concerned or whether the farms they purchased were in the province concerned . . . nowhere was the money advanced secured . . . Most of the loans were made to persons who were members of the Board or who held positions in Government or Public Service.[53]

In November 1970 the President suspended a number of senior political figures pending investigation by the DPP into their association with SPAFIF and CPAFIF. The suspended leaders included two Cabinet Ministers (Shamabanse and Dingiswayo Banda), two Ministers of State, a Permanent Secretary, a divisional police commander, and two provincial agricultural officers. The Ministers of State had formerly chaired CPAFIF and SPAFIF *ex officio*. Investigations were also conducted into the actions of Sipalo (out of office after losing his seat in the 1968 elections) and a former UNIP Regional Secretary, M. M. Kalaluka, who had links with Sipalo in provincial UNIP political organisational work.[54] Another eleven officials were also investigated though they do not appear to have been suspended. These included a Permanent Secretary, five District Governors, three provincial civil servants and two central civil servants.

In January 1971, the DPP decided that he could find no grounds for prosecution against any of the above, except for Shamabanse, Sipalo and Kalaluka— who had already appeared in court by then. He noted that all those investigated fell into one of two categories: they had either obtained loans from SPAFIF and CPAFIF which were authorised by the Board, but were not farmers at the time or did not use the money for the purpose stipulated; or they had obtained loans through the chairman or executive officers without the prior knowledge or consent of the Boards. But as there was no evidence of criminal conduct, no charges were preferred. Accordingly, the President reinstated all those suspended except Shamabanse and ordered them all to repay their loans within six months. The three charged appealed successfully against conviction for obtaining money by false pretences, but Shamabanse was ultimately convicted on other charges after two appeals.[55] But SPAFIF would appear to have continued to serve as a resource for people in high office, as a 1979 report indicated that it had outstanding debts of K191,483 and included among these debtors a Cabinet Minister, two former ministers, two MPs, four District Governors and a senior civil servant.[56]

The scandal had profound political consequences. The reinstatement of those investigated produced allegations of political favouritism and even corruption in government and the dismissal of senior political figures. This led to a judicial inquiry under Chief Justice Doyle which essentially confirmed the conclusions of the DPP. The political crisis exacerbated tensions already serious within UNIP, ultimately leading to a serious schism, the formation of a major new party (the UPP) in 1972 and the declaration of a one-party state by the government. It remains the most important and interesting single instance of the working of the spoils system for which documentation is available.

Corruption and political factionalism

The cases discussed above indicate that graft and patronage are intertwined. Indeed, it would seem difficult to separate them empirically and almost impossible to do so in terms of their political significance. The Lusaka City Council inquiry indicated a close relationship between activities designed to ensure self-advancement and those seeking to promote friends and political comrades. The Land Act controversy involved allegations of efforts made to benefit third parties rather than any official directly involved, although the issues were never fully clarified. And the SPAFIF case involved individual acts of appropriation within the context of a group activity—no fewer than twenty-one people were investigated for their use of SPAFIF and CPAFIF. Clearly patronage and political graft overlap and are common to specific acts and events and it is for this reason that I have suggested that the notion of a spoils system—in which success in gaining access to political office or political officers produces tangible material rewards for individuals—is more appropriate than the discrete concept of corruption to denote a range of activities in which public resources are privately appropriated.

This spoils system is one facet of a clientelist political system. In the context of underdevelopment there is great pressure on state resources to provide the means for individual mobility. In the context of electoral politics, however, access to public office requires the mobilisation of support and the need to provide payoffs for supporters, particularly for political lieutenants and brokers. In Zambia this mobilisation of support typically involves the construction of political networks from a local and regional base so that political factions are generally regionally, provincially, linguistically and/or ethnically defined— although the lines of demarcation fluctuate over time and across issues. Political factionalism thus has a provincial flavour and is referred to by politicians as being 'tribal' or as 'tribalism'.[57]

It is not surprising that the accumulation of spoils, in the context of resource scarcity, should involve factional competition for access to the state apparatus and that it should replicate or reproduce factional lines of cleavage. And the evidence would indicate that the struggle to accumulate state spoils has tended, in turn, to promote and reinforce this pattern of 'tribalism'. In Zambia the allocation of senior party and government positions has reflected the need to balance the claims of contending factions. The Cabinet, for instance, has been characterised by a shifting balance of posts between provinces. When shifts in influence within UNIP have produced adjustments to this balance, tensions have surfaced within the party. And when factional competition has threatened to alter the balance dramatically or seriously disadvantaged a particular faction, the party and government have been plunged into political crises.[58] The spoils system is not, therefore, an epiphenomenon; it is at the heart of the political process and its problems.

The SPAFIF affair particularly illuminates this factional influence in the spoils system. The loan beneficiaries were drawn from four provinces—Eastern, Western, Southern and Central. By 1968 these were part of a larger coalition seeking to offset gains made in the UNIP power structure by Northern Province politicians who also had a strong base in the Copperbelt working class. Two of the loan recipients, indeed, were among the most important political figures in the country during the independence struggle—Banda had strong urban and Eastern support and Sipalo had been one of the key leaders of the independence campaign. The SPAFIF scandal was, apparently, first reported by a Bemba District Governor and, when the President accepted the DPP's report, criticism was voiced in the press by two leading Bemba politicians, one of them a Cabinet Minister. These claims led the President to set up the Doyle Commission which, as noted, upheld the DPP. In 1972 a large section of this Bemba faction left UNIP to found the UPP and all three Northern politicians prominent in prosecuting the SPAFIF scandal were prominent in the new party. The UPP drew significant support from Northern and Copperbelt provinces and its challenge was sufficient to provoke the creation of a one-party state in 1972. The SPAFIF scandal thus provides a window through which this gathering crisis within UNIP can be viewed and through which the intensity of factional conflict can be understood. But it was itself more important than a symptom of the crisis inasmuch as it exacerbated and intensified grievances which spilled over into public acrimony and set in train events of profound political and constitutional importance.

Factional competition seems also to have affected the distribution of public office among competing groups. As one editorial writer in Zambia noted:

> there are these days numerous reports of corruption, nepotism and tribalism in the employment of personnel in many of our government departments and parastatal bodies as well as the private sector. Some of these are false and are made by people who have failed to secure employment because they do not qualify for the jobs they ask for. But it cannot be denied that these vices do exist in the recruitment of staff. . . . There are those who . . . employ people of their tribe or whom they expect to support them politically . . .

Then there are those who are pressed by friends or indeed people of their tribe to help them get jobs for their relatives or friends. The other class is that of people who want to get rich by accepting bribes.[59]

Certainly there was widespread belief that various groups were able to use their political position to ensure disproportionate access to office for faction members. In 1975, for instance, one MP alleged that Eastern Province was unduly favoured in its 'possession' of senior civil service posts. And since office-holders were likely to further the promotion and appointment of their own clients, such imbalances were regarded as self-perpetuating. In 1977 another MP returned to the theme of Eastern predominance, noting that it was over-represented in key sections of the bureaucracy.[60] The Prime Minister replied that this was true only if a selective sample of positions was considered, and sought to make a virtue of factional competition: 'in a way sometimes I feel that our tribalism is somewhat a safeguard because everybody is watching what the rest of the tribal bosses are doing and, therefore, this restrains . . .'.[61] Certainly factionalism made the spoils system a hazardous undertaking for participants—as the SPAFIF affair showed—but the comment also indicates that the bureaucracy is regarded in terms of its use as part of the spoils of political access rather than as an instrumentality in its own right.

Despite reassurances, factional interests continue to be regarded as a means to promote the systematic extension of influence through favouritism in appointments. Many people in Zambia came to allege that various departments and parastatal branches became factional fiefdoms as a result of the manipulation of recruitment procedures. In interviews undertaken during an election study in the Copperbelt in 1973, for example, several respondents assessed appointments and promotions purely in terms of alleged attempts by the Bemba group (often equated in the telling with the UPP) to expand its influence. And the District Secretary in one Copperbelt town expressed concern that he was occasionally required to mediate disputes within parastatal branches when members of a dominant faction protested the appointment or posting of 'outsiders'.

The problem is perhaps best illustrated by the 1978 report of a Commission of Inquiry which investigated allegations of tribalism, nepotism, corruption and theft in and by the management of Zambia Railways; the charges were brought by leaders of the Zambia Railways Amalgamated Workers' Union (ZRAWU).[62] The Report indicates that persistent claims were encountered that 'certain tribes were entrenched in certain departments . . . and were openly boasting about it', that disciplinary procedures were corrupted by 'tribalism', that appointments were made unfairly and also, by way of a counter-claim, that the allegations were themselves an attempt by certain 'tribes' to restore comrades who had been dismissed.[63] In substance, the allegations were that a particular individual who was a Tonga had ensured that his department became a Tonga stronghold. The Report concluded that

tribalism is practised on Zambia Railways by means of favouritism . . . in
relation to appointments, promotions, the exercise of disciplinary functions,
and in showing hostility and harshness to members of other tribes. In this
manner tribalism is practised on a very large scale and, in certain instances,
without any sense of shame by those concerned.[64]

Given that access to state resources is at stake, it is not surprising that factional interest often comes to be the standard by which events and decisions
are evaluated. Thus, while all condemn and abhor corruption and patronage,
they tend to do so largely when they are practised by opponents. Thus disciplinary action against public officials for misuse of office tends to be approved
in principle but resented when applied against members of one's own faction.
In the SPAFIF case this seems implicit in the attitudes of both sides. And, as
in that case, the political cost to the government has been severe: in 1966, for
example, two Ministers were dismissed for having interests in companies which
received state loans. One of them eventually went into opposition, with the
result that UNIP lost most of the seats in his province in 1968 elections. The
province clearly did not share the government's view on this matter.

Perhaps the clearest illustration of this tendency is conveyed in the Report
on the railways when it discusses the opposition of the Tonga group to the
Commission of Inquiry itself:

The Tonga group believes that the Ngoni group, aggrieved by the removal
of Mr O, their tribesman, have brought the allegations of tribalism, nepotism,
thefts and corruption against Mr A (General Manager) so that they can cause
his removal. The Tonga group argues that the persons who have been pressing
for the appointment of the Commission are [the] General Secretary of
ZRAWU, [the] General Secretary of the Zambia Congress of Trade Unions,
the Members of Parliament for Bwacha and Kabwe Central, . . . all of whom
(they say) are Ngoni. This view of the matter is held very strongly by Mr A
himself, Mr—(the Provincial Political Secretary) and Mr—, a member of
the Board. Mr O similarly believes that he was a victim of Tonga tribalism.[65]

The Report would indicate that the substance of political conflict expressed in
1973 was still very much alive in 1978.

Consequences for the state

It must be stressed again that the spoils system, of which corruption is a part,
is the outcome of a legacy of systemic deprivation and of the aspirations
which political independence excited in the elite strata from which the political
and administrative leadership was drawn. The primary requisite for access to
state spoils is public office and this in turn requires membership of the ruling
party. This institutionalisation of party patronage—expressed so graphically

in the slogan 'It Pays To Belong to UNIP'—is itself no more than an attempt to redress past disadvantages. But the systematic use of state resources to this end is endowed with clear contradictions since it often has negative implications for the state itself. We have already seen this in the discussion of how graft has exacerbated factional conflicts and brought political instability. But there are other facets of the problem as well.

Undermining efficiency

Patronage and corruption can alter the character of institutional performance in a context in which administrative efficiency is already weak as a result of a shortage of appropriate skills. This is especially so where public office is occupied by underqualified, incompetent or even corrupt officials who enjoy the protection of powerful patrons. Both the Lusaka and Railways inquiries found such instances, where lax disciplinary procedures existed for favoured individuals. The Blagden Report discusses at length the case of an acting Town Clerk—with significant stature in the party—who sought to secure the substantive appointment by securing the support of councillors and seeking to manipulate local government procedures.[66] In the process, he was considered to have acted in a questionable manner over certain appointments, over the reservation of plots for the Mayor and over the sacking of the previous Town Clerk.[67] He failed to support his staff when they were pressured by councillors, or to advise councillors when they acted improperly or to stand up to 'the pressure exerted on him by the Mayor'.

If the prevailing philosophy is too often what can be done *with* a job rather than *in* that job, there are likely to be negative effects on efficiency in administration or planning. Officers may feel that to cross a superior can be costly in career terms and may therefore agree to decisions they consider improper or erroneous. One senior parastatal official noted in 1975 that many parastatals suffered in this way as officers tried to evaluate projects in terms of the preferences they perceived their superiors to hold. Some cultivated the ability to say what was wanted rather than what was needed to a fine art, he observed, with the result that plans were often inadequately checked before being put into effect.[68] Many of the instances cited in the Reports considered above might imply such a process at work, but perhaps one small example best illustrates the point. The Auditor-General's Report for 1970 draws attention to a vegetable production scheme in Kasama where the crops in the garden were infested by eelworm and where the site had been chosen against the advice of field officers. Eleven workers employed in the garden were paid K363 per month, while the scheme earned K11 per month.[69] Inefficiency is, of course, an important element in the outcome of such schemes, but it seems clear that much inefficiency also arises from the operation of the spoils system.

Changing the ends of policy

The case studies also indicate that the incidence of graft can redirect official policy in unanticipated directions. The SPAFIF and Land Act cases, in particular, show that policy designed to broaden the social base of the public enjoying access to state resources can be hijacked in the interests of private accumulation. In the SPAFIF case this process is revealed most starkly. Funds contributed by, and intended for the benefit of, peasant producers were appropriated—albeit not illegally—by high level officials for the purchase of private farms on state land.

The Land Act was passed to check land speculation and give Zambians a greater chance of obtaining state land in prime areas. President Kaunda had earlier denounced price inflation in transfers of undeveloped property, citing an instance where one of three plots sold as a package for a total of K150,000 was itself resold alone for K100,000 on the same day (the government being the victim on this occasion).[70] The Act sought to check such speculation by suspending the land market and giving the state the power to approve all transfers. In the event, as we have seen, these powers were used to direct property to particular individuals and to set the price levels of such directed sales even where transfers had been agreed with other parties. In other words, the Act increased the pool of resources available to those with access to public office. Indeed, one MP even claimed that property expropriated from absentee landowners under the legislation was being purchased by political leaders and government officials—an indication of the climate of competition and suspicion surrounding the operation of the Act.[71]

And political ideology can also be appropriated along with policy in the service of private accumulation. The leadership publicly espouses 'the philosophy of Humanism' which champions the lot of 'the common man'. But professions of 'socialism' and ritual denunciations of 'capitalism' can be accompanied by personal accumulation and individual acquisitiveness. In the Lusaka case, having obtained a Council waiver on liquor licensing rules, the Mayor opened a K70,000 bar in 1968 and proclaimed it 'a socialist bar' where people could drink without dress restrictions.[72]

Undermining legitimacy

The redirection of public resources from global policies to individual interests creates serious problems for the operation of some political institutions, particularly administration. What its consequences are for the political system as a whole is more difficult to assess. And there seems to be little agreement among social scientists about the systemic effects of corruption; a number of them have tended to regard it as having certain positive effects on the modernisation process, in direct contrast to the classical view, espoused by Wraith and Simpkins, that corruption was essentially destructive of the public interest.[73] Merton, for example, suggests that it can be a mechanism for promoting social change and satisfying the unfulfilled needs of particular groups. Tilman observes that the bureaucratic black market acts to maintain an equilibrium between the limited supply of, and increasing demand for, government services. Huntington considers it to be an alternative to political violence as a means of making demands on the system in certain circumstances. And, in an influential paper, Nye has suggested that it may promote growth—especially where it involves high-level officials who are more likely to invest their gains than lower-level public servants who are more likely to increase their consumption. Such arguments can, of course, be generalised to the whole range of spoils discussed here.

It must be accepted that corruption does represent a response to scarcity and it gives access to the state to previously excluded groups. In this sense it may integrate them into the political system—and in Zambia it has been a mechanism for redressing generations of racial discrimination, as the Lusaka case indicated. The claim that it balances supply and demand for state resources is a truism: since spoils reduce the allocation of resources to the market principle, they confine provision to those who can pay the price, by definition. By selling citizenship, for example, officials could accumulate the resources to acquire business interests and so overcome the exclusion of Africans from the bourgeoisie. And by buying citizenship, expatriates could continue their businesses from which government policy sought to exclude them. Both groups were integrated into the system and the market mechanism used to settle mutual scarcities of resources. It is also true that the poor have a higher propensity to consume and that elite corruption is therefore more likely to produce private investment than mass corruption. It might even be inferred from this that had the Zambian government been less diligent in checking corruption, the country might have experienced higher levels of investment and might have offset some of the effects of the crippling recession that has raged since the mid-seventies.

There are at least two sets of problems with such propositions, however. Firstly, they presuppose that private property is preferable to equality of treatment—and so reflect the American origins of most of the scholars mentioned. They also conveniently ignore concerns expressed elsewhere by many of them about the problems of building rational, impersonal, achievement- rather than ascription-oriented political institutions—a project which seems to coexist uneasily with the furtherance of graft. Secondly, it is by no means clear that private investment and economic growth would result from such patterns of accumulation in the context of underdevelopment. Given the barriers to market entry constituted by the monopoly position of settler and, especially, foreign capital, investment tends to be directed more into circulation and speculation than into industry. Further, spoils tend to disperse the scarce investible surpluses concentrated in the hands of the state, even where they are appropriated by high-level officials; and patronage requires that they be further dispersed among a multitude of claimants. (Nor is it really logical to argue that private initiative would be more efficient than the state when much of the state's inefficiency is precisely the result of the eagerness with which individuals loot its resources.) Nye's argument just does not hold water. In general, it is extremely unlikely that graft aids growth in the African setting; such arguments seem to suffer from a high degree of ethnocentrism and ahistoricism.

The notion that graft is a factor in integrating disadvantaged or excluded groups into the political process is more serious. The case studies could certainly be used to argue that the spoils system was important in providing Africans with access to state resources and for permitting expatriates to preserve their links with the state in a post-colonial setting. In this sense it may well be that graft was often an alternative to political violence. (One politician characterised a scheme in which funds were widely distributed for co-operatives as being necessary to avert 'a revolution'; few of these loans were ever recovered.) If such an integrative role was indeed played by the spoils system, the case studies also indicate that its benefits were short lived from the point of view of the stability of the system. Instead, what seems to have occurred to an increasing extent was that spoils exacerbated the disillusion of many with the inability of the state to meet the overwhelming demands and hopes directed at it. Particular advantages have often been bought at the expense of inefficiency and project failures. Graft, in the context of scarce resources, implies not a market equilibrium but the ability of some people to 'jump the queue'. Thus the access gained by some previously excluded elements simply means that others are denied access. In such circumstances, the consequences for the legitimacy of the state are likely to be negative. Widely held notions that 'the government is corrupt', even where false, are likely to produce low levels of commitment to the political system. Some of this disillusion was expressed dramatically by the chairman of the Zambia Congress of Trade Unions in 1977. Commenting on the possibility that workers' representatives might run for parliament in the 1978 elections, to protect the working population from 'political mercenaries' who had made the administration 'the despair of every citizen', he observed: 'politicians are all the same. They promise to build a bridge where there is no river. In fact, politics is the conduct of public affairs for private advantage.'[74]

Class formation and class struggle

One of the main expressions of the conduct of public affairs for private advantage has been, traditionally, the pressure exerted by private business on public officials. In third world countries, multinational corporations are frequently observed to corrupt (or seek to corrupt) officials who can facilitate contracts, capital exports, market monopolies, docile labour and so on. In Zambia I encountered several reports of such pressures on public servants, particularly initiated through lavish gifts and entertainment. Some expatriate businessmen demonstrated a degree of cynicism when questioned about the probity of civil servants and one mentioned approaches from officials which, if true, indicated that some of them, like Plunkett, had seen their opportunities and were prepared to take them. But there was little possibility of verifying such allegations, often motivated by racial malice on the part of white businessmen, and so this is an area on which this chapter must largely be silent.

Nevertheless, illustrations of how public resources can be appropriated by private capital working through officials can be found in the report on the Railways. In one instance cited, a police investigation revealed that railway officers had stopped purchasing supplies from wholesalers and retailers with whom Zambia Railways operated accounts and had redirected all such orders through one commercial company. This company, it transpired, purchased the supplies from the same firms that had previously sold to the railways directly, but the new intermediary now inflated the prices enormously (by over 350 per cent in one case). An employee who queried this change was threatened by the superior who had initiated the change. In another case, the practice of buying railway sleepers from Malawi was stopped and a local company appointed supplier. This local company, however, purchased the sleepers from Malawi and, moreover, obtained import permits to do so on the strength of the Zambia Railways order. The sleepers now cost the railways K13 each instead of K7 each as they had when purchased directly. The police discovered that two employees had received motor vehicles from the intermediary company.[75] Such examples are typical of the many stories in circulation about corporate relations with government and there is little reason to doubt that they occur fairly frequently. It is clear that the state constitutes an important resource for many businessmen in Zambia, whether as a source of contracts and loans, or as a market or—as in the citizenship case—as a means of enabling business activity to occur at all.

But the cases studied and discussed here indicate a more fundamental relationship between state resources and the capitalist class, one that is part of the most significant structural change in Zambian society since Independence—the formation of an indigenous propertied class.[76] It has already been noted that the spoils system affords access to resources, position and wealth only by excluding others from that access; it is a form of 'queue jumping'. Graft is therefore not an egalitarian instrument of social mobility. Those who obtain resources in this way are often able to set up in business or farming (or to consume more) and so enter into the bourgeoisie or petit bourgeoisie from which Africans were generally excluded before independence. As Cohen has observed:

> The major activity of the ruling groups is an attempt to use the benefits of political power in an attempt to redress the insecure position they find themselves in. This can be seen in more general terms as an 'embourgeoisement' of the ruling elite. . . . Mutual back-scratching exercises are inaugurated . . . governmental contracts are appropriated or supplied to supporters. . . .

Wealth acquired from the holding of political office is used to acquire land, houses or small service industries. . . . The behaviour and activity of the ruling groups in office show their overt indebtedness to the political process as a means of developing class crystallization and solidarity.[77]

The study of Zambian companies undertaken by Carolyn Baylies and myself would indicate that access to state resources has been an important factor— though by no means the only one or even always the main one—in promoting the growth of a Zambian bourgeoisie (a process promoted vigorously through economic reforms and state loans). Access to the state has therefore been valuable as a source of upward mobility, but in many cases it has been less an end in itself than a half-way house where conditions are created for entry into business and the acquisition of property.[78]

The case studies considered have clearly exemplified this process. The Land Act controversy was most obviously concerned with the acquisition of land and businesses. The Lusaka City Council inquiry, less obviously, involved not only the first generation of Zambians in local government, but also a cross-section of the city's emerging business class. The Mayor owned a successful construction company as well as the bar. Another councillor was also a prosperous business man and, indeed, later joined the board of at least one multinational corporation. And other councillors were small traders, including one who led the UNIP co-operative society that ran four of Lusaka's markets. Access to public office thus either constituted an asset by which entry into the bourgeoisie or petit bourgeoisie could be effected or an attraction by which capital already accumulated might be defended or enlarged. The link between political office, with all its insecurities, and private property was most clearly expressed in the SPAFIF case, however. In this instance loans were taken from the funds for the specific purpose of buying farm land for the private use of public officials. Public office, in itself, was not always adequate as a means of upward mobility —not least because of its insecurity. As Sipalo indicated in court when explaining why he had taken a loan: 'round about October [1968] I was aware of the consequences of the general elections so I was looking for property for myself. I was aware that we were going to lose the elections in the Western Province and also that I was going to lose my job [as a Minister].'[79]

Yet it is not adequate to regard the spoils system as simply a means by which advantaged individuals obtain preferred access to public goods that can be converted into capital. The resources to which such access is enjoyed represent taxes and levies drawn on the public at large. The appropriation of such resources therefore constitutes a net transfer of wealth from society at large to some privileged sections of it. The state, therefore, comes to serve as an apparatus through which parts of the social product can be redistributed to incumbents of office and their supporters. In the SPAFIF case, moreover, the class character of this transfer—and the objective class conflict inherent in it—is starkly demonstrated: there was, in that instance, an expropriation of surplus from the peasantry to the emerging bourgeoisie through the apparatus of the state by means of the spoils system. This relationship was even understood, to some extent, by the Doyle Commission. Noting that it was 'discreditable' for people in public office 'to descend like locusts on a fund to which none of them had contributed and from which morally they should plainly have been excluded', the Report observed that:

> It is plain that all the persons concerned were favoured in getting loans because of their position. The ordinary African peasant farmer for whom loans under the Ordinance were really intended and whose contributions formed the funds was completely disregarded—indeed left in the dark—in favour of a horde of privileged persons in public positions.[80]

It is suggested that this observable link between spoils appropriation and class formation underlines the argument advanced here that corruption, as a concept, is of limited utility in explaining political practice. But it is of great value when understood as part (most often as a symptom) of a larger process of social change with important implications for political development and class relations. Viewed from this perspective, it is clear that while the forms of corruption may be the same over time and across countries, the social role it may perform is likely to be temporally and spatially specific. In particular, in post-colonial Africa, the Zambian case would indicate that it is an element in the way in which private capital and the capitalist class impinges on the state.

Notes

1. For a more detailed treatment of the spoils system in Zambia, see Morris Szeftel, *Conflict, Spoils and Class Formation*, Manchester University doctoral thesis, 1978; and Szeftel, 'The Political Process in Post-colonial Zambia: the Structural Bases of Factional Conflict', in *The Evolving Structure of Zambian Society*, Proceedings of a Conference at the Centre of African Studies, University of Edinburgh, May 1980.
2. On the growth of a Zambian business class, see Carolyn L. Baylies and Morris Szeftel, 'The Rise of a Zambian Capitalist Class in the 1970s', *Journal of Southern African Studies*, **8**, No. 2, 1982.
3. Arnold J. Heidenheimer (ed.), *Political Corruption: Readings in Comparative Analysis*, New York, Holt, Rinehart & Winston, 1970, pp. 3–25.
4. Arnold A. Rogow and Harold D. Laswell, 'The Definition of Corruption', in Heidenheimer, op. cit., p. 54.
5. Robert O. Tilman, 'Black Market Bureaucracy', in Heidenheimer, op. cit., pp. 62–4.
6. An outstanding example of this approach is contained in Colin Leys, 'What is the Problem about Corruption?', in Heidenheimer, op. cit., pp. 31–7.
7. James C. Scott, *Comparative Political Corruption*, Englewood Cliffs, N.J., Prentice-Hall, 1972, Ch. 1.
8. Robert C. Brooks, 'The Nature of Political Corruption', in Heidenheimer, op. cit., p. 56. One might ask how much use a legal definition of corruption would be if the law suddenly defined philately or smoking as corruption; legal definitions are a function of ideological and power considerations which are constantly changing.
9. V. O. Key, Jr, 'Techniques of Political Graft', in Heidenheimer, op. cit., pp. 46–53,

lists a number of forms of corruption: bribery, extortion, state bribery or patronage, discriminatory administration of the law, discrimination in administration of services, and auto-corruption, many of which would be excluded from narrower definitions. In Zambia, in fact, the Prime Minister enumerated a number of categories—'corrupt practices', 'corruption' and 'theft by public servant'—in reporting to the National Assembly (see text and note 49 below).

10. The notion of a set of responsibilities incumbent on the holder of an office or authority is at the heart of the concept of corruption. Thus, if garbage is collected by a local authority, it would be corrupt for a dustman to accept a cash inducement to collect my refuse twice a week (and thereby not have time to collect that belonging to someone else). But if the collector were a private company which responded to such an inducement at the expense of another consumer, although there might be liabilities under contractual obligations, the notion of corruption would not arise. It is in the concept of an impartial public service carrying out obligations towards citizens considered equal before the law, and therefore meriting equal treatment, that the modern idea of corruption is born. The expression 'bribery and corruption' expresses this difference between civil society and the state; it distinguishes between the official who is corrupt and the outside party who is doing the corrupting.

11. In fact, electoral malpractice does not seem to be a major issue in Zambia and, for this reason, I have chosen to focus on public office corruption. Where irregularities have been alleged in general elections, they have concerned partisan intimidation rather than official malpractice. After the 1968 elections, for example, complaints of intimidation led to court hearings in 1969 and resulted in some constituencies rerunning their ballots. In 1973, again, there were several complaints of pressure made to the Director of Elections, but no results were invalidated. Occasions of ballot tampering have been extremely rare: the most important case being during the elections for the UNIP Central Committee in 1967, which caused President Kaunda to order an inquiry at judicial level. The report indicated that there appeared to have been some vote-rigging but that it did not upset the results (in fact, it was predominantly on behalf of losing candidates!). Elections in Zambia have generally exhibited a high level of political propriety.

12. A broader, less legalistic version of the often-quoted definition of J. S. Nye, 'Corruption and Political Development: a Cost-benefit Analysis', in Heidenheimer, op. cit., pp. 564–78: 'Corruption is behaviour which deviates from the formal duties of a public role because of private-regarding . . . pecuniary or status gains; or violates rules against the exercise of certain types of private-regarding influence'.

13. Richard Sandbrook, 'Patrons, Clients and Factions: New Dimensions of Conflict Analysis in Africa', *Canadian Journal of Political Science*, 5, No. 1, 1972, 104–19.

14. William L. Riordan, *Plunkitt of Tammany Hall: A Series of Very Plain Talks on Very Practical Politics*, New York, Dutton, 1962, pp. 3–6.

15. I have chosen to deal only with published cases since the facts of such cases are less in dispute than those of many others reported verbally. Such cases obviously are not always representative since they are all of a sufficiently critical character to have warranted publication in the first place. But they seem to me to exemplify processes inherent in all instances I came across. It must be stressed that the discussion below makes no judgement about the legality or illegality of any actions; that is not of interest since it reveals little about the political process which these cases exemplify. For this reason also, I have sought to avoid using the names of individuals wherever possible and have only done so where it was otherwise impossible to convey the events sensibly and coherently. Again, the intention is to examine cases as representative of social processes and not as reflections on personalities.

16. In certain cases they were serious enough to warrant inquiries and this alone makes them atypical. Commissions of inquiry usually have a political purpose and so their search for the truth is necessarily coloured by the demands of state. See Tania Ocran, 'Corruption and Attendant Commissions of Inquiry', manuscript, Lusaka, undated c. 1972–3; and H. H. Werlin, 'The Roots of Corruption—the Ghanaian Enquiry', *Journal of Modern African Studies*, 10, No. 2, 1972, 247–66. On the other hand, such

inquiries do provide a great deal of systematically collected information of a kind not usually allowed publicity and they do indicate cases of singular importance to the political system.

17. Republic of Zambia, *Report of the Commission of Inquiry into the Affairs of the Lusaka City Council, November 1968*, Lusaka, 1969—The Blagden Report.
18. Ibid., p. 2.
19. Mary Elizabeth Jackman, *Recent Population Movements in Zambia: Some Aspects of the 1969 Census*, Zambian Papers No. 8, Institute of African Studies, Lusaka, Manchester, 1973.
20. The Blagden Report, op. cit., pp. 11–17.
21. Ibid., pp. 21–6, quote p. 25.
22. Ibid., p. 25.
23. Ibid., pp. 63–6.
24. Ibid., pp. 60–2, esp. p. 61.
25. United National Independence Party and African National Congress. UNIP has been the party of government ever since 1964 and in 1972 became the sole party with the creation of a one-party state. The ANC was then absorbed into it.
26. The Blagden Report, op. cit., p. 29.
27. Ibid., p. 31.
28. The report rarely uses the term 'corrupt' in its 90 pages.
29. Ibid., p. 32.
30. Ibid., p. 18.
31. Ibid., p. 20.
32. Ibid., pp. 56–9.
33. Ibid., pp. 5–7.
34. *Africa*, **69**, London, May 1977, p. 41.
35. *Zambia Daily Mail*, 3 and 16 October 1975; *Times of Zambia*, 20 October 1975.
36. *Times of Zambia*, 23 January 1976.
37. Ibid., 5 June 1976.
38. Ibid., 6 and 19 August 1976.
39. *Times of Zambia, Zambia Daily Mail*, 25 August 1976.
40. *Zambia Daily Mail*, 26 August 1976.
41. Jacob Van Klaveren, 'The Concept of Corruption', in Heidenheimer, op. cit., pp. 38–40, writes of the 'civil servant who regards his public office as a business, the income of which he will seek to maximize', p. 39.
42. *Times of Zambia*, 25 February and 5 June 1976; *Zambia Daily Mail*, 10 May 1976.
43. Republic of Zambia, *Auditor-General's Report*, First Report 1970, Lusaka, 1970, p. 15.
44. *Auditor-General's Report*, 1972, pp. 19, 44.
45. Ibid., 1973, p. 34.
46. *Zambia Daily Mail*, 20–23 May 1972, 7 and 28 November 1972 and 9 April 1976.
47. *Times of Zambia*, 29 November 1972, 5 and 6 December 1972; *Zambia Daily Mail*, 29 November 1972, 5 and 6 December 1972, 7, 14 and 28 February 1973, 1 March 1973.
48. *Zambia Daily Mail*, 2 March 1973.
49. *Times of Zambia*, 2 February 1976.
50. *Sunday Times of Zambia*, 18 April 1982.
51. Republic of Zambia, *Report of the Commission of Inquiry Into the Allegations Made by Mr Justin Chimba and Mr John Chisata*, Lusaka, May 1971, pp. 4–5, quoting from the African Farming Improvement Fund Ordinance, Section 8. The inquiry was chaired by Chief Justice Doyle and is termed the Doyle Report in the text.
52. Ibid., p. 5.
53. Ibid., p. 6.
54. *Zambia Daily Mail*, 2 January 1971.
55. *Zambia Daily Mail* and *Times of Zambia* from December 1970 through March 1971, 8 April 1972 and 14 March 1973.
56. *Zambia Daily Mail*, 9 April 1979.

57. See Robert V. Molteno, 'Cleavage and Conflict in Zambian Politics: a Study in Sectionalism', in W. Tordoff (ed.), *Politics in Zambia*, Manchester, Manchester University Press, 1974, pp. 62–106, and Szeftel (1978) op. cit., for a fuller discussion of 'tribalism'. Although 'tribalism' is often equated with ethnicity, the two should not be confused despite the fact that 'tribalism' involves a manipulation of ethnic boundaries at times. But such boundaries are extremely fluid and are often overlaid with linguistic and provincial boundaries as well. For instance, the faction known in Zambia as 'the Bemba' was made up of many Bemba-speaking people from different origins, including non-ethnic Bemba who had grown up on the Copperbelt in a Bemba milieu. It also included people from Northern and Luapula provinces until about 1969 when the Luapulans increasingly came to assert their own interests and, indeed, to take the lead in factional organisation aimed at weakening the grip of Northern Bemba on UNIP offices. This was part of a process in which different regional leaders allied to remedy the considerable success of Northern militants in the UNIP Central Committee elections of 1967. After 1969, most factional leaders were in alliance against the Northern Bemba—hardly a sign of ethnic conflict so beloved of liberal commentators on Africa. A consequence of this conflict was that many of UNIP's most militant Northern Bemba faction left UNIP to form the United Progressive Party (UPP) in 1972. But many also remained within UNIP, most notably the Bemba bourgeoisie. And the UPP was joined by some Eastern Province militants who had originally organised against the Bemba faction in UNIP! The instrumental nature of factional cleavages and the opportunism which frequently attends 'tribal' conflict must not be fetishised into a model of cultural conflict between 'primordial attachments'.

58. The most serious such crisis was the formation of the UPP which provoked the formation of a one-party state and in which the SPAFIF affair was a major moment. After 1972, the Cabinets of the one-party state have reflected a careful provincial balance within them.

59. Editorial, *Zambia Daily Mail*, 25 November 1972.

60. Republic of Zambia, National Assembly, *Daily Parliamentary Debates* (Hansard), Lusaka, col. 551, 552, 29 January and 30 January 1975 (No. 38 of bound volumes). And *Times of Zambia*, 2 December 1977.

61. *Zambia Daily Mail*, 6 December 1977, in letter from the Prime Minister.

62. Republic of Zambia, *Report of the Commission of Inquiry into the Affairs of Zambia Railways*, Lusaka, March 1978—the Mumpanshya Report.

63. Ibid., pp. 11–12.

64. Ibid., p. 59.

65. Ibid., p. 26.

66. The Blagden Report, op. cit., pp. 29, 59, 63.

67. Ibid., pp. 43–50.

68. Oral evidence, May 1975.

69. *Auditor-General's Report* 1970 (first report), p. 38.

70. Kenneth Kaunda, The *'Watershed' Speech*, Address by His Excellency the President to the National Council of UNIP, Lusaka, Government Printer, 1975, pp. 34–45.

71. *Times of Zambia*, 23 January 1976.

72. *Zambia Mail*, 1 March 1968.

73. Heidenheimer, op. cit., pp. 479–86, for a survey of this discussion.

74. *Sunday Times of Zambia*, 1 January 1978.

75. Mumpanshya Report, op. cit., pp. 27–9.

76. Baylies and Szeftel, op. cit.

77. Robin Cohen, 'Class in Africa: analytical problems and perspectives', *The Socialist Register 1972*, London, Merlin, 1972, p. 248.

78. Baylies and Szeftel, op. cit.

79. *Zambia Daily Mail*, 12 February 1971.

80. Doyle Report, op. cit., pp. 7–8.

11 'The land of waving palms': political economy, corruption inquiries and politics in Sierra Leone

STEPHEN RILEY*

Public-office corruption is a widespread, at times systemic, and significant feature of the political economy of the West African state of Sierra Leone. Observable and recordable corruption has been documented extensively since the late 1950s, and government-inspired inquiries have regularly produced evidence of culpable public officials and others outside the public sector. Public recorded corruption appears somewhat humble, however, when compared to the extensive semi-public comment and speculation about corruption and other misdemeanours. One example of the significance of corruption is that the political regime in Sierra Leone is currently (in 1982–3) operating under 'state of emergency' legislation: legislation ostensibly put into operation to cope with a series of corruption scandals that emerged in 1980 and 1981. These scandals have been described in the local press by a series of Watergate-inspired neologisms: 'Vouchergate', 'Squandergate' and so on. One might doubt that the real intention behind the imposition of a state of emergency is a desire to eliminate corruption, and instead argue that the emergency fulfils a wider political role of maintaining control over a regime threatened by economic decline and dissent. The state of emergency does, nevertheless, indicate the significance of corruption as an aspect of the political reality of Sierra Leone.

Examples of corruption such as 'Vouchergate'—which involved the diversion of government payment orders (or 'Vouchers') to enrich some junior officials—are not new or unusual; instead such instances of public recorded corruption echo many past examples. The gossip and rumour surrounding the scandals also had many echoes of the past, as did the political manipulation of the process of inquiry (and subsequent judicial procedures), which do shed light upon the nature of political power and economic leverage in the regime. In these ways the visible character and treatment of corruption in Sierra Leone share many features with corruption as documented in other West African states.

This chapter is intended to provide evidence and analysis of four main items: firstly, a sketch of the political economy of Sierra Leone is provided, along with a discussion of that (somewhat abstract) entity, the 'post-colonial state'.

*I wish to thank Pat White for her help and encouragement. The financial assistance of the Nuffield Foundation is also gratefully acknowledged. The quotation used in the title is a phrase used by a business man, quoted in Green (1981), p. 96.

Corruption in Sierra Leone appears to be intimately related to the fragile, 'permeable' character of the state, and to some unusual elements of the political economy, though Sierra Leone shares the features of a peripheral, and dependent, capitalist economy with many other regimes in West Africa. The second part of the chapter is a discussion of inquiries into corruption in Sierra Leone. The use of official inquiries to investigate allegations of corruption is widespread in West Africa, and some comparisons are made. Thirdly, an interpretation of public-office corruption in Sierra Leone is presented, covering the four regimes since independence in 1961, and relating corruption to administrative expansion and inefficiency, the manipulation of patron-client relations, economic decline and the political economy of 'alien trading minorities'. Finally, some conclusions are drawn from the evidence and analysis.

My interest is in political corruption, understood as corruption that is primarily public-office centred. The chapter does not, therefore, provide evidence of electoral or legislative corruption (despite the fact that the May 1982 one-party elections would provide many examples). My primary concern is the corruption of the individual in national public office. Corruption in this sense is the use of public office for private gain by an individual, clique or group. Nye's legal definition of corruption is used, but not uncritically, as some public opinion notions of corrupt behaviour are also discussed.[1]

I

Sierra Leone, situated on the west coast of Africa between Guinea and Liberia, has a population of 3.4 million in an area of 72,000 square kilometres (1979 figures from the World Bank's 'Berg Report' on Sub-Saharan Africa).[2] It is an example of a classically dependent economy, with its major exports being gem diamonds, coffee and cocoa, and its imports manufactured goods and, increasingly, food. Food shortages, especially of the staple, rice, have had important political consequences, with allegations of hoarding and political manipulation of food supplies being very prominent in the late 1970s. The price, and availability, of basic food items were important factors behind the urban labour unrest, leading to a General Strike in August–September 1981 (the first since Independence). Labour unrest has often been associated with student unrest at the countries' two university campuses (one in Freetown, the capital, the other up-country) who have brought the issue of public corruption to national attention. Students who participated in the 1977 demonstrations against the government of President Siaka Stevens were also behind the independent bi-weekly newspaper *The Tablet*, which documented extensive corruption in the 1970s.

Formal political activity has been dominated by three groups: the Creoles, and latterly the 'hinterland politics' of the Mende and Temne. The Creoles are the descendants of 're-settlement slaves' liberated during the late eighteenth and early nineteenth centuries. They have formed a distinct social, economic and political group, imbued with strong nineteenth-century Christian values and an ethos favouring education and achievement. The twentieth century has seen a parallel decline of the Creole's ethnic distinctiveness and political power. Politics and political dominance has been transferred to the hinterland groups.[3] One (incorrect) interpretation has suggested that political conflict has become 'tribalised', with the Mende in the south supporting the Sierra Leone People's Party (SLPP) and the Temne in the north plus Freetown supporting the All People's Congress (APC).

Four political regimes can be identified: the rule of the SLPP under Milton and Albert Margai (1961–4, 1964–7); military rule (1967–8) and the rule of the APC under Siaka Stevens (1968 to date). While such a periodisation might imply an excessively 'personalised' view of Sierra Leone politics, it is nevertheless the case that politics has been a very personalised affair: both parties are loose alliances based upon factional loyalties and personal interests rather than ideologically orientated claques. 'Frank Ly's'[4] account, for example, places great emphasis upon Stevens' role as an accommodator and persuader, operating within a situation of declining political competition, which culminated in the establishment of a one-party state in 1978.

Stevens' 'great achievement' has been to maintain his position by a range of manipulative means while engineering the growth of a not very loyal patrimonial elite, which seeks its rewards from the resources the state has to wield. One of the consequences of Stevens' manipulative politics, therefore, has been the growth of the state sector and the organisational bourgeoisie. 'Frank Ly' suggests that the Sierra Leone mode of production is one 'which increased the rate of exploitation of future rather than present productive forces'.[5]

In this context it is the nature of the resources of the state that is important, and in particular the major exports. Sierra Leone's major exports have been mainly mineral products: alluvial gem diamonds, and to a much lesser extent iron ore, as well as bauxite and alluvial gold in the 1970s. The diamonds have been mined both via an official, partly government-owned company backed by Selection Trust, and also by a scheme of 'illicit diamond mining' (as Selection Trust calls it). Politicians are active behind the scenes as financiers of illicit diamond-mining operations, as are Lebanese entrepreneurs. Future resources can be mortgaged to provide current security; it seems likely as well that the regime has been able to mortgage unsecured future resources, as in the case of the assumed gold and offshore oil deposits in the late 1970s.

Given that the rural sector is relatively undisturbed, it is in the export mineral sector that the resources of the state (and the fuel for corruption) lie. The situation in the 1970s has proved difficult for the central political actors as alluvial diamond production has declined and major companies proved reluctant to invest the expenditure necessary to finance the exploitation of the Kimberlite diamond pipes that would have continued diamond production.

IMF financial assistance has been called in and a series of orthodox financial measures imposed.

As a result of the nature of the resource base of the regime, and partly also because of their strategic position, commercial trading minorities—particularly Lebanese and Indian entrepreneurs—control many areas of economic activity, such as the import–export trade, retailing, transport, diamond mining (outside of the Selection Trust operation), and can wield large quantities of finance capital. This 'alien' business and trading community has great economic power but little formal political influence. The temptation to use informal political influence (in other words, 'corruption') is enormous, and is not resisted. The informal influence of local Lebanese entrepreneurs has been buttressed by the emerging significance of overseas capital from the Lebanon, which has replaced British and European capital to a limited extent.

II

The use of an official inquiry to investigate allegations of corrupt activity by public officials is widespread in West Africa. Usually appointed by the head of state or Prime Minister or equivalent, holding public sittings and using quasi-judicial procedures, they have been a common and dramatic feature of post-Independence politics (and, of course, of pre-Independence politics as well). As dramatic political events they have had an impact upon the politics of current regimes, or have acted as apologias for new ones. Out of a large number of examples, some of the more well known can be cited: the Nigerian Collier Commission of Inquiry of 1962, inquiring, as the title runs, 'into the affairs of Certain Statutory Corporations in Western Nigeria'; a Ghanaian example is the Commission to Enquire into 'the Kwame Nkrumah properties' in Ghana (and elsewhere), 1967;[6] and, for Sierra Leone, the Forster Commission of Inquiry on Assets of Ex-Ministers and Ex-Deputy Ministers, 1968, can be mentioned.

Numerous other examples can be given, but in general they have the common properties of being dramatic or 'scandalous' political events, having similar procedures and focuses of inquiry. In terms of the last point many corruption inquiries, if not most, are what can be described as 'rotten apple' inquiries. By this is meant the inquiries look at 'rotten apples' in basically good barrels; they look at the 'corrupt few' in a particular area of government, prompted by some scandalous disclosure, and, by implication, suggest that the remainder of the system is essentially honest. The result is to turn attention away from the possibility that corruption might be systematic or systemic in nature. One apparently significant exception to this is the final report of the Ghanaian Commission of Enquiry on Bribery and Corruption, 1975, which did attempt to provide an analysis of a 'corrupt society'.

In examining the Sierra Leone corruption inquiries, it is necessary to do three things. Firstly, to outline the nature and range of the inquiries, looking at the mechanics of the inquiries and suggesting a typology for analysing them and corruption in general. Secondly, to give some actual examples, in a social and political context, and thirdly to analyse what is overlooked, minimised or excluded.

In Sierra Leone an assortment of government inquiries and reports have been issued from the 1950s onwards. Early examples are the inquiries into the Chiefdom system and local government in the Provinces. Two reports from 1957 concern the 'conduct of certain chiefs', and the evidence, showing reasonably systematic corruption (particularly in the field of Chiefly exactions), has been discussed by Kilson and, more recently, by Tangri.[7] On central government and the parastatal sector, a large number of inquiries emerged in the 1960s and early 1970s. These are inquiries concerning the scandalous activity of certain ministers and committees (and particular officials associated with them) as well as inquiries into such diverse bodies as the Post Office and Marketing Board. In addition, there have been inquiries into areas of non-governmental activity, such as the trade unions (inquiries into two unions—the Transport and General Workers Union and the Artisans Union—were formally established in the late 1960s) and the Ex-Servicemen's Association (two inquiries apparently established undemocratic practices, maladministration and misuse of subscriptions, yet the individual concerned continued to head the Association). There are, therefore, a large range of inquiries.[8]

They can be divided into two main types: 'internal' inquiries and more open public inquiries. Internal inquiries are usually instituted by departments, ministries or public bodies, and work initially in private; whereas public inquiries are formally announced and work in the open, with witnesses and counsel. The internal inquiries tend to be leaked, making the distinction a fairly academic one, but greater difficulty is experienced in trying to obtain the reports of internal inquiries. Two examples of internal inquiries are the reports of inquiries into the Rice Corporation and the National Trading Company, both completed in 1979.[9] These two examples of the 'non-availability' of reports and sensitivity of inquiries indicate one factor which has to be borne in mind when considering inquiries in general: they aren't necessarily neutral politically, or 'objective' or comprehensive in their coverage. They are conscious political acts: the decision to establish them is a clearly political one, as is the determination of their focus and scope. This involves arguing against a view that simply accepts the reports as being accurate and fair indications of corruption in a society. Some commentators appear to simply accept corruption reports as accurate, fair evidence —an example in the case of Sierra Leone is Cox's book on civil-military relations, which simply records 'evidence' from various inquiries uncritically. Admittedly, Cox's book is on a different theme, but a chapter on 'Coups, Plots and Corruption' should show some sensitivity to questions of evidence.

Before considering this point in greater detail, a typology is presented which will, perhaps, help to explain the argument about the comprehensiveness of corruption inquiries. The typology can be used to analyse corruption itself as well as corruption inquiries (which is an important distinction). The typology is a fairly simple one, containing two distinctions or variables. The first distinction is in terms of the level of corruption—how high up the society does the corruption occur, how near is it to those who wield the fundamentals of state power? A second distinction can be made between incidental, systematic and systemic corruption. Incidental corruption occurs occasionally, almost on a random basis. It can be seen in the random solicitation and acceptance of bribes. Systematic corruption occurs when a pattern operates in a particular institution; whereas systemic corruption can be seen as a whole, regularised web of corruption surrounding key decision-makers and channelling funds in their direction. Examples will, perhaps, make the distinctions clear. A number of examples of low-level, incidental corruption were seen during my research in Sierra Leone: policemen asking for and taking bribes from vehicle drivers on up-country roads, for example. An example of reasonably high-level, systematic corruption is the corruption documented in one of the inquiries on the Marketing Board, the Report on the Marketing Board's Canteen Accounts. Despite its apparently innocuous and insignificant title it is an example of this: a pattern of private gain (in funds and goods) from an institution. An example of high-level, systemic corruption during the period since independence is the development of a system of corruption under the latter part of Albert Margai's rule. The system was based on Albert Margai and the main sources of funds were commissions on contracts, diamonds, the manipulation of the Sierra Leone Marketing Board and the use of state resources.

These examples will, it is hoped, explain the typology, which can be used to look at corruption and corruption inquiries. Corruption inquiries are useful as evidence in areas of low-level, incidental and systematic corruption; they are not, however, and indeed cannot for political reasons be used as evidence in cases of high-level systemic corruption. It is unlikely that a corrupt regime will investigate itself; it is only possible when there is a change of regime, and then the exercise is politically suspect (as an apologia for the current regime). Evidence from corruption inquiries does not present a balanced picture of corruption in a particular society: it 'individualises' or 'personalises' corruption in terms of a particular corrupt individual (or individuals). This problem with inquiries is, of course, in addition to some wider problems of studying corruption, such as definitional questions, and the sheer intractability of corruption itself, which is likely to be under-cover and secret in nature. To be successfully 'corrupt' (i.e. to do acts or accept bribes contrary to legal and other expectations of public office) you have to be secretive and skilled, unless societal norms legitimate certain ostensibly corrupt acts.

Some examples of corruption inquiries and their reports are now discussed, setting them in a particular social and political context. Inquiries in Sierra Leone are instituted when one of three conditions applies: firstly, when a 'scandal' becomes public, either in print or by widespread rumour; secondly, when a change of government takes place and political advantage can be gained and thirdly, when serious financial loss or inefficiency is known about by senior figures (and to a certain extent a process of face-saving has to take place). Political considerations are always involved, both in instituting the inquiry and, particularly, in determining the nature and scope of the inquiry.

'Scandal' seems to be a continuing and pervasive feature of Sierra Leone public life—extensive gossip about corruption and politics generally is assisted by the close-knit nature of the political community, predominantly Creole in the civil service, drawing from a small group in terms of politicians. An example of scandal instituting a corruption inquiry is the so-called 'Mr. Kilowatt' affair, concerning the misappropriation of public funds in the Electricity Corporation, among other matters. It was described as such by Sam Metzger, now editor of *We Yone*, the party newspaper, in a series of stories in that newspaper in 1974–5, Senior officials were misappropriating funds, as were meter-recorders who were either under-recording or not recording meters. A disorganised financial system led to major financial difficulties. All this was exposed by Metzger in *We Yone* and almost immediately an official inquiry was instituted. This was a politically safe thing to do in a number of ways, leading to the detention of a number of Corporation officials, but without harming politicians.[10]

The second occasion where an inquiry is instituted concerns those which are established when a change of government takes place. The most obvious change of government in post-Independence Sierra Leone is the military coup of 1967, and the restoration of civil rule in 1968, with the associated inquiry being the Forster Report on Ministerial Assets, reporting in 1968. The Forster Report is an inquiry used to gain political advantage, in this case for the APC and Siaka Stevens, over the SLPP who had constituted the government in the years from Independence in 1961 to the military coup. Sir Albert Margai, unpopular and widely (and fairly) regarded as corrupt during his period of rule, was thereby effectively prevented from resuming the leadership of the SLPP upon the return to civil rule, and the SLPP was thereby rendered leaderless. The Forster Report was notable in that it recorded that Sir Albert, in March 1967, possessed assets of some £250,000, despite having an annual salary of only £4,000.[11] The information on Sir Albert's corruption was not new; much of the evidence had previously been printed in the then opposition newspaper *We Yone*, which had had a series of articles concerning corruption in government.[12] The Forster Report can, however, be regarded as partisan and trivial, not in its treatment of Sir Albert, but in its treatment of some of the others—Ministers and Deputy Ministers—in Sir Albert's government. Perhaps because of lack of evidence—the Forster Report attempts to smear a number of politicians who cannot be regarded as 'corrupt' on the evidence as presented. Some politicians are criticised in the report for trivial matters—the unauthorised use of a government car on private business is one example—and then requested to pay back the 'corrupt' sum of less than £20 thus acquired.[13] Using a government car for a limited amount of private business is hardly a hanging offence; instead it is to be seen as a trivial matter, but used in a partisan way to provide a 'guilt by association' picture of the entire SLPP government. There is no doubt that Sir Albert and a number of senior ministers were corrupt, taking advantage of the usual benefits of Ministerial life, but there is doubt, on the evidence presented, that all those made guilty by association were similarly corrupt.

The Forster Commission is not the only one that is partisan. Other inquiries make similar comments about Sir Albert Margai. An example is the Beoku Betts Commission of inquiry into the Sierra Leone Produce Marketing Board, which examined the poor record of the years 1961–7, and to which Sir Albert was summoned to give evidence:

> Sir Albert took no part in the Commission as he made out that because of ill health he was unable to remember what had happened. The medical reports did not support his claims to ill health. Whether by his silence he was trying to save himself embarrassment we were unable to tell. However, the Commission took a decision to release him after several appearances without taking part and looking more and more sorry for himself. More so when he and his solicitors indicated that Sir Albert would abide by the decision of the Commission if he was implicated by documentary evidence.[14]

No doubt Sir Albert had a great deal to be sorry about, but the whole tenor of the report is partisan, a product, perhaps, of the times as well as documented corruption. Again, corruption is 'individualised' rather than being seen as potentially systemic or a factor related to more fundamental political problems (the need to secure continued political support) or administrative difficulties. Emphasis upon the particular and spectacular directs attention away from the way in which a web of high-level, systemic corruption was created in the latter year of Sir Albert's regime; emphasis upon Sir Albert's personal greed tends to suggest that the web of corruption dissolved in 1967 when he left political office. It did not, though some of the personnel changed. A system of corruption did consolidate itself again, almost as the APC consolidated its own position of political dominance.

The third case where an inquiry is instituted is when serious financial loss or inefficiency is known about by senior figures. There are a number of examples of this, including the early Marketing Board inquiries and the inquiry into the Post Office. The early Marketing Board inquiries were instituted when it became known that the financial operations of the board were, to say the least, running into difficulties. This was primarily due to mismanagement, corruption and excessive spending on a number of allegedly impractical schemes. All this is documented in the subsequent official inquiries, but several cases of mismanagement had been allegedly hushed up earlier, in 1965, or so *We Yone* reported (and *We Yone* had a good record for accuracy in the period). These early inquiries came at a time when the economy as a whole was facing serious difficulties, and, of course, concerned a key economic institution of corruption as the Marketing Board was the most obvious source of funds. The government managed to put off claims for public inquiries until the board was unable to meet its debts—to buying-agents and to those involved in the system of external suppliers credits. The collapse of the board was an important factor in the subsequent 1967 election. Thus the Marketing Board inquiry is an example where the government institutes an internal inquiry into a critical financial situation; trying at all costs to avoid public embarrassment at a time of increased political competition (the discussion on the one-party state proposal and the run-up to the election of 1967).[15]

The Post Office example is similar but it is a case of a public inquiry prompted by 'internal knowledge' for as the inquiry stated: 'it was agreed by all concerned, including the Director [of the Department] that the Department during the period under investigation (1961–71) was inefficient, corrupt and immoral'.[16] The three ways in which corruption inquiries were instituted are not completely analytically distinct, but they do illustrate the varying administrative and political context of corruption inquiries. Corruption inquiries and responses to scandal have to be set in context, with the major distinction between them being whether they are 'within' the regime or at a time of regime change.

Denis Martin has used the phrase 'a deforming mirror' to describe what Tanzanian elections say about Tanzanian political processes.[17] The phrase is an appropriate one; it can be similarly used to describe the relationship between Sierra Leone corruption inquiries and Sierra Leone corruption. A distorted, inaccurate view is gained from looking at corruption only via the medium of the corruption inquiries. This is partly due to their stage-management, in certain cases, to attribute particular political blame and to avoid more sensitive areas. One of the Marketing Board inquiries comments that all blame seems to be directed by individuals towards Sir Albert, almost implying that he was working alone, and was solely guilty. Perhaps like the Ghanaian inquiries of 1967 onwards, which can be described as carefully orchestrated,[18] some of the immediate post-Margai inquiries were carefully managed also. This can be suggested of the Forster Report, and also of the earlier Cole Commission into the 1961–2 Audit.

A second comment on the inquiries concerns the focus of the inquiries upon individual or institutional cases. As has been argued earlier, they make corruption appear 'individualised' rather than potentially systemic. Thirdly, the inquiries are inquiries into public-office corruption, and focus therefore on the misdemeanours of public officials. But public-office corruption is of course a transaction, involving at least two people, one of whom is in a formal public post. The other person, group or company involved in the transaction—the source of bribes—is little considered. If, as has been argued, a source of corruption is to be found in the political economy of Sierra Leone (particularly in the Lebanese role in the economy and in the politics of diamonds), then there is a situation where there is a permanent (or at least relatively permanent) source of bribes, yet an impermanent public officialdom (with changes of regime and moves of post). The sources of bribes in the 1960s are the same as sources of bribes in the 1980s. From this it is possible to suggest some personal motivation for politicians not wanting to uncover evidence of bribery by 'foreigners'.

Only one inquiry makes comments—incidental ones—about the position of the Lebanese. The Post Office inquiry found that, in Koidu town, in the centre of the diamond areas, only six telephones were working, all of which belonged to Lebanese business concerns. The inquiry commented that the official explanation—that all the telephones concerned were around the exchange—was rather less than convincing. Very little else is said about the position and economic power of the Lebanese. In the case of the Lebanese community, mentions or threats of mention in corruption inquiries might have had the effect of inducing further corruption, in view of the insecure political position of the Lebanese. A related factor to that of incidental comments regarding 'foreigners' is the sheer naivety of some of the comments made about foreign involvement in political activity. An example is in the Forster Report on the entertaining of government ministers by business concerns. The Diamond Corporation and others provided hospitality, free accommodation and entertainment, for Ministers travelling to London and New York. The Forster Report comments: 'both Dicor London and Messrs Templesman provided such hospitality to relieve Government of its burdens, and the result of their kind gesture is lost when recipients of hospitality retain allowances provided them by Government'. The Forster Report complains that ministers keep their allowances yet fails to recognise the potentially corrupting influence of free hospitality provided by companies dependent upon government goodwill for their continued operations.

A fourth comment on the inquiries is related to the clash between popular values and popular expectations of politicians and government, and what can be described as 'Weberian' values. By 'Weberian' values, I mean a view of the political system and politics that accepts a distinction between public duty and private interests, a concept of 'public service'. This can be contrasted with certain public expectations of government and politicians, which have been described above and throws a different light on ostensibly 'corrupt' acts. The inquiries mostly operate from a 'Weberian' perspective, but do make the occasional extra comment. The inquiry into the Ports Authority said:

employees caught fiddling or pilfering would not be automatically dismissed. They kept their jobs because of an apparently double standard . . . stealing from the Authority was punishable . . . but most employees did not regard fiddling or pilfering from ships as a crime. But is anyone justified in thinking those ills are borne of necessity, in an industry in which the basic wages of the worker averages only forty leones a month? [19]

This low-level, apparently systematic pilfering is described differently from most other comments on corruption. It is 'legitimated' by being carried out by people with low incomes and directed at private, foreign concerns, not 'public' authority. This raises, of course, much wider questions. So the inquiries throw only a little light on the question of rationales and indeed the 'nature' of corruption in a form other than that defined in a public office-private gain manner.

For a final comment on corruption inquiries, there is A. K. Armah's fine rhetorical and cynical statement comparing inquiries and fishing nets:

> The net had been made in the special Ghanaian way that allowed the really big corrupt people to pass through it. A net to catch only the small, dispensable fellows, trying in their anguished blindness to leap and to attain the gleam and the comfort the only way these things can be done. And the big ones floated free, like all the slogans. [20]

This is good populist rhetoric, and an easy statement to make, but are the Sierra Leone corruption inquiries like this? The 'fishing nets' seem to be similar. As a group, the inquiries are more concerned with trivial, incidental corruption: catching 'little fish'. There are some exceptions, though, with the most well known being the case of Sir Albert Margai, but the 'big fish' appear to have got off reasonably lightly, especially if one examines the corruption of the 1970s. In addition, the nets have not been cast in areas where profitable catches may take place, for example in the areas of the political economy of Sierra Leone, 'foreigners' and diamonds. Any inquiries into those areas have produced unsurprisingly poor results. The 'big fish' remain as elusive as ever, as they, politically dominant in the regime, would expect. The major documentary source on corruption in Sierra Leone is therefore demonstrated to be unsatisfactory and incomplete. A far wider and more critical perspective has to be employed.

III

In considering a survey of political corruption in Sierra Leone during the period since Independence in 1961, a number of general points need to be borne in mind—as a background. [21] Firstly, there are the difficulties involved in operating a new state structure from the 'move to independence' onwards. It is important to stress the newness, complexity and sheer size of operations of this new structure, in the light of the pressure for Sierra Leoneanisation despite a generally accepted lack of skilled manpower. Secondly, there is the alien, abstract and artificial nature of the state. The state appeared in this way from the perspective of the ordinary citizen. In an attempt to overcome this 'distance' between the state and the citizen, the politicians tried to 'personalise' the state, yet ended up using its assets as their personal property. Finally, there was, in the period, a contrast between individual expectations of the state and politicians and what has been described above as the 'Weberian inheritance'. Citizens regarded the prime duty of politicians as being to 'help their people', and they viewed the efforts of politicians primarily in instrumental rather than ideological terms. They judged in terms of roads built and services improved—and in this way judged politicians and, through them, the state. It is not surprising, therefore, that politicians acted in response to 'their people's' expectations: they may have cut corners, diverted funds and broken bureaucratic regulations, but they were (perhaps) achieving what their people wanted. This pattern of expectations conflicts with the 'Weberian inheritance': the system of administration and political behaviour inherited from the former colonial power, Britain. The allegedly impartial, efficient, rulebound and orderly system was expected to run on lines derived from British experience. As a result a conflict emerged. One might question the appropriateness of the 'Weberian model' for government in Sierra Leone (and would therefore, by implication, question the definition of corruption given above), but a response would be to sidestep the question by arguing that during the period researched this was the formal system and its legal rules. All these factors have to be borne in mind when considering the period.

In the 1950s, to use the typology given above, corruption seems to have been mainly low level in nature, for obvious reasons, including the size of state resources. Much of the recorded corruption refers in particular to provincial government and the chiefdoms.

At the start of the 1960s, the situation changes. Corruption becomes a significant feature of national level politics, as part of a host of other problems: administrative difficulties, including maladministration and inefficiency, for example. It seems to me, however, that the incidence of national-level corruption is relatively small in the early 1960s, in Sir Milton's regime, barring the exceptions of the items included in the 1960-1 audit, particularly the activities of Albert Margai as a minister. One of the problems of discussing this period is the somewhat contrasting pictures painted in the academic literature of Milton and Albert Margai as respectively the living representatives of heaven and hell—saintly Sir Milton versus his terrible brother, the brash, corrupt, wheeler-dealer Albert. However, even the most partisan friends and supporters of Sir Milton have suggested to me that Milton was not beyond reproach. Sir Milton seems to have benefited from the 'usual advantages of Ministerial life'.[22] but he pales in comparison with his brother Albert, described to me, by several people, as 'the man who loved money'.[23]

Sir Albert's corrupt activities could be called a saga of 'cows, cars and Collier'. This saga—in its many parts—was documented in the then opposition paper

We Yone in a series of articles by the columnist Taqi. The details are briefly as follows. By 'cows' is meant a traditional gift of the beasts, given to Sir Albert on a trip up-country. It was expected that the gift would be returned, but instead they were sent to the Prime Minister's farm. 'Cars' concerns the import of a large American car without paying duty (union officials seem to have had difficulties with cars also); and 'Collier' is of course Gershon Collier, Sierra Leone's ambassador in New York at the time, who was involved in dubious financial dealings with Sir Albert.[24] But the story of Sir Albert and corruption is not simply 'cows, cars and Collier'. Instead, I would argue that a web or system of corruption was created around Sir Albert, and that the incidents reported in the press were very much the epiphenomena. This is not to say that the incidents didn't have an impact—they had a widespread public impact. Here a public opinion definition of corruption comes in as well. One thing about the cows-car-Collier incidents is notable: they aren't very corrupt when viewed in monetary terms, certainly not compared to the manipulation of contracts and Marketing Board funds.

There is no doubt that Sir Albert's corruption was a significant factor in his unpopularity, leading to his replacement along with the partial demise of the system of corruption associated with him. On the whole the subsequent military regimes seem to have had a relatively low incidence of corruption: incidental corruption rather than systemic, but the latter part of Juxon Smith's regime was tainted by accusations of corruption, some of them fairly trivial.

With the coming to power of Siaka Stevens and the APC under a 'national government' banner in 1968 the political situation and the possibilities for corruption changed. In the post-Independence regime the opportunities for personal gain had expanded but they were always limited by the likelihood of censure by opposing political forces, encouraged by a vigorous press. The Stevens government set about controlling that opposition and criticism by engineering a decline in political competition (which ultimately resulted in a one-party state being declared in 1978). It also sought to gain the support of the notables who had attached themselves to the somewhat patrician SLPP, and it did this by means of promises of preferment and political manipulation. The previously critical press was also cowed, as the dominant party began to use state resources to defend and expand its position. Factional in-fighting and electoral violence were a feature of 'public politics' in the 1970s, culminating in (for West Africans) some very familiar arguments for one-party rule. Against this background, and against a further background of economic decline and vocal dissent (articulated most notably in the student protests of 1977, the opposition to the hosting of the OAU summit in 1980 and the labour protest of 1981), a substantial, systemic web of corruption was created, centred around the president, his two vice-presidents, a range of senior ministers and parastatal heads, coupled with a group of potential economic beneficiaries. Lack of accountability and emerging opportunities were significant aspects of an explanation of this situation.

Alliances between particular Lebanese entrepreneurs and senior political figures became more important as the possibility of the removal of the politicians from office receded, and as the scope for corrupt openings expanded. The openings for corruption were similar to those during the period of the Margais: manipulation of contracts, the Marketing Board and the politics of diamonds, and increasingly other mineral exports also, but the magnitude of the corrupt deals increased enormously as public expenditure and the state machine grew larger. A prime example is the expenditure surrounding the hosting of the annual Organisation of African Unity heads of state meeting in Freetown, 1–3 July 1980. Various estimates of the cost have been given but a reasonable figure would be over Le200 million for extensive public works, including the building of a 'presidential village' (now used as accommodation for senior civil servants), road improvements and the purchase of new ferries and vehicles. Quite apart from the morality of such expenditure for a transient event, substantial kick-backs and corrupt payments were part of the operation. While this situation of substantial private gain from public office may soon change with the expected retirement from office of President Stevens, or with the emergence of a populist military revolution (along Liberian, or more appropriately Ghanaian, lines), it is much more likely that with a non-accountable political system the web of systemic corruption associated with the Stevens regime will continue. The Stevens regime (since the early 1970s) has not been an enthusiastic promoter of corruption inquiries, despite widespread evidence of corruption in various institutions, some published by an independent press (now no longer in operation, after the presses were dynamited during the labour disputes of 1981).[25]

To sum up the survey of national-level corruption in Sierra Leone: the major elements are a continuity of incidental corruption, and a massive slide into a web or a system of corruption under the Albert Margai regime. Such infelicities of governance as practised by the Margais do pale into insignificance, however, when compared to the much more thorough and extensive patterns of systematic and systemic corruption that have emerged during the Stevens regimes since 1968, due to a range of factors including non-accountability as a consequence of declining political competition, the need to maintain political support via patron–clientelism and the increasing opportunities as the state machine expanded its formal roles.

IV

Certain forms of corruption appear to be a persistent feature of the political economy of Sierra Leone. At one level incidental corruption is a very obvious element of social and political behaviour. It is difficult to interpret its significance. To the consumer of government services, perhaps, it is an unhelpful addition to an already problematic life; it is unlikely to be viewed as a way of humanising official relationships, as some functionalist theories of corruption have suggested.[26] Systematic and systemic corruption is more important for our analyses. This chapter has, one hopes, documented and interpreted the range of examples that have emerged in post-Independence Sierra Leone. The corruption inquiries themselves provide a wealth of detail on corrupt acts, but they are partisan rather than neutral documents. In fact they often give a skewed view of corrupt behaviour, presenting it as an individualised pheno-menon rather than systemic in nature. Perhaps this comment on Sierra Leone corruption inquiries is capable of wider application. In my view, significant corruption in Sierra Leone politics is an ever-present problem and there have been two instances or periods when public-office corruption has had an impor-tant political impact, namely the Margai period in the 1960s and in the current political regime. Corruption in these periods appears related to the political economy of Sierra Leone, and also to the ever-burgeoning state apparatus, which now, grossly expanded, dominates the political, social and economic scene. The contradiction between economic power and political power (as seen in, for example, the ambiguous position of the Lebanese) provides the incentive to engage in what are, formally, corrupt acts, as defined by statutes derived from the British legal system.

Though the practice surrounding the statutes has weakened since Indepen-dence, it can nevertheless be asserted that many actions of public officials go beyond a threshold of acceptance of behaviour in public office and are thus corrupt. In so doing, they act in alliance with a range of external economic beneficiaries, some within the system, some without. While the assumption that corruption is a behavioural disease peculiar to Third World societies (as asserted by some theorists) is rejected, corruption in public office in Sierra Leone does have some features peculiar to itself alone, notably in the nature of the typical corrupt acts and the opportunities available. Some features are more common, however, and seen in a number of similar societies along the West African coast.

Political corruption is one aspect of what can be described as the 'paradox of politics' in Sierra Leone. In order to maintain political control with a weak economy in decline, those in key political positions have to divert and cor-ruptly use public funds. This diversion of funds affects the presumed develop-ment strategies of the regime. Success at maintaining political control has meant failures in administrative efficiency and development planning and the growth of a large parasitic 'state class'.

Notes

1. 'Corruption is behaviour which deviates from the formal duties of a public role because of private-regarding (personal, close family, private clique) pecuniary or status gains', Nye, in Heidenheimer (1978), pp. 566–7.

2. A brief outline of the political economy of Sierra Leone is provided by Christopher Allen in his contribution to Dunn (1978), pp. 193–6. An additional source is the World Bank Report No. 3375-SL, 'Sierra Leone: Prospects for Growth and Equity' (1981), but this document has a 'restricted distribution'.
3. Kilson (1966) contains a detailed account of this.
4. A pseudonym. This article is a well-informed and acutely argued account. 'Frank Ly' (1980), pp. 10–26.
5. Ibid., p. 25.
6. The Ghanaian inquiries are discussed in Le Vine (1975).
7. Kilson (1966) and Tangri (1981).
8. A list of the major 'corruption inquiries' is given.
9. The *Tablet* gave a detailed summary of both inquiry reports: *Tablet*, 7 May 1979; 2 June 1979. The availability of rice is a very sensitive issue in Sierra Leone.
10. *We Yone*, 22 January 1975; 19 February 1975.
11. Forster Report (1968).
12. For example, *We Yone*, 29 October 1966. A front page story was headlined 'Gershon Sends Sir Albert Le8642 Car'.
13. The politicians included Salia Jusu-Sheriff, who later became leader of the SLPP.
14. Beoku Betts Commission (1968), p. 4.
15. Cartwright (1970), Ch 12, gives an assessment of these moves.
16. The Post Office was subsequently reorganised, but continued to be prone to corruption scandals.
17. Martin in Hermet *et al.* (1978), p. 127.
18. Rathbone in Dunn (ed.) (1978), p. 25, comments that 'The spirit of Enquiry stalked the land and self-righteousness as well as political astuteness led to commission after commission of enquiry'.
19. Ports Inquiry Report (1977), p. 32. The sterling equivalent of a salary of Le40 a month in 1975–6 is £20.
20. A. K. Armah, *The Beautiful Ones are Not Yet Born*, London (1966).
21. The survey is based upon extensive research I have been conducting on public-office corruption and the growth of the state since the 1950s. It has involved extensive interviewing, participant observation, and the collection of a good deal of unpublished documentary material, during several research visits to Sierra Leone since 1978. Additional evidence for many of the statements made will appear in my forthcoming Birmingham doctoral thesis; space considerations have meant its exclusion here.
22. Informant, a former civil servant, interviewed Freetown, 12 February 1979.
23. Informants interviewed in Freetown and the provinces: politically active medical practitioner, Freetown, 1 February 1979; retired politician, Bo, 3 May 1979; retired journalist, Freetown, 20 June 1980.
24. *We Yone*, 20 August 1966, article entitled 'Clean Hands and Dirty Money'; 1 October 1966.
25. An assessment of the recent academic literature on Sierra Leone politics is included in my review article; Riley (1982). An additional source on the period of the 1980s is the publication of the exile movement, *SLAM. SLAM*, 1, No. 5 (undated), contains, for example, a discussion of a new bank to be formed by J. S. Mohammed, a key Afro-Lebanese entrepreneur and a close associate of President Stevens.
26. Such as Leff (1964).

Bibliography

Allen, C. (1978), 'Sierra Leone', in J. Dunn (ed.), *West African States*, Cambridge, Cambridge University Press.
Armah, A. K. (1966), *The Beautiful Ones are Not Yet Born*, London, Heinemann.
Berg, E. *et al.* (1981), *Accelerated Development in Sub Saharan Africa*, New York, The World Bank.
Cartwright, J. (1970), *Politics in Sierra Leone*, Toronto, Toronto University Press.

Cox, T. S. (1976), *Civil–Military Relations in Sierra Leone*, Cambridge, Mass., Harvard University Press.

Green, T. (1981), *The World of Diamonds*, London, Weidenfeld and Nicolson.

Kilson, M. (1966), *Political Change in a West African State*, Cambridge, Mass., Harvard University Press.

Leff, N. H. (1964), 'Economic Development through Bureaucratic Corruption', *American Behavioral Scientist*, **8**, Part 3.

Le Vine, V. T. (1975), *Political Corruption; the Ghana Case*, Stanford, Hoover Institution Publications.

'Frank Ly' (1980), 'Sierra Leone', *Monthly Review*, June.

Martin, D. (1978), 'The 1975 Tanzanian Elections', in G. Hermet *et al.* (eds), *Elections without Choice*, London, Macmillan.

Nye, J. S. (1978), 'Corruption and Political Development', in A. J. Heidenheimer (ed.), *Political Corruption*, New York, Transaction Press.

Rathbone, R. (1978), 'Ghana', in J. Dunn (ed.), *West African States*, Cambridge, Cambridge University Press.

Riley, S. P. (1982), 'Sierra Leone Politics; Some Recent Assessments', *Africa*, **52**, No. 2.

Tangri, R. (1981), 'Local Government Institutions in Sierra Leone', *Journal of Administration Overseas* (new series).

World Bank (1981), *Sierra Leone: Prospects for Growth and Equity*, Report No. 3375–SL, 31 July 1981.

List of major corruption inquiries:

Report of Commission of Enquiry into the conduct of certain chiefs, Freetown, Government Printer, 1957.

Report of the Commission appointed to enquire into and report on the matters contained in the Director of Audit's Report on the Accounts of Sierra Leone, 1960–61 (known as the Cole Commission), Freetown, Government Printer, 1963.

Report of the Commission of Enquiry into the conduct of the 1967 General Election (known as the Dove-Edwin Commission), Freetown, Government Printer, 1967.

Report of the Forster Commission of Enquiry into the Assets of Ex-Ministers and Ex-Deputy Ministers, Freetown, Government Printer, 1968.

Report of the Beoku Betts Commission of Enquiry into the Sierra Leone Produce Marketing Board, 1961–7, Freetown, Government Printer, 1968.

Report of the Percy Davies Commission of Enquiry into the activities of Freetown City Council, 1964–7, Freetown, Government Printer, 1969.

Report of the Wales Commission of Enquiry into the conduct of Immigration Quota Committee, Freetown, Government Printer, 1969.

Report of the Commission of Inquiry into the finance and administration of the Transport and General Workers Union (known as the Faulkner Commission), Freetown, Government Printer, 1971.

Report of the Commission appointed to inquire into all aspects of the affairs of the Sierra Leone Ports Authority as a viable economic establishment, Freetown, Government Printer, 1977.

12 Bureaucratic corruption and its remedies

LESLIE PALMIER

If not as old as time, then certainly bureaucratic corruption is as old as government office. We hear of it in Babylon and in Rome, in classical India of the third century BC, in the pre-Reformation Catholic Church, and in the Spanish Empire, to come no closer to our own day. In the modern era it appears in all the 'worlds', from simon-pure Sweden to genocidal Kampuchea. In a phrase, corruption is perennial and ubiquitous, to be found in any and all systems of government. The problem therefore is not to account for its presence, but rather for its extent in a specific situation at a particular time.

There is fairly general agreement in the literature on what corruption means: namely, the use of public office for private advantage. However, virtually all writers leave room for the possibility that in some circumstances such a practice may not be corrupt and that some additional criterion is required before it can be adjudged so. The *Encyclopaedia of the Social Sciences of 1931* proposed that the judgement of when public power has been 'misused' for private profit was to be left to 'the best opinion and political morality of the time'. How these were to be identified was not made clear (Senturia, 1931:448). *The Dictionary of the Social Sciences*, however, while mentioning '. . . standards of high moral conduct' (without indicating whose were to be followed), placed first emphasis on 'a breach of law' (Aikin, 1964). More recent literature has moved in this direction, defining corruption as the use of public power for private advantage in ways which transgress some formal rule or law. A number of sources could be quoted here: perhaps one of the most succinct is 'using the power of office for making private gain in breach of laws' (Andreski, 1968:92). Clarity seems to require this type of definition, otherwise one is simply imposing values from outside the situation. Uses of public office considered corrupt in one administration may be permitted in another.

Why should any use of public office for private benefit be condemned; where lies the offence? According to one political scientist prominent in this field, because of the injury done to the public interest.

Indeed, he argues that if the actions taken result in public benefit, they are not corrupt, but merely devious (Friedrich, 1966:74–5). This is to define an action only by its results. Most criminal codes, however, emphasise the breach of law; the consequences are only additional considerations, not primary. Moreover there is no agreement among authorities on how to define the public interest. One recent work argues that it is essentially a normative or ideological question; one cannot solve it by definition (Scott, 1972:3), and as another author maintains, those who attempt to do so tend 'to find, very sincerely, that there is a fortunate coincidence between their own welfare and that of others' (Penrose, 1968:268).

Perhaps a truer perspective is to be found in the *Oxford English Dictionary*. It defines corruption as the perversion or destruction of integrity or fidelity in the discharge of public duties by bribery or favour. We need not accept this limitation of corruption; officials can fill their pockets illegally without being bribed or favoured. It is the weakening of loyalty that is at the heart of the offence. When Clive in 1771 condemned the servants of the East India Company for their corruption, it was on the grounds that 'their sense of honour and duty to their employers had . . . been estranged by the too eager pursuit of their own immediate advantages' (Select Committee 1773:App. 73, para. 1). Similarly, a few years ago in the course of a trial at the London Central Criminal Court (the 'Old Bailey') of a former police officer, it was alleged that favours to him from a property developer had 'alienated the loyalty to the police' (*Daily Telegraph*, 18 September 1979).

In brief, then, corruption may be defined as the acquisition of forbidden benefits by officials or employees, so bringing into question their loyalty to their employers.

We should distinguish here between the formal offence and the moral condemnation of it. For officials to remain loyal, their employer should obviously provide emoluments sufficient to remove any compulsion to seek supplements to income. We might call this an implicit contract: adequate provision on one side, loyalty on the other. Only if it is being fulfilled by the employer, but not by the employee, should the term corruption carry censure. This consideration is seldom taken into account by the literature. A reference to the malpractice in the Roman Empire expresses the view that the governors 'exploited the provinces shamelessly for their own profit' (Senturia, 1931:449); it does not expand on the fact that they were unpaid. The treatise on government by Kautiliya, the chief minister of an Indian emperor of three centuries before Christ, which includes the oft-quoted phrase '. . . it is impossible for a government servant not to eat up, at least, a bit of the King's revenue' (Shamastry, 1967:71), does not consider the adequacy of official salaries. Neither did Clive's outburst, quoted above, against East India Company employees. In brief, too often accounts of corruption are written from the point of view of the employer; one should be on one's guard against accepting their analyses.

What circumstances impel officials to break faith with their employer and seek additional forbidden sources of income? Study of several instances suggests that three principal factors are involved. These are the salaries paid; the opportunities presented for illegal use of office; and policing, to mean both detection and punishment, with the emphasis perhaps on the former. It is important to consider these three factors simultaneously, not individually. That is to say, corruption should not be thought to be dependent only on the level of salaries, or the efficiency of the policing system or the opportunities present, but on all three together. Obviously, corruption will be most prevalent when salaries are low, opportunities great, and policing weak; it will be infrequent when the reverse applies, and salaries are generous, opportunities few, and policing strong, while any combination in between is possible. These are, of course, analytic categories, not concrete. A generous salary may not only reduce the attraction of opportunities: fear of its loss may act as a powerful element in policing.

To support this argument, we shall discuss two well documented historical instances, namely corruption in the English and Dutch East India Companies of the eighteenth century, and the situation in three contemporary administrations, namely those of India, Hong Kong and Indonesia, whose anti-corruption measures have been the subject of a special study.[1] They differ greatly in size, population, culture and forms of government; accordingly, any lesson we may draw from them may have a wider applicability.

The poor payment of the English East India Company's servants had long been a subject of complaint. In the late seventeenth century the Bengal Agent and Council had remarked to the Court of Directors in London: 'The Trueth is your Worships give youre servants such small encouragement that doth but very little animate their endeavoures; their sallaryes are so small . . .' (Foster, 1962:183). The reason was obvious enough: the Company did not wish to incur large overheads which would reduce its profits. As compensation, however, it permitted its servants to trade on their own account, though they could not use the Company's stock or credit to do so (Ghosal, 1944:417, 419). After the battle of Plassey in 1757, when Bengal fell into the Company's hands, the servants used their powers to seize the opportunities for enrichment thus provided. And since even the most senior officials were involved, there was no policing.

Corruption was curbed by reversing the situation. Clive improved senior salaries and restored policing by drastic punishment (Dodwell, 1929:178). Perhaps more important were the changes made by Lord Cornwallis twenty years later. He argued that '. . . if the principle of withholding all concealed sources of emolument from Company servants be a right one, it is no less necessary to make their avowed salaries and allowances liberal and handsome' (IOR BLR, 1789:489). The object of his reforms was to establish 'as an invariable rule . . . that the Company's servants shall be confined to public business only . . . that those in office shall on no account be permitted to be members of Agency or Banking houses, or to transact mercantile business of any kind upon their own account' (IOR HMS, 1792:515). Major corruption was ended within relatively few years. Cornwallis' successor, Lord Teignmouth, asserted: '. . . I will venture to say that there is little speculation, or sinister emoluments. In this respect the reform is not only considerable, but visible' (Teignmouth, 1843: I, 329).

As for the Dutch East India Company, an official investigation after its collapse found that '. . . there were very few offices in India whose occupants could exist on the legal income . . .'. In consequence, 'Officials were holding a plurality of offices or were drawing the Company's pay and using their time to build up their private fortunes; they were selling goods to the Company at advanced prices; they . . . were conniving at all kinds of corruption; silk was stolen from the Company's warehouse and naval stores were given away from the Company's storehouse'.

Policing was lacking here too: 'the whole system of accounting was so weak and so loosely administered that every opportunity for peculation was given the Company's servants . . . nothing was done to punish any officials or to recover . . . losses, which were simply written off the books'. Indeed, the Company accepted the corrupt practices of its servants to the extent that it laid a tax on officials holding the more lucrative positions (Day, 1904:95–105). The Company fell in 1801, and the Indies came under government rule. But it was only late in the nineteenth century that European officials were removed from all concern with the production of crops (Furnivall, 1939:192–4). This reduction of opportunities was effective here too; by the end of the century only occasional malpractices were being reported (Day, 1904:424–5).

Of the contemporary instances, we may discuss India first, if only because it has the longest history of anti-corruption work. Here we must distinguish between the decision-making levels of the administration, namely the gazetted officers (and their equivalents, the commissioned officers in the armed forces), and the lower ranks such as clerks, messengers, etc. Among the latter petty corruption, in terms of 'speed money' for the movement of files, small bribes, etc., has long been endemic. The attitude of both Imperial and independent governments has been to ignore it. It was and is widely recognised that the ministerial staff are underpaid, there is little or no possibility of the government ever providing them with adequate salaries, and petty corruption is tolerated to allow them to make ends meet.

Gazetted officers are a different matter, and the spread of corruption among them has called for counter measures. It is worth emphasising here that it has never been alleged that salaries for this group were too low, in the conventional sense of being insufficient to support a customary standard of living. It was rather that the opportunities with which they were presented suddenly proliferated. This first occurred during the Second World War, when controls were imposed on the economy. With Independence and the coming to power of the Congress Party, they were increased in pursuit of 'socialist' goals. Furthermore, the state invaded ever more sectors of the economy; the banks, for instance, were all nationalised in the 1970s. All this, as might have been predicted, led to a considerable increase in corruption.

To control the malady in 1946 the Delhi Special Police Establishment (DSPE) was set up with the specific task of investigating and prosecuting corruption in the Central Government. In 1964 it was absorbed into a newly created Central Bureau of Investigation as its investigative arm. It is perhaps a sign of government concern that this body, primarily concerned with corruption, remains the only police organization in the Central Government; all other police forces are state responsibilities. Within the Administration itself, in the 1950s an Administrative Vigilance Division (AVD) was established within the Home Ministry, with a network of Vigilance Officers in the departments of government, whose task it is also to carry out investigations. However, the AVD proved ineffective, and in 1964, also, was replaced by a Central Vigilance Commission with much the same functions, but with the Commissioner responsible only to the President.

These bodies have been reasonably effective. On the one hand, the amount of corruption in the administration is less than public belief would allow. In any one year, no more than one per cent of gazetted officers is *alleged* to be guilty of corruption. The number against whom a case can be established, and who can then be convicted, is even smaller. Secondly, despite its best efforts the CBI has been unable to discover an increasing number of corrupt officials, but if anything the reverse is true. The Bureau, it must be emphasised, has no vested interest in limiting the number of suspects it investigates and charges; it acquires prestige and resources by an ever larger number of successful prosecutions of corrupt officials. These do not seem to be forthcoming.

On the other hand, though corruption may have been contained, it has not been reduced. For this there seems to be two reasons. First, opportunities continue to abound. To take only a few instances, licences and permits are required for a great number of activities, contracts have to be placed for defence and other supplies, the nationalised banks extend credit to cultivators, many illiterate and easily duped. Those departments that deal most directly with the economy are also the most corrupt. The CBI Report for 1980 gives details of cases dealt with in the courts. Of 172 convictions, fifty-three (31 per cent) were of officials from the Ministry of Finance (thirty-six being from the public sector banks), twenty-five (15 per cent) from the Railways, twenty-one (12 per cent) from the Ministry of Communications (mainly Posts and Telegraphs) and fourteen (8 per cent) from the Ministry of Defence. The second reason is the weakness of policing. Here we must emphasise the principle steadfastly maintained by the Indian government, namely that the prevention of corruption in the administration is primarily the responsibility of departmental heads. However, their position hardly encourages them to give it absolute priority. Like departmental heads anywhere, they obtain recognition and rewards depending on their ability to meet operational targets, not on the probity of their staff. If, say, an income tax office increases its receipts, even if 'arrangements' have been made between some inspectors and payers, the head of the office is likely to be congratulated, not criticised. The failure of administrative heads to control corruption within their departments is of course attested by the creation of the external bodies mentioned above. But the effect of their establishment has been that, while the heads are still formally responsible for 'vigilance', as it is called, in practice they tend to see the fight against corruption as the task of the specialised agencies.

It is true that heads are assisted by a Chief Vigilance Officer and his staff. But it would appear that in many instances these internal controllers have been incorporated into the ethos of the department. The natural and healthy collegiality which arises among people working together also ensures not only that any of them who may be suspected of corruption are not betrayed, but also that the Vigilance Officers may well be drawn into the same net of mutual obligations. One must also mention that, since vigilance is considered, here as elsewhere, a non-productive chore, those assigned to it are not always of the highest calibre. In consequence, not only is internal control weak, but the external control bodies have a hard task piercing the self-protective departmental shell. Against this irreducible weakness of policing, we must set the continuing proliferation of opportunities, since the Indian state remains wedded to a policy of extensive intervention in the economy. There is no indication, either, that salaries are to be increased even to market rates so as to reduce temptation. It is true that some action has been taken to reduce opportunities by closing loopholes in regulations which can be used for the personal profit of officials. The Central Vigilance Commission, too, has given some attention to publicity, encouraging citizens to report instances of corruption, thus encouraging policing. But against the major factors mentioned, these do not seem likely to avail much. We must therefore expect that corruption in the administration will continue, even if perhaps it does not increase.

Political corruption is not the concern of this chapter, but obviously the example set by politicians is of importance. When corrupt, they are unable to demand honesty in their civil servants with any degree of conviction; very often they serve as a model and an excuse for the corrupt official. And it must regretfully be recorded that political corruption in India is increasing and involves even the very highest levels of government. One cannot, therefore, expect any policing effort to come from that quarter.

Hong Kong, of course, is very different: minute by comparison, and still a colony. Yet there are important similarities also. First, one has a structure of senior, mostly British, officials, who are usually, if not by any means always, honest, with subordinate Chinese staff who have long been, on the one hand, paid relatively poorly, and on the other have often been corrupt. This applied most forcefully to the Royal Hong Kong Police Force. Indeed, in recent years there appears to have been a tacit understanding that in exchange for saving the Colony from Communist mobs in 1967 the police were given a free rein to extort money as and when they could from the public. The opportunities to do so were provided by legislative attempts, with support of the Chinese Unofficial Members of the Legislative Council, to regulate the morals of the citizens, particularly by attempting to prevent them from gambling or fornicating. As is usually the case, this simply encouraged corruption. The police used the legislation as a lever to exact levies so as to turn a blind eye. Highly organised systems of 'syndicated corruption', as it was called, were established, based on police stations, with the proceeds of extortion being distributed according to rank.

Policing was so weak as to be virtually absent. The government as a whole tended, with some reason, to accept corruption as part of Chinese culture, about which nothing could be done. There is also the suspicion that it was regarded as a preferable alternative to having to raise sufficient taxes to pay subordinate employees adequately. Nor was the example set at the highest levels always of the most desirable; at least one nineteenth-century Governor left the Colony laden with corrupt booty. Concern with corruption really began only after the Second World War. Eventually this took the shape of an Anti-Corruption Bureau, later Office, within the Royal Hong Kong Police Force. That body was well known for its corruption, and the ACB/O proved as ineffective as other systems of internal control, and itself acquired a reputation for being corrupt.

Change began in the 1970s. When the Cultural Revolution started in the Chinese People's Republic, young Chinese in Hong Kong were influenced by the idealism, if not by the venom and incompetence, of that movement. At the same time, a new reforming Governor, Sir Murray MacLehose, was appointed. The stage was thus set for a violent but salutary and effective reaction to the escape from Hong Kong in 1972 of a senior police official, Peter Godber, who was under investigation for corruption. The government appointed a judge to enquire into the matter, and on the basis of his recommendations, the Governor set up the Independent Commission Against Corruption (ICAC) in 1974. He made is completely independent of the police or any government department, and responsible only to him. Technically a civilian organisation, it was given powers at least as great as those of the police, including that of detention without trial.

From its inception, the ICAC has adopted the policy that anti-corruption work requires more than just investigation and prosecution. It also has a branch concerned with prevention, that is to say reducing the opportunities for corruption, and another whose task is to involve the public. It has done so by making it very easy for people to report corruption, either in person or in writing, anonymously or authentically, and by using the mass communications media to bring home to the public not only the evil of corruption but also what was being done about it. All this has much enhanced the policing factor. With the passage of time it is clear that public confidence in the ICAC has grown greatly; the number of people reporting in person has increased substantially, as have the authentic written complaints.

Three years after its foundation, the ICAC had broken the major syndicated corruption rackets in the police force, and all that was left were conspiracies of rather smaller numbers, let us say of up to half a dozen police officers or officials. But this success led to a reaction. In 1977 the police force mutinied against the ICAC's investigations, and compelled the Governor to issue a 'partial amnesty', so that any officers not already under investigation were exempted from it. This meant, of course, that all those who had grown rich through extortion in the past and were not under enquiry would be allowed to keep their ill-gotten gains. Much ICAC preparatory work was just jettisoned. However, the Commission recovered quickly enough; certainly there are sufficient cases of present corruption to replace those of the past. It is now concerned with the smaller groups of extortionists on the one hand, and the 'satisfied customer' type of corruption, usually bribery, on the other. These are perhaps more difficult to detect and investigate than the large syndicates or the 'unexplained assets' type of cases, so spectacular results are unlikely.

Together with the vigorous prosecution of external controls, the ICAC has also gone to considerable lengths to strengthen internal policing, by arguing for the adoption of a system of personal responsibility for the actions of subordinates by their immediate superiors. It has also had much effect in reducing the opportunities for corruption. In the past, one of the sources of revenue for the corrupt police syndicates was the ban on betting anywhere outside Jockey Club premises. Now, not only has the Jockey Club been induced to open betting shops throughout the Colony, but also the playing of games of chance on social occasions has been legalised. This is, of course, in addition to the constant scrutiny of laws and regulations to suggest removal of loopholes and inapplicable legislation that simply provide opportunities for corruption. Salaries, the third factor in corruption, were outside the brief of the ICAC. Nevertheless, in the police force they have been improved substantially. In addition, the educational requirements have been considerably increased, thus adding an important element of internal control.

Much of course remains to be done. The attitude of Government departments is very similar to that of the Indian; corruption is not their concern. The notoriety of the Public Works Department for corruption is second only to that of the police. Yet, at a trial of one of their senior (British) engineers on that charge, the Department did not even send an observer. Nevertheless, the ICAC remains active and undiscouraged. Most recently, it has arrested a recent Securities Commissioner on suspicion of corruption. It seems clear that what is required is a change of attitude at the senior levels of Government.

In turning to discuss corruption in Indonesia, two important points should be made. First, unlike both India and Hong Kong, there is no continuity with the pre-war administration. The allied collapse in the face of the Japanese invasion of 1942 effectively marked the end of Dutch administration. What was built then, by the Indonesian insurgents, was a new and very different structure. As a consequence, whereas in both India and Hong Kong it is possible to distinguish between politics and administration, this is not so in Indonesia.

From the early years of the Republic, as the nationalists called their state, the spoils system was introduced into the bureaucracy. Appointment and promotion came to depend not on merit, but on party affiliation. By the same token, loyalty to the party exonerated such faults as proved corruption. In a small way, corruption had begun to spread during the Japanese occupation, a result of the inflation which obtained then. The approach of the elections of 1955 and the need for money to fight them coincided with the proliferation of economic controls, particularly over foreign trade; widespread corruption resulted. Its value was confirmed when the party which had used it most emerged as the victor of the election. At the same time, the public service, virtually the sole source of employment for the educated, was greatly expanded; it became the major source of patronage. Economic mismanagement led to inflation and the government was in no position to pay the large numbers of public servants a living wage. Corruption naturally now permeated government at every level. However, these malpractices brought the system of parliamentary government into disrepute, and was one of the factors which led to the acceptance of 'Guided Democracy' as it was called. This on the one hand increased the politicisation of the bureaucracy; on the other, under the guise of 'guided economy', it imposed even more controls. Foreign adventures in the guise of the campaigns for Western New Guinea and against the formation of Malaysia led to a considerable increase in inflation, bearing down most heavily on the many public servants. Corruption became widespread and virtually normal. Unlike India and Hong Kong, it reached to the highest levels of the administration. Such attempts as were made to fight inflation were bedevilled by politics. As soon as investigation and prosecution threatened a powerful figure, the attempt at control was discontinued.

The widespread corruption under 'Guided Democracy' was one of the reasons why its supersession, after the abortive left-wing coup of October 1965, was greeted with relief. The military regime which has ruled Indonesia since, styling itself the New Order, has had to face the same difficulties as preceding attempts at reform. When it took over, it proclaimed it wanted not only good government, but also clean government. To this end in 1967 it set up a 'Corruption Eradication Team'. This did not get far. The corrupt were shielded by men who had been powerful under Guided Democracy, and remained so under the New Order. The regime then, in 1970, appointed a Commission of Four elder statesmen to analyse the problem. They did so in some depth, and identified two root causes of corruption. The main one was the lack of efficient administrative and budgetary controls. As a result, officials at the head of departments acted as they pleased, little hindered by the ministers to whom they were nominally responsible, while their example was followed by their subordinates. Consequently, using office to make money, where possible, was the norm and not the exception.

Not only internal controls were lacking, but also external. The only institution which until 1975 was charged with investigating corruption was the Attorney General's Office. He had done little. One reason was that until 1970 Indonesian law did not recognise corruption as a crime unless it was part of criminal activity. Even after the passage of a law remedying this defect, the then Attorney General showed no greater enthusiasm for prosecution. He can do little against powerful figures who are either corrupt themselves or wish to shield their followers who are. His successor has, in 1982, reviewed the 'Corruption Eradication Team', with what results remains to be seen.

The Commission also recommended reducing opportunities for corruption by, for example, restricting the scope of the activities of BULOG, the rice procurement agency, where much money had been siphoned away by its officials. It proposed that the rice ration given to all officials be replaced by a payment in kind. Sad to say, at the time of writing, twelve years after the Commission's report, the rice ration is still being provided, and reports of corruption in BULOG continue to surface. Regarding salaries, the Commission acknowledged that they were not enough to live on. However, to raise them to an adequate level was simply not within the state's financial capacity. It suggested that what was required was a shrinkage of the public service, to have fewer people better paid. This has not occurred in any substantial degree, but the rise in the price of oil has greatly improved government salaries. The Commission's main recommendations, however, were concerned with policing. It demanded that the Attorney General be more active in taking people to court, even if there was less than a certainty of conviction; the publicity alone would deter others, and encourage the public. It also proposed new legislation to bring the great state undertakings (concerned with oil, forestry and rice) under better controls. This was duly enacted. This might well have had little effect but for the bankruptcy of Pertamina in 1975. The government had to assume its debts, and Pertamina was brought firmly back into the ministerial fold. Its buccaneer founder, Ibnu Sutowo, was dismissed, as were several of his henchmen, described as 'cannibals' by his successor.

To its credit, the regime recognised early on that corruption was a symptom of a more fundamental problem, namely the politicisation of the bureaucracy. It had become not so much an instrument of state policy, leave alone a servant of the public, as an arena for conflict between political parties coveting the sources of patronage it represented. To remedy the situation, the regime took three steps. First, it placed in leading positions in government departments officers whose loyalty was to the Army in general and the President in particular, displacing those who had been tied to political parties. Secondly, it introduced a new office, derived from military practice, of Inspector General, whose task it was to ensure that policies agreed by ministers and senior officials were implemented by their subordinates, and that money was spent on the purposes for which it was allocated. Similarly, Development Inspectors General have been appointed with the task of overseeing the many projects approved directly by the President. Thirdly, the political parties have been greatly reduced, in essence to two, and emasculated; they no longer serve as a focus for the allegiance of officials. Instead, an association of civil servants (KORPRI) was established, linked with the 'functional' group known as GOLKAR, which gives its undivided loyalty to the regime, and is in effect the official party. The government provides it with great resources and facilities, and it marshals the votes at general elections for the deliberative assemblies and the presidency. The politicisation of the civil service has thus been ended. According to the head of the State Intelligence Service, corruption is no longer of the kind that threatens the state, implying no doubt that corruption no longer fuels internecine fighting between political parties.

Nevertheless, however unpolitical, corruption continued to flourish. It was clear enough that the Inspectors General were not functioning as effectively as might have been expected. Indeed, the Minister for Administrative Reform at one time asserted that some 20 per cent of their officials were psychologically unfit for their tasks. As elsewhere, the task of internal control is most unpopular, and regarded as fit only for the less able. The reputation for corruption Indonesia was acquiring abroad led to another attempt at control. A military formation, the National Security Agency (Kopkamtib) was entrused in 1974 with the task of removing 'unofficial levies'. This term covers not only forced discounts, extortion, bribes, etc., but also levies made for perfectly proper purposes by, for example, provincial governors, but for which there was no legal sanction. This gave rise to what is now known as *Opstib*, an abbreviation of *Operasi Tertib*, or Operation Orderliness. Lightning visits to known centres of corruption, such as road weigh-stations and customs offices, followed, red-handed officials were dismissed on the spot and occasional announcements were made that the problem was now under control.

However, it is clear that the government departments took exception to these incursions into their hierarchical chain of command. *Opstib* was reined back, and its concerns limited to investigation, sending the result to the relevant department for action. Only if the response is unsatisfactory does it move in the matter, but it has done so with great effect. Surprisingly, it has even brought to justice some police generals. So far, however, no senior officers in the armed forces proper have been arraigned, though rumour is rife that they are among the most corrupt. Nevertheless, despite the improvement of salaries, the establishment of the Inspectors General and of *Opstib*, corruption in Indonesia still thrives. For opportunities remain many and great, and policing remains weak. Here one cannot avoid referring again to the close link between politics (in the sense of decision-making) and bureaucracy in Indonesia. For one of the greatest impediments to effective policing is precisely that many of the great in the country are themselves corrupt and protect their corrupt personal followers. In addition, public vigilance is virtually absent. Unlike India or Hong Kong, the press is effectively muzzled, and in particular is debarred from investigating or reporting instances of corruption unless and until they are before the courts. Without such independent intelligence, those responsible for curbing corruption, even within the political limits set, have no way of knowing the true state of affairs, since their own officials are very prone to submit only favourable reports. For all these reasons, one cannot be sanguine about the likelihood of any lessening of corruption in the country.

It follows from the proposition advanced at the beginning of this chapter that corruption could be discouraged further by reducing opportunities, increasing salaries, improving policing, or all three. With regard to opportunities, while certainly 'loopholes' can be closed, the imposition of controls, whether over imports or restaurant hygiene, is a political decision, and cannot really be removed except by a change of political mind. Then, with regard to salaries, no administration is likely to set aside its usual criteria of responsibility and seniority in favour of 'opportunity-compensation', as it may be called, for those particular officials administering controls. Indeed, in the present day, any suggestion of following the Cornwallis example would receive short shrift; the trend is to reduce differentials in civil services, not to increase them, for whatever reason.

In consequence, as we have seen, the emphasis is placed on policing. Internal controls having failed, external agencies are established. In the Indonesian case these are weakened by the protection given the corrupt by the powerful. In all three governments, these agencies find themselves restrained by the very factors which defeated internal controls, namely the emphasis on operational result, not probity, and the collegiality of officials. These are, of course, intrinsic to any bureaucracy. They permit its working; they also limit its policing, and so reduce the possibility of eliminating corruption when it is stimulated by the other factors mentioned.

Note

1. Originally supported by the SSRC, and now under preparation for publication.

References

Aikin, C. (1964), 'Corruption', in J. Gould and W. L. Kolb, *A Dictionary of the Social Sciences*, New York, UNESCO, p. 142.

Akshaya-Kumara, Ghoshal (1944), *Civil Service in India under the East India Company*, Calcutta, University of Calcutta.

Andreski, S. (1968), *The African Predicament*, London, Michael Joseph.

Day, C. (1904), *The Policy and Administration of the Dutch in Java*, London, Macmillan.

Foster, Sir W. (1926), *John Company*, London, John Lane.

Friedrich, Carl J. (1966), 'Political Pathology', *Political Quarterly*, **37**, January–March, 70–85.

IOR BLR (1789), *India Office Records: Bengal Letters Received*, **27**, p. 489. 'Secret and Separate Letter', 9 January 1789.

IOR HMS (1792), *India Office Records: Home Miscellaneous Series*, H/79, p. 515. 'Letter to Court', 2 May 1792.

Penrose, E. T. (1968), *The Large International Firm in Development Countries: the International Petroleum Industry*, London, Allen & Unwin.

Select Committee (1773), *Third Report of the Select Committee of the House of Commons*, London. Appendix, No. 73, 'Letter to Court of Directors', 30 September 1765, para. 1.

Senturia, J. J. (1931), 'Corruption, Political', *Encyclopaedia of the Social Sciences*, New York, Macmillan, Vol. 3, pp. 448-52.

Shamastry, R. (1967), *Kautiliya's Arthasastra*, Mysore Printing and Publishing House.

Teignmouth, Lord (1843), *Memoir of the Life and Correspondence of John Lord Teignmouth*, London, Hatchard and Son.

13 Corruption in the USSR: some methodological notes

ARON KATSENELINBOIGEN*

Corruption like inflation, suicide, military expenditures, etc. is among the subjects forbidden to be discussed in the official Soviet literature if they concern the USSR. That is why there are no preliminary generalisations of the phenomenon of corruption based on an investigation of the real situation in the USSR.

Our knowledge of corruption in the Soviet Union is limited mainly to abrupt dates and anecdotal stories. This situation makes theoretical analyses of corruption in the USSR by Western scholars very difficult. To my knowledge, there are only a few papers presented in the West which are completely devoted to the theoretical analysis of corruption in the USSR.[1]

This chapter is also an attempt to do some theoretical analysis of corruption in the USSR. I want to emphasise the two essential aspects of the problem that are less developed in the literature. First of all, I want to put forward a classification of different methods of payment which can be, generally speaking, treated as legal. The evolution of these payments into corruption practices is expressed in terms of rules which are used in different countries for different reasons. Secondly, I want to show the diverse range of corruption in the interactions between three leading societal institutions—individuals, enterprises and government agencies.

Vertical and horizontal components of rewards

Corruption, as a negative phenomenon, can be contrasted with a phenomenon of incentives in a normally functioning socio-economic system. The operation of a socio-economic system can be regarded as a process of exchange activities by the participants in the system. Since exchange involves people with their diverse individual interests, there arises a problem of harmonising the interests of

*This chapter is a part of research concerning social pathology which is done in the Department of Social Systems Sciences, University of Pennsylvania, under the supervision of Dr R. Ackoff, J. Charajedaghi, and myself and with participation of Dr H. Levine in particular. The results of these investigations of corruption are described in the manuscript 'Corruption: Its Nature, Causes, and Cures' (1980). A preliminary version of this chapter was presented at the Economic Planning Workshop headed by J. Gremer and H. Levine, Department of Economics, University of Pennsylvania, 18 September 1980. I am very thankful to Gregory Katsenelinboigen for the translation of this chapter into English and to Roberta Snow for its editing.

individual participants with those of the system as a whole. This harmony can be implemented either through vertical mechanisms or through horizontal ones. Vertical mechanisms are based upon the principle of subordination that guides the interactions of participants in the system. Horizontal mechanisms are based upon the assumption of equality of participants in their interactions. Generally speaking, in developed societies people simultaneously utilise both vertical and horizontal mechanisms.

A participant receives, in exchange for the results of his activities, rewards in the form of goods, services or money. The rewards can be assigned either positive or negative signs. In vertical mechanisms, a positive sign would mean that a higher participant rewards another participant on a lower level; a negative sign would mean that a participant on a lower level rewards his superior. In horizontal mechanisms, a positive sign would mean that the receiver of a product (service) rewards the producer; a negative sign would mean that the producer rewards the receiver.

One can imagine certain situations in which the participant simultaneously receives both positive rewards for one kind of activity and negative ones (e.g. fines) for another. Thus, if one considers a variety of activities performed by the participants, one has to regard an individual's rewards (both along the vertical and horizontal dimensions) as an algebraic sum. This sum can have either a negative or a positive sign.

In view of the foregoing, one can build a matrix that expresses the connections between the types of mechanism that operate in the system and the sign of reward. On the basis of this matrix in a general case, i.e. when the participants *simultaneously* take part in vertical and horizontal mechanisms, one can build four logically distinct combinations, four types of relations that characterise the participants' reward-structure:

(1) Positive in vertical mechanisms and positive in horizontal ones;
(2) Positive in vertical mechanisms and negative in horizontal ones;
(3) Negative in vertical mechanisms and positive in horizontal ones;
(4) Negative in vertical mechanisms and negative in horizontal ones.

mechanisms	signs of rewards	
	+	−
vertical		
horizontal		

Fig. 13.1   Connections between mechanisms and the signs of rewards.

These methods of earning income are based on different rules which can be powerful to various extents—eventually they can be laws. In its turn, society elaborates rules to maintain these rules, e.g. by setting fines for people who disobey the rules.

It is not our task to consider the expedience of the societal rules (including the rules to maintain these rules) and the methods by which they are changed. I take these rules as given. (Of course, I understand that changing these rules can be one of the most decisive methods of reducing corruption.) In the present analysis it is above all important to emphasise the situations where these rules can be avoided by providing additional rewards to people who might otherwise follow them. Corruption is this kind of additional reward. In general, corruption can be considered as an obstacle to development, as a social illness, because it is linked with actions which erode the mind of the individual. As with any kind of illness, corruption can be analysed within the framework of a larger system where it is sometimes considered a lesser evil, i.e. as a means to treat more dangerous illnesses (like the attempt in the beginning of the twentieth century to cure syphilis by malaria). Corruption in this case seems to be an illegal process to overcome self-imposed constraints by the system itself. Meanwhile, using the illegal methods in the process of development could incur 'painful' side effects. Eventually these effects can cause society to deteriorate enormously. But it is possible that the society in this situation cannot or does not desire to avoid corruption. In this case one could speak about a societal pathology.

Thus, every society has its own rules for paying its people. In different societies these rules can be different. That is why a method of payment considered in one country as normal would be treated in another country as corrupt and vice versa. Let me illustrate the last point by using the four combinations of rewards in the example of a restaurant.

The vertical mechanism here involves the interactions between waiters and managers; the horizontal mechanism, those between waiters and customers. The payment system for waiters, in accordance with the said four combinations, can be constructed in the following manner:

(1) On the one hand, a waiter receives a wage from the manager that exceeds the amount withheld by the manager for the damages that the waiter causes; on the other hand, the waiter receives tips from customers that exceed the inconveniences he causes them (if customers are unsatisfied with his service, e.g. they wait a long time for their meal, or suffer material damages because of his negligence, such as their suits stained, etc.).

(2) The waiter receives a wage from the manager that exceeds the amount withheld by the manager for the damages that the waiter causes; on the other hand, the waiter not only does not receive any tips from customers but actually reimburses them for damages sustained.

(3) The waiter pays the manager a certain sum (or a certain percentage of his

wage) for the privilege of having the job and/or for the damages he causes; customers reward the waiter with tips that exceed the amount he pays them for damages.

(4) The waiter pays the manager for damages in excess of his wages; and reimburses customers for bad service to an amount exceeding his tips.

The last of the above-mentioned combinations could only be sustained for a short while; it is impossible for a duration since the waiter must regularly receive positive rewards either from his manager or from his customers. All of the four types of payments that have been shown in the matrix can be prolonged to the point where they are treated as corruption and bring more negative than positive consequences.

Vertical payments with a positive sign

In this case the manager can provide the waiter at least with a minimum reward. This minimum is given to the waiter since there can be breakdowns in the operation of the restaurant for which he is not responsible. Meanwhile, the manager can corrupt the waiter by paying him additional money for serving the clients low-quality food and regulating the conflicts which can emerge in this situation.

Vertical payments with a negative sign

This type of payment rarely occurs, since it presupposes rather large tips. It existed, for example, in pre-Revolutionary Russia in some very good restaurants. The owner would not only not pay his waiters but would in fact obligate them to pay him a certain sum out of the tips that they received from their customers. Such a method of payment greatly increased the responsibility of the waiter for high quality service as well as the responsibility of the manager for good service of the waiters. This method of payment still exists in the USSR, but it is considered illegal. In accordance with the established law, a manager must pay wages to a waiter in the regular way, and a waiter need only compensate the manager for damage he does directly. However, the waiters in very good restaurants receiving high tips (which many, many times exceed their wages) regularly have to pay managers a fixed amount of money (or a part of their tips). The requirement of such illegal payments is part of an informal contract which is made when the manager is hiring the waiter.

Horizontal payments with a positive sign

These payments are made in the form of tips which customers pay the waiter depending upon their evaluation of the quality of his service. The positive aspect of this type of a reward is due to the fact that it creates strong incentives for the waiter to improve his service. Moreover, the manager doesn't have to spend any time on systematic supervision of the quality of service provided by his waiter. Since it is also true that in this case many people (customers) evaluate the waiter's services, the probability of making an erroneous estimate of his activities is reduced, in comparison with the system in which the manager himself rewards his waiter for good work.

Let us now consider some negative aspects of this type of reward. This may be due to the fact that this type of relationship can create situations in which those customers who have a reputation among waiters for being generous will get a better service to the detriment of other customers.[2] Besides that, when the customer rewards the waiter problems can arise in accounting for his income. This creates the possibility for the waiter to keep his income without it being taxed. Thus, the waiter faces a strong temptation, with all the negative consequences it involves. For these reasons (and possibly some other ones), in a number of countries/regions and during some periods of time, service is included in or constitutes a fixed surcharge to the price of the meal.

Horizontal payments with a negative sign

The positive aspect of this type of payment is the reinforced responsibility of the waiter for damage to the customer. Meanwhile, the waiter can corrupt the customer by paying him additional money if the customer promises to keep silent about the accidents which happened in the restaurant.

Thus, all methods of payment under certain conditions can be used for corruption of the participants involved in exchange relations. The analysis of the reasons which determine corruption and methods to stop it are a subject for special investigations.

The organisational structure of the society and corruption

The restaurant example touched upon the interactions between individuals and organisations. This kind of interaction frequently occurs in other instances where services are provided, e.g. taxi-cabs, barber shops, shops, etc. In passing, it may be noted that one encounters a variety of rewards primarily in those areas of the service-sector in which not only is the actual good passed on to the consumer important but also the quality of the service rendered. It may be for this reason that one rarely encounters horizontal types of legal rewards in stores, i.e. direct rewards given by the customer to the salesperson.

These combinations of mechanisms and rewards can be used for more than analysing interactions between individuals and organisations. A society has a complicated structure which links the participants who in certain situations play the role either of producers or consumers of commodities and services. This structure determines the various forms of corruption.

Let us consider this variety in relation to three major institutions that represent the societal structure of the Soviet Union. These three institutions are: private people (individuals), enterprises and governmental agencies.

The distinction between enterprises and agencies is rather blurred in the USSR; at the same time it is important for the following reasons. First, relationships between individuals and organisations and among organisations themselves are mainly based on horizontal relations. Relationships between individuals and organisations, on the one hand, and governmental agencies, on the other, are mainly based on vertical relations. Second, the extent of corruption often depends on the extent of the influence of corruption on the activities of an institution. It is no accident that in the Soviet Union (as in Western countries) corruption within industrial enterprises is developed to a lesser extent. The manager of an enterprise is first of all interested in a system of hiring people and paying them that allows him to fulfil the plan; if the manager does not fulfil the plan, his career is finished. A different situation is found in governmental agencies. The results of their activities are very difficult to check. In addition, they are subject to less control because they control others. Finally, the governmental agencies maintain the higher levels on the managerial hierarchy; they control many organisations and that is why they have more options in allocating resources and disguising the failures resulting from corruption.

There are nine possible types of relations between the three groups of producers (individuals, enterprises and government agencies) and the three groups of consumers (individuals, enterprises and government agencies). The following section considers how corruption comes about in their interactions.

Individual

Individual (consumer)–individual (producer)

Semi-legal services such as repairing apartments, renting apartments, renting a summer country house etc., have been developed in the USSR. I include these in the 'grey market'.[3] The payments for private services can be interpreted as corruption. For example, the repairman gets much more money from individuals than he receives from his basic job, making such workers less productive on their jobs. Besides, these workers often use building materials stolen from their job-sites because it is difficult for private people to find these materials in stores. The extra money which these workers earn from private individuals is used largely to purchase alcohol.

Individual–organisation

An individual often bribes the members of the admissions committee when he wants his child to be admitted to a good university. It is no accident that the main newspapers on the eve of the examination period in the universities publish leaflets which unmask bribetakers from the universities. And that is almost every year.

Individuals pay bribes to the doctors and administrators of good clinics. Hospitals in the Soviet Union usually serve the people who live near by. If somebody wants the services of a specialist who works in another hospital, he has to bribe the doctor and the administrators of that hospital. If a hospital is part of a research institute (these hospitals are usually very good), it can serve people without taking into account where they live. In this case, the doctors and administrators are bribed to avoid a long wait in the queue for services; it is often necessary to spend years waiting to be admitted to such hospitals in a regular way.

Small bribes in the form of money for drinks are often given by the workers to a foreman who provides them with more advantageous jobs.

Individual-governmental agencies

The large network of bureaucratic rules established by the Soviet government form the very environment in which bribery flourishes. Bribes are often given to the police for the right to move into the large cities. A Soviet citizen who wants to move from one city to another often falls into a vicious circle: he cannot get a job in another city until he has permission from the police to stay in the city (at least provisionally); he cannot get permission from the police to stay in the city until he has a job. A bribe to the police often can help him to break out of this circle. Bribes are given to government agencies by individuals to avoid punishment for such illegal activities as producing home distilled alcohol, disguising income from illegal private activities (e.g. private dentistry), etc. Bribing police inspectors to issue driving licences without passing exams, to overlook traffic violations, etc. is quite common.

Enterprise

Enterprise-individual

This kind of corruption is primarily linked to the illegal activities of the leader of the organisation (or its department) in which ordinary employees are involved. To get the employees to participate in the illegal activities while 'keeping silent' the manager has to pay them at least a double salary.

But there are also frequent cases where the managers corrupt the workers in order to complete legal kinds of activities. The manager of a shop in an enterprise often has to ask the employees to work overtime or to work on the weekends. Because the manager cannot pay an additional amount of money for these extra activities, the workers could decline his request. The solution is usually bribery by pure alcohol (*spirt*), the most attractive drink for many Russian workers. Pure alcohol is not sold in stores with the possible exception of the North region of the USSR. Many factories keep stocks of pure alcohol for industrial purposes. A number of glasses of pure alcohol ('glass' being a unit of measurement), given to the workers in a semi-legal manner, serves as a kind of payment for their work.

Enterprise-enterprise

Strictly speaking, the interactions between these participants can be twofold, depending upon the interplay of supply and demand. Let us look at a common situation in the USSR where the demand exceeds the supply. It is known that planning in the USSR is set up in such a way that demand and supply for capital goods are never balanced: the former invariably exceeds the latter. This is a consequence of the falsity of the plan itself (e.g. intentionally unfulfillable planned deadlines for introducing new capacities, unrealistically high percentages of planned cost-reductions, etc.) or with the absence of backstop reserves which can alleviate fluctuations that occur during the process of implementing the plan.

Though in many cases the gap between supply and demand is not all that great (say, 2–3 per cent) it is still large enough to prevent individual consumers of goods from fulfilling *their* plans, with all the attendant negative consequences. Therefore, industrial consumers have to send emissaries ('expediters') to their suppliers. Naturally, each expediter tries to get the top priority assigned to the dispatch of the goods he needs. To accomplish this he has to corrupt the vendor's employees, beginning with small offerings to secretaries and up to considerably larger rewards for the sales department personnel and, in some cases, even top management.

Still, the activities of expediters are considered semi-legal since they are thought of as a lesser evil than having the factories demonstrate that they are incapable of fulfilling the plan due to insufficient goods received.

Corruption of one enterprise by another also exists in the West. The interactions between the buyers of goods for stores and sellers of these goods will serve as an example. Here the seller of goods, wanting to increase their sales, will try to 'ingratiate' the buyer in all sorts of ways. The rewards received by the buyer from the seller are generally considered undesirable. The usual rationale for this is that the buyer can conclude the transaction to the detriment of his employer. In the previous examples using the service-sector, i.e. in the case of restaurants, it was assumed that the seller (waiter), by improving the quality of his service, could not cause significant damages to be incurred by his employer.

In spite of a certain mirror-like structure of corruption that occurs when the demand exceeds the supply (the Soviet case) and vice versa (the Western case) the consequences of these imbalances are not at all similar. In the case of excessive demand, corruption reinforces the already existing situation, which is characterised by sharply increased delays of deliveries, decrease in the quality of goods, etc.[4] Under the existing conditions the consumer-enterprise in the USSR is reluctant to penalise a supplier who has broken its contract on delivery days and/or quality specifications. A money penalty does not save the consumer–enterprise from punishment because the major criterion by which the government judges the activities of the enterprise is the fulfilment of the plan in terms of outputs.

Thus, the system of planning in the USSR which performs under the conditions of excess demand causes a lot of problems, and corruption is one among them. The West, with an excessive supply, presents quite another situation. In spite of the fact that the buyer can hurt his employer, one can still try, in principle, to normalise the rewards that the buyer of goods receives from the seller. On the other hand, this requires two things: trust toward the buyer, and a strong penalty imposed on the buyer in the event he betrays this trust. One can also imagine a kind of interaction between the buyer and his employer which will result in the third type of reward; i.e. the buyer will pay to his employer some part of what he receives from the seller of the goods.

In principle, this variety of rewards can be used to describe interactions between individuals and private organisations on the one hand, and the government on the other.

Enterprise–governmental agency

It seems to me that corruption in the USSR chiefly occurs in the relations between enterprises and governmental agencies. Bribery within these oganisations includes semi-legal and illegal activities. Bribery for semi-legal activities concerns the ministerial and party apparatus. The enterprises bribe them to get an easier plan: less output more input. Considerable literature has been devoted to this phenomenon.

A 'semi-mirror-like' structure of this phenomenon can be seen in the West: the corporations corrupt government employees (in their own country and abroad) to get better contracts: more output and more input. Government organisations are primarily involved in the production of public goods. In the process of producing these goods, however, they often have to purchase private goods. For example, government organisations carry out orders for the design and production of military hardware. These designs, as well as the weaponry itself, are private goods. Their manufacture is entrusted to a variety of organisations that compete among themselves. The representative of the government organisation which controls the allocation of military contracts has an opportunity to receive rewards from the firm that gets the contract. This situation is analogous to that of the buyer and seller in the previous example, with all the positive and negative consequences that attend the utilisation of each type of reward.

Thus, in Western countries additional payments to government employees by the firms can be interpreted as a horizontal part of their income; of course, this statement is correct if these employees do not misuse their obligations. This cannot be said of the Soviet Union where the additional payments to government employees always have to be treated as bribes because they are always orientated to reduce the effectiveness of the economy.

The major portion of bribes enterprises pay to government are for hiding their illegal activities. Stealing is most widespread in the Soviet Union in retail trade. (I will say that, practically speaking, *all* people working in the Soviet retail trade system are involved in one or another kind of theft.) That is why these people especially need protection. The managers of the stores regularly (every month) give bribes to the party apparatus, to top levels of the bureaucracy involved with retail trade, to the people involved in the judicial system, etc.

The ministerial employees often receive bribes for setting higher norms for inputs in material, equipment, labour, energy, etc. In fact, by using less of these resources the managers have an opportunity to produce a surplus which can be sold in an illegal way; this particularly concerns enterprises which produce consumer goods.

Governmental agencies

Governmental agencies–individual

The government can corrupt individuals by different means. One of them is knowingly setting prices which are lower than the required prices of equilibrium on some consumer goods. Therefore, the demand for these commodities is greater than their supply, and they become scarce. (We may note that other commodities, which have equilibrium prices, are in short supply in the sense that demand would rise with lower prices or higher incomes. Necessities such as butter, cheese and other foods are examples found in many cities.) Scarce commodities include various types of women's clothing, carpets, imported furniture, refrigerators, cars, building materials, etc. It would seem that the state could increase their prices without fear of an upsurge of public indignation since the commodities in question are not necessities.

It is nevertheless possible that the reason for this scarcity lies in the government's fear of raising prices because of the public's possible dissatisfaction. I once happened to hear the following explanation in a private conversation with a rather prominent official engaged in price determination. He felt that reduced prices resulted from the following political considerations. Reduced prices made it possible to create an illusion of accessibility, an illusion that, in principle, even a person with a small income could afford these commodities; all he had to do was to stand in a queue. There is a feeling among the public at large that the impossibility of purchasing without queuing is due merely to temporary difficulties, and that, as production of scarce commodities increases, the queues will shorten.

We shall now consider the negative aspects of the formation of scarce commodities from the point of view of the problem that is of interest to us. And we shall describe the payment that society has to make for the illusions created by the government.

The existence of scarce commodities gives rise to an illegal system of selling commodities in the state network. The mechanics of this process vary. For example, a saleswoman tells her friends when a scarce commodity will be arriving. The purchasers arrive, stand in a queue, and buy the commodity; or the salespeople 'put it aside' (e.g. a 'sold' sign is put on furniture, or clothing is put under the counter). The amount of the additional payment in such cases is lower than that charged by speculators, but it is more difficult to find salespeople who are ready to take a risk with people they do not know. Frequently the salespeople deal with a 'tried and true contingent' of speculators who could also be seen as victims of corruption.

We can boldly state that the overwhelming majority of salespeople in shops selling manufactured commodities participate in selling of scarce commodities in this way because scarce commodities appear in practically all the shops. Even if a young salesgirl is honest, she is forced to engage in this activity by the departmental head, to whom she must 'kick back' part of the income. He, in his turn, must give a 'kick back' to the shop director who, in turn, gives one to the area trade office or to the wholesale base from which he received the scarce commodities (after all, they could have given them to someone else). So it goes until one reaches the very pinnacle of the trade hierarchy. Trade malpractices revealed in the late 1950s indicated that the persons involved in this process included the USSR's deputy minister of trade.

What, then, forces the trade workers to use illegal sales methods? On the one hand, their low wages. The wages paid to a shop assistant come to approximately 1,000 roubles a year. On the other hand, there is an immediate possibility of illegally earning money (an engineer might also trade in scarce resources under the counter, but he does not have any). Moreover, there is comparative safety in these methods of selling scarce commodities, since it is difficult to prove that the salesgirl telephoned such-and-such a person or put aside the article. In addition, the police who have to combat this trade method are themselves poorly paid and can be corrupted easily.

Within the trade system, this possibility of accumulating considerable amounts of money leads to widespread perversion of its personnel. With the low cultural level of the workers in trade, the money that they have obtained by illegal methods is, to a tremendous degree, spent on alcohol. This is especially obvious in furniture stores where, because of scarce commodities, the salespeople have very high incomes (as much as several hundred roubles on individual days). Usually, the salespeople there are not completely 'dried out'; they are always 'a bit tipsy'. There has also been a sharp increase in drunkenness among women working in trade.

Government agencies–enterprise

It seems to me that corruption of enterprises by governmental agencies is not widely spread; corruption of government agencies by enterprises is more developed. Meanwhile, there are cases of Soviet government agencies corrupting enterprises. For example, a ministerial employee can offer a subordinate research institute considerable additional money from the ministry's funds to reward the employees of the institute. But in exchange the managers of the institute must return part of this money to these ministerial employees. Technically the managers of the institute can do this by adding fictitious names to the payroll (primarily by simulating the hiring process in the experimental laboratories), or by working out an informal agreement with reliable people to return part of their bonuses to the managers.

Government agencies–government agencies

Corruption between Soviet government agencies is quite extensively developed. There are instances of corruption of lower-level agencies by the top level and vice versa.

Corruption of the top level by lower-level agencies is typified by bribery for better positions in the state and party apparatus. For example, a party official who is living on the periphery can bribe the party official on the top level to get an opportunity to move to the capital of the province (Union Republic, etc.). The people in the judicial system bribe their bosses, the party apparatus, for permission to stop the investigation of certain cases to reduce the severity of punishment.

Let us further consider corruption of the people involved in government agencies' lower levels by top-level government officials. In this case corruption takes the form of higher payments to the lower-level government employees than the declared principles of equality in a socialist country should allow.

Following Marx's behests, which were based on the experience of the Paris Commune, and Lenin's principles postulated in his *State and Revolution*, it was felt in the USSR that the average wage of leading officials should not significantly exceed the wage of skilled workers. Even shortly after the revolution the new class of leading officials were not satisfied with this situation. In order to preserve outward conformity, however, to Marx's and Lenin's principles, these officials were given additional income in kind and perquisites. This situation has persisted to this very day in the USSR and is widely known in the West.[5]

The deviation of reality from declared principles can be better described if one classifies income as legal and illegal, official and unofficial. By official income I mean income that is officially declared, i.e. it is known to all. We can apply all four combinations of these two dimensions in the analysis of income. In our case one of these combinations is most interesting: the income for the leading government officials is set in a legal way but it is not officially announced. Disguising the income of leading government officials from the people corrupts these employees. This situation was well described by the famous Soviet dissident academician A. Sakharov:

I want to emphasize that I am not opposed to the socialist principle of payment based on the amount and quality of labor. Relatively higher wages for better administrators, for highly skilled workers, teachers, and physicians, for workers in dangerous or harmful occupations, for workers in science, culture, and the arts, all of whom account for a relatively small part of the total wage bill, do not threaten society if they are not accompanied by concealed privileges; moreover, higher wages benefit society if they are deserved.

The point is that every wasted minute of a leading administrator represents a major material loss for the economy, and every wasted minute of a leading figure in the arts means a loss in the emotional, philosophical, and artistic wealth of society. But when something is done in secret, the suspicion inevitably arises that things are not clean, that loyal servants of the existing system are being bribed.

It seems to me that the rational way of solving this touchy problem would be not the setting of income ceilings for Party members or some such measure, but simply the prohibition of all privileges and the establishment of unified wage rates based on the social value of labor and an economic market approach to the wage problem.[6]

Moreover, corruption of lower-level government employees by the leaders involves not only the unofficial character of payment, but also the structure of the income. We shall formulate the following law which can be regarded as one possible manifestation of the socialist principle of distribution according to quantity and quality of labour: in Soviet society the higher the place a person occupies in the social hierarchy, the higher his share of payments in kind and perquisites. Thus, while the income received at an enterprise by a machine-tool operator consists almost entirely of money, the money part of the income of a CPSU Central Committee secretary (who is not a candidate member or member of the Politburo) is on the order of one-third; two-thirds of his income consists of payments in kind and perquisites that he receives in accordance with the position he occupies.

Naturally, the high-income level of leaders makes it easier to maintain them and, at the same time, is a powerful incentive to obtain such positions. The opportunity to obtain commodities that cannot be purchased in shops is equally powerful. Moreover, the considerable payments in kind, especially the perquisites they receive, also promote the authorities' more skilful manipulation of cadres. The existence of payments in kind and perquisites does not officially allow executives to accumulate significant money resources and become more independent, but it does mean a sharp drop in their standard of living if they lose their high position.

The Soviet elite is not satisfied with such income instability. Thus, some of the elite share the view that the USSR should restore something like a service nobility stratum, whose privileges would be preserved for life whatever positions they held. Generally speaking, only upper-level members in the academies of various sciences and academicians receiving a considerable lifetime sum for their titles enjoy such privileges in the USSR.

Finally, I want to note that corruption of the top-level provincial party leaders also comes about through the policy of distribution of investments. The top official who protects a certain secretary of the provincial committee of the Communist Party makes a decision to award a large construction project to his protégé. If the secretary has this project he has much to gain (a new country house, a good road to his house, etc.) over and above what his people can gain. The secretary can obtain building materials that are in short supply; of course, he can also utilise the labour force without any payments. It is possible to assume, that one of the essential reasons for long construction timetables in the USSR is the unwillingness of provincial party leaders to finish large construction projects quickly because in so doing they will lose an important source of their wealth.

In connection with the last observation I would like to make a paradoxical statement. If a government is involved in the distribution of investments, an authoritarian regime is preferable to a democracy. Leaders of a democratic society are dependent on a greater number of forces than are the leaders of an authoritarian regime. That is why the former have to allocate more resources to insure their political stability than leaders of an authoritarian one. Thus, in the process of allocation of investments the Soviet leaders have to corrupt ministers and secretaries of leading provincial (Union Republics) committees of the Communist Party. And the leaders of Western societies, e.g. the USA, in addition to secretaries, corrupt senators, congressmen, governors, etc.

Three laws of Soviet corruption

The higher the level of the person in the society, the greater
the percentage of bribes in his total income

This proposition can be elucidated in the following manner. The employee's possibilities of influencing the distribution of resources rise in geometric progression with his promotion through the successively higher levels of the organisation. At the same time, however, his income rises only in arithmetic progression. Since the extent of corruption stands in direct ratio to the amount of resources controlled by the given employee, the higher his level in the organisation (agency), the greater the amount of bribes that will be paid out to him for appropriate services.

I can confirm the above in respect to the Soviet Union only by sporadic information from people who shared with me their knowledge of the Soviet reality. Recently, a group of prominent Western specialists in Sovietology organised an investigation concerning the Soviet second economy, based on information supplied by Soviet emigrants. I hope that this investigation will also allow us to verify this statement.

The less tyrannical authoritarian leadership, the more it uses corruption of lower-level employees as a method to increase its own power

The leaders of authoritarian states are not elected. They try by different methods to protect their power from takeover attempts by the people in lower layers of the hierarchy. These methods include corruption of the employees through higher income (involving income in kind and perks). This is corruption from above. An employee once corrupted is not necessarily frightened. To make the employee more loyal the threat of imprisonment is used. If the authoritarian regime becomes a tyranny it is usual to exterminate an unloyal person without any real violation of the law. In non-tyrannical authoritarian systems there has to be a genuine case before an employee is prosecuted. In this situation corruption of the employees by their subordinates, i.e. from below, become a powerful weapon in the hands of the authorities to increase their own stability.[7] If the employee shows disloyalty he can be accused immediately as a criminal involved in corrupt illegal activities and arrested. Several trials in the Soviet Union (for example, in Lugansk in the seventies), involving local party officials, were organised, I believe, by 'big shots' against disloyal subordinates.

It is interesting to note that if the authoritarian regime becomes a tyranny it can become less corrupt because the leader can increase his power by arbitrary extermination of disloyal people. It seems to me that there was less corruption of the officials in Stalin's time than after, when the extermination of disloyal people enormously decreased.

The lower the ratio of the population's legal income to its semi-legal and illegal income, the higher the amount of corruption

Corruption is not equally pervasive in all the regions of the USSR. The Baltic Republics are the least susceptible to corruption; Central Asia, the Caucasus, and Moldavia are mong the most susceptible. Regions of Central Russia (Great Russia proper) fall somewhere in the middle (or veering in the direction of less corrupt). The amount of corruption in a region appears to be correlated with the ratio of the population's legal income to its semi-legal and illegal income.

The USSR, which is the last large empire in the world, has a unique way of setting regional income policies. The Russians have the lowest legal income; this includes not only those who live in the Metropolis but also those in the national republics. In the Baltic area legal income is higher. Apparently, this has to do with the fact that prior to becoming part of the USSR in 1940, these regions had a higher standard of living than the USSR; and the Soviet government, for political reasons, has been afraid to reduce it drastically. Moreover, the peasants in this area are more skilled than those in Russia. In the republic in Central Asia, the Caucasus and in Moldavia the legal income is comparable to that of Central Russia. At the same time, the people in these republics have considerable opportunities to increase their income illegally and semi-legally. They can do it by producing large quantities of fruit and early vegetables in their own orchards and vegetable gardens. The sale of these products outside of the republic is restricted; and in some cases—before the collective farm delivers its shipments to the state—even prohibited. However, there is a large demand for their products and they command high prices all over the Soviet Union. For this reason most of the rural population have large incomes. In addition, there are insufficient facilities, including hotels, in resort areas. This creates an opportunity for the local population, in Soviet Georgia in particular, to rent rooms semi-legally to tourists.

The fact that a part of the population receives semi-legal or illegal income leads to the corruption of controlling agencies that cover up such activities. Furthermore, if a part of the population that receives a high semi-legal or illegal income wants to obtain services from low-income parts of the population then the latter try to exact additional payments for services. They justify doing so by claiming it produces an equitable redistribution of income.

Instead of a conclusion

I want to make three general concluding notes concerning corruption.

Vertical and horizontal rewards and corruption

Employees and employers in a developed society, being primarily involved in horizontal and vertical mechanisms, are widely subjected to the simultaneous influence of both types of reward. The complexity of the problem consists in determining the proportions of these types of reward. The latter consideration, in turn, has to do with working out certain norms and with legalisation of various kinds of reward.

Indeed, corruption takes place when horizontal and vertical components of the reward go against the established norms.

With respect to the case of restaurants, one can see that vertical and horizontal components of rewards are not always a norm in all countries. When the rules of the restaurant prohibit tipping but the waiter still expects the reward and this becomes known, he will be penalised for violating the norm. In this case, it may be assumed that the process of corruption has affected the waiter. Indeed, as we have already noted, if the ban on tipping has to do with protecting the interests of customers, tipping the waiter is nothing else but an attempt on the part of the tipper and the willing receiver to improve the service given to this customer, to the detriment of other customers. All this becomes even more obvious in interactions between individuals and organisations when the participant's personal interest in getting a horizontal reward can hurt the organisation he represents.

A great variety of reasons determine the elaboration of norms that regulate the proportions of the vertical to horizontal types of rewards. It seems to us, that one of the most decisive reasons has to do with the responsibility of the employee in discharging his obligations. The more responsible the person, the less the need (*ceteris paribus*) to give him horizontal rewards; vertical rewards are of decisive importance. An extreme case characterising this kind of situation would be that of a robot, which does not need any horizontal rewards, only vertical ones, i.e. supply of energy and maintenance on the part of the owner. If the dominant culture in the society does not demand great personal responsibility then it may perhaps be necessary to augment the horizontal component of rewards.

First and second kind of corruption and their spectrum

I would like to distinguish between actions whose harmful effect on the society are questionable and those actions that harm the society unambiguously. The above mentioned cases of corruption had to do with those actions whose harm on the society is indeed questionable. Let us call it the *first kind of corruption*. Apparently, the first kind of corruption involves the process of redesigning the system, legalising the appropriate actions of people in it.

At the same time, however, there are many actions that can cause a great deal of harm to the society. Rewards for these illegal activities can be regarded as the *second kind of corruption*. Fighting this kind of corruption poses special difficulties and reduces itself largely to the general problem of combating crime.

Needless to say, the introduction of only two kinds of corruption, as with any other binary classification of a complex phenomenon, constitutes a certain over-simplification. The more bureaucratic the country (i.e. the higher the degree of regimentation), the more difficult it is to change this regimentation to take new conditions into account, and the more developed is the spectrum of illegality in it.

The freer the country (the lesser the degree of regimentation in it and the easier it is to change), the more rigorously the established norms are observed, and the narrower the spectrum that characterises the extent of semi-legality and illegality.

If, for example, we compare the USA and the USSR, we will see the following picture. In the USSR, where bureaucracy has permeated all aspects of life, there is a wide spectrum that characterises the extent of illegality. There one encounters a wide variety of semi-legal activities because on the one hand the government does not want to legalise them (since they contradict the predominant ideological principles of the system) but on the other hand finds itself compelled to take account of its own best interests.

The sign and scale of corruption in a developed society

There are varieties of corruption. I will assume that a payment can be recognised as corruption both when it is an invariant, i.e. accepted in all countries, and when it is a singular point, i.e. accepted by one country (or a group of countries). The differences between countries, under this assumption, are determined by the *sign* (direction) and the *scale* of corruption.

Some types of corruption 'go in the same direction' in different countries. For example, this includes attempts to corrupt the authorities by criminals who commit murder. Meanwhile there are types of corruption going in different directions in different countries. For example, in the USSR the consumer-enterprise corrupts the producer-enterprise to receive deficit resources; in the Western countries the producer-enterprise corrupts the consumer-enterprise to sell its products. In the Soviet Union the enterprises corrupt the government agencies to get a reduced plan for output, in the Western countries the corporations corrupt the government agencies to get larger contracts.

Thus, the type of corruption in different countries is distinguished by its *sign*. The sign can be determined by different factors: the role of the participants—who is the corruptor and who is the corruptee, the consumer or the producer; the intentions of the participants, i.e. either to increase the output or to decrease it.

Further differences between countries are related to the *scale* of corruption. This scale of corruption is determined first of all by the number of constraints on the activities of individuals, enterprises and government agencies. Of course, the number of the constraints only potentially determine the scale of corruption. Some other conditions, including the culture of people, severity of punishment for corruption, etc. will eventually determine the real scale of corruption in a given country.

Notes and references

1. Among them are G. Grossman, 'Notes on Illegal Private Economy and Corruption', US Congress, Joint Economic Committee, The Soviet Economy in a Time of Change. Washington, US GPO, 1979, 834–55; R. Ericson, 'The "Second Economy" as a Resource Allocation Mechanism under Central Planning', Harvard Institute of Economic Research, Harvard University, Discussion Paper No. 782, 49 pp., August 1980; J. M. Montias and S. Rose Ackerman, 'Corruption in a Soviet-Type Economy: Theoretical Considerations', Paper presented at the Conference 'The Second Economy of the USSR' sponsored by Kennan Institute for Advanced Russian Studies with National Council on Soviet and East European Research, 24–25 January, 1980.
2. R. Ackoff tells the following story. Once he came to an American hotel with a wealthy person who was known by the bell-boys to be a generous tipper. The moment this man stepped into the vestibule, several bell-boys rushed toward him. At the same time they completely neglected the other guests in the hotel from whom they did not expect large tips.
3. See A. Katsenelinboigen, *Studies in Soviet Economic Planning*, White Plains, New York, M. Sharp Publications, 1978.

4. See J. Kornai, *Anti-Equilibrium*, New York, North Holland, 1972.
5. See M. Matthews, 'Top Incomes in the USSR', in *Economic Aspects of Life in the USSR*, Brussels, NATO Directorate of Economic Affairs, 1975, pp. 131–54.
6. A. Sakharov, 'Progress, Coexistence, and Intellectual Freedom', *Sakharov Speaks*, H. Salisbury (ed.), New York, Vintage Books, 1968, pp. 102–3.
7. See A. Shtromas, *Political Change and Social Development: The Case of the Soviet Union* (Europaïsches Forum, Band 1), Frankfurt, Peter Lang, 1981.

14 *Pripiski:* false statistical reporting in Soviet-type economies

STEPHEN SHENFIELD*

Introduction

> Statistics is such a thing that here you are done with phrases and exclamations, and deception is immediately exposed.
>
> V. I. Lenin, *Poln. sobr. soch.* t. 25, str. 60

One of the conditions of the collection of reliable statistics is that those who provide the primary data lack motives for systematic falsification. (Other conditions are that they be in a position to provide the data, sufficiently conscientious in the work of compiling them etc.) If the statistical agency enjoys institutional autonomy and concerns itself solely with statistical aims, then such motives need not be very prominent in the minds of respondents. The agency will take every opportunity to explain to its respondents that it takes no interest in the affairs of individual persons (households, firms etc.) but only in the characteristics of the statistical aggregates of which they form part. It is this circumscribed role of the agency that makes its promises of anonymity and confidentiality credible. The respondent will then be inclined to falsify data only if, through misunderstanding or extreme caution, he distrusts this assurance. A former company statistician tells of such a situation (Irvine *et al.*, 1979): 'I was pressed time and again to use false figures for turnover, cost of raw materials etc., for fear of the taxman. They did not realise that the taxman would never see the forms—or so I hoped.'

*This chapter forms part of continuing research into the statistical methods in use in the USSR. The draft presented at the conference was criticised on fundamental points by discussants, in particular by my supervisor, Dr Philip Hanson, and by Professor Aron Katsenelinboigen. They considered that I tended to exaggerate the impact of the phenomenon of *pripiski*, and cast doubt on the realism of my perspective for the development of an 'alternative statistical system' under Soviet conditions.

Dr Hanson and Professor Katsenelinboigen have a more thorough knowledge of the Soviet economy than I, and the view of the latter is informed by long personal experience. In the course of future work I hope to integrate the points they make into a clearer account of the issue. However, I judged it premature to attempt to revise my draft properly in the light of their comments. Accordingly the chapter that follows has been revised in minor points only, but is supplemented by the reconstructed contributions of the two main critics.

At the conference my attention was drawn to the account of false statistical reporting by Pomorski (1978). My account and his are consistent: his main emphasis is on the legal aspects, mine on the statistical. He also gives many further references.

Within the governmental structures of Western countries provision is commonly made for the autonomy of the statistical function. Nevertheless, even in the West many statistics are derived as by-products of administrative records serving other purposes affecting the interests of those who supply the information. For example, data on the distribution of wealth may be estimated on the basis of estate duty records of inheritance. There is then a motive for systematic falsification, and the reliability of the statistics produced must come under suspicion.

In economies of the Soviet type, the primary function of state statistical agencies is to monitor plan fulfilment at the level of individual enterprises as well as at higher levels of aggregation. The income, public prestige and career prospects of managers and officials responsible for forwarding statistical reports depend heavily on the assessment of their performance made on the basis of these very reports. The statistical function is not autonomous but is inextricably mixed with supervisory and disciplinary functions in the work of the statistical agencies. Thus respondents have very strong motives to distort or falsify reports of their activity so as to present themselves in a better light to their superordinates and to obtain bonuses for fulfilment or over-fulfilment of plan. Over-reporting of achievements in production goes by the name of *pripiski*, while deception in general—which includes suppressing reports of accidents, hold-ups and other negative phenomena as well as *pripiski*—is covered by the vaguer term *ochkovtiratel'stvo* ('eyewash'). Another common motive for deception is in order to cover up theft or embezzlement.

Let us note that even in Soviet-type societies quite a few statistics are the product of purely statistical operations such as the population census. Even here, however, there is some evidence of data being used for disciplinary purposes, as when the respondent's unjustified absence from work is discovered by the census enumerator. Under Soviet conditions it is difficult to ensure confidentiality and to convince people that confidentiality is guaranteed (even where it is).

Deception need not take the direct form of falsification of figures. Statistical definitions and categories may be manipulated to achieve the effect required. Thus a drive for technological progress induces a large number of trivial 'improvements' in products. When Khruschev in the early 1960s called for sharp increases in the production of meat, milk and butter, the level of reported output promptly rose by some 15 per cent as coverage and definitions were adjusted upward (Hunter, 1972).

A Western parallel to this phenomenon might be unscrupulous public-relations promotion and advertising by commercial firms. These, like *pripiski*, are designed to project a misleadingly rosy picture of performance to the audience that assesses and rewards that performance. In the West that audience may sometimes be the government (for example, as a source of research grants), sometimes potential investors or often a wider consuming or voting public. In the USSR the audience is superordinate levels of the bureaucracy and ultimately the party-state leadership. This analogy exposes the arbitrary element in definitions of 'corruption'. If we define corruption as the misuse of public office for private ends, then *pripiski* certainly constitute corruption, while the corresponding Western phenomena do not.

Although, so far as I know, no Western commentator denies the existence of *pripiski*, the conclusions which seem to us necessary are rarely drawn. Over-reporting is seldom included in the list of most acute operational problems of the Soviet-type economy and polity, and published production data are assumed reliable enough to justify their insertion in sophisticated macro-economic models.[1] It is therefore worth reviewing a tiny portion of the evidence for the vast scale of the phenomenon and for its economic and political significance. I then try to distinguish the main forms it takes and discuss the means used to combat it. The possibility of the development of an alternative autonomous statistical system free of systematic deception in the USSR is considered. Next, some tentative suggestions are made about the role that over-reporting may play in the political-economic cycles of Soviet-type societies. I conclude by asking what further research on the question is needed and feasible.

The scale of over-reporting

The prevalence of *pripiski* is universally attested to in all non-Soviet and unofficial Soviet accounts of the matter: reports in *samizdat* and by *émigrés* and Western journalists. In countries of the Soviet bloc with less severe censorship, such as Poland before the latest crisis, official statements also paint a bleak general picture. Official Soviet sources admittedly claim that only individual anti-social persons are involved in such offences (Zelenov, 1964), and that the scale of over-reporting is insignificant in comparison with the total volume of production, construction, trade and services (Babayev, 1979). The sincerity of such statements, obviously required to maintain an acceptable ideological representation of Soviet society, is belied by the large amount of space devoted to the problem in the general and economic press, in statistical and in legal literature. Where Soviet fiction deals with economic life, it too features *pripiski*. The agreement of so many different sources of evidence makes it hard to avoid the conclusion that this is an important and universal phenomenon of Soviet-type societies.

Thus, an *émigré* reproducing the monologue of a man on a Soviet train:

I am a construction worker: I repair roads. Right now, we are laying asphalt near Fryazino. I tell you honestly, if I didn't do a little fiddling, my men wouldn't make more than 50 or 60 roubles, even though they might work two shifts. That's the kind of pay they get. So I fiddle by adding to their production—on paper, of course. You can put anything on paper. Because of this my boys do not grumble, and now and again one of them presents me with a bottle of vodka. They make up to 100 roubles with me. It's not a lot but it's something.

Next, Gibian (1960) discussing a novel by Nikolayeva (1958) in his study of Soviet literature of the mid-1950s:

> [Factory managers] pad their production figures . . . Valgan, for example, used artificially lowered norms of production. Toward the end of the month he listed as 'assembled' tractors not yet completed, to overfulfil the plan. In reporting the quantity of defective goods produced, he subtracted the 'legal' percentage—the quantity of rejects and irregulars allowed for in the production plan.

From an account of Soviet life by an American journalist (Smith, 1976):

> A poultry breeder from Central Asia explained that his State farm, one of the nation's largest, regularly fudged its figures to show it had met the plan. The daily target was 100,000 eggs, and the farm consistently produced about 70,000. The Director would report plan fulfilment . . . and the next morning order 30–40,000 eggs written off as broken and fed to the chickens. Similarly, feed shipments regularly arrived at the farm with 1.5–2 out of 30 tons missing, indicating padding by the supplier.
>
>   It is a tale told in one form or another by people from all walks of Soviet life. Cooking the books and double counting, occasionally exposed in the press, are so widely practised that many disbelieve official claims about plan fulfilment.

From Poland we actually have an estimate of the proportion of statistical reports thought to be false. Hirszowicz (1980) bases her account on the official press (*Życie Warszawy, Polityka*):

> In 1976 about 65% of units . . . gave false information regarding housing investment, the implementation of economic targets and the number of livestock. In June 1977 the Chairman of the Main Statistical Office notified the Procurator-General that the falsification of statistics was continuing in respect of housing construction—in many enterprises report of completion had been given months before the buildings were ready . . . There is little evidence that anything has changed since then.

Over-reporting may be so drastic as to make an enterprise that is really persistently and seriously below plan appear a satisfactory or even exemplary concern:

> The Director of the Ozerkovskii factory for reinforced-concrete articles, Kaliningradselstroi, V. Gubeiko, not having managed to fulfil his production plan, distorted his report data over some time. The total over-reporting came

to over 100,000 roubles. As a result the enterprise was considered 'advanced', while its managers and other staff received illegal bonuses of about 10,000 roubles (Babayev, 1979).

The Director of an instruments factory in Orla, whose real plan fulfilment for September 1961 was 56 per cent, reported 100 per cent (Zelenov, 1964). While in agriculture: 'Not infrequently matters in one or another collective or State farm seem not bad on the basis of report data, but signs of an unsatisfactory situation emerge, and on inspection the crudest eyewash is revealed' (Zelenov, 1964).

In *Gulag Archipelago* Solzhenitsyn (1976, 2, 147–53) describes the process —called *tukhta* in Gulag—at work in the labour-camp timber industry of the 1940s. As all state work norms are well beyond the physical capacity of the prisoners, prisoner foremen, norm-setters and economists in solidarity introduce 'a reasonable share of *tukhta* in their accounting'. The non-existent timber is then written off later as rotten or not worth the cost of transporting it. In spite of administrative changes designed to control it, *tukhta* survived and grew over time, because everyone along the production chain—loggers, camp despatcher, expediter at the log-rafting office, log-sorters at the landing point downstream, prisoners or workers at the sawmill and the lumberyard, railway stevedores—was on impossible norms and needed it to survive. 'The Ministry of Timber Industry made serious use in their economic reports of these figures . . . They were useful to the Ministry too.' The 'surplus (non-existent) timber which no-one needed was allowed in late autumn to float downstream into the White Sea'.

An industrial Ministry, perhaps no less than an individual enterprise, has an interest in creating a good impression, a false one if necessary, of its performance. Its officials may not only connive at the *pripiski* of their subordinate enterprises but even take an active hand in the matter themselves. Thus global figures for entire economic branches are likewise subject to substantial over-reporting.

A Deputy Minister in the Ministry of Oil Industry was recently removed following the exposure of a particularly blatant piece of deception (Sevastyanov, 1981). In 1976 it had been decided that the Ministry should introduce new methods to enhance the oil yields of reservoirs in a number of regions during the coming tenth Five-Year Plan. Substantial funds and imported technology were allocated for this purpose. Reports submitted by the Ministry in the course of the five-year period showed modernisation proceeding according to schedule, and production figures fell barely short of plan indices. But an outside inspection in 1981 revealed that the Ministry had made virtually no attempt to introduce the new methods. Report data had simply been invented, and there was a shortfall of millions of tons of oil. Equipment had been left uninstalled to rust and be pilfered. Inspectors found that thousands of barrels of imported reagents had been dumped beside railway tracks, thrown into abandoned mine pits, and even encased in the foundations of railway embankments.

The resistance of Soviet industry to technical innovation is well known, and cover-up of non-fulfilment of planned modernisation tasks is a common form of *pripiski*. For example, non-existent savings of materials may be reported. In agriculture, abandoned mineral fertiliser is reported as spread, mechanisation is reported when in fact manual labour continues to predominate, and so on (Zelenov, 1964, pp. 52–3).

From time to time reports appear in the Soviet press of a form of *pripiski* more ambitious than the over-reporting of production in enterprises that do at least exist—that is, the creation (at higher administrative levels) of enterprises or even complexes of enterprises solely on paper. Thus we read of the director of the Alma-Ata provincial trust of specialised vineyard state farms submitting fictitious documents about the alleged creation in 1961 of five new vineyard farms with a total area of 5,200 hectares, and about the introduction of ten new varieties of grape (as well as ordinary over-reporting for real farms) (Zelenov, 1964).

The economic and political significance of *pripiski*

Even official Soviet sources, while denying that *pripiski* occur on a substantial scale, argue that those which do occur inflict great harm on the national economy. The financial loss through the payment of bonuses and wages on the basis of false pretences is considered a less serious matter than the disorganisation of planning attributed to *pripiski*, for the correctness of planning 'depends on the objectivity of report data' (Zelenov, 1964). On the 'ratchet principle', plan targets tend to be set as a percentage markup on the level attained in the preceding period (or markdown for such parameters as material inputs). However, this is of course the level attained *as reported*, so that over-reporting leads to increasingly more impracticable plans in successive years until the pattern is broken by exposure of the real situation. Worsening real under-fulfilment of plans entails shortfalls in the supplies transported to other enterprises or to trade.

Zelenov (1964) quotes from *Izvestiya* (11 June 1963) a typical example of the chain effect which results. If the Zaporozhye coal mines misrepresent poor-quality coal as top-grade, many factories which need high-quality coal will be unable to fulfil their plans—including the plan for the production of mining equipment, thereby closing the circle. False data are one of the principal obstacles to the effective co-ordination of production and supplies in the Soviet economy.

In turn, we may add, shortfalls and delays in supplies and impracticable plan targets, by making real plan fulfilment so difficult, heighten the motivation to engage in *pripiski*. The planning process is caught up in a vicious circle.

Over-reporting also confuses any attempt at objective assessment of the performance and capabilities of managers and officials (among many other confusing factors also at work). The selection of the most capable people for promotion to more responsible posts is thereby impeded, entailing enormous if imponderable opportunity costs for the Soviet economy.

As Hirszowicz (1980) points out, the falsification of statistics 'leads to self-deception on a massive scale, and this becomes one of the main obstacles in the way of successful economic policies'. The more (self-) deceived the leadership, the more unrealistic the policies upon which they may be encouraged to embark. The more ambitious the policies, in turn, the greater the pressures generated within the system for the submission of falsely optimistic reports (the 'launching of satellites', as it is called in China).

The process takes the most dramatic forms when 'voluntarist' leaders are in power, impatient to achieve miracles in record time and easily led to believe by their sycophants that the miracles are indeed happening. Khruschev's campaign to 'catch up with and overtake America' in agriculture is a case in point. Another, of yet a greater order of magnitude, was Mao's 'Great Leap Forward' of 1958–61, when the diversion of labour and resources to the construction of 'backyard furnaces' led only to masses of unusable scrap steel and famine.

Forms taken by false statistical reporting

So far we have considered only the false reporting of economic units trying to exaggerate the extent to which they have fulfilled their plan targets. Although probably the most important type of misreporting, it is not the only one. It leads to upward biases in statistics of production volume, quality or productivity, and to downward biases in statistics of costs, accidents or other quantities the *reduction* of which is rewarded. Other types of deception, however, may lead to biases in the opposite direction.

One type of under-reporting of output which seems just conceivable to us, though we have no evidence for it (as yet), might arise as a result of the known tendency of enterprises to avoid over-fulfilling their plans by more than a small margin. Substantial over-fulfilment can be expected, on the ratchet principle, to lead to impossibly high targets in the succeeding year, a danger not sufficiently compensated for by the moderate additional bonuses for over-fulfilment (small relative to the bonus for simple fulfilment). This consideration places a limit on worthwhile *pripiski*: while it may be in the interest of a manager to report 75 per cent fulfilment as 100 per cent, it will not be in his interest to report 100 per cent fulfilment as 125 per cent. Moreover, consider the optimal strategy for an enterprise which *has* (for whatever reason, perhaps unintentionally) overshot the wise margin of over-fulfilment. By *under*-reporting its plan over-fulfilment as, say, 101 per cent, it loses some bonus, but strengthens its position for the succeeding year, when circumstances (for example, punctuality of arrival of supplies) may have become more difficult. Not only will next year's plan be less demanding (by the ratchet) but the excess un-reported production can be put to next year's credit.

Pripiski, however, are often aimed not at manipulating the official system of rewards (unjustified bonuses, affecting future plans) but at covering up some more direct form of theft or fraud. Thus, the procuracy uncovered the fictitious nature of a cotton production operation in Tadzhikistan, involving procurement agencies and cotton-processing factories as well as collective farm managers. Over 700,000 roubles were paid out by the state for non-existent products, of which about 150,000 roubles were given as 'wages' to persons supposedly recruited (on the basis of forged documents) to pick the cotton. Daily summary 'reports' of cotton picked, transported and so on were com-piled, with quantities matching those shown on the forged receipts. (Arrange-ments are often made for the circulation of fictitious receipts and other documents in order to protect *pripiski* of all types from exposure.)

We note here that false reporting tends to take different forms in state industry and in collective-farm agriculture, formally under the group oẃner-ship of collective-farm members. In industry money plays a mainly accounting function, to facilitate the monitoring of fulfilment of plans which are funda-mentally in physical terms: payment for goods received can be made only by drafts of the state bank, and these cannot be cashed. In such a 'documonetary' economy there is little scope for direct fraud (as distinct from indirect fraud of the state through the bonus system). There is much greater scope for fraud in collective-farm agriculture, as collective farms can obtain cash payment from the procurement agencies for the products they deliver. Thus Zelenov's discussion of direct fraud centres on agriculture, though construction, road freight transport and trade also seem to provide ample opportunities.

Misreporting which serves the purpose of covering up *theft* of real products for private use or illegal resale must *under*-report real production or supplies in order to create the necessary 'reserve'. Thus, in livestock rearing, growth in the number of animals may be *over*-reported (by inventing births and/or con-cealing deaths) if the deception has the purpose of simulating plan fulfilment or that of implementing fraud (as in the Tadzhikistan cotton case), but will be *under*-reported (by concealing births and/or inventing deaths) if the purpose is to create a reserve for theft.

A common method of creating a reserve of agricultural products for theft seems to be the manipulation of quality data at the reception points for pro-curements. Thus, laboratory staff may exaggerate the humidity of a batch of wheat they are testing, or underestimate the fat content of milk received, to cover up the siphoning off for theft of part of the delivery (Zelenov, 1964). Such tricks must be harder to detect than the direct falsification of quantity data, though this occurs as well.

The pattern of data distortion during the procurement process depends on whether the procurement agency is carrying out the deception on its own or in collaboration with the supplying farms. If the procurement agency alone is involved, underestimation of deliveries received from the farms tends to be combined with overestimation of quantities despatched onwards for processing etc. As the collective farms are paid for procurements on the basis of documents issued at the reception points, they are thereby cheated. For example, the weight of cattle delivered may be distorted by delaying weighing while failing to feed or water the waiting cattle; the cattle are well fed and watered after the first weighing to create the misleading impression that they have been fattened at the reception point.

If the farms are to avoid being cheated, they must establish a collaborative relationship with the staff of the reception points. When all parties are brought into the operation, over-reporting occurs all down the line from farm to food factory, with false documents arranged by bribery and other means, and the non-existent 'products' are 'disposed of' as 'losses in processing', the validity of which is hard to check. Part of the waste usually attributed to the inefficiency of the Soviet distribution system is therefore fictional.

False reporting in construction and road freight transport is often designed to facilitate theft of building materials and of petrol respectively, both goods in high demand on the black market.

The over-reporting involved in some types of deception and the under-reporting involved in others must to some extent cancel out in their effect on global statistics. However, cancelling out is limited by the fact that the conditions in some economic branches seem more favourable to one type of deception, conditions in other economic branches to another type. On deeper study we may be able to make differential assessments by economic branch of the net effect of *pripiski* on production statistics.

Although the main emphasis in this chapter is on the falsification of production data, the point should be made that other types of data that reflect on the performance of reporting organisations undergo a like distortion. In particular, there is a strong motivation to under-report any negative phenomena for which the reporting organisation may be (justly or unjustly) held to blame. Three examples may be cited: expulsions of pupils from school, industrial accidents and working time during which equipment stands idle.

(a) Zelenov cites a case from *Uchitelskaya gazeta* (Teachers' Magazine) of 27 August 1963 of a town education authority which reported that there had been no expulsions of pupils from its schools. However, the semblance of this was achieved by transferring, against the instructions of the Ministry of Education, undisciplined and failed pupils to evening school.

(b) An article in the newspaper *Trud* of 11 February 1981 (Vasilenko) deals with the cover-up of accidents at a forge-equipment factory in Voronezh: only five accidents were registered in a year in one workshop when in fact

there were at least twice as many. This is explained by the fact that enterprises for which reported accidents exceed a set limit are penalised: for
example, they are disqualified from winning in 'socialist competitions'.

(c) Sonin (1977) compares different data sources on losses of working time as
a result of hold-ups in production. Three enterprises he mentions (in the oil,
gas and agricultural machinery industries respectively) reported virtually no
time lost at all: 0.00 per cent, 0.11 per cent and 0.02 per cent! The annual
sample surveys ('photography of the working day') conducted by enterprises give figures of 5–6 per cent of working time lost. However, sample
surveys conducted by outside research institutes reveal 20 per cent of time
lost in industry and even more in construction. In 1962 the Central Statistical Administration (TsSU) conducted surveys of the use of basic equipment at 500 engineering factories. These showed that on average 46 per
cent of metal-cutting machine-tools stayed idle throughout a whole shift,
and only 30 per cent were in use throughout a whole shift (Nekotorye . . .,
1963).

This example dramatically demonstrates how we gradually arrive at realistic
figures as we move from enterprise reports to surveys conducted by autonomous
agencies. Enterprise reports of stoppages are compiled from forms (*prostoinye
listki*) which are supposed to be filled in for each stoppage, and under-reporting
can easily be achieved by deliberate negligence in filling them in. Special sample
surveys are harder to falsify, but when they are conducted by the enterprises
themselves under-estimates are obtained by choosing an especially busy time
of year (the pre-holiday period at the end of October) to conduct the surveys.
Figures corresponding to the known seriousness of the problem of stoppages
in Soviet industry are obtained only when independent agencies (research
institutes, TsSU) directly collect the data.

The struggle against eyewash and over-reporting

Statistical record-keeping and reporting in the USSR are regulated in detail by
administrative and criminal law (Holubnychy, 1958). Reports are signed by
individuals—managers, accountants, planners etc. of the organisation concerned—who are held legally responsible for the information contained in
them, and who are liable to prison sentences of up to eight years (as well as
to a range of lesser penalties) for the deliberate falsification of data. Why is
the deterrent effect of such laws so often insufficient to outweigh the immediate
incentives to falsify?

This weakness of the law is all the more remarkable in view of the wide array
of bodies which have the power to inspect and check the records, accounts and
reports of Soviet enterprises and organisations and to bring any derelictions
they discover to the attention of judicial bodies. The administrative bodies to

which an enterprise is directly subordinated—trusts, administrations, Ministries, Departments and so on—have these powers over it, as do the statistical offices at different levels and the inspectors of the Ministry of Finance. Finally, there are the bodies of party and state control under the Central Committee of the party and the Council of Ministers. These are assisted by auxiliary groups and committees in the enterprises, and even in workshops and sections of enterprises (Zelenov, 1964). *Pravda* (27 February 1964) stated that four million people in all were taking part in the work of inspection.

Yet in relatively few cases, it appears, are false reports exposed, and in an unknown—but certainly very large—proportion even of these cases the culprits escape severe punishment.[2] In accounting for the ineffectiveness of the enforcement system, we must consider first the motivation of its agents and then the difficulties facing them.

We would expect that the inspections of most of the millions of people supposedly involved in the work of inspection are rather formal in nature when we consider that they are inspecting themselves, or at best colleagues on good relations with whom they are dependent. Only a quixotic 'whistleblower' (Lampert, 1982) is likely to be over-zealous in tracking down the fiddles of the managers to whom he is subordinate. Krotkov (1967) mentions a party-state Control Committee of thirty-two people 'elected to keep an eye on the 250 other workers' in a brick-making plant. His informant commented: 'They select the members (of the committee) from among the most "politically conscious". And these are the ones who themselves carry bricks away from the factory in their pockets. It's silly—as if committees would do any good!'

Nor can inspection by administrative superordinates be relied upon. As the performance of higher managing bodies is assessed on the basis of the apparent performance of the enterprises subordinate to them, they share an interest in *pripiski* with the latter, and are more likely to make their own contribution to the eyewashing effort (or at least connive at it) than to make any effort to correct falsifications. Zelenov (1964) himself recognises the futility of relying on departmental checks when he comments that managers of construction trusts fail to take serious measures against *pripiski*: their checking is too aggregated to stand much chance of detecting them, and any discrepancies are superficially explained away.

Inspectors from the Ministry of Finance and the responsible staff in the statistical offices are more likely to take their inspection responsibilities seriously, and we read of many cases exposed and prosecuted by them. Indeed, Zelenov (1964) complains that over-enthusiastic statistical staff 'discover' non-existent *pripiski* and send the materials on to the procuracy for prosecution. Whatever we may make of this, it can be no easy task to distinguish real from apparent falsifications. However, Zelenov also complains about statistical offices being superficial in their checks, covering up cases and failing to prosecute.[3]

Moreover, the judicial agencies are accused by him of often taking too 'liberal' an approach to the cases referred to them. The procuracy too often fail to prosecute; the penalties imposed by the courts are too lenient. Thus, the Kirovograd Town Procuracy refused to prosecute those guilty of concealing a large quantity of metal tubes and non-ferrous metal from those taking a census of materials at a factory, on the grounds—obviously regarded as invalid by the commentator Kunin (1965)—of 'absence of harmful consequences'. The chairman of a collective farm in Kirgizia over-reported hundreds of centners of produce over a period of three years, but the *raion* (county) procurator prosecuted his accusers instead (presumably for slander) (Zelenov, 1964).

Instead of prosecuting, the procurator may merely refer culprits to Party or administrative discipline. Or the director of the enterprise, who organised the deception, goes scot-free while subordinate collaborators get sentenced. Up to 1961 the courts sometimes sent culprits to be 're-educated' in enterprises which they had been managing—and continued to manage. In 1961 a decree of the Plenum of the Supreme Court of the RSFSR (Russian Republic) ruled out 're-education' in the same enterprise as before, but it did not rule out 're-education' in some other enterprise. But perhaps the harshest fate of all met the director of the Alma-Ata trust who invented five fictitious vineyard farms: when public opinion exposed him, the order awarding him a medal was withdrawn.

In such cases one suspects that members of a local elite—who include directors of local enterprises, local party officials, the head of the local statistical office and the local procurator—have made a concerted effort to protect one of their own from accusers who are perhaps regarded as opportunists or over-conscientious troublemakers. The accusers—the 'whistleblowers' to use Nick Lampert's expression—hope to break the stranglehold of the local elite by appealing over their heads to authorities at higher levels. The cases we read about in Soviet literature are ones in which the whistleblowers have, at least to some extent (for the press is one such higher authority), succeeded in doing this. There must be many more cases where they fail, and about which we cannot read.

The *pripiski* of the director of the instruments factory in Orla has already been mentioned. In spite of the fact that she 'lacked technical education and work experience', she had been appointed to this post apparently on the strength of being an official (a *lektor*) of the town committee of the party. Some staff from the factory warned the town committee that she was failing in the job and covering the fact up by false reports, but they received no support. She had gathered around her a group of collaborators, including a 'foreman for *pripiski*'. The secretary and the majority of the members of the factory party committee assisted her, while the one member who objected was held guilty by the others of factionalism (*gruppovshchina*) and sacked. The town committee was aware of the facts, but the first secretary covered up for her. Kunin (1965) rebukes Zelenov for failing to note that 'the criminals were severely punished', but he does not tell us what the punishment was. At any rate, the case brings out the importance of the local party apparatus as an instrument through which the local elite protects its members.

Let us proceed to the difficulties facing even those inspectors who are motivated to uncover falsifications. We already have some idea of the political difficulties they face. As for technical difficulties, the three mentioned most often in the literature are:

(a) the time lag between falsification and its detection;
(b) imperfect record-keeping systems which make detection more difficult than it need be; and
(c) the huge volume of report data—the 'information flood'—which creates conditions conducive to falsifications going undetected.

(a) We saw that it took five years before the deception in the oil industry about modernisation was uncovered. Apart from the time discount which he may implicitly place on future disutility ('let's cross that bridge when we come to it'), the culprit knows that by the time his crime is discovered (if it is) he may well have moved on—perhaps indeed to that higher post he had his eye on when he was trying so hard to make a good impression, and in which he is relatively invulnerable to 'slander'. By then, in any case, it may be extremely difficult to determine who was responsible.

Kuczynski (1978) further points out that, by the time a falsification is discovered, it may no longer be of much interest to the authorities, concerned above all with current problems. The central authorities are unable to destroy the 'informational freedom' of the enterprise: their efforts do enable them to 'cumulate truth' over time, but continual change in circumstances devalues this gain and prevents them from ever catching up.

Solzhenitsyn (1976) reveals how prisoners too are protected by the passage of time: 'Accountants' inspections and audits turn up *tukhta* after a delay of months or years, when all that can be done is to bring charges against a free employee or smudge it up and write it off'.

(b) In the contest between falsifiers and inspectors, much depends on who is more skilled in using documentation: the falsifier in trying to make his deceptions consistent both with one another and with information beyond his control, or the inspector in spotting inconsistencies and tracing their causes. Zelenov (1964) gives inspectors advice on what sort of inconsistencies to look out for—for example, whether journey times and petrol used in road haulage are consistent with the facts of geography.

The maintenance of suitable procedures of documentation is accordingly regarded as a condition of effective inspection work (Babayev, 1979). Record-keeping should be well organised on a regular system; the documentation systems of different organisations should be unified as far as possible for ease of cross-checking and procedures should be clear, for lack of clarity will be exploited by falsifiers. The transition to 'integrated mechanised processing of accounts' is thought to make falsification more difficult; this may partly explain resistance to automation of data processing.

(c) The 'information flood' which deluges Soviet organisations is recognised to militate against the careful examination and cross-checking of data, and against the ability of people to distinguish the important from the trivial, and thereby to create favourable conditions for deception. The late party secretary of Belorussia, P. M. Masherov, made comments on these lines in a lecture in 1978, taking the Belorussian Ministry of Meat and Milk Industry as his example (Masherov, 1978).

The view taken by Zelenov on this problem points up the contradictions in the situation. Thus, on the one hand he regards a reduction in the volume of reporting in livestock husbandry as desirable. On the other hand, the consistency checks he advises depend on the existence of a multiplicity of overlapping documents, one of the principle causes of the information flood. For example, data on material outlays in industrial enterprises are to be cross-checked among reporting forms, supply documents, the documents for release of materials from store and so on. Concern about deception feeds opposing tendencies for both the expansion and the contraction of the volume of data in circulation, the domination of one tendency alternating with that of the other.

An alternative statistical system?

'The struggle against eyewash and over-reporting' seems a pretty hopeless one given the existing Soviet social system. This does not preclude, however, the possibility that more reliable sources of statistical data may be developed even in the absence of basic systemic change. We have in mind the gradual emergence of an alternative statistical system parallel to, but separate and different in character from, the existing system of statistical reporting. This new system would enjoy relative institutional autonomy, and (unlike the old system) its only purposes would be statistical ones. As data collected would be used solely for the study of socio-economic issues at the macro level, respondents (including enterprises) could be effectively assured that their confidentiality and anonymity were guaranteed and that their interests would in no way be affected by the information they provided. Reliable data of adequate precision would be yielded by efficiently designed sample surveys, in contrast to the complete enumeration required by the system of statistical reporting.

The alternative statistical system, possibly though not necessarily located in the academic world, could be expected to justify its relatively moderate cost (by comparison with the enormous cost of the existing system of complete reporting) by the much more reliable orientation to, and much more meaningful analysis of, the real situation it would provide. As a secondary benefit, it would furnish a means of assessing and monitoring the operation of the standard statistical system.

This is not pure speculation: the alternative system could already be said to exist in embryonic form wherever special sample surveys are conducted as a check or supplement to complete reporting. To the extent that such surveys, whether conducted by academic institutes, by TsSU or elsewhere, fulfil the conditions of autonomous statistical work, they yield more reliable data that show up the shortcomings of statistical reporting. We have seen how this is so in the study of industrial stoppages, and could illustrate the point in other fields (for example, as regards the collection of general morbidity statistics). Opinion polls and other sociological surveys can be viewed in the same perspective.

We see no real technical obstacle to the development of this embryonic alternative. The question is rather the political and ideological one of openly facing up to the inevitability of *pripiski* on a massive scale under the existing economic and statistical systems. But, were the leadership to be possessed of such insight and honesty, they would most likely initiate an economic reform that would put an end to the situation in which people's interests are at stake in the reports they submit of their own activity.

False reporting and political-economic cycles

A number of writers have argued that Soviet-type economies tend to undergo political-economic cycles (for example, Ellman, 1979). The basic theory—on to which different analysts superimpose different additional ideas—focusses on the generation of alternately dominating pressures to increase and then to reduce investment. Under favourable circumstances—recent successes in plan fulfilment, access to new resources, a good harvest, a healthy balance of payments—the leadership takes an optimistic view of feasible growth rates. The growth ambitions of the top leadership give broad scope for interest groups at intermediate levels—branch ministries of different industries, *oblast* (province) and republican party committees etc.—to press for increased investment in their sectors. Increased investment is desirable to these groups for many reasons: it strengthens their power base, raises their prestige, improves their access to scarce supplies. They submit misleadingly low cost estimates for the investment projects they propose to the central planners in order to improve their chances of being allotted the necessary funds from the state budget. This deception results in an investment plan for the country for which the resources really available are inadequate. Delays in construction follow that disorganise planning. In the effort to keep things moving, resources are shifted away from consumption, perhaps leading to popular unrest (riots, strikes etc.). The deteriorating situation eventually induces a pessimistic frame of mind among the leadership. They take measures to avert the coming crisis: reduction of investment, concentration of effort on a few key projects, a shift of resources back into the neglected sectors. Stabilisation is achieved, but the ambitions and pressures that caused the trouble gradually re-emerge and a new turn of the cycle begins.

254 Stephen Shenfield

In putting forward my own elaboration of the cycle theory, I wish to avoid making a firm commitment to the still controversial idea that a cycle of this nature plays an essential role in the dynamics of the Soviet-type economy. The strongest evidence in favour of the cycle relates to Poland, and factors specific to this country may well be involved. There is some indication of a cycle in some other East European countries (East Germany, Czechoslovakia), but the evidence for the USSR is not clear.

Let us then consider how we should adjust the formulation of the cycle theory to allow for the impact of false reporting. The leadership cannot directly perceive and react to the actual situation, but must largely rely on the statistical (and other) reports they receive of the situation. During that part of the cycle when plans are over-ambitious and especially difficult to fulfil with the resources really available, the political pressure to fulfil them (or appear to fulfil them) is especially strong. Thus there is the greatest motivation for resorting to *pripiski*, and the leadership will be in a mood to accept the optimistically distorted reports they receive.

Over time, however, evidence pointing towards the real situation becomes harder and harder to conceal, explain away or ignore: that is, 'truth cumulates'. The mood and policies of the leadership become more realistic when they reach a full realisation of the real state of affairs. Then the amount of over-reporting declines as plans become less taut and the leadership more ready to accept bad news. But there is a delay, more or less prolonged, between the point at which the situation has become serious and the point at which the leadership comes to grasp this fact. During this period the leadership continue to act under the influence of badly distorted information. This would account partly for their 'curiously suicidal' behaviour (Hanson, 1978)—that is, their seeming failure to learn from experience and to halt the trend of over-investment well before the crisis point is reached.

It is commonly argued that, however great the effect of falsifications may be on absolute production figures, they can be expected to maintain over time a fairly constant ratio to the reported figures, so that (other sources of distortion aside) reported growth rates are still reasonably reliable (Alec Nove's 'Law of Equal Cheating'). My argument suggests that this supposition may be invalid when considering growth over periods shorter than one cycle, or over periods with end-points situated at different phases of the cycle.

It is more difficult to judge whether reported growth rates between corresponding phases of successive cycles are reliable. There are two reasons for suspecting that upward biases may be tending to worsen over time, leading to exaggerated growth rates as well as exaggerated absolute figures. Firstly, the weight in the economy of economic branches especially prone to compensating downward falsifications motivated by theft cover-ups—agriculture being the main such branch—is falling over time. Secondly, there may be a tendency, even after correcting for changes in the branch structure of the economy, for *pripiski* to become more widespread and more audacious in scale. Vague impressions by commentators of deepening social demoralisation point in this direction, and the growth of economic complexity and the information flood must made the task of detecting falsified data increasingly difficult. Only further research might be able to clarify such points.

Future research work

My purpose in this chapter has been only to present a few tentative hypotheses on the basis of a very partial examination of the literature. It would be worthwhile to assemble and keep updated a catalogue of all cases of *pripiski* mentioned in the Soviet press, and to analyse the details provided by region, branch, circumstances, scale of falsification and so on. Nick Lampert has started work on a catalogue of 'whistleblowing' cases that will provide a large overlap with the catalogue being proposed. The catalogue could not be regarded as a representative sample of all *pripiski*, but it might be reasonable to assume that it approximated to a representative sample of all successfully exposed *pripiski*.

There are now in the West (mainly the USA and Israel) a considerable number of Soviet *émigrés* who in their former jobs would have been in a position to know about the occurrence of *pripiski* at their workplaces. An interview survey of such people would provide us with much new information and many new insights. It is hoped to conduct such interviews within the framework of the Soviet Interview Project directed by Professor James Millar of the University of Chicago.

Comparison of the results of the *émigré* interviews with the results of the study of the Soviet press would help to assess both sources. Three categories of cases could be identified for comparative study: (a) unexposed cases revealed by *émigrés*; (b) exposed cases revealed by *émigrés* for which no Soviet press reference can be found; and (c) cases exposed in the Soviet press.

During the recent period of 'renewal' in Poland, uniquely favourable conditions existed for the study of a Soviet-type economy: continued operation of an economic system of the Soviet type coincided with a relaxation of censorship and freer discussion of socio-economic problems. Unfortunately this period has been brought to an end and it is no longer possible to research such problems in Poland under relatively favourable conditions. However, close study of Polish literature of the renewal period should have very high priority for students of the Soviet system. Interviews of Polish *émigrés* are obviously another line worth pursuing.

It is too soon to tell whether the research which Western analysts of the Soviet-type economy are able to undertake can yield only qualitative insights, or whether it might not be possible to arrive at very approximate quantitative conclusions. Might we be able to assess the scale of the phenomenon of false reporting in different branches of the economy, and the way in which it is changing over time? Might we even perhaps be able to arrive at rough corrective coefficients which can be applied to the published production figures? If Soviet officials know how to apply such coefficients, why not us? We may then find ourselves with different and more accurate perceptions of the Soviet system.

Dr Hanson

Under-reporting of production to create reserves for theft must be much more common with easily sold consumer goods than with producer goods.

We do know a considerable amount about how to correct distorted Soviet statistics, for example, about how to apply adjustments to data of coal and grain output that take account of the inclusion in them of waste materials.[4]

The activity in the West that corresponds most closely to Soviet statistical reporting of production is not the work of State statistical agencies but the reporting to headquarters by managers of different profit centres within large conglomerates and nationalised industries. To provide standards of comparison such reporting needs to be studied, as well as statistical reporting in East European countries that have abandoned the Soviet economic model—that is, Hungary and Yugoslavia.

I doubt the long-term viability of the alternative parallel statistical system which you envisage. As it would be known to yield more reliable data than the traditional system, there would be a strong tendency to use it not only for broad analysis but also for detailed current planning. As a result it would lose its original advantages and become similar to the old system.

Professor Katsenelinboigen

Let us take care not to exaggerate the problem of *pripiski*. The scope for them varies enormously from one sphere of activity to another.

In mass production, cover-up of wildly false reports is impeded by the ability of recipients of output to make checks. To simulate plan fulfilment it is typically necessary to over-report by just one or one-and-a-half days' production at the end of the month. One then 'goes to the priest'(*v papu*)—that is, the director of quality control—to prevail upon him to sign the report of plan fulfilment ahead of time.

In the production of unique items such as buildings, the difficulty of checking up after the event on what work was done leaves more scope for *pripiski*, but even here there are limits. The state of new apartment blocks and their dates of completion may be falsely reported, but scarcely the number of blocks built.

Construction and agriculture are both areas in which opportunities for deception abound, and it is hard to find out later what actually happened. Many tricks are possible in construction and there is no clear definition of the point at which one can consider a building completed.[5] There are many reasonable explanations for the disappearance of agricultural produce—destruction of harvested crops by rain, the writing-off of eggs as broken or of milk as drunk by calves etc. One can claim that 50 per cent of eggs have been broken, but one cannot make such a claim about cars!

Soviet leaders are confident that their information is reliable in those areas which concern them the most. They trust the 70–100 figures for the physical output of key heavy industrial products, which the Chairman of the Council of Ministers reviews every ten days. *Pripiski* are less important for these high priority goods than for consumer goods. *Pripiski* must be rarest of all in military industry, in consequence of the control exercised here by representatives of the military (the *voyenpredy*). Similarly, key industrial projects are subject to special high-level control. In areas where *pripiski* are more prevalent, Soviet officials apply correction factors to compensate for them.

Though no doubt many minor industrial accidents are successfully covered up, it is unlikely that this could be achieved with a major accident in which people are killed.

As for the development of independent alternative sources of data, this is considered too dangerous politically by the leadership. Work of an academic nature cannot be kept secret enough. This is why the Institute of Sociology was destroyed. The demographer Ryabushkin complained at a meeting of the Academy of Sciences that the USSR was the only country in the world to lack an independent institute of demography, but nothing has been done to change the situation.

Notes

1. Deliberate falsification is not the only important source of unreliability in Soviet statistics, though it is the one with which we are here concerned. Methodological problems (for example, double counting of output at different stages of its production, or misleading methods of constructing indices) are legion. Accidental errors—for example, mistakes in arithmetic by bookkeepers, or errors in assigning computer codes—may occur at many points in the long process of data collection and processing. Their net effect, while often self-cancelling, will sometimes happen to be cumulative. Accidental errors are regarded as disciplinary lapses in the USSR, but are exempt from legal action.
2. Exemplarily severe punishments *are* meted out: for example, the Kaliningrad *oblast* (province) court sentenced the factory director Gubeiko to the maximum penalty of an eight-year term (Babayev, 1979). We do not know how common this is.
3. The statistical bodies are in fact accused of these failings in a decree (19 May 1961) of the Central Committee and the Council of Ministers. Kunin (1965), reviewing Zelenov's book in the journal of the Central Statistical Administration *Vestnik statistiki*, understandably complains that Zelenov understates the part played by the statistical offices in the struggle for reliable data, and especially the contribution of their 'Social Inspectors of State Statistics'—volunteer auxiliaries, often retired from relevant jobs in accountancy and statistics, who check data and help accounting staff at enterprises.
4. e.g. US Central Intelligence Agency, *The Soviet Union Grain Balance* 1960–73, CIA (1975).
5. For recent exposés of *pripiski* in construction in the Soviet press, see Redkina (1981) and Chekalin (1982).

258   *Stephen Shenfield*

References

Babayev, V., 'Povyshat' kachestvo otchetnykh dannykh', *Vestnik statistiki*, **8** (1979), 40.

Chekalin, A., 'Po trudu', *Pravda* (6 July 1982), 2.

Ellman, M., *Socialist planning*, Cambridge, Cambridge University Press, 1979.

Gibian, G., *Interval of Freedom—Soviet Literature During the Thaw 1954-7*, Minneapolis, University of Minnesota Press, 1960.

Hanson, P., comment on article by Mieczkowski, *Soviet Studies* (July 1978).

Hirszowicz, M., *The Bureaucratic Leviathan—a study in the Sociology of Communism*, New York, New York University Press, 1980, p. 143.

Holubnychy, V., 'Organisation of Statistical Observation in the USSR', *American Statistician* (June 1958).

Hunter, H., 'Soviet Economic Statistics: an Introduction', p. 3 in Treml and Hardt, op. cit.

Irvine, J., Miles, I., Evans, J. (eds), *Demystifying Social Statistics*, London, Pluto Press, 1979.

Krotkov, Y., *The Angry Exile—a View of the Russian Miracle*, London, Heinemann, 1967, pp. 113, 132.

Kunin, S., review of V. P. Zelenov, 1964, *Vestnik statistiki* (1965), 6, 85.

Kuczynski, W., 'The State Enterprise under Socialism', *Soviet Studies* (July 1978).

Lampert, N., 'The Whistleblowers: Corruption and Citizens' Complaints in the USSR', Chapter 16 of this book.

Masherov, P. M., text of lecture, *Sovetskaya Belorussiya*, 6 December 1978, p. 4.

Nekotorye dannye vyborochnogo obsledovaniya ispolzovaniya proizvodstvennogo oborudovaniya v mashinostroyenii, *Vestnik statistiki* (1963), 7, 86.

Nikolayeva, G., *Bitva v puti*, Moscow, 1958.

Pomorski, S., 'Crimes Against the Central Planner: "ochkovtiratelstvo" ', p. 291 in D. D. Barry *et al.* (eds), *Soviet Law after Stalin*, Part II, Rockville, Md., Sijthoff and Noordhoff, 1978.

Redkina, N., ' "Pripiska" i otpiska', *Komsomolskaya Pravda* (8 September 1981), p. 2.

Sevastyanov, V., 'The Costs of Connivance', *Sotsialisticheskaya industriya*, 4 October 1981, p. 2, translated in *Current Digest of the Soviet Press*, 33, No. 41, p. 9.

Smith, H., *The Russians*, London, Sphere, 1976, pp. 281-2.

Solzhenitsyn, A., *The Gulag Archipelago*, Vol. 2, London, Collins/Fontana, 1976, pp. 147-53.

Treml, V. G. and Hardt, J. P. (eds), *Soviet Economic Statistics*, Durham, N.C., Duke University Press, 1972.

Zelenov, V. P., *Borba s ochkovtiratelstvom i pripiskami*, Moscow, 1964.

15 How a Soviet economy really works: cases and implications

GERALD MARS AND YOCHANAN ALTMAN

Introduction

This is a chapter that reports an overview of some of our early findings from a projected three-year study of Soviet Georgia and its economy.[1] Our basic problem was: why should Soviet Georgia in comparison with other Soviet Republics appear to have such an ebullient economy? That this is a suitable description is beyond argument. On measures such as the number of private cars per capita, for instance, it leads all Soviet Republics (Kipnis, 1978), while Wiles notes that 'it is obvious to the eye of any traveller that Georgians are considerably richer than the population of RSFSR' (Wiles, 1981). Such commentators have been unanimous that this ebullience is linked to a parallel effervescence in Georgia's second economy, which Soviet watchers have again, continually affirmed as being particularly dominant compared with those of other Soviet Republics (Grossman, 1977; Kaiser, 1976; Smith, 1976; Wiles, 1980). Our concern therefore was, particularly through the use of case studies, to examine the social and cultural bases and the operation of this second economy and to note how it articulates with the formal economy.

The method we have adopted is what we term 'retrospective reconstruction'. Its mode is primarily anthropological. This is to say that it depends for its primary data upon anthropological fieldwork—in this case among recently arrived immigrants from Soviet Georgia to Israel. It involved residence and social participation among them for a period of over sixteen months. This has been supplemented by one of us visiting Soviet Georgia, by continuous searches into the Georgian and Soviet press and by regular contact with specialists on Georgia including native Georgians in the UK.

We believe that the unique contribution of anthropological fieldwork as a primary tool to such an enquiry is twofold: firstly, the core of its methodology depends on building rapport over time within the context of a close-knit community, which allows the build-up of good will and of trust. At the same time it offers the opportunity to cross check and validate the data obtained. It can therefore look in depth into questions that other methods of data collection may only hope to scratch on the surface. Secondly, anthropology's principal claim to academic specialism is that it concentrates on culture, that is, on the transmission of shared values and attitudes and on the characteristic ways by which people confront their everyday existential issues. In doing so it applies a conceptual approach to data that is holistic and therefore encourages a linkage across the main institutional areas of social life. The operation of the formal and informal economies can thus be considered more readily within their social and cultural milieu.

An outline of Georgia's culture

Soviet Georgia is an 'honour and shame' type society, such as is found around the Mediterranean (Peristiany, 1966). While Georgians trace descent on both sides, Georgian families stress the male line and within it an emphasis on agnates —on the solidarity and mutual obligations of brothers. Women are important in Georgian society but primarily as the articulation points between groups of males and as the ensurers of male descent. Whereas the honour of men is achieved by the characteristic macho qualities of assertion, dominance and competition, the honour of women is passive and associated mainly with sexual modesty. Both a man's and a woman's honour reflect on the wider honour of their family and therefore their menfolk, and to a lesser extent on that of their associates.

Honour and its corollary shame are constant preoccupations in Georgia. Within families spheres of action are well defined, do not overlap and are non-competitive—everyone knows his place. Beyond the family, however, these limitations are reversed. Insecurity and instability in the perpetual ranking and re-ranking of personal relationships is the norm. An individual has therefore constantly to prove himself as *Katzo*—a man. He is, in this respect, perpetually 'on show'. He has constantly to demonstrate his worthiness to public opinion in general and to his colleagues and peers in particular. This requires the extravagant use of goods and resources in display and consumption, which are judged as exhibitions of 'manliness'. One of the principal foci of such conspicuous consumption is in the almost frenetic feasting and drinking sessions that serve to extend linkages between males and are thus a principal method of extending personal support networks. (Mars and Altman in Douglas (ed.), 1983.)

Networks and economic manipulation

Appreciating these basic cultural features allows us also to appreciate and identify the underlying need for extra resources as well as the mechanisms for their achievement through a developed parallel economy. To be a some-body, to be a man, to be *Katzo*—one has to display. But this is very difficult if one can depend only on one's official salary. This means taking risks. But taking risks is in the very nature of this society, actually a clear macho virtue. 'Screwing the system' has therefore not only obvious economic benefits, but the very honour of a man demands it and the social environment supports it.

It is for these reasons, then, that in a familial, macho-based 'honour and shame' society, a centrally organised hierarchy such as the Soviet economic system has little chance of working as it is designed to work. Not only is there necessarily a fusion of work life and private life, but positions and relations at work form only one dimension, and not the most important one of an individual's total role set. Here nepotism is perceived as a moral duty and interpersonal relations dominate decisions at the workplace. There is no room for abstraction; all relationships are personalised[2] in such a culture and formal organisational structures are bent, modified and adapted to serve personal and familial needs.

The mechanism through which such adaptation occurs and which permits Georgia's second economy to develop and thrive is quite naturally the social networks binding individuals and families together. In a highly personalised society, the body of people to whom a person can intimately relate and through them extend relations with others who might latently prove significant becomes his major social resource. We have shown elsewhere how the 'weight' and scope of a person's network are primary determinators of the type of occupation he may hope to enter (Mars and Altman, 1982).

This linkage through personal networks of the formal and relatively rigid organisational level of Georgian society and its informal and flexible second economy, raises problems when we come to define corruption. Corruption viewed from without has a negative connotation; it is seen as damaging to the operation of a formal system. The problem arises when we realise that we are dealing not with deviance but with the norm, with a daily pattern of behaviour to be found in every corner of life. It has been observed (McMullan, 1965) that a bribe, for instance, can be easily confused as a customary gift since in many cultural systems this issue is genuinely ambiguous. In Georgia we have a similar confusion. If the expectations of Soviet law, labour regulations, or Communist morals are taken as the ideal standard, then the norm varies widely from this in Georgia and, further, the operation of this norm is regarded as laudatory.

Let us look into some ordinary common occurrences, as these were related by our Israeli informants. A storekeeper explains: 'even a shop-floor worker, if he has some brains and some guts, will take a few items from his workplace so he can enter a shop and exchange them for other goods'. A village general store manager tells us: 'one day my old school headmaster entered my office. He took me aside and handed me over a handful of notes. "These are my savings for the last three years. Take whatever is required but get me a decent suit of import quality" '.[3]

A taxi driver says: 'you always get more than the traffic meter shows. Instead of one rouble, you will be given 1.20R or 1.30R. Instead of two roubles—2.5R perhaps 3R. Even a government official who calls me on official travel will give me extra'. Tipping accounted for a third of his informal income and 30 per cent more than his formal income. A young GP discloses: 'after you complete a person's check-up and before he leaves, he will slide five roubles into your pocket—sometimes less, sometimes more'.[4]

A recent visit to Tbilisi revealed an ostentatious carelessness in the paying of restaurant bills, a generous overtipping of taxi drivers, a widespread use of ferro-concrete iron supports in the railings outside private houses and a high propensity to ignore the ringing up of accounts in shops.

We would emphasise that not all of these activities are illegal in the Soviet Union though they are all formally immoral, but they all indicate a fluidity in cash transactions that increases personal incomes well above the average official norm (in 1982) of 170 roubles a month. True, they are all ancedotal—a point well disposed of by Wiles (1980)—but we have found a unanimity among our informants both in Israel and in the UK that they are not considered as examples of deviance and are certainly not reflective of the activities of Jews alone, and are part of normal everyday practice. And nor should any of this surprise us. The operation of macho competitiveness in an economy that is formally controlled from the centre must necessarily take to itself a process of resource allocation that encourages men to pay more for personal services and to revel in acquiring scarce resources.

A case study: the private biscuit factory

The most obvious—and least risky—way to beat the system and to acquire private resources in a formally centralised Soviet State, is to maximise one's informal linkages to the formal system. If this is done one can then use the formal system as a cover for informal activities. We offer the following case in outline to show how this was effected by some of our informants. In cross checking this material with others, we have confirmed not only its detail but also its typicality. A fuller account of this case will be published elsewhere.

The case focusses upon a medium-sized factory employing several hundred staff that produced biscuits.[5] In addition to the requirements of its formal plan it illicitly produced extra biscuits in the ratio of 10:4, that is, four informal biscuits to ten formal ones.[6] In order to make such surplus production the management needed a surplus of raw materials—flour, sugar, fats, eggs, yeast and water. It could obtain these by reducing the quality or quantity of its components—by using less sugar or eggs, for instance, or by using cheap substitutes for expensive ones. But these methods are easily detectable. Therefore, the more typical response in the manufacture of foodstuffs is to obtain extra raw materials from an outside source. But how? And from where? One obvious source is to partly exchange the final product when delivering it to shops for ordinary raw materials sold by the shops. However, in order to transport these the co-operation of the drivers who drive the company's vehicles is required.

After these problems have been satisfactorily settled, management has to articulate black production with its formal production. One way to start is to guarantee that fulfilment targets will stay low. This means the co-operation of the production engineers in the factory as well as at least the direct next in command. Then they have to consider when to make the extra produce. However understated the formal targets of production may be, overtime work may still be required (that is, overtime or work at weekends), which means that at least some of the shop-floor work force has to be involved in the conspiracy. After extra produce has been made, there are still other issues to tackle before goods leave the factory. One is how to balance all the elements of production, so that when stock control comes, the proportions of final stock and the ratio of raw material to other stocks will be accurate or at least conceivable.

A frequent and universal hurdle is involved in obtaining ingredients that make up the final product but are not made in the factory. In this particular case these would comprise the packing and labels; they are supplied according to the official quantities produced. So it would be necessary to get in touch with a printing workshop and perhaps also with a packing paper manufacturer.

Let us recapitulate some of the informal relations which have to be involved. Inside the factory these are: the production-line manager, production engineers who set and monitor the production targets, the warehouse manager who should monitor the movement of extra materials and produce, and the maintenance person who should account for additional wear and tear due to excessive use of machinery. Add to these at least some of the shop-floor workers who have to work overtime and also the driver(s) who are requested to do extra rounds and deliveries. And last but not least the book-keeper[7] who should not only keep a set of books that makes sense to external controllers but who should also keep a set that accounts for illicit expenses and incomes. This is particularly important since, according to our information, most of these private enterprises are run on the basis of partnership.

Already at this stage it becomes clear that such an operation requires many social resources and many contacts. The puzzling questions are: (a) how does one get all these people to co-operate and (b) how does one ensure they are reliable in the first place and that they keep their loyalty? The answer to the first question is that one has to have an adequate network to support such an undertaking. This network must be powerful and extensive enough to reach all the people needed to ensure their co-operation. This, however, is likely to be beyond the reach of a single individual's network. This is, therefore, why one characteristic we constantly meet at the enterprise level is *partnership*, which means the co-operation of several individuals, each of whom has the backing of an adequate network. Only by working together and only by combining their networks can they make their task possible. And the fact that a network exists means that in this culture its members will be subject to normative pressure to do their best in the interests of their members. This is not because of any meticulously worked out conspiracy; it is simply a manifestation of the personalistic approach of this society. And this goes a long way to explain why loyalty can be expected.

Remunerations are distributed on a regular basis, known in second economy jargon as 'salaries'. Different people get different salaries. The work force who menially produce the extra production will be paid for extra hours—at a rate not usually higher than the official rate so as not to raise their suspicions and probably their appetites as well. But they would be allowed to take home some products and raw materials as a normal practice. More important people in the hierarchy get cash regularly at the beginning of the month, as with any normal salary—the exact level depending upon a combination of the person's necessity to the operation, his standing in the formal hierarchy and his negotiating power. Outside the factory some regular figures are always found to be on the pay roll. These comprise members of the police force, the municipality, and significant members of other impinging bureaucracies. Their role is scheduled to be discussed further elsewhere.

Distribution

After production comes distribution. The whole question of the delivery of illicit materials is one that is presently being researched. It involves the role of police road patrols, false bills of lading, metaphorical and actual gatekeepers, and the selection, recruitment and rates of pay of these. These will be considered in a further paper as will the varying merits of different forms of transport and the different kinds of network on which they depend.

The most common way to distribute extra production is to supply shops with which a factory has formal contact with the additional produce, and in doing so to replicate, as far as possible, normal delivery procedures. Obviously, here enters the issue of market demand. If the product is in much demand, there should, in principle, be no difficulty in selling it. If, however, demand is not high—or fluctuations in the production process or the market cause a problem of storage—then inevitably prices become lower than the official price. If this happens the private product competes with the state product.

At the level of the shop, the shop manager has one major need: how to obtain marketable goods. To sell them will prove to be no problem. Accordingly, the main feature of the successful Georgian storekeeper is chasing goods. Not surprisingly we will hardly find him at the shop at all; he spends most of his days looking for goods. This is in neat contrast to the position of his Western counterpart. In an economy of surplus we find the Western storekeeper remaining in his store and sales representatives visiting him; in an economy of scarcity the reverse applies and the Soviet storekeeper has to leave his shop to buy his goods.

What characterises the shop level, as regards 'remunerations', are that illicit payments are made mostly on an *ad hoc* basis, as opposed to the regular payment of 'salaries' at the factory level. Similarly the price of each transaction with the factory will also be determined on the spot. And a similar arrangement applies if goods are purchased through the state machinery of the central warehouse, as they normally should be. This *ad hoc* method of payment arises because while overall production in a factory can be arranged on a regular flow basis, the variability of supply to individual shops is likely to be much more erratic. This erraticness occurs for two linked reasons. The first reflects local changes in demand. The second is because producers in an economy of scarcity are able to heat up competition between their different retail customers. The level of illicit income to a store is therefore likely to vary, which makes for erraticness in the payment of those who are involved. Thus, if the demand for biscuits is high, the producer would negotiate an extra price on an *ad hoc* basis derived from what the market will bear. And this price too would reflect unforseeable difficulties—perhaps with transport. Detection by a road patrol for instance would involve an on-the-spot settlement. One case we know of involved such a payment of 5,000 roubles. There tend to be few people on the pay roll at the shop level, compared to those at a factory. Not only are shops smaller in scale but they are less complex and have fewer sensitive points of contact outside their boundaries. Their activities are less risky and for all of these reasons we therefore find fewer partnerships and fewer partners. The ability of one or of a few linked networks can sustain a shop but not a factory.

Conclusions and implications

(1) So far assessments of the relationships between formal and informal economies within the Soviet Union have focussed upon the articulation of the informal in the service of the formal. Perhaps the most explored phenomenon is the *Tolcach* (Berliner, 1957; Nove, 1976; Kaiser, 1976 and others), the 'pusher', who bends the system in order to achieve formal production levels. This approach has emphasised the role of a single individual within an organisation who uses illicit means for desired ends. Our work, however, demonstrates that in Soviet Georgia, at least, it is the whole organisation that is utilised in the service of illicit private informal economic activity with the management team occupying an integrated role. This is why there are no *tolcachi*—and no need for them—in Georgia.

We now argue that a fresh look is required at the social nature of management within the Soviet Union, at least as this should focus on Georgia. It would appear that success in the processes of recruitment, selection, promotion and career development might depend on necessary universalistic criteria though these would not of themselves be sufficient. Network criteria appear to be of overriding importance. The ability of an individual to progress in his career (or the reverse) might thus be seen to be a product of the strengthening or weakening of his personal support network. In maintaining and developing this resource he has some control but this demands the investment of time and material resources. The necessary skills of a Georgian manager are therefore differently ordered than one would expect from his counterpart in the West and perhaps indeed from those of managers in other Soviet Republics.

(2) The Soviet political economy has developed a complex system of independent check points which could, in principle, combat corruption. It is what Rose-Ackerman (1978: 1980) has called a fragmented type of hierarchy, where independent controls operate with independence. In Soviet Georgia, however, we find how a central social institution, the personal support network, has adapted itself to combat such fragmentation. It does this by extending its contacts to overcome such independent control points. In doing this it not only negates their powers but it captures their personnel and their positions of power.

(3) We hope to have demonstrated that the workings of an economic system —whether formal or informal—cannot be understood without an appreciation of the dynamics of its cultural base. We would argue that such understanding cannot be obtained without dependence upon the patient collection of data obtained through the anthropological method of extensive and involved participant observation.

Notes

1. Funded by the Nuffield Foundation.
2. Georgia, for instance, is referred to in toasts at drinking parties as 'mother-earth' or 'parents' ground' or both (Mars and Altman, 1983).
3. The headmaster might not be making illicit profits, but he has to use the illicit economy to provide himself with clothes adequate to his position.
4. The way this informal transaction is carried out expresses the high respect offered to physicians. It is no wonder, then, that both our London and Israeli informants agree that the informal entrance fee to the only medical institute in Georgia is in the order of 15,000 roubles, a point also confirmed by Simis (1982: 169).
5. We have disguised the product and other features in this case so that the factory cannot be identified—for obvious reasons.
6. We have cases of factories where production has been up to ten times higher than this— up to a maximum of 1:4.
7. This function, in our experience, is normally held by one of the key figures in the business, like the warehouse manager, the production manager, etc.

Bibliography

Berliner, J., *Factory and Factory Managers in the Soviet Union*, Cambridge, Mass., Harvard University Press, 1957.
Grossman, G., 'The Second Economy of the USSR', *Problems of Communism*, September-October 1977, pp. 25-50.
Kaiser, R. G., *Russia; The People and the Power*, New York, Atheneum, 1976.
Kipnis, M., 'The Georgian National Movement: Problems and Trends', *Crossroads*, 1 (1978), 193-215, at p. 197.
Mars, G. and Altman, Y., 'The Social Bases of Soviet Georgia's Second Economy', a paper presented at the Western Slavic Association Conference, Honolulu, Hawaii, 1982.
— —, 'Drinking and Feast Giving: Personal Networks in Soviet Georgia', in M. Douglas (ed.), *The Anthropology of Drinking*, Cambridge, Cambridge University Press, 1983.
McMullen, M., 'A Theory of Corruption', in N. J. Smelser (ed.), *Readings on Economic Sociology*, Englewood Cliffs, N.J., Prentice-Hall, 1965.

Montias, J. M. and Rose-Ackerman, S., 'Corruption in a Soviet-type Economy: Theoretical Considerations', *Kennan Institute Paper No. 110*, 1980.

Nove, A., *The Soviet Economic System*, London, Allen and Unwin, 1977.

Peristiany, J. G. (ed.), *Honour and Shame*, London, Weidenfeld and Nicolson, 1966.

Rose-Ackerman, S., *Corruption*, New York, Academic Press, 1978.

Simis, K., *USSR: Secrets of a Corrupt Society*, London, J. M. Dent, 1982.

Staats, S. J., 'Corruption in the Soviet System', *Problems of Communism*, January–February 1972.

Smith, H., *The Russians*, New York, Quadrangle, 1976.

Wiles, P., *Die Parallelwirtschaft*, Cologne, Sonderveroffentlich des Bundesinstituts für Oswissenschafliche und Internationale Studien, 1981.

16 The whistleblowers: corruption and citizens' complaints in the USSR

NICK LAMPERT

The aim of this chapter is to throw some light on the conditions and consequences of corruption in the USSR.[1] For the purpose of my discussion corruption is to be understood in a broad sense. It refers not only to the granting of favours in return for illicit forms of influence, but to the whole range of breaches of Soviet criminal law that involve abuse of office. I shall adopt a particular angle of vision, focussing upon complaints brought by Soviet citizens that in one way or another arise out of a context of abuse of office. My contention is that if we look closely at the origins and outcome of such complaints they can provide us with a kind of anatomy of the social relationships that produce and reproduce corruption under Soviet conditions. We may also get some clues about the broader political consequences of pervasive breaches of the law. I shall first give an overview of the line of thought with which I am working, and then spell out some parts of it in more detail.

(1) The starting point is a commonplace: there is a large and intricate edifice of law in the USSR that has been established in order to regulate social behaviour, yet the rules by which people live conflict systematically with the rules written into law. Such a gap is not peculiar to the USSR; but it takes on a particular significance in the Soviet Union because of the highly ambitious character of central political control over economic activity and over social life as a whole. This gives rise to a kind of paradox. Central control can only work if the behaviour of individuals and organisations is bound by legal norms, since this alone makes possible the predictability of behaviour on which effective central direction depends. Yet the Soviet form of political direction, within a context of widespread and endemic shortages, constantly encourages or permits illegal practices. These are part of the fabric of official production and exchange, but they also help to undermine the foundations on which effective central political control might rest.

(2) The existence of these conflicting pressures seems to explain the following state of affairs. On the one hand, the self-styled representatives of the general interest issue a stream of injunctions instructing the law enforcement agencies to put a stop to illegal activities by management and local officials. On the other hand, the representatives of the centre constantly protest that these agencies are unwilling to act vigorously; that illegal practices are condoned and often encouraged by administrative superiors and local controllers; that